THE FENCE

ROBERT LEE MARIL

THE FENCE

National Security, Public Safety,
and Illegal Immigration along
the U.S.-Mexico Border

Texas Tech University Press

This book is typeset in Melior. The paper used in this book meets the minimum
requirements of ANSI/NISO Z39.48-1992 (R1997). ∞

Designed by Kasey McBeath
Composition by NK Graphics, Brattleboro, Vermont

Library of Congress Cataloging-in-Publication Data
Maril, Robert Lee.
    The fence : national security, public safety, and illegal immigration along the
U.S.-Mexico border / Robert Lee Maril.
        p. cm.
    Summary: "Investigates the reality of the proposed 2,000-mile-long border
'fence' between the United States and Mexico. First-person interviews and
rigorous analysis of government documents uncover fiscal mismanagement,
wasteful spending, and unkept promises. Suggests new public policies based
on reasoned compromise and concern for human life"—Provided by publisher.
    Includes bibliographical references and index.
    ISBN 978-0-89672-680-2 (hardcover : alk. paper)
1. Border security—Mexican-American Border Region. 2. Border security—
Government policy—United States. 3. Immigration enforcement—Mexican-
American Border Region. 4. Mexican-American Border Region—Emigration
and immigration. 5. Fences—Mexican-American Border Region. I. Title.
    JV6565.M37 2011
    363.28'509721—dc22   2010049037

    ISBN 978-0-89672-776-2 (paperback) First paperback printing, 2012

Printed in the United States of America
12 13 14 15 16 17 18 19 20 / 9 8 7 6 5 4 3 2 1

Texas Tech University Press
Box 41037 | Lubbock, Texas 79409-1037 USA
800.832.4042 | ttup@ttu.edu | www.ttupress.org

For Dindy Reich

There is always an easy solution to every
human problem—neat, plausible, and wrong.
  H. L. Mencken

Beware the aged critic with his hair of winebar
sawdust. Beware the nun and the witchy
buckles of her shoes. Beware the man at the
callbox with the suitcase: this man is you. The
planesaw whines, whining for its planesaw
mummy. And then there is the information,
which is nothing, and comes at night.
  Martin Amis

I could give all to Time except - except
What I myself have held. But why declare
The things forbidden that while the Customs slept
I have crossed to Safety with? For I am There
And what I would not part with I have kept.
  Robert Frost

Contents

Illustrations   xi

Part One: A Virtual American Dream

1: A Simple Solution   3

2: Manny's Disguise Isn't One   24

3: Anzalduas   38

4: Olga Rivera Garcia's Fence
   and Omar Sanchez's Fence   60

5: ISIS   88

6: Dubuque   111

Part Two: Crossing to Safety

7: More Virtual Fences   135

8: CBP Agent Nora Muñoz   179

9: Juliet Garcia's Fence and
   Michael Chertoff's Wall   198

10: Three Different Walls   230

11: It's Getting Crowded along
    the Border   258

12: Crossing to Safety   279

Epilogue   301
Notes   309
Bibliography   341
Acknowledgments   353
Index   355

Illustrations

1.1. Cameron County levee with
Border Patrol road, 2009.   15

3.1. Border wall at Tijuana,
Mexico, 2009.   57

9.1. University of Texas at
Brownsville–Texas Southmost
College border fence, 2009.   205

9.2. Workers pouring concrete for
Hidalgo County hydraulic wall, 2008.   210

9.3. Construction of hydraulic wall
at Anzalduas County Park, 2009.   211

10.1. Workers constructing hydraulic
wall near McAllen, Texas, 2008.   236

10.2. Workers on concrete forms fronting
old levee near Weslaco, Texas, 2008.   246

10.3. View from north side of Hidalgo
County hydraulic wall, 2009.   247

10.4. Border wall separating Nogales,
Arizona, from Nogales, Mexico, 2009.   254

11.1. Project 28 towers outside
of Sasabe, Arizona, 2009.   276

Maps

1. The U.S.-Mexico Borderlands   2

2. Terrain near Brownsville, Texas,
   and Matamoros, Tamaulipas   39

3. Terrain near Nogales, Arizona,
   and Nogales, Sonora   252

Part One

A Virtual American Dream

Map 1. The U.S.-Mexico Borderlands. (Map by Margret
Mulcahy, East Carolina University Center for Geographic
Information Science)

Chapter 1
A Simple Solution

Perhaps the core implications of Time do not occur until, straining to hear the unintelligible ramblings of the youthful radiation oncologist, we are forced to face down the possibility of our own death. Or perhaps Time's reminder is the inevitable passing of a parent or beloved friend, or even the family pet, one second romping with the kids, another inexplicably expiring on the freshly cut front lawn, legs jerking among the roots of the bermuda as unspoken words collect on the tongues of the gathering children. The vapid democracy of illness and death produces in the living an understanding of Time as the distillate of life.

Time can be particularly cruel to those residing in the U.S.-Mexico borderlands. Those living along the northern banks of the Rio Grande, the Big River, as well as those on the Mexican side of the Río Bravo, the Fierce River, may experience Time in very different and more direct ways than those in the interior of border states and those in nonborder states. The countenance of Time may be far different in the South Texas border towns of La Paloma, Relampago, Blue Town, Mercedes, San Benito, Brownsville, Harlingen, Santa Rosa, McAllen, Donna, Pharr, Rio Grande City, Santa Maria, Progresso, Zapata, Granjeno, Sullivan City, and San Juan than in Dallas, Dubuque, and Washington, D.C.[1]

For undocumented workers along the border, Time may be counted in units of mesmerizing panic while crossing the Río Bravo on inflated inner tubes linked by lines of thin, wet twine, one eye fixed on a six-year-old child, the other on the *coyote*, the human smuggler.[2] Traversing a dangerous river is followed by a crazed dash toward a new life, beginning with a wild ride in a fifteen-year-old Ford van, motor revving, the *coyote* sweating in the vehicle's air-conditioned interior as his passengers pray out loud to their patron saint. Illegal entry also may be an attempt to rejoin an abandoned life in the United States after the *abuela*, the grandmother, has died and the sons have rushed back home to the funeral in San Luís Potosí. How then will these same sons get back safely to their families and jobs in Des Moines, Iowa?

If there is not a dangerous river to cross along some parts of the border, there may be an even more hostile desert in locales such as Nogales, where thousands have already died illegally crossing the borderline.

For a Latino Border Patrol agent sworn to apprehend these workers and their families, Time's foreshortened memory may end in uncounted bravery or a coward's desperation when shadowy figures suddenly emerge from the banks of the Rio Grande or the deep canyons south of San Diego. Anonymous to the public in his or her green nylon uniform, often despised by local residents for a history of other agents' transgressions, this federal law enforcer must immediately decide what action to take.[3] Are these human outlines heavily armed cocaine smugglers, or are they nameless men, women, and children looking for work in a new land? Alone in the desert under a dark moon, the agent knows that, whatever decision he or she makes, backup cannot arrive in less than forty-five minutes.

For those on both sides of this international boundary—whether community residents, undocumented workers, law enforcement officers, or tourists—personal safety cannot be assumed or taken for granted. The borderlands have always been a very dangerous place in which to live.[4]

In the border villages, towns, and cities from Brownsville to San Diego, from Matamoros to Tijuana, Time is also sensed as centuries of family, community, and regional history unique to the American experience. Those who live in Nogales, Arizona, may have as much or more in common with those residing in Nogales, Sonora, than with those of nearby Tucson.

Although Time reigns supreme in the borderlands, geography and topography cannot be ignored. Isolated from mainstream Mexican and American culture and politics, these borderlands form nothing less than a slim wedge between two very different nations, one first-world, one in the third-.[5] The rural landscape ranges from rich delta farmland with two growing seasons to high Sonoran desert. Neither entirely Mexican nor entirely American, the people of the border, *sui generis*, and the landscape in which they are embedded are perpetually misunderstood, underestimated, and even distrusted by federal officials in the distant capitals of México, D.F., and Washington, D.C.

Arbitrary but binding decisions made in the two national capitals have the ability to directly form, shape, and change the lives of residents on both sides of the border—and, more tellingly but in ways less understood, the lives of those far from these borderlands. The prevalent supposition that residents on both sides of this international boundary are passive recipients of their respective nation's laws and policies arrogantly disregards history. Repeatedly these people of the borderlands have negotiated, mitigated, ignored, stalled, passively tolerated, blunted, changed, or fought to the bitter end laws, regulations, and policies they deemed unacceptable. They also repelled invading armies, armed bands of outlaws, and bureaucrats with MBAs and law degrees. The complexities of life in the borderlands are frequently far too intricate to be understood or appreciated in federal offices in Washington and Mexico City.[6]

Olga Rivera graduated from Brownsville's Porter High School in the spring of 1978. Her life across Time plays out in edited closeups and broad pans of the camera's eye, first as a novice eighteen-year-old field researcher, then a part-time assistant and secretary, then later a full-time college employee at the University of Texas, Brownsville–Texas Southmost College (UTB-TSC), less than a city block from the bridge to Matamoros, Tamaulipas, Mexico.[7] Just over five feet tall, with long, black hair framing her dark eyes, Olga dressed in crisp blue jeans and a white blouse little different from those of the other Latinas roaming the academic halls of UTB-TSC.

Beneath my office window amid a verdant patio formed by what was once the juncture of the morgue at Fort Brown and the officers' infirmary, I saw Olga return from lunch with her boyfriend Carlos, kiss him quickly, then skip up the stairs to greet me with a smile. Looking down through the royal palms, bougainvillea, and acacia, I saw Carlos, his steps falling silently on the terra cotta tile, walk briskly in the direction of Olin Library.

From the very beginning Olga was the star of a summer research program funded by Washington dollars siphoned through Brownsville City

Hall. Antonio "Tony" Zavaleta, one of my colleagues at UTB-TSC, had re-cruited a group of ten high school graduates who badly needed summer jobs in a region in which systemic poverty is pervasive. Tony and I sent Olga and our other high school interviewers to selected households in Brownsville neighborhoods, where they introduced themselves, as they had been trained to do, then conducted a twenty-minute interview before exiting gracefully. This survey questionnaire was no easy matter, a tough sell to barrio residents with many other things to do than answer questions from an unknown teen-ager who had appeared uninvited on their doorstep. A tireless but cheerful motivator, Olga was both the best interviewer and the best leader among the recruits.[8]

I regularly dropped off Olga and the other teens in neighborhoods they had never before seen, then picked them up at a certain street corner at an arranged time. As I drove up, Olga always stood patiently under the slim shade of a tall palm, her stack of completed interviews clutched to her chest. The others students huddled in the shade to avoid the stifling heat, heads down, often worn out and dispirited. For every one interview her fellow high school graduates completed, Olga completed three.

In later years, Olga married her high school boyfriend Carlos Garcia, raised two daughters, worked full time, and took college classes. Graduating in 1981, she was immediately hired by her alma mater as a data entry opera-tor in the new Department of Information Technology. Thriving on staff training and professional development workshops, Olga also tried her hand at teaching in the classroom and, over the years, moved in and out of various positions and titles. Again and again Olga demonstrated a steadfast compe-tency along with a disdain for academic laziness in all its forms and shapes.

Stumbling into law enforcement, Carlos worked first for the Brownsville Police Department, then with the Cameron County sheriff's office before fi-nally landing a coveted job with the Immigration and Naturalization Service as a customs officer at Brownsville's bridges to Matamoros. Such employ-ment was coveted because job security and a federal pension speak loudly when the most common local work is picking grapefruit, oranges, cabbages, and onions at a piece rate in Rio Grande Valley orchards and fields. Carlos's job was to scrutinize all those leaving and entering the territorial boundaries of the United States, allowing only those with the proper legal documents and goods to pass. His brothers and brothers-in-law soon followed him into federal law enforcement.

Born and raised in Brownsville, Carlos is a second-generation citizen of the United States. Olga, Carlos, and their two daughters reside in a two-bedroom wood-framed house on a quiet street in a Brownsville barrio. Car-los's parents live barely two miles distant from them in another Brownsville neighborhood. Covered in dust and poinsettias, Olga and Carlos's house is a stone's throw from the banks of the Rio Grande.

Unlike Carlos, Olga was born in Matamoros, *en el otro lado*, on the other side, of the Rio Grande. After Olga married Carlos, she became an American citizen. But she was not one before. For more than ten years Olga and certain members of her family lived illegally in Brownsville. When first brought to this country by her parents, Olga did not speak a word of English and was thrown into public school in Brownsville with no formal preparation. She recalls, "They put me on the back row of all my classes. I had no idea what was going on. I got no help in English." By high school graduation, Olga spoke fluent English.

Border Time is transnational, unhindered in South Texas by a political line of demarcation assigned to the Rio Grande/Río Bravo. Olga and Carlos's story is only one among many; on the border, each individual and place can be very distinct from another. Twenty miles upriver from Olga and Carlos's neighborhood, at Anzalduas County Park, *coyotes* smuggle in thousands of workers each year while *narcotrafficantes*, drug smugglers, find this particular bend in the river an excellent site at which to cross tons of marijuana and cocaine. Part of a Spanish land grant awarded to the original colonists in 1767, a centuries-old Oblate chapel next to the park has morphed into a staging area for illegal aliens and drugs.[9]

Olga Rivera Garcia's singular transnational story is also typical: lives of new immigrants to the United States often reveal a complexity not easily circumscribed within the popular Horatio Alger myth of success guaranteed by hard work. One, two, or more generations removed from their families' immigration experiences, Americans may forget or selectively disremember the joys and tragedies of their immigrant status—or whether they entered legally or *sin papeles*, without documents.

Olga, Carlos, and their kids live geographically less than five miles from Olga's place of birth. Yet the distance economically from Olga's Mexican family in the poorest sections of Matamoros is much greater. In this border city, third-world poverty prevails behind the broad avenues, a tourist curtain of prosperity masking the economic status of the majority of Mexican citizens who, if fortunate enough to be employed, work hard for several dollars a day. Those who are the most fortunate work in the twin plants, the Mexican- and American-owned maquiladoras, where they earn the exceptional wage of several dollars an hour.[10]

This pervasive poverty often goes unseen by the average American tourist to Matamoros or other cities of the Mexican border, such as Juárez or Tijuana, or the Mexican communities more modest in size. It is partially invisible; you have to know where to look. For example, throwaway cardboard salvaged from the back alleys of my former Brownsville neighborhood on a Monday can, by Tuesday, become exterior building material for one-room shacks in Matamoros. Cinder blocks purchased at Walmart, Lowe's, or Home Depot are the preferred building material but far too expensive when the average Matamoros job pays so little. Those who can afford cinder-block houses on both sides of the river often build them one wall at a time. In the poorest neighborhoods of Matamoros extension cords from one structure to the next serve as the only source of electricity, and clean water is scarce for drinking, cooking, or bathing. When it rains, the narrow pathways flood, the dirt floors turn to mud, and the cardboard, tin, and cinder-block construc-tions that are the homes of many residents frequently collapse.[11]

Oklahomans I grew up with in the 1960s would call Olga and Carlos Garcia "wetbacks." For me, born and raised in Oklahoma City suburbs, where wetbacks were uncommon but not unheard of on the nearby farms and ranches, this derogatory term held no real substance or meaning. In a state founded as recently as 1907, my own family ignored its immigrant roots. Only much later in my adult life did I learn one side of my family were fourth-generation Americans, land-poor Okie "Boomers" from England by way of Arkansas, and the other side were only second-generation Americans descended from Lithuanian peasants. In Oklahoma, which recently cele-brated its centennial, country of origin and date of citizenship can frequently be trumped by land, oil, cattle, and other sources of wealth. Intentionally ignorant of the specifics of their own state history, including the exodus of many impoverished Okies to California during the Great Depression, my fel-low Oklahomans have long held personal wealth and its accoutrements to be the ticket to social acceptance and prominence.[12]

Labeling based on perceived notions of race, class, nativity, or other markers can be tricky within certain regions and histories. Definitions of race and ethnicity, whether in Oklahoma or on the Mexican border, are far more elusive than many Americans would like, or want, to believe. In the Lower Rio Grande Valley, often called simply the Valley, Olga Rivera Garcia, not unjustifiably, considers herself no more or less a Mexican national than she did before she married Carlos. During this same time Carlos, in contrast, identified himself as Mexican American or, less frequently, Hispanic, even though those in other parts of Texas, New Mexico, Arizona, and California may have selected other labels. At one time the term *Chicano* was used in the Valley to refer to college-educated young adults who were also politi-cally active or Hispanics living in far-away Austin, 350 miles to the north, or in San Antonio, Dallas, Houston, or Los Angeles. Most recently, while I was living in the Valley border city of McAllen, it became clear that the label

Mexican American had been replaced by the more common *Hispanic* or *Latino*.[13]

In the 1970s and 1980s in Brownsville, Texas, Olga and Carlos, like the three Valley teenagers my wife and I welcomed into our home, or our neighbors, campus colleagues, and friends throughout Brownsville, were individuals about whom I cared rather than labels, people first rather than Mexican American, Mexican national, Chicano, or Anglo. Certainly I never thought of Olga's citizenship status, or that of any of those with whom I was acquainted, as crucial or necessary. For their part, my college students at UTB-TSC referred to me as Anglo, a label I hated but one with which I was forced to live while in the Valley. The validity of these racial and ethnic labels went largely unquestioned in the Valley at that time, as in the suburbs of Oklahoma and many other places throughout the United States.

Like all the other instructors at the college in Brownsville, Tony Zavaleta and I taught a busy schedule of five courses a semester, plus one to three course overloads. Finding time to exercise between the demands of work and family life was always challenging. During lunchtime we sometimes jogged together around the city golf course, which lay squeezed between a *resaca*, a small lake, bordering the campus and the banks of the Rio Grande. The golf course on our left, the Rio Grande on our right, we ran down a narrow, sandy road talking at first about nothing in particular, then fell silent as the demands of running under a tropical sun commanded our attention. Our view of the waters of the Rio Grande was limited by the thick vegetation and earthen levees designed to prevent Brownsville from flooding.

One lunch period in October 1978, two young men came slowly out of the weeds and brush lining the sandy road, saw us, then continued in our direction. Perhaps realizing that we were crazy Americans with nothing better to do than jog during the heat of the day (the temperature was close to one hundred degrees), they did not panic at the sight of us. Their only other choice, once we had seen them, was to retrace their steps back to the banks of the river. Never missing a stride, Tony waved to them. The two waved back. As we rounded another curve in the road bordering the river, I looked back to see them trudging across the fairway, both dressed in tan pants, cuffs still rolled up above their knees, cheap sneakers, T-shirts, and baseball caps. Soaked to their chests, their shirts were marked by a thick line of river water and mud. A few minutes earlier they had waded across the river under the international bridge linking Matamoros to Brownsville.[14] Once they had crossed the golf course, the two men were less than a block from the safety of downtown streets.

I was shocked by the sight of two men so openly crossing the international border at high noon on a Tuesday, but, exhausted from the run in the heat, I never asked Tony, not until many years later, about this brief encounter. By his utter lack of alarm or concern—the mere wave of his hand—it was clear to me that the two young men were an unremarkable sight. Born and raised in Brownsville, he never gave a second thought to the illegal crossers because it was an insignificant event, one he had witnessed many times.

Those two young undocumented workers are joined inextricably by shared history, family, culture, and blood with hundreds of thousands of other residents on both sides of the border from Brownsville to San Diego, over centuries a commingling of millions of lives never completely separated by the nations in which they reside. This sediment of Time, embodied in families like that of Olga Rivera Garcia and her husband Carlos, or that of Antonio Zavaleta, or those of eighth-generation Valley Mexican Americans, reduced my sighting of one illegal crossing to a mere blip on a far grander parade of life.[15]

The vast, unique history of the U.S.-Mexico borderlands clearly demonstrates that the international boundary between Mexico and the United States is frequently a figment of the political imaginations of decision makers in Mexico City and in Washington. In reality and practice it is a boundary regularly crossed and recrossed each day of the year by border residents pursuing their routine lives. It is no surprise that deterrence theory, the major theoretical underpinning upon which the U.S. Border Patrol struggles to maintain order and law, has been largely ineffective in the borderlands. That is, it is ineffective except in the minds of political leaders and institutions invested in certain imprecise theories of law enforcement, border labels, stereotypes, and myths with little basis in reality.[16]

In South Texas, Rio Grande City was colonized by Spanish soldiers and settlers in 1757. Not until 164 years after its founding were two border agents assigned there, along with two agents to nearby Brownsville and four to Hidalgo. A year later, in 1922, a handful of other agents were sent to Harlingen, Mission, Kingsville, and Alice. In 1924 Congress formally created the Border Patrol, and by 1975 the department had 1,746 agents. Since the events of 9/11 the number of agents has increased to approximately 20,000.

But the influx of undocumented workers and vast amounts of illegal drugs has not been deterred regardless of the number of agents patrolling the line. Of the approximately 29 million foreign-born who entered the United States in the last twenty-five years, about 12 million migrated illegally. Half of them, roughly 6 million in number, are from Mexico; another 12 percent are from El Salvador, Guatemala, Honduras, and the Philippines. The vast majority of the undocumented aliens from Mexico and Latin America crossed into the United States by way of our southern border with Mexico. Drugs annually crossing from Mexico into the hands of the American consumer are valued in the billions of dollars. The amount and value of drugs also have not been reduced since the War on Drugs was initiated several decades in the past.[17]

Now, highlighted by the horrific events of September 11, 2001, the overriding concern is with international terrorists who might enter this country by way of the Mexican border to cause irreparable harm to our homeland. They are a major threat to our national security. We must deter them.

Time structures and frames border and nonborder communities alike, populating both with those who share similar histories, cultures, languages, wisdoms, and perceptions. Those Americans who live in nonborder cultures, particularly those who have lost or conveniently forgotten their own family narratives—as has been the case with my own family in suburban Oklahoma—are in a difficult position. Since they are forced to rely on experiences other than their own, they can fall victim to social information and expertise supplied to them by trusted social institutions and/or rely on social myths, labels, and "common sense." Border stereotypes abound and thrive not only in nonborder communities, but also within border communities.

In remarkable contrast to the simplistic labels that may fuel these misreadings of the borderlands, border factory workers, ranch laborers, migrant farmworkers, service workers, single working mothers, municipal and county employees, public school teachers, construction workers, street vendors, the elderly, the young—all those who make up the populations of border Latinos and Anglos—are as American in their own special ways as any of the tens of thousands of Americans claiming ancestral passage on the tiny *Mayflower*. Regardless of place, Time is always translucent.[18]

In early January of 2006 I received an unsolicited email from a vice president at Honeywell, Inc., a global conglomerate with annual revenues of 30 billion dollars that manufactures products ranging from household thermostats to engines for NASA spacecraft.[19] This corporation's original 1885 contribution to the marketplace was, in fact, a kind of coal furnace thermostat called the "damper flapper." The email read in part: "I am leading some initiatives at Honeywell on border protection. . . . Tools such as ground sensors, radar and video for example. . . . Would you be willing to talk to me or maybe even my team sometime?"

After the events of 9/11, the George W. Bush administration formed the Department of Homeland Security (DHS) by enveloping twenty-two separate federal law enforcement agencies and programs, along with their more than two hundred thousand employees, into one unwieldy bureaucracy. After a series of miserable failures, DHS eventually birthed the Secure Border Initiative (SBI), designed as "a comprehensive multi-year plan to secure America's borders and to reduce illegal immigration." DHS decided that it would secure the U.S.-Mexico borderlands by constructing a concrete and steel fence along with a "virtual" fence to be called SBInet. This combination of low tech and sophisticated high tech would aid Border Patrol agents in controlling the flow of illegal immigrants and drugs and inhibit international terrorists from illegally crossing into the homeland.[20]

Honeywell, Inc., now stood in line with other major defense contractors for a $250 million federal contract to construct a virtual fence that, it was vehemently hoped by politicians of both major parties in Washington, would finally resolve the myriad problems and issues at our southern border. Major contractors, including Honeywell, believed that this initial $250 million contract, modest by standards of the defense industry, would soon lead to multibillion-dollar contracts to construct a virtual wall stretching from Brownsville to San Diego.

SBInet, illegal immigration, and the fence are exactly why I sat fiddling with my PowerPoint presentation in Clearwater, Florida, one sunny Thursday morning in March 2007, a small crowd of Honeywell employees cautiously eyeing me from around a conference table. Although dressed like professional golfers, most of these engineers were executives who led their divisions. There was Randy from the Honeywell Smart Lab in Albuquerque; Chris from Government Relations in Washington, D.C.; Jason from Marketing; Len and Joe from the Space and Defense Division; Kevin in Security Software; Todd and Scott from Sales; Ray in Military Tech Services; Danny from Business Development; and Bob, the local connection, the manager of Honeywell's Clearwater plant. George, the team leader who originally invited me to give the presentation, sat at the opposite end of the table, patiently waiting for me to begin.

Unfortunately I couldn't fire up Honeywell's state-of-the-art computer, because my own university-issue PowerPoint software was an older version and seemed hopelessly incompatible. I looked around at the fifteen white male executives immersed in their BlackBerries and laptops and asked, "Could someone please get your IT person?"

I had jumped on the flight to Florida because I believed I had something vital to convey to Honeywell's executives about the proposed fence between two countries. After riding shotgun with Border Patrol agents for two years and witnessing firsthand the problems they confronted daily, I had published my findings in the first comprehensive study of this federal law enforcement agency. During my stint with the agents I eyeballed the *coyotes*, those apprehended *sin papeles*, the drug smugglers tied to the *narcotraffi-cantes*, and all the rest of the criminal element populating the borderline.[21]

Given unprecedented access to the Border Patrol for two years, I'd documented the data, then analyzed it along with additional data underlying the foundation of specific immigration and Border Patrol policies and regulations, many of which were based upon deterrence theory. I described in detail how Border Patrol agents daily placed themselves in high-risk situations while patrolling the line. At the same time I documented the many ways in which undocumented workers also were placed in constant danger as they sought to enter the United States.[22] As the talk in Washington of an international fence morphed into political reality, I believed my research might contribute to the planning and development of a virtual border fence designed to be secure and as reasonably safe as possible for all concerned.

I remained optimistic that a detailed description of my recent findings, presented within the context of my thirty-five years of borderland studies, might provide Honeywell engineers insights otherwise unavailable. My goal at Honeywell was to establish the requirements for a virtual fence that, on the one hand, would be a strong barrier to *narcotrafficantes*, drug smugglers, the *coyotes*, and international terrorists. That same research told me it was possible to develop that secure barrier and virtual fence in ways that would, on the other hand, maintain the safety and dignity of those seeking honest employment in this country without putting Border Patrol agents at risk.[23]

It was first necessary to appreciate and consider the bravery and heroism of agents, something that frequently went unacknowledged. From my two years with agents patrolling the line I also was familiar with why it was so difficult, even when agents put their own lives at risk, to apprehend even a small percentage of those trying illegally to cross the border. Observing and interviewing undocumented workers, I was also informed by their fear, their physical exhaustion, and their human suffering: I had heard the cries of infants and children and seen the faces of women who believed that upon their arrest they would be sexually assaulted and/or killed.[24]

Having witnessed successes and failures of the system and policies in place along the border, I was concerned that Honeywell would seek out high-tech engineering solutions that could be bolstered by misleading Border Patrol measurements of success, such as apprehension rates.[25] I was equally concerned that these engineering solutions would take a toll in human suffering for which, for whatever reasons, the engineers would not be concerned. In short, Honeywell's solution to SBInet might be a glorious engineering feat for the ages, but one treating both agents of the U.S. Border Patrol and undocumented workers as expendable blips on a computer screen.

George had shaken my hand firmly when he met me at the Tampa airport the night before. A tall, handsome man in his late thirties, George sported short, blond hair in a faux military cut, expensive slacks and shirt, and a Bluetooth glued to his right ear. We were delayed in rush-hour traffic but were soon ensconced in George's favorite restaurant overlooking the ocean. Over little parasol drinks after dinner we exchanged pleasantries as Larry, another Honeywell employee just in from Turkey, scanned me from head to toe. Larry was less than forthcoming about his own personal job history, leaving me to take at face value that he was in "international security." I was left to assume Larry was one of those former CIA or military intelligence types who since 9/11 have become ubiquitous, popping up in the private sector and on university campuses where they teach courses in "security studies."[26] Larry soon excused himself, and I never saw him again. Apparently he had assessed that I was no risk.

The next morning in the conference room, after Honeywell's IT guy jump-started my antiquated software, I was finally able to ask a rudimentary question to those seated around me: "How many of you have ever traveled to the Mexican border?" No one spoke up, no hands were raised around the conference table. These decision makers, while champing at the bit to construct an airtight security system spanning more than two thousand miles, had never personally seen the low banks and steep gorges of the Rio Grande, or its islands and sandbars, or the formidable Chihuahuan and Sonoran deserts, or the rugged mountain ranges. Nor had they ever walked through any of the border cities, towns, and villages.

Neither were any of them acquainted with the diverse populations on both sides of the border, nor did any of them have a fundamental understanding of the political and economic conditions in Central and Latin America that motivated illegal immigrants to travel thousands of miles just to reach the American border—a journey along which they are harassed, extorted, robbed, kidnapped, beaten, sexually assaulted, and killed, often by Mexican law enforcement officers.[27]

No border fence was going to keep out all undocumented workers. No stationary structure would prove a match for human ingenuity and motivation. Illegal workers are, in fact, crucial to the welfare of many Mexican communities long since grown dependent upon remittances.[28] In addition, countless subsidiary jobs, such as that of "tube wrangler," rely upon illegal crossers. Tube wranglers make their daily living selling inner tubes at a premium to illegal border crossers on the south side of the Río Bravo. After the tubes are left on the north side, following their one-way trip, the wranglers cautiously swim from one country to the other to retrieve them, reinflating the used tubes by means of unwieldy air tanks hidden in the riverbank cane.

Fig. 1.1 Cameron County levee with Border Patrol road
before fence construction. Near the Rio Grande,
Brownsville, Texas, 2009.

They then tie their tubes into long rafts and tug them back across to the
Mexican shore to resell to the next customers to come along.[29]

Stories among Border Patrol agents are already circulating about an en-
terprising group of Mexicans drug smugglers who build a steel ramp for a
van or truck to span border barriers already in place. Then, before the authorities can get to the scene, they dismantle the ramp and move it to another site. For decades smuggling and employment related to it have been
big business in Mexico.

I show photographs of U.S. Border Patrol agents in body armor posed
with M-16s in front of an Econoline van filled with over a ton of marijuana,
and I explain why these same agents are very worried they are about to take
incoming fire from the south banks of the Rio Grande. I tell the Honeywell
engineers, who have never spent five minutes in the U.S.-Mexico borderlands, about the first dead worker I saw lying in the Valley weeds along State
Highway 281 after a high-speed chase. Eight men had been stuffed into a

1991 Toyota Corolla by their *coyote*; three more were packed into the trunk. When the *coyote* at the wheel "bailed out," a common practice, the car rolled into the highway median, and one of the undocumented workers in the front seat, an old man, panicked, jumped out of the car, and ran into oncoming traffic. When the first car hit the old man at full speed, the impact was so severe it flung his body fifty feet into the weeds at the side of the highway. The exact point where he was struck on State Highway 281 was marked by his left tennis shoe, out of which he literally had been slammed. Next to his tennis shoe was his upper dental plate.[30]

And I tell them about the "floater," a human corpse found in the Rio Grande, vividly discussed at the Border Patrol muster along with detailed photos of the bloated body. Identified as an "amateur" drug runner ("amateur" because he carried less than twenty pounds of marijuana in his knapsack), the body was eventually turned over to the Mexican authorities at the border for identification and burial by his family. Many bodies and body parts discovered are never identified.

I tell them also about the *ropa usada*, giant bales of used clothes smuggled into Mexico by the rental truckload, the tons of frozen chicken bound for *turista* restaurants in Mexican border cities, the avocados headed north, guns smuggled south, the Mexican prostitutes at the highway bars, all part of the endless goods and services smuggled back and forth across the Rio Grande year after year, decade after decade.[31]

And, last but not least, I tell them about the Mexican military and other armed groups that regularly cross with impunity into the United States.[32]

I want these engineers, obviously impatient and itching to get out of here by early afternoon, to know about the forests of border cacti that can rip apart your arm, the boulders and the ravines that cause falls that can result in disability or surgery, the soaring temperatures that bring dehydration within forty-eight hours, the poisonous snakes, and the crying infants in the arms of trembling women—always the first apprehended when a group of undocumented workers runs for its freedom. I cannot forget the toddler tossed out by border carjackers and not discovered by Border Patrol agents for several hot summer days; the two agents who finally came upon his corpse first thought they were looking at an old doll strapped in a child's car seat.[33]

Since 1996, the first year that statistics of dead workers were collected, an average of more than four hundred illegal crossers have died each year attempting to cross the Mexican border into the United States.[34] I knew in fact these figures to be undercounts, because law enforcers never find all the bodies in this vast, unforgiving frontier. The ways, furthermore, in which the bodies of undocumented workers are counted or not counted in the collection of these statistics leaves much to the imagination: the old man struck by a passing motorist after the *coyote* bailed out on the Valley's Highway 281 was never included among those who died. His death was not defined by the number crunchers as directly attributable to his illegal entry because the accident was fifteen miles from the border.[35]

In recent years, I tell the executives around the conference table, there have been significant positive changes in the Border Patrol. Budget increases have been translated into newer, higher-quality equipment, including communications systems, boats, planes, drones, and agency computers. Yet American technology in place along the border is, I know from firsthand experience, still a dismal failure despite Border Patrol claims to the contrary.[36] Ground sensors, the foundation of the Border Patrol's system of border security, are Vietnam-era trash. They simply do not work. Most determined undocumented workers still find ways to cross the border, their total numbers lessening only from a combination of economic recession and more agents. Not even the recession, however, stanched the mind-boggling flow of illegal immigrants and illegal drugs.[37] Honeywell faces formidable challenges in building what I suggest should be not only an effective border fence, but also a safe one.

We break for lunch. Several of the engineers are curious about my presentation; most are not. One of the curious sums it up in an aside: "I didn't know the Mexican border and the Border Patrol were so screwed up." While the group around the table is certainly competent and qualified as engineers with many years of corporate experience, they are not necessarily sensitive to the human implications or consequences of their products. Another Honeywell engineer provides a broader context in which to judge the group at the table: "These guys here haven't the slightest idea of what it's like out there. They think they do, but they don't."

After a quick, tasty lunch in the company cafeteria, I walk along the long corridors of the Honeywell plant to get a feel for the place. Passing by hundreds of workers behind glass walls, most dressed in sanitary white from head to toe, more than a few with white masks covering their faces, I have more questions than answers. The Honeywell men and women stand hunched over space-age optical devices or sit at tables next to small piles of chip boards on which they perform intricate tasks and operations. A few wave as I walk by, and I wave back.

George, the team leader, a take-charge kind of guy, after summing up my morning presentation demands that his team develop a formal business plan. He writes on the left side of the white board the sources of the information necessary to bring a "superior security system," the virtual border fence, to market. Various team members talk about "value," then much more about "marketing the security product."

Jason, from Marketing, waxes eloquently in business-school speak on "off-the-shelf Honeywell products" and how to integrate them "with existing technologies." Honeywell, according to Jason, should be able in a very short time to "get it up and running in the field." All that then remains is to "tweak it and work out the bugs."

As specific tactics and solutions unfold around the table, I have no intention of remaining silent. I am not a member of this team, only a short-term outside consultant. As such, Honeywell hired me to provide my expertise and honest opinions about the border fence. I do not give one hoot about corporate protocol, deference to higher-ups, and all the other restraints by which the full-time employees, regardless of their stature within Honeywell, might feel constrained. So I remind the team that the real experts are not the engineers sitting around the table in Clearwater, Florida, but the federal agents who spend their careers patrolling the line, along with the millions of undocumented workers who successfully cross the Mexican border time after time.

"Okay," says one of the engineers from Government Relations who listens carefully to what I have to say. "No problem. We'll buy us a Border Patrol agent." (Honeywell could always hire an agent or former agent as a consultant. But all Border Patrol agents are not carbon copies of each other, nor are they trained to question those who pay their salaries.)

A robust discussion of other marketing and pricing concerns immediately follows. Honeywell must, in order to pay its one hundred thousand employees, develop and manufacture products that sell for no less than $20 million a pop. Otherwise, they lose money on the deal. (Later that night, one of the engineers tells me, "Simple economies of scale. We're too big in some ways, too small in others. Our start-up costs are high. We're slower and more expensive than some of our small competitors. So we have to be very careful about whether this border fence project is going to be big enough for us to make a profit.")

Suddenly the Clearwater plant manager, so far silent as a clam, says in a jolly voice, "Anybody want to see our new secret weapon? It's right outside the door and across the parking lot." I certainly would like to see Honeywell's "new secret weapon." But first it is time for the team to watch, according to George, "some simulations the guys at the Virtual Lab in Albuquerque have been working on for the last six months." The large screen at the end of the narrow room comes to life as a childlike outline of a missile silo "somewhere in the Midwest" comes into focus. The silo, housing one of hundreds of intercontinental ballistic missiles (ICBMs) left over from the Cold War, is nuked to the nines and ready to blow. Honeywell's task is to develop security software to crush any threat to these dinosaur missiles, thereby avoiding a radioactive nightmare in our own backyard.

Played out in images resembling the first generation of video Pong (but without the annoying sound effects that drove a generation of parents crazy), a pickup truck filled with local yokels stumbles by accident onto an ICBM silo site. Honeywell's innovative technology quickly determines that the intruders are beer-guzzling nimrods from Nebraska. However, when a vehicle carrying Taliban terrorists crosses Honeywell's invisible security screen, heavily armed rent-a-cops quickly save the day.

One of the engineers sitting next to me leans over to fill in the missing details. It is very expensive to protect each one of the hundreds of ICBM silos throughout the Midwest on a 24/7 basis with "on-site human security." Honeywell's Virtual Lab has developed a system in which one guard watches a hundred missile silos. No alarm sounds on any security screens as long as rednecks chug beers atop an armed ICBM. But if the bad guys appear, then Honeywell technology telephones the cavalry.

The lights in the conference room come back on as the plant manager stands and stretches. Then he says, "How about that secret weapon?" Eagerly, I follow the engineers out the door.

Later in the day, the Tampa restaurant where George has made dinner reservations resembles a *CSI Miami* set. The place is all polished, poured concrete tabletops, polished stainless steel, and enough glass to resemble the Scripps Oceanographic Institute. Our dinner swims in postmodern fish tanks abutting our tables. Surrounded by South Beach wannabes, the Honeywell engineers are very picky about their wines.

I order the house merlot and talk to Ray, a former Air Force general and fighter pilot turned Honeywell employee. Ray differs from the rest of the team because he has lived through real conflicts and wars rather than virtual Pong simulations of terrorist attacks. In fact, Ray appears to be the only member of the team whose life was shaped and formed outside of the encompassing corporate world of Honeywell, its subsidiaries, and its competitors.

Sitting across from Ray is another executive who, as the wine flows, grows more talkative. I ask him about the "actual price of the security product" Honeywell is considering, a topic never once discussed during the afternoon session. I ask him how what they call "market price" is determined if Honeywell's virtual border fence actually comes to fruition.

"That's not really my area," he says right off. But I can tell he really wants to set the university professor straight on this subject, so I push him a little harder. According to this VP, "market price" actually has nothing to do with "cost" in Honeywell's business plan. It's all about "value," he repeatedly tells me. Warming to the subject, he says, "At some point we've got to sit around the table and come up with the market value of this product."

"You mean the cost to you, plus your profit?" I ask.

"Value has nothing to do with that," he says, now seeming really to enjoy himself. "Value is simply what the customer will pay for the product."

The plates have been cleared and more bottles of expensive wine appear. Cigars in the restaurant's smoking bar are in the offing.

"Look," he says with patience, "every MBA knows that value is not just about cost. Sure, you have to cover your costs. That's fundamental. Value is about what the market will pay for your product regardless of what it costs to produce, including R&D [research and development], and regardless of the profit you need to make. What we try to do is keep our costs under control because we're so big. We do that in part by limiting the R&D on what we sell. We take a product off the shelf, that we've already developed and paid for, reconfigure it for the job, then determine what it's worth to the customer."[38]

"So just for purposes of the discussion, does this mean you could make as much as 50 percent profit on a product?"

The VP smiles at me as if I am the next best thing to an imbecile.

"Much more," is what he finally says. For Honeywell, Inc., along with all the other defense contractors, it is not about cost plus profit, it is always about value. If the market can bear it, in this case the market being the federal government desiring to build a virtual fence along the Mexican border, the markup may be 100 percent, or 500 percent, or 1,000 percent. Or higher.

I am wildly wrong about Honeywell. Over the weekend it becomes clear they do not seek a highly sophisticated, whiz-bang, technological solution to a complex set of border security problems called the virtual fence. Instead, Honeywell simply desires the cheapest engineering solution its best engineers can patch together from their existing, off-the-shelf inventory. Honeywell can then assign a price to their product, the border fence, based upon their assessment of how much the customer, the feds, will pay. For very little corporate effort and cost, they may make outlandish profits.

The planning and development of Honeywell's virtual border fence really is over before it ever begins. There is little need for research into those border crossers who might challenge the integrity of the virtual fence, those who would police it, those who might operate it, or anyone else. Honeywell engineers indeed can always "find an engineering solution."

Honeywell's solution, and by extension that of any other defense industry contract bidder, is always going to be the damper flapper—whatever product is gathering dust in inventory and, through minimal efforts, can be adapted as part of the engineering solution. Or whatever products the corporation immediately can get its hands on through its suppliers. In this corporate political economy the virtual border fence is always and only about maximizing profit by determining market value. People, if considered at all, finish a distant second.

Time can be a facile trickster even when it comes to transnational corporations. Honeywell, Inc., producers of damper flappers and rocket engines, took another look at its global competitors and decided not to submit a bid for the virtual border fence under SBInet. Nine months after the team meeting in Clearwater, Florida, the Department of Homeland Security, after holding a "business fair" for all potential contractors, awarded the primary contract, an initial $250 million, for building the virtual border fence to Boeing, Inc., the nation's largest aerospace corporation.[39]

But what exactly is this virtual border fence Boeing will build? Boeing is not talking. Neither is the DHS except to reiterate that the virtual border fence will integrate sophisticated technological systems with existing, proven security devices. No federal agency or Boeing defines the virtual border fence except in broad, rather meaningless terms. The project slips quickly out of sight into the realm of the semisecret.

According to a primary contractor, however, the prototype for the virtual border fence will be constructed near Tucson, Arizona, after a working prototype is completed in Florida. Boeing names its virtual fence prototype "Project 28." The DHS soon announces that it will supervise the building of low-tech border fencing in parts of South Texas, New Mexico, and Arizona. In South Texas low-tech fence construction will first begin in Cameron and Hidalgo Counties.

The American public, whether residing in Brownsville, Texas, the county seat of Cameron County, or Dubuque, Iowa, or New York, yearns for simple solutions to complex problems. By nature politicians ache for such solutions. But ignoring the lessons of borderlands history, culture, politics, and geography likely dooms any simple solution to failure. In fact, a simple resolution to border problems in the form of a high-tech border fence had already been constructed a decade earlier. Developed in 1999, it was called the Integrated Surveillance Intelligence System (ISIS).[40] While the Honeywell and Boeing engineers were creating their business plans for a virtual border fence, most remnants of this failed high-tech fence were rusting in a border wind.

While the public continued to yearn for simple resolutions to immigration, drugs, and national security along the border, elected officials, some with presidential aspirations, began envisioning the possibilities for producing political hay. Real issues and concerns about the border fence, both the low- and high-tech versions, soon began to creep out like so many Greeks from the gut of the Trojan horse.

Randomly cruel, always deadly, ephemeral, translucent, by trade a known trickster, Time reminds us in the personages of our own families, our neighbors across the street or down the block, along with all with whom we interact daily, that immigrants and immigration are an integral part of American society. In whatever form, the border fence between Mexico and the United States, its notorious history, its rationalizations and justifications, planning, design, standards, goals, best practices, bidding processes, appropriations, oversight, construction, operation, and maintenance are all an embodiment of competing individuals, institutions, and forces. As such, this border fence is a clear reflection of American polity.

Any border fence can be no less than a symbol in concrete, steel, microchips, and fiber optics of all that is right and wrong with contemporary immigration policy. Regardless of the engineers, there is a human face to this story that cannot be ignored. It includes the community residents on both sides of the border, such as Olga Rivera Garcia's family, Antonio Zavaleta, the two illegal workers I saw crossing into Brownsville, elected politicians, local public officials, and many more. It also includes Boeing, the employees of the Department of Homeland Security, the U.S. Border Patrol, the American military, the Environmental Protection Agency, intelligence experts, media pundits, the Minutemen, members of Congress, immigrant rights groups, and many others.

These disparate, often contradictory voices reflect very different interests and concerns. Each is best judged, weighed, and valued according to the available facts and, as well, discernible self-interests.

A host of questions about the Mexican border fence have gone unanswered, but three remain primary: What exactly is this new border fence being built from Brownsville to San Diego? More to the point, is human safety along the Mexican border in fact anathema to national security? And third, are the issues surrounding the Mexican border fence such diabolical opposites that there is no path down the middle of the dusty border road, no common ground for consensus and agreement? There is a long list of additional unanswered questions, enough to muddy the already murky waters of the Rio Grande.

Certain themes inductively reveal themselves throughout this book. In the final chapter I detail them and make suggestions for relevant policy.

Even as this new Mexican border fence, this virtual American dream now stretching almost seven hundred miles, is modeled, built, and finally operated, it is not too late to guard against the erosion of historical memory by closely examining it from a variety of unheralded perspectives.[41] Everyone concerned with immigration issues, illegal drugs, and national security can join in the public discussion of the history, policy, and consequences of this massive construction project along our southern border. Questioning the consequences and implications of this colossal effort in the U.S.-Mexico borderlands has never been more crucial. Should we, for example, support and promote the construction of the rest of the border fence, or define it as magnificent folly? Might not our best solution lie somewhere in between these two irreconcilable positions?

It is long past time to confront the many challenging contemporary realities of an immigrant America, an America also facing debilitating drug use and drug violence even as it continues to be threatened by enemies outside our borders. By objectively judging the border fence between Mexico and the United States for what it can and can never be, by closely listening to those who most often go unheard along with those who always make themselves heard, we take a small but significant step in confronting, understanding, and resolving this crucial national issue.

Chapter 2

Manny's Disguise Isn't One

The last thing Manuel "Manny" A. Rodriguez needs on the jet to Memphis is a
hard case across the aisle giving him the
prison yard stare. According to Manny,
these days everything is turned around. Now the
lawbreakers have more rights than the law enforcers. Agents are not only targets patrolling the line,
but also targets for members of the general public
who disagree with national immigration policy.
What incenses Manny is the scumbag drug smuggler whose testimony sent two border agents in El
Paso to a federal penitentiary.[1]

"I don't make laws," he tells me. "My job is
to enforce the laws. The public don't seem to
get that."

"Lou Dobbs for President," he says as an afterthought. "You seen Lou's show on TV? He doesn't
pull any punches. Or how about Rush?"

Even with Manny's new green uniforms carefully folded away in his rolling suitcase, there is
no doubt he is pure Border Patrol from the top of
his gimme cap to the worn leather of his hand-

tooled boots. Manny is old-school Border Patrol, legacy, eons of spit and polish distant from the "wimps" graduating like clockwork from the academy in Artesia, New Mexico.[2]

Manny is incapable of disguising who he really is on his recruiting trips to Memphis, Dallas, and Chicago. In his civilian garb at the airport, Manny wears a white, tightly pressed western shirt, "made in Malaysia, wherever the hell that is," neatly tucked into a pair of faded Levi's jeans, also hand-pressed in his kitchen that very morning. His favorite boots, custom made in Laredo, fit him like a glove when the bootmaker sized Manny in 1996. But years of patrolling the line have long since flattened his feet, and now Manny's favorite boots give him blisters if he wears them during his shift.

One thing Manny knows for damned sure: he will never buy boots across the river in Nuevo Laredo, not even if they are half the price of what he pays in Laredo. It is American-made for Manny, whether it is his truck or his cowboy boots—that is, not counting the countries he never heard of, such as Malaysia. In 2009 Manny still refers to french fries as "freedom fries."[3]

It isn't just his shirt with cuff snaps, his high-and-tight military haircut, or even the pressed jeans that scream Border Patrol agent. The disguise buster is his belt buckle with the Border Patrol logo. On shiny, gold metal plate with an embossment of Border Patrol green, the buckle is easily the size of a mature grapefruit. His gut has grown larger since he was promoted to supervisor, so his belt buckle is as impossible to overlook as a shiny front bumper on a forty-year-old pickup.

The same Border Patrol emblem is replicated on his leather cell phone case, shined, like his old boots, to a mirror finish. Manny wears the cell phone case on his hip in place of his holstered service weapon. After more than a decade and a half of patrolling the line, Manny feels naked without his gun on his right hip, so the empty cell phone case with the Border Patrol logo is a hocus-pocus placebo. That way Manny can fiddle with the cell phone case the same way he does with his holstered service weapon, unconsciously readjusting it multiple times when standing in line at the ticket counter at the Laredo airport, then messing with it again before squeezing into the narrow coach seat next to me.

Manny certainly doesn't look like a DEA agent, many of whom along the Mexican border still dress like Don Johnson in television's *Miami Vice*, or an air marshal before the marshals finally convinced their director that terrorists could spot them easily in their mandatory crew cuts, sports jackets, and running shoes.[4]

No, it isn't just the clothes, the logos, or the remnants of military bearing that identify Manny as a career Border Patrol agent. It is his constant checking and rechecking of every passenger he can see from the vantage point of his narrow seat. Who are they? Are they acting in an inconsistent fashion since he last eyeballed them? Does he recognize them from somewhere before?

Mid-flight, raising himself up on the fulcrum of his two powerful arms, he bench presses his full weight against the seat so that it creaks and groans. From this temporary vantage point Manny surveys the path to the jet's rest room the same way he checks out his chances before walking through a cane field fifty yards from the Rio Grande.

Just to confirm what I already know, I finally ask Manny what kind of work he does for a living. He leans over to whisper his answer, his words tucked safely within the drone of the jet. "I work for the Border Patrol. I'm on a recruiting trip." Then he retracts his neck like a turtle into its shell as if waiting for the insults or the blows. None come, but he is ready for them.

Despite the television ads with agents steering ATVs through scenic green passages along the Rio Grande, piloting go-fast boats, or galloping horses along the slopes of picturesque mountains, and despite his own Madison Avenue hyperbole, Manny knows from his own years along the borderline just how tough and demanding the work of a Border Patrol agent can be. So his recruiting sales pitch is designed to rope in high school graduates who may be extreme bikers, skaters, or skiers, former members of the military, members of the local police department, outdoor hunters and fishermen, gamers of military videos, and other kinds of real or virtual risk takers. But Manny knows, in truth, a Border Patrol agent spends most of his or her shift chasing individuals desperate not to be caught.

Ninety-nine percent of the illegal crossers Manny and other agents see along the border are undocumented workers and members of their families. Manny knows you run after these men, women, and children on foot. You chase them, they hide, then you chase them some more. In all weather conditions and at all times of the day and night you hightail it through brush and river cane, around rocks and other impediments peppering the desert terrain. You dodge the cacti, which come in twenty different forms and sizes, along with the thorny bushes and stunted trees. You fall in the ravines and ditches, then you get up. You get scratched and torn. Sometimes you get busted up pretty good—not stove up so you need to be rolled into the local emergency room on a gurney, but the kind of hurt that is a preamble, a wakeup call, to chronic injury.

Throughout their career in the Border Patrol agents gamble injury to their knees, back, and shoulders against a decent paycheck. Probationary graduates of the Border Patrol academy start out at about $55,000 with a federal pension awaiting them after twenty years of service. One year after graduation, agents at the GL-11 level with overtime may earn $70,000 annually. With only a high school education to most of their names, the Border

Patrol is a good bet for those who already know where dead-end, minimum-wage jobs in the service sector lead, or for those who have gotten used to regular military paychecks with housing allowances and other perks.

Looked at from the distance of time and experience, however, a career in the Border Patrol can also be a sucker's bet. The cumulative effect of patrolling the line, of all that chasing and all that stumbling over nighttime terrain, catches up with you. So can the fists, bricks, knives, and bullets. And so can what you see. Somewhere down the road to a federal pension some agents begin to wonder if they bet their law enforcement careers on the wrong horse.

Day-to-day injuries suffered by Border Patrol agents never grab headlines, but ultimately can be as life-changing as shootouts with drug smugglers. Manny knows from his years patrolling the line in South Texas that chasing after desperate people is almost always about falling. Not the Tom Cruise *Mission Impossible* kind of stunt in which you roll, tumble, and right yourself like a human cat before firing off five rounds, but twisting or straining the lumbar discs as you land in a heap. In the desert outside Laredo, along the banks of the Rio Grande, or in the middle of irrigated citrus orchards, the only variation in falling is the kind of fall. In a tilled field just after the cotton seed is planted, an agent staggers as he jumps from the top of one row of earthen clots to the other, eventually misjudging the distance between rows. Overcompensating, he glimpses the perps escaping. He falls forward, hands out front to protect his face as the weight of his armored vest and tool belt throw him to the ground with more force than expected—no Tomcat screen immortalization, just a sloppy ending. It is this same twenty pounds of equipment an agent normally carries on his or her tool belt that, along with the Rio Grande currents, drowned two agents after their boat capsized near the International Bridge in Brownsville.[5]

In the Border Patrol there are lots of situations leading to falls by those even in the best of physical conditioning, lots of ways to get banged up. Some agents, however, are not in good condition when they fall. Although the Border Patrol academy demands certain physical standards be met before graduation, agents are never again tested throughout their twenty-year careers in uniform.

Over time the cumulative cost of what seem to be minor falls can exact a high price. Returning to work before wounds or muscles properly heal increases the probability of chronic leg and back problems. Manny, after many falls, twists, and bad steps, like most other agents did not want to use up his sick days or annual vacation to rest his knees. So he went back to the line still limping.

What Manny, like many other agents, is paying for now is years of falling badly.

But it is always more complicated than that. When you run like crazy to apprehend suspects you must constantly check on the people around you as well as the immoveable objects. As time slows to a standstill in the crucial moments during a chase, you check and recheck all your surroundings, gauging possibilities, figuring possible behaviors and reactions. "They can get in your way. The families, friends, anybody. You have to keep an eye out for them. It's because everybody thinks the Border Patrol makes all these immigration laws. That's what the guys in Washington do. My job every shift is to do what I'm told. If the public doesn't like it, then they should stop giving me a hard time and call up Cornyn [Sen. John Cornyn, R-Texas] or one of those guys."

Manny is, must be, cautious at all times, even when off the job and out of uniform. The only times he really relaxes his guard is when he is in the company of other agents he trusts or in the privacy of his own home. Members of border communities come at agents when they are drinking coffee in restaurants, standing in line at the movies, shopping at Walmart, or socializing after church services. First it is the look of disapproval, often followed by a comment in a voice meant to be overheard. Then maybe a calling-out, or some other form of confrontation. Agents are very aware of the fact that many border community residents hate them for what they think agents do or have done.[6]

Attacks against agents have substantially increased since Manny signed on with the Border Patrol. In ever greater numbers agents are punched, kicked, stabbed, stoned, and shot at. The greater the number of agents—the Border Patrol has more than tripled in less than ten years—the more the violence directed at agents has escalated.[7] Random gunshots have always been fired from *el otro lado*, but now the agents are targets. While Border Patrol statistics are frequently difficult to pin down, they indicate that in 2004 there were 384 assaults against agents, but three years later there were 987 attacks. Department of Homeland Security secretary Michael Chertoff summarized the violence directed towards Border Patrol agents: "We've had occasions of people shooting at agents, trying to run agents down with vehicles, throwing large rocks or pieces of brick or concrete at agents, which actually can be fatal, and I've seen some pretty serious injuries that have resulted from it. The levels have consistently increased."[8]

Agents must always be cautious in public settings. In uniform or out, Manny is subject to harassment or personal threats at the mall, on the street, in grocery stores, at the movies, in restaurants, bars, and nightclubs.

So are Manny's family. Says Manny, "One time I was across in Nuevo Laredo with my wife and two girls. My girls were maybe nine and ten. We were standing in line at a store where my wife was buying something for the house. And this guy walks over to me. With my girls standing right next to me, he says, 'Don't I know you?'

"I know him alright. I busted him at least three times crossing the river. I tell him, 'No, I never seen you before.' But I can see by the look in his eyes he recognized me. He didn't say another word. Just walked away. I'm thinking he's going to get his gun in his truck or he's coming back with a bunch of his friends. I grabbed my wife and girls and got the hell back to Laredo."

In addition to chronic injuries and violence directed towards agents, other occupational hazards include drug abuse, alcoholism, divorce, depression, and suicide. Then there are a rising number of attempts by criminal organizations to bribe agents to participate in human trafficking or drug smuggling.[9]

As it becomes more difficult to cross the border, *coyotes* charge undocumented workers higher prices for their services. The personal safety of illegal immigrants is always a problem. Likely to be victims before they ever reach the Mexican border, they face increasing risk north of the river as security tightens on the American side. At the same time, the risk to agents in chasing ever more desperate undocumented workers also increases substantially. So, too, does the likelihood of encountering armed drug smugglers.

So far, Manny tells me, he has dodged any serious diseases. Poor people from third-world countries such as Mexico, El Salvador, and Guatemala are much more likely than others to have contagious diseases, including tuberculosis. Every day Border Patrol agents are exposed to individuals who could not afford professional medical care even if it were available. Agents patrolling the line frequently do not have the luxury of grabbing a pair of latex gloves and rarely, if ever, have the option of wearing a mask such as those worn by public health workers among similar populations.

After two hours on the flight from Dallas to Memphis, Manny's right knee is screaming at him. For years Manny's doctor and ex-wife have been telling him to get surgery. His ex Manny could deal with. She wants the child support to keep on coming, believing Manny will be back at work stronger than ever after the surgery as if Manny is a real-life version of the Bionic Man, with an indestructible knee joint. Manny does not begrudge his ex the child support. On his supe pay with overtime he grosses more than $75,000 a year, so Manny has the $1,236 a month for his two girls. If Manny's ex wants to spend his check on partying with her new boyfriend, then that is her business.

The doc is something else. Manny trusts him about as far as he can throw him out the office door. As soon as the doc heard Manny was a Border Patrol agent, he told Manny to get the surgery over with as quickly as possible, or he would be a cripple for the rest of his life. He said this to Manny after his own nurse told Manny in the examination room, before he even saw the doc, that her boss paid twenty thousand dollars a year for his deer lease near Lake Amistad.

Manny asked the doctor exactly what his knee would be like after the surgery. He knew three agents, plus an old buddy from his army days, who had the same knee surgery. They all told Manny the same thing: "It's way overrated." Manny was not going to have a bionic leg after the doc cut on him, not unless his buddies were liars and the doc with a deer lease up his butt was telling him the truth.

So for three years Manny delayed having the surgery on his bum knee. Instead, he bought a membership at Gold's Gym off the interstate in Laredo and pestered a personal trainer to show him how to use the space-age machines. In six months Manny lost twenty-eight pounds. But after a ten-hour night shift, the last thing in the world Manny wanted to do, especially since his divorce, was work out. Manny kept going to Gold's by telling himself that since he was single, he was killing two birds with one stone. He was putting less weight on his bad knee, and he was looking good for the ladies who expected biceps the size of hubcaps.

Pure and simple, Manny admits to being a party animal. On the job you certainly are not going to meet available females, and if you do run into the rare female agent or staffer not already involved in a serious relationship, there is way too much competition from all the other agents. That leaves the Laredo bars and clubs.

Manny's other single male friends, all agents, are in the same boat. "The best thing about recruiting," says Manny, "is going to these big cities that have more night life than Laredo. In Laredo I got to watch myself everywhere I go. Everywhere. You know what I mean. But when I fly to one of these big cities, well, that's another thing. Especially now I'm single again. I always liked to party.

"Don't get me wrong. I put in my hours, but when I'm not working a shift I'm ready to kick back. They got places in Memphis like Beale Street or in Chicago they got clubs in Old Town. Wherever I go, I take advantage like I can't do in Laredo. Never know who's looking at me there."

If you are in the Border Patrol, kicking back with your bros is essential. Otherwise you go nuts from the job, because most of the time you have very next to nothing, or nothing at all, to show for all your hard work. Nothing but the paycheck and the pension.

Because when you combine the sensors that haven't worked for years with the bad terrain, the weather, the attitude of the local residents, the injuries, the insects, the poisonous snakes, the dark of the night, the trickiness of the *coyotes*, the risk of running into heavily armed cocaine *narcotraficantes*, and a supe with a bone to pick, well, it can all add up to wondering if it's really worth it all.

Often agents at the end of their shift can say only that they "deterred" for the last ten hours—that their presence along the line minimized the likelihood of illegal entry by workers, drug smuggling, or other crimes. Many times agents apprehend no one, seize no drugs, and arrest no international terrorists. Besides the usual scrapes and bruises, all an agent may have to show for his ten hours on the line is a sour stomach from too much bad coffee.

Manny does not tell the recruits he talks to about how much time during a normal shift is spent just waiting around for something, anything, to happen. You can spend a ferocious amount of a shift "killing time." Manny is good at it, an expert. He perfected it in the army. Killing time is what an agent does before the chasing starts. An agent kills time talking with his fellow agents on his radio or, if it's private and not meant for the supe back at the station who is eavesdropping on your conversation, on his personal cell. He kills time talking with his wife, girlfriend, ex-wife, ex-girlfriend, kids, or the kids' teachers when the kids get into trouble, the car mechanic, the landlord, and the plumber. Because if you are working ten hours all hours of the clock, plus the commute, there never is enough time to attend to your personal or family obligations.

Killing time is also about talking to other agents, rehashing events that should or shouldn't have happened, daydreaming, reading, playing video games on your personal laptop, and drinking coffee at the nearest McDonalds, What-A-Burger, Burger King, or convenience store—the kind of convenience store where the self-serve coffee has been cooking for hours on the burner along the back wall next to the Styrofoam coolers and the cases of canned dog food.

Or killing time is the mountains of paperwork facing Manny and other agents and keeping them from patrolling the line. Manny must account for every minute of his shift and justify to the penny every federal dollar he spends. Last year when Manny was a principal in a drug bust, he spent five hours at the station filling out the damn forms. Then there are the travel forms and all the rest of it; an endless array of electronic forms measure Manny's work productivity but, in reality, consume it, because Manny is busy filling out the forms instead of chasing OTMs, other-than-Mexicans.[10]

Killing time can be productive. Besides taking care of domestic responsibilities, you can also meet with other agents to discuss how to catch a known drug smuggler who lives in a house where people come and go like flies, even if the talk turns occasionally to who's going to win the Super Bowl. It soon turns back to why Supe Torres is acting weird and when the drag road that washed out during the last hard flood finally will get repaired.

In the army Manny also learned how to fall asleep at the drop of a hat. On the plane to Memphis he drops off in less than five seconds, but not before he eyeballs everyone in his line of sight, then pulls his neck into his body and his gimme cap low over his eyes. In thirty seconds he is snoring loudly.

It does not help that legacies like Manny are mostly two-, three-, or four-finger keyboarders, not like the new generation of recruits who text with lightning thumbs. Before he made supe, every time Manny apprehended an OTM he spent two hours in front of a computer screen processing forms at the station. The keyboard paperwork required for his supervisory work and recruiting would take him far less time and effort if he could use ten fingers instead of two.

If Manny was telling his recruits in Memphis, Chicago, and Kansas City anything close to the truth about the Border Patrol, if his sales pitch about what to expect when they joined the Border Patrol was based on his real experiences rather than the manufactured dreams and fantasies of the advertising firm hired by the Border Patrol, Manny would be telling them three things. First, be patient, as in wait for the illegal aliens to reach your concealed positions rather than running around after them in the middle of nowhere. Second, avoid burnout, although Manny is not quite sure how to do that himself. And third, make sure you stay in good enough condition healthwise to enjoy your hard-earned federal pension.

Manny never tells the new recruits the simple fact that most of the undocumented workers get away. It is the dirty little secret that the public, at least in the nonborder states, does not understand. One way or another, most undocumented workers successfully cross over into the United States. That's why so many of them are here.

The same is true with the drug runners and their loads. Most of the illegal drugs make it into this country. That's why drugs are so cheap.

And throughout his career along the line, Manny has never seen an international terrorist.

The good news is that the days of "catch-and-release" are over. In the bad old days spanning most of Border Patrol history, agents nabbed OTMs, who then were bonded out on their own recognizance. When their hearings came up on their immigration status, very few OTMs who had been bonded out showed up to face possible deportation. In sharp contrast to the catch-and-release policy for OTMs, Mexican workers, the vast majority of those apprehended by the Border Patrol, were "voluntarily returned" (VRed). When apprehended, Mexican illegal workers signed a legal document admitting their guilt, then they were taken by Border Patrol agents to the nearest bridge to Mexico and released to Mexican officials. In effect the Border

Patrol chauffeured Mexican illegal aliens back to Mexico, where they were freed to recross into the United States. Most undocumented workers caught the first time by Manny and his fellow agents made it back to the United States sooner or later—if not on a second try, then on a third or fourth.

Border Patrol agents, of course, found this policy demoralizing and alienating because it undermined all their efforts. Why chase down illegals if, after catching them, they were just going to return during your next shift with no penalties?

Secretary of Homeland Security Michael Chertoff put a stop to catch-and-release shortly after his appointment by President Bush. Now all OTMs apprehended are processed at the station, then placed as required in new, privately operated detention centers. There they are brought before a judge, and their immigration status is determined. Eventually they are either jailed or deported, but they may spend several months or longer waiting for adjudication. One crucial breakdown in the current system is that there are not enough INS judges to try all cases fairly. Another is that OTMs frequently do not receive adequate legal counsel.

Biometrics of every illegal crosser now are recorded in a computer database. Those OTMs who are caught a second time face increasingly harsher jail sentences and other legal penalties that affect their immigrant status.

Mexican illegal workers, the majority of all those caught by Border Patrol agents, face an increasing likelihood of mandatory deportation in some places along the border. Those Mexicans found to have committed crimes in this country may face criminal prosecution under programs such as Operation Streamline. There is evidence to suggest that in the first years of the Obama administration, workplace arrests of undocumented workers and roundups of illegal immigrants increased significantly in some border and interior communities.

The new system in place does not work perfectly. Most undocumented workers, in spite of the new policies, still cross the borderlands at their choosing. Only now it is more difficult to enter the United States, and more expensive, than it used to be.

Since the Border Patrol's budget has been significantly increased, Manny tells me, he has already "lost" two illegal workers he arrested because of the "human error" of drivers of buses transporting detainees to detention centers, buses operated by private contractors. In one case during the confusion of boarding, two workers with the same last name, one of them with a criminal record, simply walked away.

Now catch-and-release is just an agent's bad dream, but there are still a dozen other policies, procedures, and routines endured for years by Manny and the other old-timers—policies nothing less than counterproductive.

What these ways of working have in common is a gap in understanding between the reality of the border, public policy, and a Border Patrol resistant to change of any kind. These policies and traditions include, in addition to those already suggested, promoting favorites based upon a good-old-boy system, lack of cooperation with Mexican officials, unreasonably long work shifts, ignorance of the ways of private contractors, special assignments for favored agents, poor training of new recruits, an unwillingness to support professional development, and an organizational culture hostile to female agents.

And that is just the beginning of a long, deep list. Although Manny has seen some positive changes since 9/11, especially in regard to professional equipment, resources, and facilities, there are still many deeply troubling issues that the Border Patrol will not even admit and that compromise efficiency and promote dissatisfaction among agents along the line.

Manny also does not bother to tell the new recruits that their chances of making a big drug bust are about as great as those of finding a diamond under their pillow. The Border Patrol has bad intel on drug traffic. Even worse, the intel from the local police departments and county sheriffs may be designed to divert an agent's attention elsewhere while drugs are offloaded on turf he or she is assigned at muster to patrol.[11] If an agent does participate in a drug bust, it is most likely because of dumb luck, the stupidity of the drug smugglers, or one rival drug gang's snitching on another to eliminate the competition.

And forget about the possibility of nabbing an international terrorist. It does not happen. And even if it did, it would be kept secret.[12]

If Manny's recruiting pitch were beholden to bare facts, he would tell prospective recruits that anyone dumb enough to complain, criticize, or in any form convey a negative comment about the Border Patrol to a supe or higher-up may as well kiss his career goodbye. This federal agency is not interested in feedback from its agents about line conditions, remedies to common problems, policies, strategies, best practices, reforms, or any other job-related issues. A top-down hierarchy, the Border Patrol affirms, promotes, rewards, and compensates only those who follow orders, keep their mouths shut, and demonstrate personal loyalty to their immediate superiors. While Border Patrol managers like to think their agency is closely modeled after, and resembles, the U.S. Army, it is not the U.S. Army of the new millennium but that of World War II.

Female agents are at a distinct disadvantage in this antiquated federal law enforcement agency, an organization that nourishes gender values and attitudes popular in the 1940s. Heavily recruited, female agents find careers in the U.S. Border Patrol problematic, so they leave in droves; female agents number no more than 5 percent.[13]

In this cultural climate the National Border Patrol Council,[14] the voluntary union, is also treated poorly. By definition union reps are troublemakers and rarely promoted into management. If union reps are promoted it is because they are three times better at their jobs than their peers.

Waking up an hour later in his seat on the jet, Manny winces at the pain in his knee as he readjusts his bulk. He tells me how he is beginning to think it may be time to have that knee surgery. But he still has his reservations: "I'd like to hang on for a few more years. If I make it to retirement, then I get my pension, and I get my surgery paid for. It could be twenty, twenty-five grand. I'm not sure what it is. I'll get the surgery before I retire.

"What else can I do? There is no way after the surgery I can work anything but a desk job. I mean, right now I'm doing some desk work as a supe, but I'm talking about a desk job where you sit in a chair all day drinking coffee, writing reports, and talking on the phone. I can't do that. That'd kill me. I'm an outside guy. I'm one of those supes that really gets out there and keeps an eye on things. That's just the way I am. Only now it hurts me every time I get out of my truck."

Soon after his trip to Memphis, Manny decided he couldn't wait any longer on his knee. I visited him a month after his surgery. Since the operation, he'd been popping pain pills and using a walker to get around his house. His two teenage girls are visiting him from Killeen for the weekend. Sitting in his living room filled with tray tables, old pizza boxes, milk cartons, and other flotsam accumulated since coming home from the hospital, Manny has a bad case of cabin fever.

Manny yells at his daughters in the kitchen. "What are you guys doing in there? Have you done your homework for Monday? I promised your momma that you'd do your homework. Have you?"

There is complete silence in the kitchen.

"You answer me in there. What are you doing?"

"Eating, Daddy," comes a small voice.

"Eating what? Don't you go and ruin your dinner. Who said that, Maria or Elena?"

"Me, Daddy. Elena."

"Both of you come in here right now and show me your homework."

The two girls dutifully march into the room, notebooks in hand. Manny sifts through the pages of their notebooks, saying things such as, "Good job," "What is this word here the teacher wrote?" and "I'm proud of you for being such a good student." The two young girls disappear into the back of the house.

"I'm thinking about retiring from the Border Patrol," he tells me as he puts down their notebooks. "I can't do shit with this knee. I got the rehab yet, but I can already tell how it's going to be. I'd go crazy sitting at a desk all day. There's this friend of mine who says he can get me a job with his new company. It's security work with regular hours. He says I can make a hundred thousand dollars a year no problem. Maybe have to put in some weekends and nights, but regular hours. Not like an agent up all hours of the night. I'm thinking about turning in my letter after I get out of rehab."

I tell Manny I think he would also make a good teacher. It's a secure job, no chasing or falling, no hiding in public places, and the students make sure you never get bored. The public schools need more math and science teachers, and Manny would have no trouble getting financial aid at the local university. Besides, I remind him, he can teach for two or three years, then if he doesn't like the classroom, he can apply for a position as an assistant principal. Manny is dubious. He's never considered teaching as a profession. He offers me some day-old pizza from the TV tray table next to his meds.

"I don't see it, Doc," Manny tells me. "I'm smart enough. I'm not saying I have the best education, but I've got the brains for it. I like kids in general. But I've got to make some real money. I appreciate your telling me about it and encouraging me. You never know. That other thing might fall apart."

Manny speaks fluent Spanish. He can separate an El Salvadoran from a Mexican by asking three questions or fewer. He knows basic first aid, including CPR, from his days in the military and from his training in the Border Patrol. Looking at documents he is handed, he can identify the real from the fake almost instantaneously. Manny tells me, "You know, some of the stuff just don't look right. I get to looking at it, and pretty soon I figure out what's missing."

Manny knows his immigration law backwards and forwards, rides a horse, and has a canny nose when it comes to traffic stops. He fires his service weapon and shotgun with reasonable accuracy on the test range and was recently certified on the new automatic weapons the Border Patrol purchased. Always a team player, he is a good supe and a better than average recruiter. Although he types no more than eight to ten words a minute, he is not afraid to learn new office technology. A backyard mechanic, Manny will drive twenty miles to help another agent who is broken down in the boonies.

Manny is loyal to his fellow agents and friends, cannot tolerate pencil pushers and bean counters, and voted Republican since the day he first turned eighteen. A good if perhaps overprotective father to his kids when they visit, he works hard and parties hard. He distrusts the majority of the new recruits to his station and has grave doubts about the Obama administration.

If Manny stays in the Border Patrol, he'll be a desk guy for the rest of his career. He'll never patrol the line again. If Manny leaves the Border Patrol before his twenty are up, he'll take with him the friendship and trust of his fellow legacy agents—along with a permanent limp.

Since joining the Border Patrol, Manny has always done his job, done what he was told to do by his superiors, never complained, simply taken the good with the bad. If he ever complained, it was in private to his fellow agents after a few drinks, when everyone around the table was bitching because they'd feel better for it the next day.

Legacies like Manny want to see changes to their jobs, but it is not clear whether those changes are going to occur. What they also desire, although they are not prone to admit it, is the support and affirmation of the public. These agents consider themselves unsung blue-collar heroes protecting the homeland, but many border residents treat them like federal thugs.

What legacies like Manny find most difficult to cope with are the rapid ways in which the Border Patrol appears to be transitioning itself into a different kind of law enforcement agency. In fact, Manny and his fellow agents are no longer Border Patrol agents but agents of the new Customs and Border Protection. As CBP agents they are not sure, however, where this rapid institutional change is heading. Some farsighted CBP agents believe the agency will become a high-tech paramilitary organization specifically trained to defend the Mexican border. But another scenario is equally likely. CBP agents could become untrained prison guards, patrolling the new border fence in the same way that guards walk prison walls and yards.[15]

From where I sit in Manny's living room, looking at him after his job-related knee surgery, this is what seems obvious: Manny and his fellow agents should be able to believe their law enforcement careers are meaningful and worthy of all their blood and sweat, that sticking it out twenty years is about more than pay grade and the pension. CBP agents should feel they are living lives of consequence.

And what does Manny think about the new border fence soon to be constructed a few miles from his Border Patrol station? Manny is too busy thinking about his knee, the rehab, and his future to give it much thought. Finally, he says, "The fence should help us, but I guess it just depends on what it ends up looking like. I mean, it could be a big help, or just another pain in the butt."

Then CBP agent Manuel A. "Manny" Rodriguez slowly gets to his feet and, using the walker, limps his way to the kitchen.

Chapter 3
Anzalduas

"The past is never dead. It's not even past."

William Faulkner

There is a rich history to every twist and bend of the Rio Grande/Río Bravo in South Texas and northern Mexico. Although the official history of the region—the version taught from textbooks in Valley public schools—may be better known, another version, one of subjugation and ruthless exploitation, is not forgotten among populations who for generations have lived it. On both sides of the river the region's past provides a crucial context for understanding the success or failure of any proposed border fence.

Anzalduas County Park is one site among hundreds in the borderlands where mainstream documented history fails to account for how these lands form an intricate and binding relationship between Mexico and the United States. At one level of historical understanding Anzalduas County Park is simply a longtime favorite of Hidalgo County residents from nearby Mission, McAllen, and other Valley communities—a place where one can take all the family on weekends without worrying about

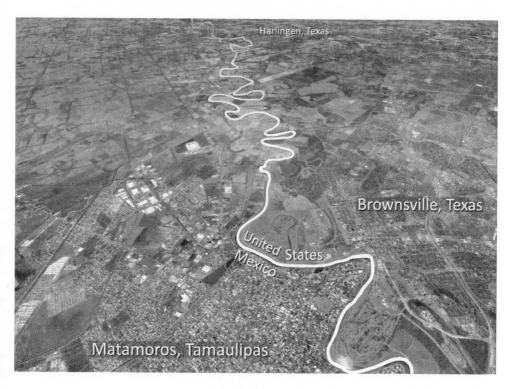

Map 2. Terrain near Brownsville, Texas, and Matamoros, Tamaulipas. (Map by Margret Mulcahy, East Carolina University Center for Geographic Information Science)

unruly drunks or gangs. Relatives and friends can gather around brick barbecue pits and enjoy a few cold ones while the kids play safely. Smoke from the barbecuing scents Anzalduas with cilantro and sizzling fajitas. Weekend *pachangas,* parties, fill the park with the voices of men and women discussing the merits of local politicos or what kind of football team McHigh (McAllen High School) will field in the fall. All the while the *abuelos,* grandparents, sit comfortably at the picnic tables eating, laughing, and smoking their cigarettes.

Anzalduas was once also a place to fish from wooden benches along a concrete embankment overlooking the Rio Grande. There was even a boat ramp where, once you had launched into the waters of the river, you could find temporary respite from the heat. For many Hidalgo County residents, Anzalduas remains a place to enjoy a well-deserved break from a long, hard work week in the company of family and friends before the all-too-short weekend turns into Monday morning.

Barely twenty yards away, citizens of Mexico also enjoy the weekend with family and friends. Groups of young boys swim in the Río Bravo, shouting and diving into the shallow water. When a group of girls wades near them, the boys shout even louder. Since there are only a few picnic tables or barbecue pits on the Mexican side of the river, families stand in groups next to their trucks and cars while they eat and drink. Occasionally the hulls of their worn-out pleasure boats are gingerly offloaded into the water, then with fanfare slowly paraded up and down the Río Bravo before the sun sets between the palm trees and the carrizo cane. One or two other boats also stand ready at the shore, smoke rising from the revving engines as their captains lazily drink beer under the hot sun.

There is other human activity in this particular bend in the Rio Grande/Río Bravo that historians have neglected. By keeping a close eye on the southern banks of the river, it is possible to glimpse another Anzalduas County Park, one that has nothing to do with recreational activities for residents of Hidalgo County or northern Tamaulipas. For many, many years during the steaming months from mid-March through November—when the park is filled with visitors—men, women, and children rushed on cue aboard one of the old Mexican boats idling at the sandy riverbank. In five seconds or less a practiced *coyote* captained his rickety boat with the smoking outboard across the few yards of international water to deposit his passengers skillfully on the concrete embankment of the park. Disembarking quickly, the men, women, and children dashed across the caliche to the cover of the picnic tables beneath the gnarled, ancient mesquites. Easily mixing in with the families gathered around the picnic tables and barbeque pits, the undocumented workers and their children disappeared into the park as if they had never existed. Swiftly the smoking speedboat then returned to the Mexican side of the river, where its captain opened another can of beer, and the lazy afternoon continued to meander towards dusk.[1]

Although the smuggling strategies have changed since the construction of the border fence at Anzalduas County Park, sentries and lookouts for the *coyotes* and the *narcotrafficantes* still line the Río Bravo, some among the palms and mesquite, others camouflaged among those enjoying the afternoon. Still other scouts brazenly patrol the river on Jet Skis.

The Border Patrol used to place special operations agents on the two roads leading into the park, one from along the river, the other from the north, but these watchdogs are themselves easy to locate. During the daylight hours the smugglers simply wait until the area is free of the Border Patrol. It does not really matter if the waiting takes hours or days, because eventually the Border Patrol agents and special ops will grow frustrated and leave. In the meantime, the smugglers lie low.

Longtime visitors to Anzalduas accept the sight of these undocumented workers crossing the Rio Grande with no more surprise or concern than Professor Antonio Zavaleta showed thirty years earlier as we jogged around the Brownsville golf course. At Anzalduas such activity is as common as the grackles, the cactus, and the stifling heat. At numerous other landings along the Rio Grande in Cameron and Hidalgo Counties, human smuggling does not bear mentioning by the locals but is, nevertheless, an integral part of life.

At night the *narcotrafficantes*, regardless of the changes in resources and public policy along the border, still control Anzalduas Park. The park is a prime location to smuggle their burlap bags of cocaine and marijuana, which lightning quick they offload from high-powered cigarette boats.

The Border Patrol has found it, and still finds it, next to impossible to stop the human smuggling or the drug trafficking at Anzalduas. Regardless of the strategies employed, the mad dash of humans shipped from one side of the river to the other in rusting pleasure boats in a matter of seconds plays out day after day, month after month from March through November even as quantities of illegal drugs, measured by the ton, come and go year-round from the boats with the powerful engines.

The geography of Anzalduas County Park is ideal for smugglers. On the south side the park is bordered by dense brush, cacti, and scrub, almost impenetrable to the uninitiated, while to the west and northwest the twists and bends of the river create ideal landings only a stone's throw from Mexico. When the coast is clear of agents, illegal aliens and drug loads may be floated across the river on tire tubes, rubber rafts, and plastic jugs used as flotation devices. Humans and drugs are then shuttled along a maze of trails leading to waiting vans and cars. If drug smugglers suspect they are about to be caught, they hide their loads in the thick South Texas brush to retrieve at a later time, then hightail it back across the river. Or sometimes, if cornered, they may even drive their loads into the river, their bosses taking the loss as a cost of doing business.

From the picnic tables and the barbeque pits the only signs of smuggling at Anzalduas are the gaps in the barbed wire fence along the south side of the park. Every twenty feet or so the strands of wire have been cut or the metal fence posts bent double. No work of the deer or javelina that populate this stretch of riverside land, this intentional destruction is another indication of the volume of illegal workers and drug smugglers passing through the park.

Over the decades so many thousands of illegal workers and drug mules have passed along the trails in Anzalduas County Park that the parched ground has been beaten by their feet into smooth grooves. The smugglers' trails are littered with decaying green garbage bags that once bore the dry belongings of illegal aliens. Pieces of clothing, empty food cans, and plastic gallon bottles are also scattered along the grooved trails.

Droves of tourists from across the nation also find their way to Anzalduas and the surrounding area, but they rarely collide with the smugglers. By day birders walk the very paths along which smugglers and their cargo scurry in the dark of night. The trails through the thick brush all cross, one way or the other, at the doors of La Lomita (Little Hill) Chapel to the north of the park. Once open to the public for solitary worship, La Lomita is now tightly boarded shut.

Anzalduas County Park was formerly part of a Spanish land grant awarded to the original colonists in 1767. French Oblates purchased the land in 1884 from the original settlers "for the propagation of the faith among the barbarians," and soon built this modest chapel.[2] By the last decades of the twentieth century, La Lomita was no longer an Oblate place of contemplation and worship, but the meeting place for *coyotes* and *narcotrafficantes* awaiting transportation to local safe houses. Behind No Trespassing signs, the walls of the old stone building are now covered by layers of gang graffiti.

In April 2008 after passing through the main entrance, I try at the end of my visit to drive the river road out of Anzalduas County Park, but the Border Patrol has blockaded it with different kinds of barriers. Officially it is closed to the public. I circumvent the signs and concrete posts in my rental car but can drive only another one hundred yards before the road becomes impassable. As they had in the spring of 2006 and again on subsequent visits, the Border Patrol confirmed that Anzalduas was still a hot spot for illegal aliens and drugs. This time as I walk through the park I see where the barbed wire fencing along the south side has been patched and where it is cut anew. I beat my way into the dense brush, find a trail, and follow it. Along the way I see garbage bags, a tennis shoe, a shirt, water bottles, and all the other signs of recent and frequent traffic.[3]

In the last several years there have been only superficial changes made at Anzalduas Park. The concrete fishing embankment, from which generations of Hidalgo County families tossed their lines into the river waters, is now fenced off from the public by rusting chain link nailed crudely to two-by-eights. A No Trespassing sign hangs from this crude fence. The concrete bank lies crumbling, while the wooden benches behind it are uprooted. The roof that once provided shade to generations of Valley fishermen is filled with gaping holes. Every flat surface along the river frontage is covered by gang graffiti. The boat ramp is also a wreck. Garbage fills the ramp, and a hefty tree trunk floats belly up a foot from the shore. A telephone pole has been buried deep into the river's silt to block entrance to the ramp from the Rio Grande.

The other side of the Río Bravo is a mirror of times past. At four on this April afternoon, the thermometer approaching one hundred degrees, boys swim and play in the Río Bravo while men talk and drink beer beside their trucks. Out of nowhere a sleek white and blue cigarette boat appears directly opposite me. As it seems to hover midriver, I can see six men aboard, all dressed in dark suits. Casually the men stare back at me. No apparition, the powerful boat zooms suddenly upriver to disappear around a bend, its wake breaking hard against the crumbling concrete embankment. One of the boys playing in the water, now spotting me, waves. I wave back.

Although Anzalduas Park is empty at this hour, soon Hidalgo County families will arrive in convoys, just as quickly as they can get cleaned up after work and load their coolers with ice, meat, beer, salsa, and all the other fixings for *pachangas.*

Back in my rental, I exit the park and turn south, but the construction of a new international bridge linking Reynosa, Mexico—now approaching 600,000 in population—to Mission in Hidalgo County forces a detour. This new bridge, fifteen years in the planning, is jointly financed by U.S. federal, Hidalgo County, and Mexican funds totaling $80 million.[4] The multilane bridge will soar over the wild brushland south of the park, terrain that for many years has hidden smugglers' trails and landings. Designed to ease the North American Free Trade Agreement (NAFTA) truck traffic, this bridge is just a mile from upscale Sharyland Plantation, a residential area built by Hunt Valley Development, owned by the superrich Hunt family of Dallas. Directly across the border from Sharyland Plantation by way of the new bridge is a new sixteen-thousand-acre residential development owned by Grupo Río Juan.

When the international bridge opens, exposing long-hidden trails to law enforcement and the public, what will it mean to smugglers and their operations? Not much. Indefatigable, they will simply move a mile up- or down-river to the next-best landing sites available and resume business.

It was at Anzalduas County Park that President George W. Bush on August 3, 2006, made the last major speech regarding his pending legislation before the U.S. Congress. Falling on sympathetic Valley ears, President Bush's speech followed by just two days the final summer field hearing on immigration policies held by House leadership in Dubuque, Iowa.

At 1:40 p.m. Air Force One touched down at Miller International Airport in McAllen. Then the president's twenty-three-vehicle entourage motored along Expressway 83 before turning left, south, at Shary Road, then again at the Old Military Highway before reaching Anzalduas Park. The presidential motorcade followed, in fact, the same route CBP agents take every day and night from the McAllen Border Patrol station to patrol the park. On this day, however, small crowds of respectful Valley well-wishers waving flags and holding hand-lettered signs and placards supporting President Bush and his policies temporarily replaced the sentries and other spies of the smugglers of humans and drugs.

At Anzalduas Park a crowd of fawning city and county politicians, CBP agents, party contributors, and other selected guests, ignoring the hundred-degree South Texas heat, applauded loudly as President Bush spoke about his new immigration legislation. The president emphatically defended his proposed management program for guest workers. He also called for border fencing. He told the crowd, "There is an important debate facing our nation, and the debate is, can we secure this border and, at the same time, honor our history of being a land of immigrants? And the answer is, absolutely, we can do both. And we will do both."[5]

That President Bush gave his last immigration speech in dicey Anzalduas County Park, a place long known by Hidalgo County residents for its rampant human and drug smuggling, speaks to the White House's complete misreading of the illegal traffic that along the Mexican border is as constant as the river itself. It also reveals yet another Washington administration, as was the case with the Clinton presidency, out of touch with the historical subjugation and contemporary challenges besetting an impoverished Latino citizenry.

Anzalduas County Park proves, if anything, that border security is in the eye of the beholder. While the Bush administration, and the Clinton administration before it, may have believed that resolving immigration issues is as simple as signing federal legislation at the nation's capital, one hundred yards from the podium where President Bush speaks, cut fences and mounting detritus along worn trails suggest otherwise.

Despite the enthusiasm of the president's audience, the majority of Valley citizens know border security is a chimera. Throwing more money, more agents, and more resources at Anzalduas is only part of the solution. The situation is more complex. It is equally doubtful that a border fence at Anzalduas, or elsewhere in the Valley, will do much to bolster border security except perhaps in the eyes of Washington politicians and those across the rest of the country who find them convincing. Declaring difficult problems to be soon resolved, or framing a complex situation as resolvable if only certain specific conditions are met, is a story Valley citizens have heard many times before from their elected officials.

Planning any portion of a new border fence in Hidalgo County or adjacent Cameron County courts failure. The geography of the Rio Grande is at times beyond belief, especially to those who have never seen firsthand how it tortuously twists and bends its way to the Gulf of Mexico. From the air one can easily see the juts of Mexican and American riparian land that ram into each other, often surrounding the other nation's land on two if not three sides. Narrow and shallow in so many places, with abundant islands of sand midriver, the Rio Grande as it passes through South Texas is a smuggler's dream.

At the same time, the river is unpredictable, prone to seasonal flooding capable of washing away or surmounting old levees to leave residents on both the northern and southern banks hip deep in river water and mud. At times like these it becomes impossible for CBP agents to patrol the line.[6]

In the heart of Hidalgo and Cameron Counties, as in many locales in the borderlands, it is foolhardy to suggest a border fence will not only ensure border security but at the same time "honor our history of being a land of immigrants." The historical record in South Texas is second to none in lawlessness and bloodshed, and the majority of the violence has been directed toward Mexican citizens on both sides of the river and Mexican Americans. Over the centuries resident immigrants along the border, both legal and illegal, have suffered grievously. It is this same bloody history that accounts in part for the primacy and efficacy of human smuggling and drug trafficking in the local economy, a pairing of binational crime and criminals with systemic graft and corruption.

Graft and corruption, permeating many of the Valley's contemporary social, political, and economic institutions, are rooted in a legacy of political bossism. Ruling Anglo elites founded Cameron County in 1848 and Hidalgo County four years later. These same elites governed these counties with an iron hand for more than a century and a half. This particular style of bossism used municipal, county, state, and federal law enforcement to subjugate its citizenry, the majority of whom were low-income and impoverished Mexican Americans and Mexicans.

Before this rampant bossism, South Texas residents faced wars, border skirmishes, banditry, lawlessness, and repeated attacks from displaced Indians. Over the centuries these pervasive and bloody conflicts nurtured simultaneous xenophobic, racial, and class conflicts that continue unabated.[7]

Wherever one turns in this border region, there is evidence of systemic violence married to corruption. One example that still festers is the notorious C Shift, the midnight shift, of the McAllen Police Department. In a style and manner identical to nineteenth-century bossism, Mayor Othal Brand and his cronies subjugated the local citizenry throughout the 1970s and 1980s using local law enforcement. Forced to live in segregated, substandard housing across the tracks, the majority of the McAllen Hispanic population were disenfranchised, brutalized, and discriminated against in politics, business, public education, and the criminal justice system.

During the more than two decades in which Mayor Brand, protégé of Valley kingpin Lloyd Bentsen, Sr., held sway in McAllen, factions in the McAllen Police Department systematically terrorized the city's Hispanic residents. Arbitrarily arrested on McAllen streets in the early 1980s for alleged minor infractions of the law, placed in police custody, and booked at the front desk of the McAllen Police Department, hundreds of handcuffed Latinos then were beaten by McAllen police officers on the C Shift. Concerned with the threat of possible litigation brought by the victims of these beatings, the McAllen Police Department videotaped the crimes it perpetrated.

Finally, in 1983 a handful of these police tapes were anonymously leaked to a network television affiliate in nearby Harlingen. Soon after on the six o'clock national news the American public saw handcuffed McAllen Mexican Americans taunted, demeaned, and cruelly beaten while in the custody of their own police department. Once the tapes were nationally broadcast, a Texas district judge was forced to step in to clean up the horrific travesty of justice. All but two of the officers on the C Shift were fired. But in the end, only five McAllen policemen were indicted, tried, and convicted. Many more, including McAllen police officers and elected officials, were directly involved in these crimes or complicit in their knowledge of the ongoing abuse. Top elected officials, including Mayor Brand, were never indicted.[8]

Eventually voted out of the mayor's office in the late 1980s, Othal Brand again ran for mayor in 2002. Although in his eighties, he still commanded the vestiges of a formidable political machine capable of restoring him to his former position of power in the tradition of South Texas bossism. The hallmark of his well-financed campaign was a signature television ad in which he ripped away his white shirt and tie to reveal himself in the costume of Superman. Although Brand was narrowly defeated, his reprehensible form of justice speaks to the ceaseless, violent push and pull of lawlessness in South Texas and Tamaulipas, Mexico.

In this region, where violence and intimidation of the impoverished have played out for centuries on both sides of the border, the atrocities of a local drug ring do much to explain why some citizens might well have supported Brand and the McAllen C Shift. Under a petty Mexican drug dealer named Adolfo Constanzo, a pseudo-Santería cult of Mexicans and Americans preyed on local citizens as well as vacationing American college students. One victim of this drug ring, Mark Kilroy, a University of Texas student on spring break at South Padre Island, was kidnapped from the streets of Matamoros on March 12, 1989, as he and a group of his friends were walking back to the Brownsville International Bridge after a night of drinking.

Two months later the cannibalized remains of Kilroy and a number of other victims, including Mexicans and Mexican Americans, were found in a large metal pot in a ranch shed outside Matamoros. Mr. Kilroy had been ritualistically slaughtered with a machete in the same shed. Constanzo, the cult's self-styled leader, convinced his followers that his magical powers were so strong that the bullets of the police on both sides of the river could not harm them. In fact just another local drug trafficker, Constanzo, under the mantle of religion, manipulated his binational gang of petty thugs into committing heinous acts of torture and murder. The number of the cult's victims has been estimated at twenty.[9]

Both the cult and the McAllen C Shift are best understood within the context of the violent lawlessness and institutional corruption that have always pervaded this region—one inevitably inviting the other. Even though the Treaty of Guadalupe Hidalgo was signed in 1848, signifying the end of the Mexican War, rag-tag gangs and bands of former American and Mexican soldiers ravaged this area for many years. Each new attempt at revolution in Mexico brought more violence to the border.[10]

Even greater societal violence resulted from the influx of Anglos who swarmed into the Valley after the Mexican War. The treaty ending the Mexican War formally guaranteed the original Spanish colonists and landowners not only rights to their lands, but American citizenship as well. Only a handful of the most powerful, however, were able to retain any remnants of their Spanish land grants as opportunistic Anglos, aided by a corrupt district court in Brownsville, managed to appropriate most of their land and wealth. Anglos employed unscrupulous lawyers and judges, along with local and federal law enforcement, including *Los Rinches*, the Texas Rangers, to threaten, beat, and murder those who kept insisting upon their legal rights.

The political and social structures that emerged from this constant turmoil, conflict, and legitimized robbery in small towns and on *rancheros* were at once racist and elitist. This idiosyncratic hierarchy ruled a citizenry resembling peasants more than freedmen. Although a small class of artisans and merchants thrived in the small towns, they were controlled by a tiny group of new Anglo landowners who sometimes, in order to consolidate their power, intermarried with the few remaining Spanish land grant families. In the river towns of Brownsville, Rio Grande City, and Roma, then later in McAllen and the mid-Valley towns laid out before World War I, the freedoms and rights of the Hispanic majority were premised upon the needs and desires of a rich and powerful Anglo minority.[11]

In Brownsville after the end of the Civil War, for example, many residents were "voted" when elections periodically rolled around.[12] Brownsville's poor were literally corralled and fed, then transported to the polls. This tradition of enforced loyalty and allegiance by the disenfranchised and impoverished majority to a *patrón* was predicated upon selling one's vote in exchange for the pittance of a party, a meal, and a drink. This kind of political subjugation lasted well into the twentieth century.

The business of smuggling was fundamental to this border region. Since the mid-nineteenth century a wide variety of goods and services were smuggled in both directions, including wood, furniture, leather, alcohol, tobacco, agricultural products, *ropa usada*, and guns. Long before illegal immigrants and illegal drugs were smuggled from the Mexican side of the river to the American, long before there was any concern about the threat of international terrorists, laws of supply and demand determined which goods and services were secretly and illegally transported back and forth across the Rio Grande.

Over time a smuggling culture based upon the primacy of family ties established itself on both sides of the river, facilitating the success of this alternative economy. Certain families in Valley river towns and communities developed special expertise, coming to know every twist and turn of the river, which sand islands were best for hiding contraband, the surest crossings in drought and flood, and innovative as well as proven methods of eluding law enforcers.

It can hardly be surprising that smuggling grew to be both cancer and lifeblood in these mostly destitute river communities and towns, alternately sapping and supplementing the regional economy. While the majority of the Hispanic population faced lives of back-breaking labor with limited freedoms and rights, smugglers often were respected if not admired members in their communities. Impoverished Valley Mexican Americans came to view local smugglers, their neighbors, as entrepreneurs and businessmen. Contraband was simply their inventory. To many the real criminals were the police, the county deputy sheriffs, Los Rinches, and *Los Patrullos Fronteros*, the Border Patrol, because all these agencies of law functioned interchangeably as the hired guns of the Anglo elites, their political bosses, and their henchmen.

Valley Hispanics hated Los Rinches for the murderous atrocities they had perpetrated year after year. Beatings, shootings, and lynchings heightened after an alleged insurrection was revealed.[13] In 1915 Basilio Ramos was arrested in McAllen with a copy of the Plan of San Diego, a suspect political strategy in which Mexicans and Mexican Americans throughout the American Southwest were to foment a revolution against Anglo elites. In South

Texas the Plan of San Diego was one means by which the Anglo elites legitimated a reign of terror against the Hispanic population. Los Rinches, acting as judge and jury, lynched and shot hundreds of innocent Latinos.

Eventually a Texas legislative committee, chaired by Brownsville state representative J. T. Canales, investigated the atrocities of Los Rinches in the Valley, and as a result the Texas Rangers were forced to reorganize. Several decades later they were placed under the governance of the Texas Department of Public Safety. To this day the Texas Rangers remain a law enforcement agency whose impact is more symbolic than real. This did not, however, keep the Texas Rangers from functioning as union busters well into the 1960s, as Valley migrant farmworkers consistently attempted to organize for higher wages and safer working conditions—including protection from such hazards as pesticides, herbicides, and short-handled hoes—and an end to substandard housing provided by growers. The brutality of Los Rinches as strikebreakers is more than evident in the brutal actions of Captain Allee of the Texas Rangers against alleged union organizers, as documented in *Medrano v. Allee*.[14]

During Prohibition Congress became so concerned with the border smuggling of alcohol that it mandated the creation of the U.S. Border Patrol in 1924. At that time fewer than five hundred agents patrolled the entire Mexican border. However, very little is known about the history of the Border Patrol because historians have paid scant attention to it. In contrast to the history of Los Rinches, there is no trail of legal cases that might serve as a rich source of historical documentation of the Border Patrol. Amateur historians, including agents who have penned their own autobiographies upon retirement, have exaggerated and romanticized the historical deeds of the Border Patrol. Mostly self-serving, these autobiographies represent border agents as replicas of U.S. Marshals enforcing law upon the heathen.[15]

What is known about the Border Patrol in the Valley is that this federal agency was despised and hated as much as Los Rinches. The perspective of border crossers—illegal or legal—and poor residents of border communities and ranches is best encapsulated in the legacy of *corridos,* folk songs, handed down in the custom of the oral tradition from one generation to the next. This historical record is at least as accurate a depiction of the Border Patrol as the self-aggrandizing autobiographies penned by border agents. These popular ballads focus on specific encounters in which the Border Patrol most frequently treats Hispanics, regardless of citizenship, cruelly and violently.[16]

These same border *corridos* find support in recent interviews of Valley respondents. The hatred of the Border Patrol is predicated upon the brutality respondents or other family members endured or witnessed as passed down by word of mouth from one generation to the next. Valley respondents who were interviewed frequently mentioned Border Patrol brutality as central to their personal family history.[17]

After Los Rinches were constrained, the Border Patrol simply denied its own legacy of brutality, which, although undocumented by historians, remains nonetheless vivid in the memories of many Valley families and Latinos who have settled throughout the country. There is, fortunately, evidence that Border Patrol violence and brutality have indeed declined since the mid-1980s. This is in part because agents in the Border Patrol no longer remain silent about the crimes of fellow agents and because victims, and advocacy groups representing them, are much more likely to be heard. For example, at the trial in 2001 of McAllen Border Patrol agent David Sipe, accused of beating a fifty-year-old, one-armed undocumented worker with a large flashlight, several Border Patrol agents testified for the prosecution.

These agents and other witnesses testified that Agent Sipe bragged to them about a "tonk" he repeatedly hit with his heavy flashlight. Presiding judge Ricardo Hinojosa interrupted one witness during the trial to ask, "What is a tonk?" The witness replied, "He [Sipe] told us a tonk is the sound an alien makes when you hit him over the head with a flashlight." Continued the witness, "He [Sipe] says it was him that should be upset because his flashlight might have broke."[18]

Border Patrol violence against undocumented workers and border residents remains a serious concern. Equally troubling is the relatively large number of criminal cases, including some for graft and corruption, pending all along the border against Border Patrol agents. According to the CBP, thirteen agents were arrested on corruption charges in 2007, twenty-one in 2008, and fourteen in 2009. Although conviction rates of agents since 2004 are about 75 percent, CBP historically has been reluctant to bring charges against supervisory agents or those in management positions above them, so these arrest statistics at best are only the tip of the iceberg. In one case in 2001, for example, the Border Patrol in Hidalgo County never brought official charges against the suspected agent holding a management position, but instead allowed him to retire. Already since 2007 CBP has arrested more than four CBP agents who were hired by the Mexican drug cartels to infiltrate the agency.[19]

It is impossible to assess whether these investigations and prosecutions represent a real and significant increase in criminal behavior by Border Patrol agents, an upturn in media attention, or greater efforts by the Border Patrol to police itself. It also may be true the number of cases reflects the fact that victims feel safer in reporting these crimes than in previous years. Other factors may be the large number of new recruits who have received limited training and who have not been socialized with professional law enforcement values.

If that is the case, further increases in crimes against undocumented workers and members of border communities, including rising rates of graft and corruption, can reasonably be expected. Criminal organizations, as competition becomes more and more difficult and the border harder to cross, may also play a more significant role in the corruption of CBP agents.

At about the time Los Rinches were muzzled in South Texas, speculators, including Lloyd Bentsen, Sr., bought and resold the majority of Valley ranchlands. An infusion of capital in the 1920s by new Midwestern landowners financed irrigation systems and agricultural infrastructure. Water from the Rio Grande opened up the Valley to industrialized systems of agriculture, with multiple growing seasons for row crops possible in the tropical climate. As outside capital flowed into the Valley, it commanded a considerable labor force of Valley residents and Mexican immigrants.

Mexicans and Mexican Americans were exploited. With shovels, mules, and wagons to clear the thick brush, cactus, and mesquite, the quasi-serfs who built the modern agricultural infrastructure, the majority of which is still intact, labored from sunup to sundown. Then this same labor force of legal Valley citizens and illegal Mexicans, the vast majority Hispanics, dug the irrigation canals to bring river water to the new crops, which included cotton, vegetables, and citrus, and built the intricate system of levees along the Rio Grande to control seasonal flooding.

In practice this economic transformation of the land, which took more than a decade to complete, was accomplished by the recruitment of peasants from northern Mexico with promises the developers never intended to fulfill. These Mexicans joined an exploited workforce of Valley Mexican Americans who also toiled within a system of poverty designed to keep them from any possibility of upward mobility. One such promise to Mexicans who were recruited to the Valley was high wages; other necessities were to be provided along with the new jobs.[20] Mexican workers may have received higher wages for their labor than in Mexico, but working conditions were far harsher, necessities few, and legal rights virtually ignored. Laborers who worked fourteen to fifteen hours a day, six and one-half days every week, were commonly paid fifty cents a day. Even by the standards of the times, this was a poverty wage in the United States, barely covering food for the workers and their families or rent for their dilapidated shacks. Many of these workers, Mexicans and Mexican Americans alike, soon fell into debt to the developers and farmers, as had the ranch workers before them.

During and after the transformation of the Valley from ranchland to agriculture, a form of debt peonage thrived in the Valley, a quasi-feudal relationship between farmworkers and Anglo landowners in which small favors were given, such as money for weddings and funerals, but constitutional rights and freedoms were set aside. The Anglo landowners paid their chattel a poverty wage, provided them substandard housing, and often settled disputes between workers outside the court system.[21]

Hispanic workers who attempted to escape from the system in place were arrested by the county sheriff, thrown into jail until the landowner or his representative could be summoned by the sheriff, then given the option by the sheriff of returning to work on the landowner's farm or serving a jail sentence.[22] Judge James B. Wells was one of the most prominent political bosses in Cameron and Hidalgo Counties to enforce this feudalist system, while in nearby Starr County, Manuel Guerra held sway.

Poor Hispanics along the Rio Grande were kept in line by municipal police and sheriff's departments and a rigid system of political bossism that commanded almost all aspects of society. Jobs were in short supply and controlled—in practice, owned—by Anglo elites. The public schools, for example, although funded by taxpayers, were overseen by Anglo school boards hiring Anglo superintendents. In turn, Anglo superintendents hired Anglo teachers in the public high schools, junior highs, and elementary schools. Custodial and other service jobs in public schools were doled out to Hispanics as part of the system of political spoils. Anglos in most Valley communities spatially distanced themselves from the poor by forcing Hispanics to live and, if given permission, to operate modest businesses—on the other side of town railroad tracks.[23]

When social services to the poor expanded during the Great Depression in the 1930s as a result of federal legislation, Anglo elites seized control over these new resources and jobs. Anglo boards controlled federal and state social service agencies, employment in hospitals, most retail businesses and trade, mainstream churches, and newspapers. When absolutely necessary, city and county governments hired *bolios*, Mexican Americans who owed their employment to their Anglo employer and were expected to act in their employer's best interest. The town newspapers similarly represented the best interests of the Anglo elites and political bosses. Mexican Americans who sought to change this prevailing system were, as necessary, blacklisted from jobs, marginalized, intimidated, beaten, run out of town, or murdered.[24]

New Valley towns in the mid-Valley, including Harlingen, San Benito, La Feria, Weslaco, Donna, Alamo, and San Juan, were laid out as agricultural trade centers after the ranchland had been transformed by a subjugated workforce. To some degree the peonage system on the new farms reinforced the elitist racial systems in place in these new communities. As in Brownsville, a Hispanic middle class remained rudimentary and without real political power. Middle-income Valley Hispanics, although lacking the votes to elect representatives, sought to find ways to change the dominant system of prejudice and discrimination. Meeting in Harlingen in 1927, they formed the first chapter of the League of United Latin American Citizens (LULAC). Two years later in Corpus Christi, meeting at the first statewide conference of LULAC, they pledged to fight racism, which was "contrary to the true spirit of Democracy, our Constitution, and our privileges." These attempts to build organizations and institutions to fight racism found further support when Hispanic G.I.s returned from World War II.[25]

The Bracero Program was instituted by the U.S. Congress to specifically address labor shortages in agriculture during World War II. From 1942 to 1964 citizens of Mexico were actively recruited by farmers, then brought to this country legally to work in fields in the Valley and throughout the United States.[26] Although some *braceros* returned to Mexico, others stayed and settled in major American cities and small towns. Many of these former braceros and their family members eventually became citizens.

When troops came home from the Korean War in the early 1950s, causing national unemployment rates to rise dramatically, hundreds of thousands of Mexicans, including some Mexican American citizens throughout the United States, were summarily rounded up by the Immigration and Naturalization Service and the Border Patrol in Operation Wetback and deported to Mexico. In 1954 the INS and Border Patrol forced more than seventy thousand individuals to leave the United States. Some were detained on ships docked at Port Brownsville before being transported on the ships to Mexican cities, including Veracruz.[27]

Chicanismo and the civil rights movement did not reach Hidalgo and Cameron Counties until the late 1960s and early 1970s. Attempts to end bossism and racism in the 1970s met with mixed and brutal results. In Pharr, for example, a group of protesters demanding an end to police brutality were themselves beaten by the police on the night of February 6, 1971. This legal protest began outside the Pharr city jail after several Latino suspects had been jailed and beaten by guards the previous week. Hundreds of outside law enforcement officers from municipalities and counties throughout Texas were called in by Pharr chief of police Alfonso Ramirez to quell the peaceful protest. One innocent Latino bystander, twenty-year-old Alfonso Flores, was shot and killed by Anglo deputy sheriff Robert Johnson. Those who fit the profile of young Chicanos were arrested, jailed, and eventually tried before biased juries. The Pharr legal system, controlled by Anglo elites throughout much of this decade, summarily found the youthful protestors, including bystanders Efraim Fernandez and Alonzo Lopez, guilty. Deputy Sheriff Robert

Johnson, who witnesses testified intentionally aimed at and shot Flores, was never indicted.[28]

Only in the 1980s did young, educated Latinos finally begin to win elections against longtime politicos supported by the Anglo establishment. This new generation of Latinos also found strong support in Texas RioGrande Legal Aid, a branch of Federal Legal Services, which opened its first Valley office in the late 1960s. Texas RioGrande Legal Aid was at the forefront of demanding legal rights for all citizens of the Valley regardless of race or class. In so doing, it took on the crooked system of justice supported by Anglos. During the 1980s Valley Hispanics also began to replace Anglos in elected or appointed positions in Valley social service agencies, school systems, and hospitals and in other job areas previously closed to them.

During this same period, as the DEA and other federal agencies succeeded in disrupting the production and distribution of drugs by the Columbian cartels, Mexican criminal organizations gradually began taking over the Columbian smuggling channels into the United States. Local smuggling families in river communities were in many instances pushed out of the drug trade by the Mexican *narcotrafficantes*. Growing rapidly in power, size, and influence, the Mexican criminal organizations soon became not only the biggest distributors of illegal drugs to the United States, but also the major producers of illegal drugs. By 2005, for example, Mexican drug cartels produced large quantities of methamphetamines, which they trafficked into the United States. As the Mexican drug cartels grew more dominant, they completely subordinated Valley drug smugglers, forcing them to scale down their illegal drug businesses, traffic in other goods, or invest their working capital in legitimate business enterprises. At present, once dominant Valley smuggling families have been relegated to the role of outsiders in the drug trade, at best mid- to low-level employees of highly organized Mexican criminal cartels.[29]

Since 9/11 and the creation of the Department of Homeland Security, Mexican drug cartel money continues to foster corrosive graft and corruption in this region's law enforcement. At the same time, the drug cartels support a pervasive culture sympathetic to bossism and favoritism sweetened by crime, bribery, and theft of public funds. County sheriff is an elected position. Sheriff Brig Marmolejo of Hidalgo County is just one example of a corrupt public official.[30]

Equally alarming was the indictment, trial, and conviction of Sheriff Conrado Cantu, Cameron County's top elected law enforcer from 2001 to 2004, who was sentenced in 2006 to twenty-four years in prison without parole. Sheriff Cantu was found guilty of accepting bribes from drug smugglers, laundering drug money, protecting illegal video gamblers, and covering up "a shootout between one of Cantu's political supporters and the deputies." Cantu was also found guilty, after holding office less than one month, of accepting a ten-thousand-dollar bribe to protect a drug smuggler. The presiding judge characterized Cantu's criminal behavior as "egregious activity that only served to promote the illegal narcotics trade."[31]

Graft and corruption still permeate not just law enforcement, but all facets of Valley society. Again in Pharr, a typical community in Hidalgo County, Hispanic custodians sued the Pharr–San Juan–Alamo Public School District in 2004. Paid a minimum wage, these male custodians, several of whom were undocumented workers, detailed at trial the crimes committed against them nightly on the job. The head custodian, a close friend of the principal with no previous supervisory experience, harassed, physically abused, and sexually assaulted a number of these custodians for more than three years— even as the victims reported these incidents to a number of high school administrators, including the principal, verbally and in signed letters.

Various high school and district administrators were, in short, aware of these crimes against the custodians but failed to protect the victims or even investigate their charges. Instead, according to the trial evidence, they covered up the incidents and warned the victims not to complain. Although victims of these crimes, all the custodians feared they would be fired from their job. Several undocumented custodians from Mexico testified that they were afraid to complain because they feared not only losing their job, but also being deported because of their illegal status. Before the jury, on which I served, was allowed to reach a verdict, attorneys representing the defendants reached an undisclosed financial settlement that favored the high school custodians.[32]

True to the patronage system, the high school administrators who hired, supervised, and covered up the crimes of the alleged perpetrator were never fired from their positions or punished in any way. These individuals continued at their jobs in the high school as if nothing had happened. Neither, too, was the alleged perpetrator of these crimes against the custodians ever brought to trial in either a criminal or a civil court. Instead, this individual was transferred to another Valley school system, again to a position for which he had no legitimate qualifications.

Several years after this trial one of the same high school administrators, Arturo Guajardo, now elevated to the position of superintendent of the Pharr–San Juan–Alamo School District, summarily retired after pleading guilty to receiving kickbacks from a construction company building a school under his direct supervision. These kickbacks to Guajardo and others included $123,000, a free four-day trip to Las Vegas, and tickets to various sporting events. Two other Pharr school board members—Rogelio "Little Roy" Rodriguez and Raul "Big Roy" Navarro—also pled guilty.[33]

Previous Border Fences

The new Mexican border fence did not spring full blown in 2006. Both the low-tech fence and the virtual fence have substantial political and institutional histories. The first low-tech border fencing was constructed in 1990 in the Border Patrol's San Diego Sector. Called primary fencing, it extended for fourteen miles and was part of the Border Patrol's so-called Prevention through Deterrence strategy. In theory, this fourteen miles of border fence, along with an increase in agents who patrolled it, was supposed to reduce greatly illegal immigration from Tijuana. The Illegal Immigration Reform and Immigrant Responsibility Act enacted by Congress in 1996 gave legal power to the U.S. attorney general, and subsequently to the secretary of the Department of Homeland Security, to construct additional physical barriers along the U.S.-Mexico border wherever deemed necessary. As well, this same act authorized secondary fencing to be built to complement the fourteen-mile San Diego fence already in place.[34]

In 2005 Congress passed the Real ID Act. This little-known piece of legislation gave power to Secretary Chertoff of the DHS to waive any and all laws that might hamper border fence construction. These laws included all environmental requirements and provisions under the EPA. This legislation was followed by the Secure Fence Act, passed by Congress in 2006, which originally mandated 850 miles of border fencing. But this act was soon superseded by the 2007 Consolidated Appropriations Act, which required DHS to build no less than seven hundred miles of border fence.

According to the CBP, there are three categories of border fencing in place. Primary fencing is constructed directly on the borderline to discourage individuals, "pedestrians," from crossing into the United States. Secondary fencing, or Sandia fencing (named for the national laboratory where it was developed), is constructed behind primary fencing. Finally, the third kind of fencing is vehicle-barrier fencing.[35]

Primary fencing currently accounts for 90 percent of fencing along the Mexican border. A small section of this fencing, broadcast and photographed to the point that it has become iconic, is the steel fencing south of San Diego. This barrier includes five miles of landing mat fence. Landing mat fencing is constructed of Vietnam-era carbon steel strips, twelve feet long by twenty inches wide by one-quarter inch thick. These surplus steel planks (originally designed to pave the surface of temporary airfields) are welded to steel pipes, each buried eight feet into the terrain at six-foot intervals. It takes 3,080 steel panels to complete one mile of this type of fencing.[36]

Ten miles of secondary, or Sandia, fencing have also been constructed south of San Diego. Between the landing mat fence and the secondary fence lies enough space for an access road that agents patrol by vehicle. The sec-

Fig. 3.1 Border fence at Tijuana, Mexico, showing
multiple barriers and CBP road in between, 2009.

ondary fence, of chain link, rises ten feet high before angling another few
feet toward Mexico to make it almost impossible to climb from that side. As
of 2009 there is also secondary fencing in the El Paso Sector; the total of
secondary fencing in both San Diego and El Paso is thirty-two miles.[37]

Two types of vehicle barrier fencing, the third category, are already in
place along the border. The first type, a permanent vehicle barrier, is erected
to discourage drug traffickers from driving their loads across the border.
Steel posts, bollards, are sunk five feet into the ground into concrete forms.
Above ground the posts differ in height to make it more difficult for smugglers to erect ramps over the barriers. Temporary vehicle barriers, the second
type, are built by agents at sector Border Patrol stations from railroad tracks,
telephone poles, or pipes. These barriers, moveable only by forklift, are installed along trails to slow or discourage smuggling. When the smugglers
change their strategy and move elsewhere, the Border Patrol moves these
barriers to new spots.[38]

By February of 2009 the CBP reported it had built 306 miles of pedestrian fencing and 301 miles of permanent and temporary vehicle barriers along the Mexican border. This leaves, according to the CBP, 64 miles of fencing still to be completed by the end of the year.[39]

The second major component of border fencing, the high-tech, virtual fence, dates to 1998. Much of this Mexican border fence was constructed in West Texas. Called the Integrated Surveillance and Intelligence System, or ISIS, this first attempt at building a high-tech barrier along the border is a massive program failure that Secretary Chertoff's DHS covered up. Most of the high-tech border fence constructed under the ISIS program now lies forgotten and rotting in the West Texas wind.[40]

President Bush Goes Home

The majority of Valley residents, as well as residents all along the Mexican border, know their rich family narratives and region's past far better than does anyone in the White House. Valley immigrants, and those on the other side of the river, endured the bloody Mexican War, the Civil War, the Cortina Wars, Anglo retaliation to the alleged Plan of San Diego, a virulent system of bossism and peonage, Los Rinches, Operation Wetback, the McAllen C Shift, *narcotrafficantes* turned cannibals, and Los Patrullos Fronteros. This same population also endured thousands of lesser acts of brutality and injustice such as those involving the Pharr high school custodians.

Many of these acts of violence against the regional population were hidden behind a thick curtain of legalism; peonage, lynchings, theft of land, beatings, murders, harassment—all escaped the historical record. Nevertheless, this violent past, along with a system of oppression engendered by Anglo bosses, is entrenched in the memories of Valley residents. Within this historical context President Bush's assurances at Anzalduas County Park that a new border fence would simultaneously provide security to residents and honor the history of border immigrants were received as yet another Washington promise in a long line of promises never kept.

At Anzalduas Park President Bush's speech was received with enthusiastic applause by those invited to attend, but throughout the Valley and *en el otro lado* his words were met with skepticism and disdain. Few in the Valley beyond the president's close supporters believed that, under the protection of a new border fence erected by the federal government, the vulnerable Valley population either would be protected or would cease to be victimized by both federal neglect and arbitrary federal policies. For all the reasons suggested, there was widespread doubt among the Valley public that a federally mandated fence along the Rio Grande would contribute in any way to the region's, or the nation's, security and safety.

Valley residents wondered aloud if this border fence would actually resolve border problems facing Valley residents or simply bring additional burdens to the region. How would this new fence protect them if it cut them off from their families and their cultural heritage on the other side of the Rio Grande? Did President Bush and members of Congress have any concern for the existing social problems endemic to the borderlands, challenges far more grave than the telegraphed federal construction of a new border fence? And, finally, some local residents questioned what kind of new border fence would be constructed if the corrupt patronage system embedded in local and county government were entrusted with hundreds of millions of federal dollars.

President Bush, for all the banners and flags erected at Anzalduas, delivered his promises from a podium located on land notorious for decades for human smuggling and drug trafficking. In all respects Anzalduas County Park, with its specific history, is typical of the numerous landings in the Valley and the hundreds more along the Mexican border, landings where undocumented workers cross each night and day, where drugs are off-loaded with impunity, and where international terrorists can presumably find easy entry. Excepting his immediate admirers and supporters, President Bush's words fell on the skeptical ears of the region's residents who have lived, and are still living, the real immigrant experience in America.

President Bush's speech at Anzalduas lasted no more than twenty minutes. Returning in his cavalcade to the Miller International Airport in McAllen, the president and his entourage lifted off the tarmac in Air Force One at 3:40 p.m., exactly two hours after landing in the Valley. Air Force One headed straight to Crawford, Texas. There, President Bush and his family spent the rest of the month of August on vacation at his ranch.

At Anzalduas County Park the human smuggling and drug trafficking resumed in full force as soon as the U.S. Secret Service and other federal, local, and state law enforcement agencies vacated the area.

Chapter 4

Olga Rivera Garcia's Fence and
Omar Sanchez's Fence

In a stiff wind from Mexico, the banks of the Rio Grande less than one hundred yards due south, the American flag and the UTB-TSC university flag pull and groan in unison against the rope anchoring them to the same aluminum pole. Olga Rivera Garcia skirts the busload of visiting Brownsville high school students in her aging golf cart, swerves to the left to avoid hitting two college students on their cells, then slams hard on the brakes at the campus flagpole.

Olga dropped everything when I called this morning, and here she is now in front of the administration building motioning me to climb into the dilapidated golf cart with its faded canvas top. Rainwater has pooled on the rusty metal floor of the cart, and the seats, foam long since exposed, are saturated. The only thing I find in my backpack to soak up the rainwater is sheets of paper from my legal pad, which I offer to Olga before stuffing some of them under my seat.

Olga has insisted on taking me on a tour of the campus to show me where the new border fence will be built. But first she must check back at her office for any new messages from her boss. "I could retire now," she tells me in her cramped, tiny office in the Tandy Building bordering International Boulevard. Just a few class-rooms down the hall from where we sit, I spent twelve years teaching courses in sociology, social problems, marriage and family, and human sexuality to first-generation Hispanics like Olga. Although that teaching was more than thirty years in my deep past, the images linger.

"I could apply for a disability," Olga tells me, jerking me back to the present.

"You going to do that?"

"No, of course not." Olga chuckles, then points with pride to an eight-by-ten color photograph taped to the wall above her head. In the photo Olga stands enfolded in the left arm of Chelsea Clinton. Chelsea wears a "Hillary for President" baseball cap atop her head. "That was two months ago," Olga tells me with obvious pride. "Chelsea is wearing my campaign hat. She lost hers, so I gave her mine. The *Brownsville Herald* wrote that I gave it to her, but I just loaned it. Never did get it back."

It has been almost ten years since I last saw Olga. Her hair is longer than I remember it, and grayer. At fifty she is a little stoop-shouldered. Sitting beneath Chelsea's photo, she tells me quietly, "First the doctor said the pain was fibromyalgia. Then he said it was rheumatoid arthritis. Finally it was something else." Whatever her doctor's diagnosis, every morning Olga takes a fistful of pills and questions whether she should keep working. Some days the pain is too great, so she stays home and cleans her house. She also likes working in her garden.

Before calling Olga, I dropped by President Juliet Garcia's office to find out more about UTB-TSC's official position regarding the new border fence. Dr. Garcia, no relation to Olga's husband Carlos, and her staff unfortunately were occupied by a "campus emergency" in the conference room. Since they had been discussing solutions to the emergency for two hours, President Garcia's administrative assistant told me they probably would remain at the table until the end of the day. But the door opened, and there was Antonio Zavaleta, now vice chancellor for external affairs at UTB-TSC. He motioned me into the meeting, and when I entered the room President Garcia and the others present greeted me warmly with the traditional *abrazo*.

Then I looked at Dr. Garcia for the first time in many years. I had known her long before she became the head of the university. She was always a very determined and direct person, never one not to speak her mind. Dressed in a no-nonsense black suit, her dark, long hair in a tight bun, she looked like someone who was not about to back away from the Department of Homeland Security.

Born and raised in Brownsville, Juliet Garcia is the first Latina ever to lead a university in the United States. In her tenure as president of UTB-TSC enrollment has jumped by more than 50 percent, and the number of graduates has substantially increased. President Garcia has doubled the university budget and enlarged the campus from 49 acres to 382. After earning her doctorate in English from the University of Texas at Austin, she returned to teach as a member of the Texas Southmost College faculty in the early 1980s. After she rose quickly through the administrative ranks, her postdoctoral studies took her to the Kennedy School of Government at Harvard, to MIT, and eventually to the London School of Business. She served on several national committees, including the White House Initiative on Educational Excellence for Hispanic Americans and several international efforts, including work in South Africa.

Dr. Garcia has been a member of the board of directors of the Ford Foundation for almost a decade, as well as vice chair of the Carnegie Foundation for the Advancement of Teaching, and she has extensive professional expertise beyond the confines of the campus. At the same time, she is deeply rooted in the politics of Brownsville and the borderlands. Married to a Brownsville native who owns the local feed store, mother of two and grandmother of four, this university administrator possesses an unusual combination of skills and talents.[1] It was not in President Garcia's borderlands bones to walk away from a fight.

Dr. Garcia introduced me to the other administrators around the long table, some of whom I knew. Ten minutes later I left the room a little dazed, memories of my old colleagues awkwardly awash in my skull. But I also left convinced President Garcia would always put the welfare of her university, the institution to which she had dedicated her professional career, before the immediate needs of a large federal bureaucracy.

As the sun makes a brief appearance on an otherwise cloudy day, Olga's campus tour takes us first to all the new classroom buildings, the remodeled art gallery and studios, the sculpture garden in memory of former faculty artist George Truan, the new student bookstore, complete with Starbucks overlooking the large *resaca* (oxbow lake), more new classroom buildings, the new addition to the old gymnasium, the new student wellness center under construction, the new student recreation facility, the construction site of the new library, the old Fort Brown Hotel, which is in transition to student dorms, and much more.

Scattered around the lush, green campus are hundreds of palm trees, flowering cactuses, banana trees, bougainvilleas, poinsettias, and other tropical plants in small courtyards decorated with colorful Spanish tiles. Unlike most public universities, this one has a cohesive architectural design that reflects the region's rich culture and history. UTB-TSC's campus, jammed tightly against the banks of the Rio Grande, has become an educational oasis in a binational metroplex. On one side are the 120,000 residents of Brownsville, and *en el otro lado*, across a thin international border, are the 1 million residents of Matamoros.

While showing me the future location of the university day care center, Olga powers the golf cart between two utility poles on the sidewalk. Luckily it only cost the cart another few dents and a patch of paint. Darting across a busy street, she then zooms down a narrow dirt path and up a levee. From its modest height we see, to our left, the city golf course where Antonio Zavaleta and I thirty years ago crossed paths with two undocumented workers fresh from the Rio Grande. In spite of intermittent showers, golfers cover every inch of the well-groomed fairways and greens as golf carts motor along asphalt pathways through mazes of sand traps and waterholes fed by the adjacent Rio Grande.

The new border fence proposed by the Department of Homeland Security will cut off the golf course, now owned by the university, from the rest of the campus. Once the new fence is in place, it is not clear how students will get from the golf course on one side of the campus to the library and the classrooms on the other.

Across the street from the university golf course, the baseball coaches put the UTB-TSC Scorpions through infield drills. The baseball stadium, less than fifty yards from the golf course, also will be separated from the campus by the proposed new border fence. Behind the backstop at home plate is an abandoned greenhouse and the National Guard armory, its parking lot filled with Humvees, large military transports, and other trucks painted in camouflage. The National Guard armory will be on the same side of the new border fence as the university's baseball park and the golf course. Then there is the International Technology, Education, and Commerce facility (ITEC).

My foot braced against the dashboard, hand on the side rail, we slide through mud on top of the Rio Grande levee. For a brief second I am convinced we are going to flip sideways down the steep side of the levee, but the wheels gain traction as Olga stomps on the accelerator.

"You want to go talk to them?" Olga asks me, pointing to agents in a Border Patrol truck parked south of us atop the same levee. "They're probably taking a coffee break." Carlos, Olga's husband, has worked for the Customs Service and now CBP for more than ten years, so Olga knows many of the Border Patrol agents on a first-name basis.

"No, I want to take a look at the river," I tell her, stepping out of the golf cart as it is still moving forward. A swift, dirty current passes below us heading for the Gulf of Mexico ten miles downstream. The banks of the Rio Grande lie thick with mesquite and shrubs, the muddy ground covered by a carpet of footprints, a plastic water jug, and other trash. Across no more than thirty feet of roiling water I see narrow trails leading into tall grass and sparse Carrizo cane, then running up the embankment into the back alleys of Matamoros. A block from there are the popular tourist boulevards of Matamoros with their restaurants, bars, and three-story curio shops for tourists.

"Where are they going to build the fence?" I ask Olga once more, wanting to be sure of its exact location.

"On top of that levee which we just drove over. Not this one we are on, that one there. It's going to cut off all the golf course and some of the baseball field. They say the government is going to destroy some of the university trees and plants when they build it, but I don't know anything about that. I heard the fence is going to take a piece out of the parking lot at the day care center. They had a big meeting about it."

Knowing it was far beyond her control, Olga is fatalistic about the new border fence. Instead of dwelling on it, she tells me about the small house in Matamoros a mile to the southwest that she inherited when her mother died. Olga lets her aunt and uncle, both in their eighties, live in the house rent-free. She has other close family members in Matamoros and visits them whenever she can. "It's taking longer and longer to cross," she tells me.

We cannot see the ITEC buildings, but they are located less than half a mile northeast of where we now stand. The university purchased the forty-two-acre ITEC site, formerly Amigoland Mall, a popular destination of Matamoros and Brownsville shoppers, in 2002. Part of the former mall is now fifty thousand square feet of technical training programs, classrooms, labs, offices, the Brownsville police academy, and a small business incubator. ITEC is bordered on two sides, the south and east, by the Rio Grande.[2]

The border fence originally proposed by the DHS would have cut off the ITEC campus from the UTB-TSC campus and, as well, from the rest of the city of Brownsville. As originally planned, the border fence did not follow the path of the winding river, but cut directly northwestward towards McAllen. By choosing not to follow the twisting banks of the river, the DHS presumably thought to save on construction costs. But in so doing, it put costs before the educational needs of Latino university students.

The Border Patrol has stated that students with special IDs will be allowed to travel back and forth from one part of the campus to the other by way of special gates installed in the fence, but at the time of this writing no specific details or plans have been produced by the Border Patrol to explain how this system will work on a daily basis.

Once more I stare at the river, listen to the ambient street noise from Matamoros, then gaze over my shoulder at the university golf course and the Scorpions now taking batting practice. Making small talk, I kid Olga about once seeing her from my office window kissing Carlos during her lunch hour: this remembrance of Olga and Carlos is frozen in my brain as if it were yesterday. But my memory is in error.

Olga blushes crimson. "That wasn't Carlos," she tells me.

"No?"

"Another guy. A Mexican playboy type I knew back then. A lawyer. I didn't meet Carlos until I graduated college." Olga convinces me she is right and I am wrong. Time can be a trickster.

Later, after Olga's campus tour, we walk down busy International Boulevard to lunch at a new cafe. The restaurant we used to go to, a lesser clone of Matamoros's well-known Drive In, with house mariachis, caged peacocks, and tuxedoed waiters, has long since closed its doors. Olga introduces me to the cafe owner, her friend from high school, who tells us that although they have been open a full year, it is impossible to compete with the likes of Mc-Donald's and Wendy's on International Boulevard. Then he brings us two plates of tasty chicken tacos topped with goat cheese.

Later, after lunch, after her friend clears our table, Olga quietly begins to cry. I was asking her if she ever ran into Antonio Zavaleta on campus. "He's very good to me. He always asks me about my sister and, before my mother died, he always asked about her. My oldest is graduating with a pharmacy degree from UT-Austin, and Dr. Zavaleta always asks about her. The youngest, I don't know about her. She's a freshman at UTPA in Edinburg and thinks for some reason she doesn't have to get good grades. But Dr. Zavaleta always asks about them." Her mouth tenses at this exact moment, her eyes fill, and the tears flow.

Olga blows her nose on a paper napkin. "I just get so mad. My supervisor, you know who I'm talking about, has been giving me the same crap all these years. More than twenty years now. Every time I do something good, he ignores it. I'm on the university alumni committee, and he's been trying to get me taken off. But Dr. Zavaleta told me he'd take care of it and he did. I love that committee. They send me to Austin and other places. I learn so much. I care so much for this place. Now they are sending me over to the library."

"Why?"

"It's supposed to be an office reorganization, but it's just an excuse to put me away somewhere. I'll be officed in the library. Which is just as well. He knows he can't fire me. I've decided I'm going to retire in eighteen months. I want to learn to cook like an Italian chef. I always wanted to learn. And work more in my garden at home.

"Carlos retires in seven years. Then the kids will be out of school and we can travel. I've never been anywhere except Texas and Atlanta and a few cities. First I want to see Italy. Carlos wants to play more golf, but he'll go with me. Carlos loves golf. He used to play with his father before his father hurt his shoulder.

"You know what pisses me off? The women around here with their long fingernails. How can they work with fingers like that? I can't waste money that way. We always avoid debt. We still live in the same house we built. If Carlos's friends don't like it when they come over, then we don't see them again."

Situated amid the reconstructed remnants of old Fort Brown, the university is a border mix of Mexican Americans, Mexicans, and Anglos, a population mired in centuries of racial intolerance, violence, and nationalism.[3] The university student body is 80 percent Mexican American, 10 percent Mexican, and 10 percent Anglo. Faculty, staff, and administration are heavily skewed towards Mexican Americans and Anglos, Anglos predominating on the faculty, Mexican Americans in administration. Mexican nationals are most often found in staff positions at the lowest rungs of this hierarchy.[4]

Olga, an American citizen for more than a quarter of a century, has endured a university career of adversity, at least in part because she is discriminated against by some campus Mexican Americans and Anglos. Her American citizenship notwithstanding, Olga will always be treated by many on campus as Mexican. In the borderlands there is not only the expected racism of Anglos toward Mexicans, but also Latinos toward Mexicans. Many justify their discrimination based upon pride in their American citizenship by birth, their unique culture, and their history; Anglos join in this discrimination against Mexicans.

Another little secret is that many Mexicans return the favor and more, labeling Mexican Americans, along with border Anglos, among those who have long since lost their own culture and beliefs to questionable imperialistic and capitalistic values and customs.[5] UTB-TSC is, like all universities, a complex arrangement of personal relationships and attitudes not subject to instantaneous change by education alone; as such, it reflects the standards of the region.

For Olga at this point the proposed fence is no more than another potential inconvenience, one among many for a former illegal immigrant who moved a total of three miles from her place of birth to a new life, new citizenship, and new home in another country. On a daily basis the new fence may mean Olga will have to wait in line longer to cross and recross the river.

University staff living in Matamoros will face the same inconvenience. But while Olga's view of the river and the city in which she was born may be obstructed by the new border fence, Olga has too many other things in her life to worry about.

If Olga Rivera Garcia has suffered from twenty-five years of indignities at her university job solely because of her country of origin, she never once questions whether she is better off on the north side of the river than on the south. By moving three miles, Olga knows she inestimably improved her life, the lives of her children, and the lives of other members of her family, including those who remain in Matamoros. So Olga at one and the same time is hardened to certain inevitabilities, including the border fence, even as she encourages her two daughters to pursue careers as educated professionals.

After lunch Olga disappears into the confines of the Tandy Building. I spend the rest of the afternoon gathering documents from university administrators. Not surprisingly I learn that President Garcia has grave reservations about the proposed border fence on the UTB-TSC campus. She writes in a recent press release:

> We were notified of plans by the Department of Homeland Security to build a fence 18 feet high on top of the levee north of the ITEC campus, essentially placing ITEC on the Mexican side of the fence. In addition, the plans would also build a fence 18 feet high on top of the levee just south of the baseball field and of the EDBC (Education and Business Complex) parking lot, essentially placing all of the golf course on the Mexican side of the fence.
>
> In October [2007], we received a letter from the U.S. Customs and Border Protection asking for right of entry onto University property. The request sought access to survey University land for 18 months for the possible construction of the fence, to store equipment and supplies, take samples and to do any other work they found necessary for the proposed construction of the fence.
>
> The same letter informed us that they would not be responsible for any damage done during this time by their activities. Finally, the letter stated that should they determine need for any University land, the University would be paid market value for the land.
>
> I did not sign the letter that would have granted access for several reasons. I felt the action posed serious harm to the University on many fronts.[6]

After President Garcia refused to allow unlimited DHS entry onto university land, along with its other nonnegotiated demands, DHS took the university to federal district court. After a day in court, President Garcia was guardedly optimistic about the proposed campus border fence, saying, "I believe that we have begun to make progress toward a meaningful, consultative conversation to achieve the mutual objectives of the DHS and the University."[7] Dr. Garcia and her other administrators believe, in fact, that the court hearing is a legal victory for the university. UTB-TSC and DHS are ordered by the judge to reach a joint compromise, a negotiated resolution the details of which they will report back to the judge in a timely fashion.

DHS assumed it could steamroll in a federal court of law Dr. Garcia's legal objections to the border fence. Instead, Judge Andrew S. Hanem, after hearing testimony from both sides, required DHS to negotiate with the university. Negotiation, however, is simply not among DHS secretary Michael Chertoff's strategies in constructing the new border fence. Nevertheless, Judge Hanem ordered DHS to sit down at the same table with university representatives to find solutions that were amenable to both sides.

Less than three weeks later, Secretary Chertoff stated that, based upon his interpretation of the Real ID Act of 2005, all environmental reviews would be bypassed so that construction of the fence could be completed as soon as possible. Chertoff further declared, "Criminal activity at the border does not stop for endless debate or protracted litigation."[8] In other words, Chertoff intended to construct a fence anywhere DHS deemed appropriate, splitting the UTB-TSC campus into two separate parts in the name of national security.

By his statements Chertoff believed that by increasing pressure on UTB-TSC, he could bully President Garcia and circumvent any genuine negotiation. Certainly it is not clear what options this left President Garcia with regards to achieving her "meaningful, consultative conversation to achieve the mutual objectives of the DHS and the University." When Chertoff's staff met on several different occasions with UTB-TSC administrators, the DHS officials did little but make demands and were unwilling to compromise on any points. What Secretary Chertoff did not seem to realize is that President Garcia and her staff are competent, experienced administrators, have faced off many times in the past against demands from various agencies of the state and the federal government, and are not about to be pushed around.

Secretary Chertoff's statements and the actions of his DHS representatives suggest he believed he was dealing with a bunch of border bumpkins incapable of understanding either the ins and outs of national politics, the rights of a public university, or the options open to them. Chertoff and DHS were, on the other hand, oblivious to the fact that along the Mexican border, given its long history of conflicts and violence, attempts at legal intimidation by the federal government are at most seen as foreplay. While certainly true that President Garcia and her administrators are not beltway insiders, what they do know is that in South Texas the legal and judicial systems at the local, county, state, and federal levels are, and always have been, subject to power politics.

The university administrators know, for example, that the judge hearing their case resides in Brownsville, not Washington, D.C. Regardless of the exacting letter of the law, this same judge, who is appointed for life, will, long after Secretary Chertoff has left public office, still make his home in Brownsville and still have to explain his court decisions to his family, his close friends, his neighbors, his church congregation, and the rest of the Brownsville crowd looking over his legal shoulder. Secretary Chertoff, a foreigner to the borderlands, simply did not understand that in South Texas the force of law embodied in the legal system has always played second or third fiddle to border politics.[9]

Dr. Garcia had several cards to play, not the least of which was the impact of national opinion when it became widely known that DHS had plans to split a poor, minority university with a controversial border fence. With access to local, state, and national politicians, all aware of the Latino vote come election time, Dr. Garcia was not without options. These same university administrators know how to use the media to shape public opinion; from the very beginning they documented their contact with DHS from their own university's website.

Chertoff's strategy to site a border fence was crystal clear from the start: first, send an ominous letter to the landowner threatening a federal suit along with the concomitant costs of defending against it; second, push hard and fast for the property owner, in this case a public university, to make a quick, binding decision; third, take to court all property owners who refuse to sign away their legal property rights and obtain a quick decision against them; and fourth, act at all times as if there are no options or choices other than those demanded by DHS.

Perhaps further emboldened by President Bush's reelection to a second term of office, Chertoff's DHS presupposed a one-size-fits-all legal strategy to eliminate any borderlands opposition to the new fence. In so doing, the DHS underestimated both the broad and diverse public reaction to the border fence among border populations, the strategic resources available to regional dissenters, and the extent to which acute desperation may drive those involved. Most important, Chertoff's DHS did not understand the historical role, the politicized role, of the force of law within borderlands society. In the borderlands, as in many other regions of the United States, one size never fits all.

"Jerkoff is what stinks about this whole mess," David Hall tells me a day later in Weslaco, ten miles upriver from Brownsville. David has worked as the executive director of Texas RioGrande Legal Aid in South Texas since 1969.

"Jerkoff?" I say.

"Yeah, Jerkoff. Michael Jerkoff," David tells me without a smile. "Secretary of Homeland Security. DHS comes in like gangbusters and starts dictating to property owners what they can and cannot do on their own land. Refuses to negotiate with them. Tells them if they don't sign on the dotted line, then they will sue them in court. And that's what DHS did. They sued any landowner in the Valley that refused to sign. This is Texas, for God's sake, not the goddam East Coast!

"I know the guy who is their lead prosecutor. Charlie Wendlandt. assistant United States attorney based in Houston. He's an okay guy. Known him a long time. He's quiet in court but knows the law. You should have heard him in the judge's chambers. Charlie was pissed."

David and Rebecca Weber, another legal services lawyer based in Weslaco, order their lunch at the Blue Onion right off Highway 83 before David returns to the subject at hand. Rebecca, behind thick sunglasses, keeps very quiet.

"Pissed about what?"

"About being kept in the dark. The judge wanted to know the hard facts about the wall. Where, when, how, etc. But Charlie told Judge Hanem he did not know anything about it. You see, Jerkoff isn't even telling his own lawyers what DHS is doing. Jerkoff has this attitude. The whole administration in Washington has it. They get it from Cheney. They don't have to tell you squat. Nada. You're just supposed to follow their orders. If you don't, they threaten to indict, take you to federal court, investigate you, whatever it takes to put you in your place. Stuff it down your throat. It's that simple."

David is getting himself worked up. I'd seen it before. I worked on a project with David in the mid-1990s when a group of borderland developers, many of them local private attorneys, were systematically defrauding low-income Latinos. The majority of the buyers were undocumented workers, some of whom had lived and worked in this country for many years. After accepting a five-hundred-dollar down payment on the lot, the crooked developers had the impoverished buyers sign a two-page, single-spaced legal document in English—most did not read English—that included the right to foreclose if the buyer missed a single payment. These lots were in *colonias*, unincorporated rural land developments that frequently lacked basic infrastructure, including running water, sewage systems, and electricity.[10] David and his legal staff initiated state legislation that closed many of the loopholes to these fraudulent real estate practices, which intentionally took advantage of the migrant farmworkers.

Rebecca squirms in her seat. She's heard this all before.

"How long you been here?" I ask her. She removes her thick sunglasses to look at me.

"Six months."

"Where did you go to law school?"

"Yale."

"This a surprise to you?"

"No. After I graduated, I was a congressional staffer for two years in Washington."

"So what's your legal strategy in all this?" I ask David. No use beating around the bush.

"Legal strategy? My legal strategy is one day at a time." Combative in court, always lightning quick to defend the little guy against big business and big government, David looks less like a vintage civil rights lawyer, which he is, than a 1950s Beatnik poet.

"One day at a time?"

"Yeah. Five days in a week. We got a possible week's delay strategy we're working on right now. But one day at a time is the time frame we're on. Hold them off until January 1, 2009. Then we hopefully get a new president and this bullshit ends. We want to keep them from starting to build the thing [the fence]. Because once they start it, it's hard to stop it."

"I heard in Brownsville [Cameron County] that in Hidalgo County it's all about the levees. That right?"

"It's unbelievable. No, I take that back. It's very believable. One of the Hidalgo County commissioners gets on the bandwagon after the Border Patrol approaches them last fall.[11] J. D. Salinas. The system of levees in Hidalgo County has not been improved since the 1960s. The Army Corps of Engineers rebuilt the levee system after the flooding hit the valley from Hurricane Beulah. Then after Katrina, the Corps reevaluates the status of all levees nationwide, including the ones here in the Valley. That's when FEMA [Federal Emergency Management Agency] starts threatening to recategorize a bunch of Valley homes as being in a flood plain. Because the Valley levee system is in such bad shape. If there's another hurricane, FEMA is saying that the levees will not hold the flooding back. If FEMA goes by their new study of the levees here, it will substantially raise home insurance premiums for a lot of people in Hidalgo County.

"Of course, the truth is that if the county water district people had been taking care of the levees in the first place like they should have, the levees would be in good shape now. But we know what they were doing with their funding, and it wasn't keeping an eye on the levees. Everybody knows that. So this J. D. Salinas sees a big opportunity to get himself some votes for the next election. Maybe run for higher office. He panders to the Feds, the Feds pretend it's his idea, and all of a sudden the wall is all about saving the taxpayers of Hidalgo County millions of dollars. DHS gets its wall in Hidalgo County, the taxpayers get an improved levee system, and a bunch of Hidalgo County homeowners dodge higher rates. Everybody wins, according to J. D. Salinas. Including him. If this really happens he can get elected to any state job he wants."

"Except my property owners are getting screwed," David adds. "Plus we get the damn wall."

The food server brings us plate-sized, hand-made flour tortillas filled with the house salsa, fresh fried fish, shrimp, and fajitas. Hunching his shoulders, David would rather talk than eat.

"You know what this place is like because you lived here. It's going to mean millions in contracts siphoned through the Hidalgo County commissioners. And all their friends. Imagine that. That'll be fun to watch."

Ignoring his food, David says, "DHS, by way of the Border Patrol, contacted every property owner along the river in Hidalgo County. Basically they told them, 'Sign this document or we are going to sue you.' No negotiation. No nothing. We're representing several landowners."

The first hearing in Hidalgo County occurred on March 17, 2008, in the U.S. District Court, Southern District of Texas in McAllen.[12] The DHS sued any Hidalgo property owners who refused to sign a letter of agreement allowing immediate entry and surveying of their land by DHS, just as they did UTB-TSC in Brownsville. The real flavor of the DHS's suit was revealed in the testimony at the hearing.

Baldomero Muñiz, a migrant farmworker and U.S. citizen, owns a few acres of property near the small town of Los Ebanos on the Rio Grande. DHS sent Mr. Muñiz, who does not speak or read English, a single-spaced form letter in English demanding that he allow DHS to enter his property and perform certain unspecified functions. If Mr. Muñiz did not allow them entry, DHS would sue him in federal court. There were no negotiations by DHS with Muñiz about entry onto his land, or even any attempts at negotiation. Muñiz was simply told to sign the letter and return it immediately. There also was no statement of what DHS planned to do on his land or how, if at all, they might change it, including leveling buildings or chopping down valuable trees. Muñiz was told by DHS he would receive one hundred dollars for signing the enclosed document.

Requiring a court interpreter, Mr. Muñiz responded at the court hearing that the post office notified him they had some "papers" waiting for him:

Lawyer: Did you understand what those papers said?

Mr. Muñiz: The gentleman at the post office asked me to sign some papers so that I could be able to receive them from him. Since I knew nothing of that—of those things, I asked one of my little ones, one of my little girls, the littlest one since she knows some English, and so I went on ahead and I signed so that I could take them home with me.

Lawyer: And did your daughter explain to you what was in those papers?

Mr. Muñiz: Yes. I believe that they indicated that if I would give permission for them to enter, but I didn't. I said no.

Lawyer: Did—was it clear to you exactly what they wanted to do there on your land?

Mr. Muñiz: I didn't know what it was that they indicated that they wanted.

Lawyer: Sir, just to clarify, how long have you owned that property?

Mr. Muñiz: That property I purchased in '80.

Lawyer: And is that where you have your house, your homestead residence?

Mr. Muñiz: Yes. I purchased it and then I went to Michigan. And after some number of years, we built the little house there on the basis of what I earned while I was in Michigan.

Lawyer: Besides the house that's on the property, do you keep any animals there?

Mr. Muñiz: Yes. I have just a few kids, no more. Little goats.

Lawyer: Had the government ever offered you any money to come onto your property for the purposes of surveying?

Mr. Muñiz: No, no, none of that. The government has not offered me anything.[13]

Pamela Rivas, another small property owner along the Rio Grande, faced a different set of circumstances:

Lawyer: Who contacted you?

Pamela Rivas: It was a Border Patrol that contacted me, and we talked over—they handed me—over lunch, one hour lunch, and they explained to me what they were—briefly the papers that they were wanting me to sign.

Lawyer: And what did they tell you?

Pamela Rivas: That they were wanting access to the land to do some surveying and things of that sort.

Lawyer: Did they tell you exactly what they were going to do besides surveying?

Pamela Rivas: Do some land testings. They were very vague, very— didn't have a whole lot.

Lawyer: Did they do most of the talking during that meeting?

Pamela Rivas: Yes, they did.

Lawyer: You did most of the listening?

Pamela Rivas: Yes.

Lawyer: Did you have a chance to ask them questions?

Pamela Rivas: Yes, I did, but they could not give me a definite answer.

Lawyer: What was their reasoning for not being able to give you a definite answer?

Pamela Rivas: I don't know. They were just kind of very vague.

Lawyer: When they gave that [the letter] to you, did they—did they tell you that if you didn't like something in it, you could change it?

Pamela Rivas: I don't recall that.

Lawyer: Do you recall whether they asked you how much money they would pay you for this?

Pamela Rivas: That was not discussed.

Lawyer: About how long after you received this document were you sued by the government?

Pamela Rivas: I think it was immediately after. Very short time.

Lawyer: In between the time you received that document and the time you were sued, did they contact you at all in any other way?

Pamela Rivas: No.[14]

Noel A. Gonzalez is the superintendent of schools for the Rio Grande Consolidated Independent School District in Starr County, which lies along the Rio Grande directly west of Hidalgo County. Starr County historically is, like neighboring Hidalgo and Cameron Counties, one of the very poorest of all of the five thousand counties in the nation.[15] Mr. Gonzalez was approached by two representatives of the Army Corps of Engineers, who wanted to meet with the Starr County School District. The Starr County School District owns a large portion of land along the Rio Grande which includes a school campus, school buildings, school grounds, a wildlife refuge, and several nationally registered historical sites. In their meeting, according to Gonzalez's sworn testimony, this is what transpired:

> Lawyer: Okay. Did either of these ladies [from the Army Corps of Engineers] explain to the board that this was the beginning of a process of negotiation for entry onto the property [owned by the Board of Education]?
>
> Mr. Gonzalez: No. That word was never shared at that meeting.
>
> Lawyer: What was the gist of their presentation to the board?
>
> Mr. Gonzalez: It was for information. It was a general overview of what was going to happen.
>
> Lawyer: Okay. And were they telling the board what was going to happen, or were they asking the board for suggestions on how to do this?
>
> Mr. Gonzalez: No. They were telling them what was going to happen, and it was just a survey.
>
> Lawyer: Okay. And did they explain what kind of survey it was going to be?
>
> Mr. Gonzalez: No, they did not.
>
> Lawyer: Did they explain what the survey would entail?
>
> Mr. Gonzalez: No, they did not.
>
> Lawyer: How many students are on this particular parcel of property on a daily basis?
>
> Mr. Gonzalez: 1,000 plus.
>
> Lawyer: Mr. Gonzalez, can you tell the court what your general concern is about the government entering on the property without sitting down and having negotiations and discussions about these particular issues?
>
> Mr. Gonzalez: Sure. The first one that comes right up to my mind is my children. I have a thousand children there. Who's coming when? How many people are coming? Are they going to interact with my children? Where are they going to be at? I have to answer to my parents who are my taxpayers. How am I going to answer to them if I don't know who's what or who's where or what's going to happen? What's the game plan? I really thought we were going to be able to sit down and talk. I thought that you would get an attorney. I have an attorney. We'd all sit down, and then we could have a conversation and then go to the school board. No one ever called me. No one ever wanted to meet with me. You know, that would have been a process. And my number

one concern besides all the wonderful buildings and the chacha-laca [a bird] refuge, sir, is the children.[16]

Steamrolling their way to gain access to private property along the Rio Grande, DHS treated everyone the same, whether poor landowner with a small herd of goats, the superintendent of public schools, or a public university. That this tactic may rub against the grain of a district federal judge never seemed to pierce the thick armor of DHS's one-size-fits-all legal strategy.

"You got any other problems with the fence?" I ask David and Rebecca as we finish lunch.

"Just one small thing," says David. "They are going to raise the levees in this county so that it won't flood. That's good for Hidalgo County. But what about the folks in Reynosa? What's going to happen when they raise the levees to prevent flooding in McAllen but don't protect the other side of the river?" Floods, with or without new levees on the north side of the river, periodically damaged Reynosa, a city of 750,000 mostly poor residents directly across from McAllen.

"Anybody talking about that problem?"

"No. Jerkoff doesn't care. But we're concerned. And what about downstream? What about in Cameron County and on the other side? Nobody's talking much about that. But where do you think the water is going to go?"

The check came, and David went to get his truck. As he sat perched behind the wheel, I asked him a final time, just to be sure he is not tugging at the strings of hyperbole, "Are you really without a long-term strategy against DHS?"

"One day at a time. He's got the law on his side on this thing. That's all we got going against Jerkoff."

Two days after I speak with these and other lawyers at Texas RioGrande Legal Aid, officials from the Weslaco Border Patrol Station show me how they believe the Hidalgo County border fence will help control undocumented workers, drug smugglers, and terrorists and at the same time prevent flooding in Hidalgo County.[17] Driving a brand new truck cherry-picked from the motor pool, the field operations supervisor (FOS), Omar Sanchez, drives over every inch of the border from Weslaco to McAllen. Backseat in the cage, the public affairs officer (PAO), Dan Doty, fills in the gaps in conversation.

"Tell me about the fence at the UTB-TSC campus," I ask the PAO before we have driven ten feet. A large man with a round face, he sits separated from us by a thick plastic shield. I am hopeful that both agents, neither of whom I know, will speak honestly and openly, because they must be frustrated by local news coverage critical of the border fence, DHS, and the Border Patrol. It is in the interests of Agents Sanchez and Doty that the public hear their side of the story.

"Just a big misunderstanding," says PAO Doty right off. "If you look at the map, you'll see that there is no real problem there. They [the UTB-TSC administrators] should have enlarged it [the map], then they'd see that there was no problem."

"But it splits the campus in half."

"Not really," interjects FOS Sanchez. "There are going to be access gates. The students will be able to get back and forth from one campus to another with no problem. They'll have special I.D.s."

"How's that going to work exactly?" I said, more than dubious after Olga's campus tour at UTB-TSC.

"We'll work it out with them," is what FOS Sanchez tells me. It quickly becomes apparent that FOS Sanchez is a career Border Patrol agent who is used to, and comfortable with, speaking his mind. He seems surprised that there might be a problem with UTB-TSC students getting from ITEC or the baseball field to campus classrooms, the library, the day care center, or the student health center.

So I ask him again, "But how exactly? Are there going to be agents at these gates 24/7? What will these special I.D.s look like? Who will hand them out?

"Once we get the fence built," FOS Sanchez tells me, "these kinds of things will work themselves out."

"What about the Hidalgo County farmers with land on the south side of the fence? Between the fence and the river?" FOS Sanchez stops the truck to take in a view of the river levees west of Weslaco. Surrounded by open fields of onions and sugarcane, we've been motoring slowly atop the levees south of Weslaco. In some cases the old levees are as much as a half mile to a mile from the bending and twisting riverbanks. Thanks to County Commissioner J. D. Salinas, the plan in Hidalgo County is for the border fence to be an integral part of this levee system regardless of how distant the levee actually stands from the riverbank. By definition this means valuable farmland, black soil rejuvenated over the years by seasonal flooding, will be located on the south side of the border fence.

Not missing a beat, the FOS says, "Again, not a problem. There'll be plenty of gates. Believe me. The farmers will contact us, we open the gates, they roll in their heavy equipment or whatever they have, then we close the gates. When they need to get back out again, they just contact us and we open it up for them."

"Who are they are going to call?" I ask. The Border Patrol already have big problems with the landowners. During my previous research of the Border Patrol in South Texas, I observed many undocumented workers escape from agents because agents did not have the right keys to unlock the gates to the onion and cane fields. The suspected undocumented workers get away, especially at night. I ask FOS Sanchez, "Will they call dispatch or sector headquarters? A special phone number to agents in the field? What's the system going to look like and how's it going to work?"

For the first time there is complete silence in this vehicle. Then FOS Sanchez says, with no hesitation in his voice, "We do not have in all honesty those specific details worked out at this point in time. First we've got to get the fence built. Then we'll work out this other stuff."

By "this other stuff," FOS Sanchez means not just university students traveling from one side of campus to another with a border fence in between, but landowners preparing their lands for planting, daily irrigation, pesticide application, defoliation, harvesting, and all the other countless hours spent to ensure a financially rewarding crop.

There are other even more important issues that the CBP has not seriously considered. How will the Border Patrol police this new area? Surely this agency will need to create new strategies and tactics. For example, how will the Border Patrol safely transfer a group of undocumented workers apprehended near the river to the other side of the new fence? What will happen if one or more of those apprehended is in need of emergency medical attention? What will happen if an agent is seriously injured on the south side of the border fence? Notwithstanding FOS Sanchez's dismissive response, "this other stuff" is as germane, arguably more so, than the new construction itself. Issues of reducing risk to Border Patrol agents, strategies of apprehension that also increase the safety of illegal border crossers, should not simply be reduced to "this other stuff." The well-being and lives of agents, illegal crossers, and the general public are at stake.

Another possible scenario: How will the CBP transport a captured drug load around or through the proposed fence without exposing agents to prolonged gunfire from Mexico? What is notably missing from FOS Sanchez and PAO Dotty is any sign of detailed planning, including the Border Patrol's response to very predictable scenarios. This planning, to avoid the risk of serious injury and the unnecessary loss of lives, is best accomplished before the border fence is completed rather than as an afterthought when the injuries and deaths begin to embarrass the Border Patrol and DHS publicly.

The devil, of course, is always in the details. Unfortunately, institutional planning is not given priority in the Border Patrol but summarily discounted as needless and trivial. Precise planning could form the core of how the Border Patrol will police the new border fence and the space between it and the river. Similar planning might foresee the inherent problems in dividing a university campus by a border fence—not to mention the negative publicity associated with no planning.

Miles and miles of levees in Hidalgo County crisscross fertile river bottom that annually produces bountiful harvests of onions, melons, sugarcane, row crops, and citrus, forming the foundation of the region's economy.[18] The onion harvest is in full swing around us as we drive along the Hidalgo border. On 23rd Street in McAllen seasonal employees at the onion shed next to the railroad tracks process onions 24/7 to accommodate this year's bumper crop. Thousands upon thousands of bags of plump, golden-skinned onions, named 1015 for their recommended annual planting date of October 15, are harvested by armies of farmworkers from the fields around us. Once the border fence is constructed, how will these tons of onions, along with all the Valley's other fresh produce, be transported from one side of the border fence to the other? The Border Patrol has no clue.

Thirty-mile-an-hour winds blow onion skins and fragments down the drag road as we continue west, following the twisting Rio Grande. The dusty trail we leave in our wake rises up momentarily behind us, then is whipped out of sight by the wind. Between the gusts, the scent of onions fills the hot air.

"What about the irrigation workers?" I ask FOS Omar Sanchez, refusing to let him off the hook. Onions and all the other Valley crops are labor intensive not just during the planting and harvesting seasons, but throughout the entire year. Workers dressed in traditional white pants and shirts are constantly in the fields switching the irrigation pipes from one spot to water another, shoring up failed irrigation dams, repairing pipe, maintaining and repairing the ubiquitous water pumps, and other necessary tasks.

Human smugglers and drug traffickers hire some of these same agricultural workers as lookouts and informants. More than a few of these minimum-wage workers are caught every year by the Border Patrol transporting drug loads from the onion, sugarcane, and melon fields to Old Military Highway.

"We'll work those details out," again affirms the field operations supervisor, impatience finally creeping into his voice. A reservist in the army with the rank of major, FOS Sanchez has just returned from a one-year tour of duty in Iraq. After only a week off to spend time with his family, he reported for work at the Weslaco Border Patrol Station. From his responses it is already clear that FOS Sanchez is not pleased by either my questions or the doubts I openly express. Although annoyed, he is not going to show it.

"You've got to keep your eye on the big picture," is what he tells me as we approach the construction site of the new bridge at Donna. Here, where the new bridge will soon cross into Mexico, there are river levees on both sides of the construction, levees that will soon become part of the new border fence.

"Look, no system is perfect. The border fence is not going to be perfect. But it's going to help us control what goes on out here. We call it deterrence. You know what a mess it is. The fence is not a 100 percent solution, but it's going to allow us to better control the situation. You've got to look at the big picture. The fence is going to be one more hurdle that the bad guys are going to have to deal with. It's going to make it harder for them to cross. Not impossible, just harder. You start adding up the hurdles, and hopefully it will be enough deterrent. Is it a perfect solution? No way."

"Isn't the fence here at Donna just going to push people up river or down river where it's easier to cross?"

"Of course it is. Wherever the fence is up and running, here or at Anzalduas or wherever, the majority of the traffic is going to go somewhere else. But those places are getting fewer and fewer. There'll always be some guys that find a way to get over the fence. That's just human nature. But we're making it harder and that's what it's all about. And I can personally tell you from my experience in Iraq that this is the right thing to do."

I keep silent. I feel there is a prepared speech coming my way, but there is nowhere to hide.

"Maybe I'm talking out of line," FOS Sanchez says, looking across at me as we slowly motor along the drag road next to the river. "But believe me, you have no idea what it's like when you can't control a population. I do. In Iraq I've seen it up close. It's not pretty. What I'm scared to death of is having that same situation re-create itself right here at home. This is where I come from and live with my family. The Valley is my home. We've got an open border at this point in time. Anybody can come into our country. I'm not worried about the guys who just want to find work. They're not the problem. Not even the drug smugglers. The way I see it, if people are going to smoke dope and use drugs, then they'll always find a way to do it. My mind is more on the terrorists. It's too easy for them now. Think about it. An Arab doesn't look that different from a Mexican American or a Mexican. I was over there and I know it for a fact. After blending in with the Mexicans on the other side, terrorists can cross the river here, then blend in right away and we would never know it. Some of them look just like us. Look at Saddam Hussein. Saddam Hussein looks just like one of my uncles."

"You still have those old vests?" I ask him, not wanting to hear the rest of his speech.

"We were all issued new ones," comes from PAO Doty in the backseat. "Kevlar. None of that old stuff anymore."

I look over my shoulder at the PAO in the backseat. "You wearing it or sitting on it?" I kid him.

"No sir," he says laughing, but uncomfortably. "It's around here somewhere." He pretends to search for his vest. Bulletproof vests are at all times to be worn by agents on duty, but just as often they are used as seat cushions because they are bulky and hot.[19] Agents used to receive surplus vests or buy their own; new vests retail for about a thousand dollars. For the first time in the agency's history, agents are finally working in the field wearing state-of-the-art vests and using other professional-grade equipment.

"What about the ground sensors?" I ask them both as we bump along the drag road five miles south of McAllen. "Have the sensors been replaced yet?"

"No. They still suck."

"Radio communications?"

"Negative," says FOS Sanchez matter-of-factly. "But we've seen major improvements in other areas. Agents who qualify on the range now carry an M4 [carbine]. I know you went on the boat patrols. We've got the Coast Guard "go-fast" boats instead of those local bass boats they make in Harlingen. The go-fasts are twenty-two feet and really move. So we're competitive with the bad guys on that end of things."[20]

"What really bugs me," says the FOS, "is those new recruits coming out of the academy in New Mexico. You know how much training they are getting?"

"Five and a half to six months?"

"Negative. Fifty-five days."

"You're kidding me."

"That's what it is. Fifty-five days."

Fifty-five days to turn a Walmart employee or security guard into an agent of the U.S. Border Patrol is a travesty. Military veterans who are recruited into the Border Patrol academy are another thing, although the professional training of a soldier has very little to do with the work of an agent patrolling the line. It will be a matter of time before poorly trained recruits shoot an innocent victim or fellow agent, take a bribe, or commit some other major, perhaps fatal, infraction of the law.

"We mentor them longer. That's a positive," says the FOS. "Two years instead of one. But we don't have enough mentors to do the job the way it should be done. Guess who made supe last year? You're not going to believe it when I tell you.

"No idea."

"How about the last guy in the world you'd expect to be a supe at the McAllen Station?"

"Herman Morningside?"

"Yeah. Last year."

"I thought he was retired by now. That's what he told me he was going to do. Start his own business. I spent a lot of time with Morningside. He's a good guy, but not a supervisor."

"He started his business. But, yeah, he's a supervisor now. That should tell you how short-handed we are. We don't have the experienced guys to mentor the ones coming out of training because the good supes are getting out as fast as they can."

I ask FOS Sanchez to stop the truck so I can get out. We are not far from an old water pumping station along the river that for many years was a popular crossing point for human traffickers and drug smugglers.[21]

"This place still hot?" I ask.

"Yeah, it is," says Sanchez.

"What about Anzalduas?"

"Yeah."

"Chimney Park? Riverside? Pinetas? Bull's Balls? Granjeno? Miller's Farm?" I name a dozen other places.

"Same."

We climb back into the truck, motor down the drag road, then pull onto the top of a levee south of downtown McAllen. A uniformed McAllen utility crew digs up rusty pipes on one side of the levee, while a crew on the other side installs a culvert. To the south is a large onion field stretching to the tree line marking the river. Adjacent to the onion field is a hundred acres of knee-high sugarcane blowing in the wind. In another six weeks the sugarcane will have grown eight feet high and be a perfect location to stash a load of drugs or twenty undocumented workers heading north.

"You see that tree line?" the FOS asks me. "That's the river. It's probably going to go up right here where we're standing. In a few weeks." The "it" is the new border fence.

With renewed interest I inspect the levee on which we stand. No different than the miles of levees we already have traversed, this particular mound of dirt is twelve to fifteen feet high, with a very steep drop-off to the irrigated fields below.

"I'm most worried about security," the FOS tells me as he surveys the old levee. "I'm worried they will protest right in the middle of the heavy construction equipment and someone will get hurt. We're going to fence the construction site off and keep a low profile about it. But this is probably where it's going to start in Hidalgo County."

As we walk atop the levee, the work crews pay little attention. I eyeball them as carefully as possible. My best guess, and it's only a guess—but it is a guess based upon years of experience living in this region of the border—is that at least one-third of this city crew are undocumented workers. Maybe more.

"You're writing another book," The FOS declares straightforwardly. I nod my head. "Make sure you get it right. This is about protecting our homeland. It's about our families. Our children. It's about filtering out the background people. We've got to stop the criminals and the gangs and the terrorists. Some people are going to get over this fence. It's just another barrier. We'll have to see how it goes."

That same night I meet with Agent Sparrow at a popular cantina in McAllen. Sparrow has put in sixteen years with the Border Patrol in three different posts along the border. He's the kind of agent that earns more than his share of reprimands—not for creating messes like Agent Morningside's, but for speaking up and out when it is the untimely thing to do. Such as telling the supe in the middle of a muster that there's no reason to patrol a certain area along the river because the traffic left two months earlier. Or coming back from a workshop on first aid and letting it be known that it was a complete waste of time. Or asking too many questions about certain paperwork that takes up too much time. The Border Patrol is filled with minute procedures and policies that make little sense, but to question them is to doom one's career.

The cantina is a loud place full of diners wolfing down ten-ounce hamburgers with sides of onion blossoms, fries, and frosted mugs of Coors and Bud Lite. The beer flows in the adjoining bar along with country music from a jukebox heavily sprinkled with the accordion of local legend Flaco Jiménez. We squeeze into a booth at the back where no one can hear us. Agent Sparrow spends the next hour shifting his bulk around in a space designed for a normal-sized man.

There's no time to beat around the bush. Agent Sparrow's shift starts in two hours, so he gets right down to business.

"They are screwing us on the contracts," he tells me right off.

"Who? What contracts?"

"You know. The fence and these new contractors. Especially the big ones, the defense contractors in Washington. We've got all these contracts with these big companies worth millions. Because of the fence that is coming and all the money Congress is appropriating for it, the contracts are going to get bigger real fast. But, see, we don't have the trained managers to negotiate with them. We're talking millions. It's pathetic. I mean really pathetic. We purchase services from a defense contractor for, let's say, ten million dollars. In return, they send us a poster for free. In color.

"I actually saw one of our managers bragging about this free poster he got. Kind of a friend of a friend is the way I know him, but I know the guy personally. 'What did that cost them?' I ask him. Maybe fifty, a hundred dollars at most? They take a big cut out of the ten-million-dollar contract they get, then hand the job off to a subcontractor, who hands it off to someone else down the line. But my guy doesn't get it. He's sitting there pleased about the free poster. In fact, he's bragging about it. Not understanding the fact that they are making a big fat profit for doing nothing, and he's sitting there with a freebie poster thinking he's in high cotton.

"What I'm telling you is, it's almost a crime the way they're taking advantage of us. We got a contract manager with a high school degree, plus maybe a few weekend workshops in Dallas or somewhere. He is providing what they call 'financial oversight' to a slick defense contractor with beaucoups of lobbyists in Washington, D.C. I'm telling you that we are totally outgunned on this end of it. We are not prepared to do this thing the right way, the way it should be done. Now I'm not saying the military is always perfect, but at least they train their managers to negotiate with the big suppliers. At least they have some standards for managers to provide oversight of these contracts so they don't get ripped off as much. They're not intimidated by the law degrees, the MBAs, and the accounting degrees these corporation guys have. And the thousand-dollar Armani suits they wear every day of the week and their expense accounts. I'm telling you right now we're playing out of our league. It's just going to get worse as this fence thing goes along."

"What do you think the Border Patrol should be doing?" I ask Agent Sparrow as the beer and the coffee arrive. Agent Sparrow closely eyes my beer while sipping his hot coffee.

"Send our agents to school. That's one answer to this. Build up their self-confidence and knowledge. I mean, we've got to require them to get a college degree and then send them to business school, where they are going to learn how to stand up to these slick contractors, negotiate a contract, all that stuff. Or law school. Whatever it takes. Otherwise the game is rigged against us. Give us the skilled people we need to sit down with the big suppliers to negotiate the best deals possible. The best business deals for the least amount of money. Then have contract managers with the skills to follow the deals through and keep an eye on the products, the quality of the materials, the final test to make sure they did what they promised, the maintenance contract, and all the rest of it. The fence is going to be a boondoggle unless we start educating ourselves how the game is played in the big leagues. I'm telling you, we are way out of our league, and nobody is saying it. We're afraid to admit it. It's pathetic."

The onion blossom arrives, and Agent Sparrow digs right in. Then he looks up and asks me, "You hear about the Arab woman they caught at the airport?"

"No. Which airport?"

"McAllen. Three and one-half miles from where we are sitting. They finally identified her. She was a terrorist."

"A terrorist?" I say, genuinely surprised. PAO Dan Dotty had failed to mention anything about a terrorist. So had Supe Sanchez.

"She was between flights. Coming from Mexico City. There are two agents on duty as usual. One checks her documents while the other eyeballs her for anything out of the ordinary. They both have some problems with her, but it's a full flight and it's almost the end of their shift, so they let her walk. You know, if they take her back to the interrogation room at the airport, it's going to be more paperwork for them. And they are not entirely convinced there's a problem. Just a hunch. But then ten minutes before the flight takes off for Houston, one of them has an attack of the 'what ifs' and calls up his supe back at the station.

"You could say it was his training that made him do it, or maybe he was protecting his own rear. Your call. The supe listens to the story, then talks to his FOS. It's not like the supe wants to do anything about her. He's thinking more about all the time and the paperwork it'll cost him. He's going to protect his own sorry rear on this to keep his dream alive of making FOS before he retires. You know it's all SOP and everybody is protecting their own rear ends once it gets up past patrol agent. Anyway, the FOS hears the story from the supe, jumps in his truck, and hightails it to the airport to see for himself what the hell is going on."

"What's the problem with her?"

"She sets off alarm bells all over the place when you take a close look at her. The FOS tells me that himself. First time he sees her, he's right off telling himself 'Holy shit, this is one of them.' The supe tells me later that he heard through the feds that she's wearing the wrong kind of *burqa*—you know, the thing the Middle Eastern women cover their heads with. It's supposed to be made of silk, but she's wearing one made of linen. She's carrying six thousand dollars in cash—five thousand in American dollars, and a thousand in krugers.

"Then there is her travel itinerary. According to her documents, she first starts off in South Africa, then she flies to Mexico City. Then here. Then to Houston. It makes no sense and she's got no explanation. She's not talking, staring down at the floor. Of course all the supes on the shift want to let her go, but the FOS says to them, 'Forget it, we're taking this to the top.' There's a big argument about that at the airport when the shift supes from the station arrive to take a look at her. Then a bigger one back at the station. But the FOS has the rank, and it's his call. He decides to hold on to her and let sector make the final decision. Takes some guts to do that."

"And?" I prompt him.

"Then the sector higher-ups start arguing about it. Meanwhile, she's sitting in a holding cell at the McAllen Station still not talking. Finally [she] lawyers up. That gets their attention. The egos start to rev up at sector. You know how they are afraid of lawyers and getting sued. But while all this is going on at sector, the FOS is sticking to his guns and saying that she stinks, the documents stink, and there's that money. Not to mention her attitude. She's not defending herself like an honest person would. You know, crying, denying, yelling, getting mad, showing some kind of emotion. What the FOS is really doing is making all the supes his witnesses on this if it ever goes to a grievance or to court. Got to give him credit on that part of it."

"So what happens?" I ask him as he stuffs more onion blossom into his mouth after first dipping a clump in a heavy dose of ketchup.

"Sector finally decides it's got to protect itself, since the FOS is holding her overnight and writing her up. If she is a terrorist and they let her go, then how are they going to look to Washington? They call the feds in, and the feds waste no time in picking her right up. She disappears into the system, and the feds stop talking about it. Never happened. There are three lines in the *Monitor* about the whole thing, but that's all. She's history. Meanwhile, back at the station the supes are yapping like a pack of hounds. From the start of it they wanted to let her go, pretend she never existed.

"But I got sources. Very reliable sources. They tell me the whole thing is classified. But they are all telling me the same thing. She is definitely not a tourist. She's the real thing."

"The real thing?" I say.

"Yeah. A goddam terrorist. Right here in McAllen. Maybe linking people up with information or money. Planning stuff. Who knows."

"What happened to the FOS?" I say, knowing how the Border Patrol functions and fearing the worst. His station chief might give him forced vacation time, a reprimand for his personnel file, or worse.

"Sector is still pissed off because of all the paperwork they had to do on account of the FOS. Some of the station supes are too, but it's the higher-ups that are still talking about it. You know, like 'Who does this guy think he is?' and 'Look at all the work we did and for what?' That kind of thing."

"But he made the right decision."

"Come on. You know that's not what it's all about. The FOS made everybody else look bad. From the supes on up to the sector chief and his group of suck-ups. It's not about being right or wrong, it's about making them look bad to the folks further up the line."

"So what is the FOS saying about this?"

"He's not saying shit. The guy knows when to keep his mouth shut. He knows nobody is going to apologize to him for giving him a hard time for doing the right thing. The bullshit about a letter of reprimand, all that kind of stuff, he knows it will go away. Plus he's got the satisfaction that he came out ahead in the end."

"Meaning . . . ?"

"Meaning they give him an award. The Border Patrol gives him a goddam friggin' award for catching this terrorist. The people in Washington insist on it. No choice. But sector is not going to publicize it. And the FOS has to keep his mouth shut about it or he's in deep shit. It's all hush-hush is what I'm telling you."

"What kind of an award?"

"Agent of the Year."

"Shit," I say, genuinely surprised.

"Damn right," says Agent Sparrow, taking a real close look at my half mug of cold beer as he reaches for the last of the onion blossom. "It's pure Border Patrol. They give you a hard-ass time for doing the right thing, then give you a big-ass award with an *abrazo* from the sector chief. But you can't tell anyone about the award, and it gets absolutely no press. Wouldn't want your citizens thinking they'd been sitting on the plane next to a real terrorist. Bad for the public to think that terrorists can buy plane tickets, fly around, cross international boundaries, all that kind of thing. Might make the public feel they were vulnerable or something. Can't have that."

Chapter 5
ISIS

So which do you think I should get, the bull or the cow?" asks CBP agent Tony Jasso, turning into the parking lot in front of La Hacienda Restaurant on Old Military Highway. Although completely empty at a little before 2:00 a.m., the parking lot is lit up like a Christmas tree.

"Well, bro," says Agent Henry Rocha, "I'd say the cow. You buy the bull, the meat is stringier. Tougher. The cow is better. I'd say the cow." A seasoned agent, Rocha was born and raised in Brownsville. Agent Jasso, with three years of experience compared to Rocha's seven, is from Dallas. The two have been friends ever since Jasso was posted to South Texas.

Agent Rocha parks the Tahoe near the entrance to La Hacienda, then they both sit talking, ears constantly tuned to the radio dispatcher. The dispatcher sporadically calls out sensors, the number of hits, and the time of the hits. For the last hour all the sensor hits have been ten miles to the west of their assigned turf.

"Okay," says Tony over the voice of the dispatcher. "You convinced me. I'm going to buy the cow. You got room in your freezer?"

"It's a big one," says Henry, flexing his shoulder to loosen a cramped muscle. Their night shift half over, so far the two have very little to show for their work. Earlier they checked out four different sensors along the river, each of which took at least five hits. But by the time they reached the river landings where the sensors are buried, there was no one there to apprehend.

Except for the third sensor. The third sensor had taken twenty-three hits in less than ten minutes. Agents Jasso and Rocha rushed down to the banks of the Rio Grande in their truck, scanning the brush with their powerful Mag-lites. In the moonless night a startled cow glared back at them, then returned to its nighttime grazing. That's what got them started on the cow talk in the first place.

"Now it's only big enough for a quarter," Agent Henry Rocha tells his partner. "I got four fifteen-pound snappers in there I caught yesterday. They take up a lot of space. What a trip! Too bad you couldn't get time off. It was two hours out to the snapper banks. Rough going all the way. Three spring breakers on board and me. Those college kids started drinking soon as we left the dock at South Padre Island. Started puking a half hour later. Stayed sick most of the rest of the trip. Two hours out, four hours of fishing time, then two hours back to the dock. I think between the three of them they caught two fish. Maybe three."

"Yeah, but they deserved it. A lot of those spring breakers leave their brains back at the dorm. I'd say you got your money's worth. I'd like to. . . ."

Agent Jasso never finishes his sentence. The dispatcher calls out sensor no. 308, less than half a mile from La Hacienda Restaurant. It has already taken three hits.

Gravel flying, Rocha guns out of the empty parking lot, takes two left turns, and a few minutes later switches off the headlights as he eases the truck behind the cover of two mesquite trees. Knowing the traffic setting off sensor no. 308 must cross the irrigation canal at the footbridge to reach the trails leading to Old Military Highway, he heads directly for the footbridge. He positions his partner on the other side of the footbridge, fifty yards south between the canal and the dense vegetation bordering the lone escape route. Henry kneels down twenty feet from the bridge, checks his watch, radios Tony to make sure he is in place, then calls for backup from two agents who are the closest to them on patrol. They tell Henry they are rolling and will be there in ten minutes.

For twenty minutes Agents Jasso and Rocha wait silently in the dark near the riverbank. During those twenty minutes, which seem like an hour, they see no one and hear nothing but the bullfrogs and the night birds rustling in the trees. Agent Rocha then radios Agent Jasso to assume a new position north of the footbridge. Again they wait.

Finally, standing up as he lights a cigarette, Henry Rocha says, "They must have got by us." He checks for fresh sign with his flashlight and follows tracks leading one hundred yards to the north of the canal.

"This looks fresh. It could be them or traffic earlier. Can't tell."

Tony appears from out of the darkness. "I got some sign, but it went nowhere. It looks old."

Henry and Tony head back to their vehicle to talk it over. Two minutes into their conversation the same sensor, no. 308, takes three more hits. Henry decides the best thing to do is to backtrack from their position to the sensor buried at the landing. He follows a path along the irrigation ditch, crosses the footbridge, then a sandy trail that leads down to the banks of the Rio Grande. Kneeling on one knee from a low bluff, he scans the river with his NVGs, night vision goggles.

A soft breeze rustles the palms along the riverbanks. After the recent hurricane rains, large numbers of mosquitoes have joined the bullfrogs. The mosquitoes don't seem to mind the bug spray. Agent Rocha takes a few absentminded swats at his neck. A mourning dove calls between the basso profundo of the frogs.

CBP agents Jasso and Rocha find no undocumented workers hunkered down in the carrizo cane, no mules clutching burlap bags of marijuana or cocaine. After forty-five minutes of more waiting, they return to their vehicle. Ninety minutes later, backup arrives, hears the news, then heads back to their assigned turf.

"Wonder what they been doing?" says Jasso.

"No idea," says Rocha.

Rocha and Jasso have two more hours left on the midnight shift. They spend their time chasing down three more hits on nearby sensors, come close to getting stuck in the sand, and spot a jaguarundi, an endangered wild cat slightly larger than the domestic variety. The only thing Agents Rocha and Jasso find in the maze of levees, ditches, irrigation canals, sugarcane fields, and smuggler trails are countless human footprints. Some are old, some new.

After the ten-hour midnight shift, which includes overtime, the two men wash the grime off their truck at the car wash in the station motor pool, then head for their lockers.

"I guess we don't have much to show for tonight," says Agent Rocha, standing in front of his locker. "But we gave it our best shot. And we deterred. You got to give us that. Yeah, we deterred."

Deterrence Theory

Deterrence theory serves as the fundamental rationalization for the work engaged in by all CBP agents patrolling the line. As an explanation of criminal behavior it contains a set of tacit assumptions that justify why agents must constantly patrol the line for undocumented workers, drug smugglers, and, since 9/11, international terrorists. Even if Agents Rocha and Jasso do not encounter one lone illegal border crosser during their ten-hour shift, they can be assured, according to the tenets of deterrence theory, that their hard work serves to discourage, that is, deter, potential crossers who otherwise might have considered illegally entering the United States.

In 1764 Cesare Beccaria first laid out the major principles of deterrence theory when he published his classic treaty *On Crimes and Punishments.*[1] Beccaria posited that all human behavior is premised upon the predominance of free will. In turn, free will directly relates to the avoidance of pain and the attraction of pleasure. Later, the English utilitarian Jeremy Bentham, in his book *Political Thought*, argued the same point, asserting that before committing their criminal acts, all criminals make rational decisions based upon their own free will.[2] When considering breaking any law, according to this line of established thought, criminals may choose to act in any number of legal and illegal ways.

There are three major tenets of deterrence theory: First, the greater the perception of punishment, the less likely the criminal will be to choose to commit the crime. By extension, all societal laws must be clearly stated and understood by the potential criminal, and, as well, all laws must be consistently enforced. Second, the swifter the perception of punishment is likely to be, the less likely the criminal will choose to commit the crime. Swift and immediate punishment decreases the possibility of criminal violations because criminals, making rational choices based upon free will, will choose not to commit a particular crime when they realize they will be quickly punished. Finally, the third tenet asserts that the severity of the punishment is less important in the criminal's decision to commit a crime than the certainty and the speed with which the criminal perceives he or she will be punished. It is much more important to assure criminals that they will be quickly caught and punished for their crime than it is to threaten them with severe punishment, including death.

Based upon these tenets, CBP agents assure, by their presence on the line, that all potential illegal border crossers will be forced to consider their decisions rationally, and many, if not the majority, will choose not to illegally enter the United States regardless of whether their purpose is to find work, smuggle drugs, or blow up a power grid in a major city.

These eighteenth-century European concepts have been tested repeatedly by twentieth- and twenty-first-century criminologists and other social scientists. The ability of deterrence theory to explain the actions of real criminals, however, is at best highly questionable. For example, researchers studying battering offenses against females, or drunk driving, or white-collar crimes have found only limited support for deterrence theory. Researchers examining the effects of capital punishment upon criminals have consistently found deterrence theory not useful in explaining criminal behavior.[3] Regardless of the presumptive deterrence of the death penalty, in other words, criminals nevertheless commit the most horrific of crimes.

Deterrence theory in the real world, in short, is overly simplistic in its characterization of human behavior. The theory of criminal behavior fails adequately to account for the complexity of those who commit different kinds of crimes. At the same time, it discounts the structural, cultural, and historical contexts in which these crimes are committed.

When this theory is directly applied to the U.S.-Mexico borderlands in the twenty-first century, there is no allowance for the diversity of motivations governing those seeking illegal entry into the United States. The complexity of human choices and motivations suggests that those seeking work, those smuggling drugs, and those committed to acts of terrorism may possess completely different sets of expectations and behaviors. Would two young Mexicans returning from Mexico to their jobs in Houston be deterred by the sight of Agents Rocha and Jasso? Quite possibly, at least temporarily, until the Border Patrol truck was out of sight. But would armed mules carrying bags of cocaine be similarly influenced? Or highly trained terrorists? In particular, the motivations and behaviors of international terrorists, which may include a commitment to religious beliefs, clearly do not fit within the definitions and boundaries of deterrence theory.[4]

Studies of illegal border crossers seeking employment in this country suggest that the increased presence of the Border Patrol does not necessarily keep some border crossers from seeking entry repeatedly. Other considerations than those taken into account by deterrence theory may motivate or inhibit illegal immigration. Undocumented workers and their families, for example, may be influenced by economic motives to seek employment regardless of the number of agents on the line or any other perceived danger of which they are aware. Or, because of rising costs charged by *coyotes*, they may remain at home for a season because they cannot raise the funds necessary. Or, in the case of children, spouses, and other family members of undocumented workers in the United States, the primary motivation may be to rejoin a father, mother, parent, brothers and sisters, or other family members.[5]

The decline in illegal immigration from Mexico in 2008 and 2009 directly relates to the impact of the economic recession in the United States.

According to interviews of illegal immigrants by social scientists, the American recession trumps the impact of increased border enforcement along the line.[6] At the same time, the price *coyotes* charge for their services has increased in pace with border enforcement and undoubtedly contributes to the decline. *Coyotes* charge their human cargo from three thousand to five thousand dollars, a price that at least some undocumented workers cannot pay or are unwilling to pay.

In short, deterrence theory is the fundamental concept upon which law enforcement bases its strategies and tactics for patrolling the border and simultaneously uses to attempt to explain the efficacy of these same strategies and tactics. Deterrence theory fails in both regards, but this does not stop law enforcers from using it to justify their choices in strategies or from attempting to explain contemporary trends and patterns among illegal crossers by this same theory.

In spite of the inability of deterrence theory adequately to explain complex human behavior among border crossers, Silvestre Reyes, chief of the El Paso Sector, created a new patrolling strategy based upon his perception of the rational choices border crossers make before illegally entering the United States. In 1993 Chief Reyes named his new strategy Operation Blockade.[7] This same strategy, based upon the precepts of deterrence theory, was soon put in place in all twenty Border Patrol sectors along the Mexican border.

Chief Reyes believed that the best way to stop undocumented workers from crossing into the city of El Paso from Juárez was to increase the number and visibility of CBP agents at certain crossing locations. To this end Chief Reyes moved the vast majority of his force to popular crossing points, then, in sharp contrast to previous policy, required his agents to make sure they could be clearly observed from *el otro lado* by potential illegal crossers. In theory, illegal workers would observe the large number of agents, with their lighted vehicles, massed to arrest them; potential crossers, seeing this show of force, would make the most rational choice available to them. This most rational choice, Reyes inferred from deterrence theory, was to turn back, to return to their city or village of origin rather than illegally cross the Rio Grande to face certain arrest. If these same individuals chose not to return to their village of origin but to cross further upstream or downstream where agents were in far fewer numbers, then at the very least they were successfully deterred from crossing into the streets of El Paso.

When Chief Reyes initiated this new strategy in El Paso, he placed his professional career in the Border Patrol in serious jeopardy. Having served as a regional director of the Border Patrol in Dallas for five years and also as chief of the McAllen Sector, Reyes knew the agency hierarchy frowns upon the slightest change in policy or procedures not mandated from the highest levels of administration.[8] Even though El Paso and other major border cities were experiencing growing numbers of illegal aliens at that time, Border Patrol executives at the regional and national offices had no new strategies on the drawing board, no model projects in the planning stages, no new policies, no new procedures to address the problem. Nevertheless, new ideas and new ways of doing things were seen as undesirable and threatening by the leadership.

To the dismay and disappointment of upper management, Chief Reyes's new strategy was immediately successful. The numbers of undocumented workers, as enumerated in Border Patrol statistics, substantially declined in the city of El Paso. By perching agents in lighted trucks on top of the concrete levees and canals that separated El Paso from Juárez, Reyes appeared to have discovered an effective method of reducing the number of illegal immigrants. The biggest skeptics among upper management in the Border Patrol in Dallas and Washington soon became Chief Reyes's strongest supporters.

Critics outside the Border Patrol asked questions those within the Border Patrol, including Chief Reyes and his bosses, chose to ignore. For example, if potential illegal workers do not cross into El Paso from Juárez, are they genuinely deterred, or do they merely cross somewhere else along the Rio Grande? And if the majority cross elsewhere, what impact does this have on border communities, upon the safety of the illegal crossers in remote, dangerous locations, and the safety of agents who must track them? These kinds of concerns received little attention as other sector chiefs, observing Reyes's success and national attention, rushed to set up strategies mirroring Operation Blockade.

Operation Gatekeeper was soon initiated south of San Diego, followed by Operation Safeguard in 1995 in Nogales. This identical strategy spread to other sectors, including Douglas and Naco, Arizona.[9] In 1997 McAllen Sector chief Joe E. Garza put into place his own version of Reyes's strategy, which Chief Garza named Operation Rio Grande. McAllen Sector agents soon referred to Chief Garza's new system as "doing Xes." By 2001 eight Border Patrol vehicles were regularly assigned to the international bridge from McAllen to Reynosa. Each driver was required by the supe to maintain his or her exact fixed position, the X, for the duration of the ten-hour shift. Agents sat in their truck cabs at quarter-mile intervals on top of the levee on both sides of the bridge, headlights and flashing emergency lights clearly visible from the streets of Reynosa.

Every thirty minutes agents shifted over one position, one X on the levee, thereby freeing up the agent closest in proximity to the Burger King to use the rest room and also grab some hot coffee. At musters agents were repeatedly cautioned to remain in their vehicles except for Burger King breaks. Agents were told in no uncertain terms they were required to receive permission from their supe before pursuing any illegal crosser they observed from the front seat of their truck.

With absolutely nothing to do over the course of their shifts but sit behind the wheel, agents were left to pass the long night hours listening to talk radio—Rush Limbaugh and Dr. Laura were big favorites—reading magazines and books, and engaging in endless conversations with their fellow agents to fight off boredom and sleep. One agent I interviewed at the time brought his personal laptop to the X to play video games and check his email so he could remain lucid.

The vast majority of agents at the McAllen Sector were angered by the new strategy. They had been trained at the academy to surveil, track, and chase, not to sit for ten hours at a time in their trucks twiddling their thumbs. They felt, they said, more like prison guards than professionals in the U.S. Border Patrol. Several agents ignored the order to stay in their cabs, instead pursuing undocumented workers whenever they saw them. These agents were routinely warned and threatened with reprimands by their supes if they persisted in leaving their cabs to apprehend illegal border crossers.

In their own defense, McAllen Sector agents showed me well-worn trails running from the banks of the Rio Grande between or around their fixed Xes, providing strong evidence many illegal border crossers were not deterred by the Border Patrol's visible show of force and strength in numbers. After spending a significant number of night shifts with agents restricted to Xes, it became very clear that large numbers of undocumented workers developed counterstrategies to Chief Garza's Operation Rio Grande. They were not deterred; they simply walked around or between the fixed positions to avoid apprehension, or they crossed the Rio Grande a hundred yards downstream or upstream from where the X ended. Many agents, in fact, pointed out that the new strategy made illegal entry easier for both undocumented workers and drug smugglers because they knew exactly where the Border Patrol was positioned.

Worse still, illegal workers were far less likely to be apprehended by the Border Patrol at a later time because, once having successfully broken through the line of agents along the river, few agents were left to pursue or arrest them. Silvestre Reyes's new strategy greatly reduced apprehensions by all traditional methods in the interior, including searches and sweeps of known places, such as farms and ranches, frequented by undocumented workers. At the same time, the number of interior secondary checkpoints along roads and highways was also reduced so that more agents could be assigned to Xes on the borderline.

Documented apprehensions, as mirrored in Border Patrol statistics in the McAllen Sector, declined dramatically after Operation Rio Grande was initiated in 1997. That year they numbered 246,210, but they fell in 1998 to 207,005, then to 172,867 in 1999. By 2002 there were 86,117 apprehensions of undocumented workers in the McAllen Sector. But after a low of 77,749 in 2003, apprehensions began to rise in 2004, reaching 134,188 in 2005 and 110, 531 in 2006. Then, in 2007, the most recent year for which apprehension statistics are available, there was a major decline to 74,131 apprehensions.[10]

Prior to Chief Reyes's new strategy, increases in apprehension rates and drug interdictions were the most important performance measurements used to buttress agency appeals for increased budgets from Congress. Once Reyes's new strategy was in place, Border Patrol officials had to change their justifications for increased budgets. Declining numbers of apprehensions of undocumented workers suddenly became the single most important measurement to demonstrate, according to the Border Patrol, that it was accomplishing its objectives. According to this new line of reasoning, declining apprehensions showed that the new strategy was achieving its stated objectives. To do their job better, according to this inverted logic, the Border Patrol required larger budgets to hire more agents. The more agents hired, the greater the number of border crossers deterred. Even though Border Patrol officials drastically changed the fundamental interpretation of their own statistics after Reyes initiated the strategic change in patrolling the line, Congress and outside critics remained strangely silent.[11]

Another more legitimate interpretation of these same data, not based upon institutional self-interests, is suggested by agents who patrol the line at the McAllen Sector. Their experience tells them that during Operation Rio Grande, because agents were confined to their truck cabs, they could not chase and catch large numbers of illegal border crossers, who were not arrested and therefore are not represented in the Border Patrol's monthly and annual apprehension statistics. The touted deterrence strategy did not really reduce the actual numbers of illegal workers so much as it artificially produced misleading statistics suggesting this trend when interpreted by Border Patrol leadership before Congress.

Another major problem with the Border Patrol's interpretation of the data it collected is its assertion that increases in the value of illegal drugs it interdicted demonstrated the efficacy of its new strategy. As a result of the new strategy, according to the Border Patrol, drug smugglers, like undocumented workers, were deterred by the large force of agents massed at certain points on the line. Drug interdictions along the border, however, actually rose from 1993 to 2001. In the McAllen Sector, for example, the number of drug interdiction cases increased from 1,583 with a value of $234,678,887 in

1997 to 1,659 with a value of $492,570,628 in 2002.[12] If the Border Patrol's reasoning and rationale were correct, the drug data should reflect the reverse trend. The new strategy in fact did not deter illegal drugs as much as it appeared to stimulate more drug smuggling, resulting in higher rates of confiscation. Drug smugglers knew where the Border Patrol agents were positioned, so they crossed their loads in ever greater numbers at places that were patrolled by few agents.

The Border Patrol reasonably could have argued that illegal drug interdictions rose primarily because of greater market demand in the United States. But if the agency had made this argument with regard to illegal drugs, they would logically have been forced to make a similar argument with regards to illegal workers. This line of reasoning, although closer to an understanding of the complexity of human behavior along the border, undermines the precepts of deterrence theory.

Chief Reyes's new strategy assumed that the prescribed changes in policing the line would dramatically reduce the flow of undocumented workers entering this country as well as reduce the amount of illegal drugs smuggled across the river. Eyewitness accounts by agents at the scene, in conjunction with the agency's own data, argue against a decrease in the overall flow of undocumented workers into the United States. At the same time, the data suggest Chief Reyes's strategy may have been a significant contributor to increased drug smuggling. Regardless of these outcomes as a result of the new strategy, Border Patrol leadership remained adamant before Congress that frontal deployment was highly successful.

In part, the justifications offered before Congress by the Border Patrol in exchange for budgetary benevolence did not matter. Because of the events of 9/11 apprehension rates of workers and the tonnage of illegal drugs played second fiddle to risk from acts of international terrorism. National security increasingly drove requests for larger and larger Border Patrol budgets, including demands for more agents, more equipment, and, very soon, a border fence. The overriding sales pitch was for more agents patrolling the line backed up by high-tech surveillance equipment.

At this same time, many of the best Border Patrol agents jumped ship. Because of their strong sense of patriotism, many agents were unwilling to be hampered by patrolling strategies that minimized their professional skills at the very time the nation might be attacked by terrorists crossing the Mexican border. Agents voted with their feet, abandoning the Border Patrol in large numbers after 9/11. Many left to pursue what they hoped would be more rewarding and productive careers in other federal law enforcement agencies, including the Air Marshals.[13]

Agents who remained at the McAllen Station gradually began, on their own initiative and with at least the tacit support of some supes, to patrol the line using the "soft X." Although this procedure was never a recognized part of official policy under Operation Rio Grande, agents, without asking permission of their supes, left the confines of their vehicles to pursue undocumented workers and drug smugglers. These law enforcement professionals refused to sit idly by in their fixed positions, watching illegal crossers escape into the brush and fields of sugarcane and onions.

"Bubbles," which eventually replaced soft Xes in the McAllen Sector, were necessitated both by the exodus of agents after 9/11 and, at the same time, by the agents' unwillingness to work within the limitations of soft Xes. Agents *post facto* were encouraged by their supes to track and pursue illegal workers and drug smugglers whenever necessary. However, since not all portions of the McAllen Sector could be covered by agents because of the high attrition, at times agents were given the latitude to patrol areas not assigned them during their shift. Agents in the years immediately after 9/11 frequently found themselves without shift partners, and because backup was often unavailable, soft Xes placed agents at much greater risk in patrolling the line. Bubbles, in contrast, allowed more support from other agents as needed. Eventually new recruits rushed through the Border Patrol academy began to fill the empty slots and eventually exceeded the number of agents stationed at the McAllen Sector before 9/11. But bubbles remained.

At the height of the success of Chief Reyes's new patrolling strategy based upon deterrence theory, Reyes retired. Soon after, he was elected to Congress. Only in subsequent years did it become apparent that Congressman Reyes's strategy had succeeded less in stemming illegal immigration than in directing illegal immigrants to cross at other places along the border. The Border Patrol then began to claim that directing and redirecting flows of illegal immigrants along the Mexican border was all along a part of a larger, as yet unnamed, strategy.

Many of the crossing sites sought out by illegal workers, and the *coyotes* who frequently led them, were extremely dangerous compared to the streets of the border cities and towns. In Arizona alone, 260 illegal aliens died in 2005 attempting to cross the border. That same year there were a total of 473 immigrant deaths along the Mexican border. During the same period the Border Patrol rescued another 2,570 illegal immigrants; dehydration in the desert was the most common risk to them. The number of deaths of illegal immigrants along the Mexican border rose at least in part because of the Border Patrol's new deterrence strategy.[14]

The foundation of the Border Patrol's post-Reyes strategy of deterrence still relied upon an extensive system of underground sensors. The official description of these sensors is, "seismic and magnetic, buried in the ground."

Their official purpose is to "provide primary remote detection capability. When a sensor detects activity, alerts are sent via radio transmission."[15] The sensors in the McAllen Sector, Vietnam-era surplus, are placed near the river landings of undocumented workers and drug traffickers and along the trails the smugglers use to reach Old Military Highway. From above ground the sensor looks to the untrained eye like a single blade of grass.

Agents Jasso and Rocha, along with every other agent who patrols the line, know from their work experience that this system of sensors is a complete failure. The aging sensors are in constant need of repair and, as suggested earlier, cannot distinguish between a man and a cow. Agents know that sensors may activate for no discernible reason or, at the other extreme, fail to respond when dozens of illegal aliens pass by. Unfortunately, making use of the sensors even more difficult, five to fifteen minutes may intervene between reception of the hits on the sensors by the station dispatcher and the dispatcher's report to the agents in the field. This interval gives the intruder, if human, more than enough time to escape capture.

Maps of the exact locations of the Border Patrol sensors are in the hands of criminal organizations and have been for some time. Professional *coyotes* and the drug cartels avoid setting off the sensors by walking around them. Those who trip the sensors and get caught are much more likely to be amateur *coyotes* and small-time drug smugglers.

The sensors, the total number of which along the Mexican border is estimated at eleven thousand, have never been an effective means of policing the line. Claims to the contrary, by late 2009 little has changed.[16] In the real world along the border the sensor system, the main line of defense of the Border Patrol, is a forty-year-old bureaucratic pipe dream.

When the sensors go off for no discernible reason other than the dysfunctionality of the sensor system, the Border Patrol calls the signals "false alarms."[17] Lending support to the assertion that the Border Patrol was very aware of its own failures, there are absolutely no studies quantifying the number of sensor false alarms before 2005.[18] If objective studies had been completed on the functionality of the sensor system, they undoubtedly would have revealed how bad it was.

Agents told me, based upon their experience before 2005, that the rate of false alarms ranged from 50 percent to 80 percent. Upper management in the Border Patrol, of course, has known its sensors are relatively useless for many years, yet the Border Patrol failed to correct the existing system or replace it with a more reliable system. The INS, parent agency of the Border Patrol before DHS until 2002, also failed to correct this fundamental security system. For decades agents in the field have reported to their supes that the sensors were faulty to the point of not being worth their time or effort.

Intelligence gathering that would facilitate apprehensions of illegal workers and drug trafficking has never been an objective of the Border Patrol. As one senior agent told me, "Intelligence [gathering] and the Border Patrol do not belong in the same sentence." Cooperation with the Drug Enforcement Agency and other federal agencies that might share intelligence has been, and remains, rare.[19]

The Border Patrol remains in 2010, as repeatedly noted, a top-down decision-making institution: agents are excluded from all decisions, policy making, and development of procedures. Instead, their suggestions, based upon their work experiences in the field, are routinely ignored and might, in fact, place them in hot water with their supes. Agents who persist in reporting problematic procedures or policies to their supes, including the absolute failure of the sensor system, are themselves defined as a problem. Problematic agents, considered troublemakers by the Border Patrol, may become the targets of ridicule and harassment by managers, be assigned the most undesirable tasks and shift assignments, be given letters of reprimand in their official files, and/or be denied promotions for which they are qualified. Troublemakers also may be repeatedly encouraged to transfer out or retire early from the Border Patrol ranks.

No thanks to the sensor system, agents along the border apprehend undocumented workers and interdict drug smugglers as a result of hard work, field experience, and mutual cooperation with other agents. Sometimes, lacking reliable intelligence, agents also just get lucky. Yet in spite of the clear fact that the sensor system does not work, the Border Patrol continued to heap praise on it. Until Chief Reyes offered up Operation Blockade in 1993, the Border Patrol and its parent INS had not changed the basic strategy of patrolling the line since its inception in 1924.

The Integrated Surveillance Intelligence System

In 1998 the INS under the Clinton administration finally announced the development of a new system of border security employing a new generation of ground sensors to be bolstered by advances in other surveillance technologies. The Integrated Surveillance Intelligence System, ISIS, was to consist of new magnetic and infrared ground sensors, towers mounted with video cameras, and computers with databases designed to "help prevent contraband and illegal immigrants from crossing U.S. borders."[20]

President Clinton's INS awarded International Microwave Corporation (IMC), of East Norwalk, Connecticut, the initial contract to develop ISIS. This small private company received $2 million from INS. The federal contract awarded to IMC by INS was "noncompetitive." That is, other corporations were not invited to submit bids for ISIS.

Walt Drabik, INS Electronics Systems Section chief and project director of ISIS, upon embarking on this ambitious program, never critiqued the sensor system in place for forty years, nor did he suggest the exact nature of its many problems. Instead, Drabik implied that ISIS was a high-tech solution to the real problem in the Border Patrol along the Mexican border: that there were too few agents patrolling the line. At the time, before 9/11, there were forty-eight hundred Border Patrol agents covering the Mexican Border.[21] Drabik's chief justification for ISIS was as a so-called force multiplier. ISIS, in short, was going to be a new, sophisticated technology that would allow the more efficient and productive use of border agents. With ISIS, presumably, forty-eight hundred agents would be enough.

Two years later, in 2000, Drabik reported that the thirteen thousand new sensors along the borders, both Canadian and Mexican, "can detect movement and heat sources within a 50 foot radius and metal within 250 feet"[22] He claimed that the old sensors had been replaced with a brand new, and more sophisticated, system much more sensitive to all intruders. The new sensors would produce far fewer false alarms than the old system. These new sensors, the first completed component of ISIS, were, according to Drabik, fully operational.

The remote video surveillance system, RVS, was the second key component of ISIS as proposed by Drabik. RVS consisted of regular and thermal infrared cameras on poles sixty to eighty feet high. Included in the RVS were "repeater towers, control room monitors, and toggling keyboards to zoom, pan, and tilt the cameras."[23] According to Drabik, ISIS was "73 high resolution and infrared cameras on poles. Agents at Border Patrol Stations in 21 sectors remotely control the cameras, which scan up to a five-mile radius. The combination of cameras and sensors tells the agents the location of any activity, the number of people and whether they are armed. These critical bits of information help station agents decide which officers to dispatch."[24]

What Drabik failed to mention in his attempts to promote the genius of ISIS was that before ISIS, as early as 1989 during the administration of President George H. W. Bush, the sensor system was supposed to have been integrated by the Intelligent Computer-Aided Detection system, ICAD. The data produced by ICAD was supposed to be interpreted by special law enforcement communications assistants (LECAs), who would quickly pass on the information to Border Patrol agents. ICAD II, alleged to improve upon ICAD, was developed under the Clinton administration in 1994 to "provide analysis of any one of more than 100,000 records within minutes."[25]

As Drabik led ISIS in 1999, he was either not aware of previous attempts by his own agency to achieve the same goal or he failed to consider such previous programs important to the success of ISIS.

What is most interesting about the capabilities claimed for ICAD and ICAD II is that both were predicated upon a border sensor system that was totally unreliable. Said another way, the two data systems generated mountains of bad data from broken sensors, then dumped these bad data to Border Patrol agents in the field. ICAD and ICAD II thus generated ever increasing amounts of unreliable data. Adding more bad data to the Border Patrol pile could logically never result in better data or better analysis of the data. Nor could more bad data in any way help agents in the field.

The Clinton administration's ICAD III was designed to be the third key component of ISIS, according to Walt Drabik, and would contain all of the ICAD II data. ICAD III, according to a report of the time, "supports mapping applications and communicates with INS' national database server. . . . ICAD III will be the first version to be managed on a national level, giving once-isolated regions a broader perspective." This information would allow "Border Patrol sectors to compare and contrast trends depicted graphically."[26] ICAD III thus incorporated all the bad data from ICAD I and ICAD II and from this bad data created other additional and larger data sets upon which Border Patrol managers at the national level would rely. These managers, from these data sets, would then report on general trends that through their analyses would become apparent.

Under ISIS, Border Patrol agents would receive data, including the numbers of illegal border crossers, their location, their potential risk to agents, and other crucial information. This information, according to Drabik, would increase the efficiency of the agents, provide for their greater safety, and also increase the safety of those who were apprehended. ISIS was a force multiplier that would make up for any lack of agents patrolling the line. ISIS, powered by ICAD III, would integrate, monitor, and analyze all of the data to determine patterns and trends in apprehensions and illegal drugs. For the first time the Border Patrol would itself generate intel data.

Early on in the development of ISIS, Walt Drabik recommended that Rebecca Reyes be hired as the primary link between INS and IMC. Reyes eventually became the vice president for contracts at IMC. During that same period Silvestre Reyes, Jr., was also hired by IMC as a technician. Rebecca Reyes and Silvestre Reyes, Jr., are, of course, the daughter and son of Congressman Silvestre Reyes. Congressman Reyes, the innovator of the newest Border Patrol strategy, was now a member of the highly influential House Select Committee on Intelligence. (Under the Bush administration Congressman Reyes was soon appointed chairman of the House Select Committee on Intelligence in 2006.)[27]

In late 2000, less than two years into the creation of ISIS, Walt Drabik was unceremoniously removed as the project director of the Clinton administration's ISIS. IMC was absorbed two years later into L-3 Communications Holdings, Inc. In turn, L-3 Communications Holdings soon became a part of the much larger Government Services, Inc., in order to, according to the sworn testimony of its president, Joseph Saponaro, "better support the [ISIS] program." According to Saponaro, all managers of L-3 Communications Holdings, the company holding the original contract for ISIS that was subsumed by IMC, were fired.[28] L-3 Communications, before morphing into Government Services, received $200 million in budget year 2000 to continue developing ISIS. Those federal funds were, yet again, not a part of the competitive federal bidding process.

Beginning in late 2004 and early 2005, during the administration of President George W. Bush, reports surfaced from government sources and sworn testimony to congressional subcommittees suggesting that the ISIS program was a failure of grand proportions. Not only were its objectives never met, but also considerable federal funds had been squandered. After audits of L-3 Communications Holdings and the Border Patrol, the DHS and the General Services Administration (GSA) concluded that much of the federal funding for ISIS, now estimated at $239 million, had been spent by contractors. But the much-touted ISIS was functionally inoperable.[29]

Testimony in 2005 by Richard L. Skinner, DHS inspector general (IG), outlines the serious flaws associated with ISIS. The primary one was in the promised integration of sensors, cameras, and databases into a single system that would provide valuable information to agents in the field. Skinner testified:

> To date, ISIS components have not been integrated to the level predicted at the program's onset. RVS [remote video surveillance] cameras and sensors are not linked whereby a sensor alert automatically activates a corresponding RVS camera to pan and tilt in the direction of the triggered sensor. However, even if ISIS was fully integrated, due to a limited number of operational RVS sites (255 nationwide), integration opportunities would be limited to the areas near these sites.
>
> The lack of automated integration undercuts the effectiveness and potential of ISIS. Since no automated integration exists between RVS cameras and sensors, the integration of information from these two sources becomes the responsibility of the LECAs.[30]

LECAs (law enforcement communications assistants) were employees with no previous field experience in patrolling, no practical knowledge of the tricks of the trade of undocumented workers and drug smugglers, nor firsthand knowledge of the terrain. But these LECAs were nevertheless expected to "manually maneuver the camera in the direction of the sensor, and then attempt to identify the cause of the sensor alert."[31]

Walt Drabik's argument that ISIS was a force multiplier—that its sophisticated technology would improve the efficiency of border agents—was one of the most persuasive arguments used to convince Congress to fund ISIS. The LECAs, left to operate the border surveillance cameras manually, clearly demonstrated that ISIS was not, in fact, a force multiplier at all. Inspector General Skinner noted that "LECAs may not always have time to advise an OBP [Office of the Border Patrol] agent of sensor alerts or camera observations. Similarly, OBP agents may not be available to respond."

Speaking to the core integrity of ISIS, the IG reported, "*More than 90 percent of the responses to sensor alerts resulted in false alarms*, something other than illegal alien activity, such as local traffic, outbound traffic, a train, or animals. *On the southwest border, only two percent of sensor alerts resulted in apprehensions*." Furthermore, LECAs using ISIS cameras were not able to consistently and successfully distinguish between "illegal activity and legitimate events."[32]

In short, the new ISIS, after soaking up $239 million dollars, produced a higher rate of sensor false alarms than did the old sensor system.

ICAD III data from the new sensor and surveillance system was virtually useless in providing integrated comparable data for intelligence purposes. In practice, one Border Patrol sector cataloged information in ICAD in a completely different way than did a neighboring sector. Stated the IG of the Department of Homeland Security: "They [INS and the Border Patrol] also acknowledge that ICAD data would be of limited value and that conclusions drawn from this data would vary."[33]

The lack of sound management and oversight practices at all levels led directly to the failure of ISIS. For example, IMC, the original federal contractor, bragged about a new supply system from five technology companies it claimed would result in 16 percent discounts below the federal price list. Upon review of procurement documents of Government Services, Inc., and the Border Patrol, however, the IG concluded that inept management practices left "large portions of the border without camera coverage."[34] The DHS audit sampled contracts for seven ISIS installations using RVS technology. Six installations, according to the audit, were never completed. Work that was completed was not finished on time. Approximately $37 million still remained unspent five years after the initial contract was awarded.

Border Patrol managers also contributed to the failure of ISIS by providing inadequate oversight of contractors and subcontractors. The IG found that the Border Patrol did not regularly approve contractor invoices; all invoices for ISIS were supposed to be approved before they were paid. In the same sample of six ISIS installations, only six contractor invoices were actually approved by the Border Patrol, but sixty-five were paid in full.

In 2003, four years after the initial contract award to IMC, the Border Patrol wrote a letter to L-3 Communications citing them with "inefficient financial tracking and cost control, inefficient inventory control, a failure to meet required deadlines and deliverable due dates, and a failure to notify the government of impediments to installations."[35] While the inspector general lauded this effort by the Border Patrol to bring L-3 Communications into full contract compliance, at the same time he concluded that its efforts were incomplete and poorly timed and failed to achieve their desired purpose.

Equally damning, the installations constructed by L-3 Communications were remarkable for their high cost and slow construction. Construction sites took an average of twenty months to complete because, according to the audit, preconstruction steps that should have been accomplished concurrently were, instead, completed sequentially. The DHS IG seriously questioned the fundamental design of ISIS. He especially critiqued the basic concept of a fixed fence or barrier along the border buttressed by permanent towers for RVS cameras. He stated that the towers could not be moved to cover "changes in the traffic patterns of illegal aliens."[36] Undocumented workers, he reasoned, would quickly learn to cross the border in places where there were no towers or cameras or develop other strategies that would make ISIS towers inefficient and outdated.

The ISIS program designed by Walt Drabik incorporated little flexibility to respond to changes in human behavior, thus rapidly becoming obsolete. For all the alleged sophistication of the new technology promised by Drabik, it was poorly designed to meet the real needs of the Border Patrol. Not surprisingly, Border Patrol agents with extensive field experience and knowledge of the tactics of *coyotes* and other illegal border crossers were excluded from the ISIS planning process.

The DHS inspector general made seven specific recommendations that in part addressed the failure of ISIS and its construction: that future technologies involving cameras, agents, and databases be integrated; that variables measuring illegal intrusions be standardized; that a true measure of force multiplication and response effectiveness of agents be developed; that problems with contractors be resolved and that the unspent $37 million be returned to DHS; that construction time of ISIS installations be reduced; that future ISIS installations be shared by government departments to reduce costs; and that mobile surveillance platforms be used instead of fixed towers with RVS cameras.[37]

Joseph Saponaro, president of Government Services, Inc., defended his corporation's development and implementation of ISIS before Congress. Saponaro testified that the real problem with ISIS was that the original contract for the RVS cameras was a "small contract" of $5 million but quickly grew to $150 million, along the way "taxing seriously the management capacity of both IMC and the administering government office." However, Saponaro said that regardless of these challenges, his company installed RVS cameras at a total of 246 sites. "Where properly maintained, this system is operational today," he testified.

In sworn testimony Saponaro stated that his corporation did not have sufficient time to respond in detail to the charges of the DHS inspector general before DHS released their report to the public. Said Mr. Saponaro, "Our responses to these allegations show with specific detail and backup collaborations that their claims are wrong. Regrettably, the GSA IG never allowed us to comment prior to issuing this report. The damage by this report has been done."[38]

According to Saponaro's testimony, his corporation continued to submit evidence to the government demonstrating their sound management practices and the ways in which ISIS project goals and objectives had been achieved. Although funds were cut off to L-3 Communications in 2004, according to Saponaro, and they were owed millions of dollars by the federal government, his company continued to work on the technological development of RVS cameras. Summarizing, Saponaro stated, "We demand the highest ethical standards. L-3 is successful because we live these standards in everything we do."[39]

Michael D. Rogers, Republican congressman from Alabama and chair of the House Select Committee on Homeland Security, took issue with Saponaro's testimony. Rogers accused L-3 Communications of ending the ISIS contract by their own choice in 2004, thus effectively leaving seventy border sites without any functioning equipment. According to Rogers, L-3 Communications forced the Border Patrol to accept truckloads of useless equipment that "now sits gathering dust."

Congressman Rogers also described in considerable detail cameras delivered to the Border Patrol in Washington State that did not function properly in all kinds of weather, along with various other equipment provided by L-3 Communications that required frequent and costly repairs. In Detroit surveillance cameras had been delivered, but construction work and installation of the cameras reached a standstill for no discernible reason. In Arizona and Texas equipment had been delivered by L-3 Communications to sites, but, as in the Detroit case, was never installed. Further, tower poles had been purchased and paid for, but electrical equipment supplied by L-3 Communications did not meet code. Cost overruns, according to Rogers, were "numerous."

Summarizing the performance of L-3 Communications in the planning, development, implementation, and contract oversight of ISIS, Rogers stated, "What we have here, plain and simple, is a case of gross mismanagement of a $200 million contract. *This agreement has violated federal contracting rules.*"[40]

Although the critiques of ISIS by the DHS inspector general and others are damning, they fail to address several other matters of structural and organizational culture involving the general contractor, the Border Patrol, DHS, and other federal agencies. In spite of the promised capabilities of ISIS, as promoted most notably by INS's Walt Drabik, L-3 Communications never adapted or developed computer technology to integrate the system. At the same time, L-3 Communications also failed to construct the major infrastructure for ISIS, leaving many installations unfinished, inoperable, and literally rusting in the wind. Neither could L-3 Communications develop individual components of ISIS, including the RVS cameras, or adapt them so that they functioned properly. There is considerable evidence to suggest that once some of the cameras were up and running, they still required expensive maintenance and repair, which took months to complete. Nor could this same contractor coordinate the night vision cameras on the towers into an integrated system that was fully operable by LECAs.

ICAD III, the data system that would, according to Drabik, fully integrate ISIS, could never get off the ground in part because no workable codes had ever been devised summarizing the behavior of undocumented workers, drug smugglers, and terrorists so that they could be placed within discrete statistical categories. Descriptors of these behaviors were, therefore, not comparable between one Border Patrol sector and another. In the rare times that ICAD III was operable, lack of discrete data categories doomed it to generate mountains of bad and/or useless data for agents in the field. In this respect ICAD III resembled the previous ICAD I and ICAD II. However, ICAD III was different than its failed predecessors because it cost more and also produced larger amounts of worthless data.

ISIS's reliance on high-tech solutions neglected or ignored the observations of agents over decades of patrolling the line. The planners and designers of ISIS, the L-3 engineers, grossly underestimated the motivation, talents, and relentlessness of those seeking illegal entry into this country. In addition, ICAD III's promise to generate comparable data for all Border Patrol sectors was a pie-in-the-sky dream from computer engineers with no practical field expertise in the borderlands. Where were the trained information technology professionals in the Border Patrol who could combine boots-on-the-ground law enforcement, IT, and knowledge of statistics above the level of colorful pie charts?

ISIS also demonstrated the Border Patrol's inability to supervise and monitor contractors and subcontractors. Sector chiefs and their staffs did not have the professional training in contract oversight practices and procedures to prevent or challenge the documented mismanagement of L-3 Communications. They at best possessed a college degree and some military and/or federal law enforcement training. They were not equipped to analyze budgets, monitor invoices, and, most important, force contractors and subcontractors to maintain ethical business standards while achieving contract objectives and goals.

One agent describes the situation this way:

> You've got these agents who think they know what the business world is all about. But they don't. They are clueless. You see, maybe they have a college education, maybe not. But they probably never even took a business course. These guys aren't trained accountants. They majored in criminal justice or sociology or social work or something like that. Deer in the headlights. They are in charge of a project that the contractor is making millions of dollars off of. I've personally seen it with my own eyes. It's unbelievable. These agents have no idea who they are dealing with or what they should be doing. It's painful to watch."[41]

Even if an agent confronts a contractor about questionable business practices, the Border Patrol is not structured either to advise or to support the agent. Agents spend the majority of their careers in the Border Patrol taking orders from those above them, then carrying out those orders. They are trained to respect, not question, their superiors and keep their mouths shut. Contract representatives are seen by agents as their workplace superiors and, as well, their social superiors. Rarely have Border Patrol agents been around business people who sport substantial expense accounts.

Besides the Border Patrol, the federal government also failed to provide personnel trained in ISIS contract oversight. It is legitimate to ask why the DHS and the GSA waited six years before auditing ISIS. By the time that audit was completed, the major damage by L-3 Communications had left ISIS in shambles. If future contract disasters are to be avoided, then the federal government has to put in place policies and procedures that will assure timely audits and general oversight of contractors.

While the federal audit suggested L-3 Communications was involved in serious mismanagement of a $200 million project and at the same time members of Congress, including Congressman Rogers, reported that this same mismanagement was criminal, no charges were ever brought against L-3 Communications, their subcontractors, agents of the Border Patrol, DHS, or any other individuals, agencies, or programs involved with ISIS.[42] In light of the long list of documented problems associated with ISIS, it is truly remarkable that criminal charges never materialized and that government employees, including agents of the Border Patrol, were never penalized for their shoddy performances in supervising ISIS contracts. ISIS failed miserably, but no one was responsible.

It is equally remarkable that Mary Reyes, daughter of Congressman Silvestre Reyes, was hired by L-3 Communications to a key management position over a noncompetitive federal contract worth $200 million. That Mary Reyes's brother was then hired by the same company also calls into question the integrity of the ISIS bidding process. Taken even at face value, this documented relationship between a congressman's family members and a key defense contractor warrants rigorous public scrutiny.

The remnants of ISIS that stand useless and rotting along our southern borders include abandoned towers and rusting camera equipment. In stark contrast to the failures of ISIS, Government Services, Inc., the holding company for L-3 Communications, achieved financial success in spite of its gross mismanagement of ISIS. As of 2008, Government Services, Inc., had $8 billion in federal contracts, a majority of which are with the DHS and the Department of Defense. In 2008 Government Service, Inc., then the nation's sixth largest defense contractor, was a "$14 billion dollar company" with 65,000 employees.[43]

Years after ISIS's inception and subsequent failure neither the Border Patrol nor Michael Chertoff's DHS had incorporated substantive structural or cultural changes that might lead to different outcomes. The Border Patrol still did not have in place an experienced cadre of oversight contract managers prepared to supervise and monitor large projects in different geographical areas along the southern border. Border Patrol managers responsible for contract oversight were limited in their financial education, training, and expertise and possessed little if any practical experience in working with corporate contractors and subcontractors. These managers compose an infinitesimal segment of an organization trained always to defer to the judgment of their superiors. In a similar vein, DHS has made few substantive changes since the failures of ISIS. During oversight of ISIS it had no more than four managers supervising the prime contractor. DHS was rumored to have hired no more than five new managers for future large contracts involving the Border Patrol.[44]

DHS remains oblivious, as suggested earlier, to the history of graft and corruption characterizing municipal and county governments in South Texas. These local governmental bodies in Cameron and Hidalgo Counties, for example, each with its own unique and long history of the misapplication of county, state, and federal funds, will be charged in the construction of the border fence with monitoring the daily work and standards of hundreds of specific projects by different local and regional subcontractors. At the same time, because the total costs for a border fence, based on some estimates, might reach $50 billion to $100 billion, payoffs and favors to elected officials and others associated with the project all along the border seem much more likely than they were with ISIS.

In the planning and designing of ISIS, high-tech solutions were the linchpins of border security. As defense contractors began hearing Washington rumors in late 2005 about a new high-tech fence to be built along the Mexican border, their engineers, like those I consulted at Honeywell's Florida plant, began to bandy about sophisticated technological solutions, including satellite uplinks, high-speed computers capable of collecting vast amounts of data, surface radar, drones, and night-vision remote cameras. All these components would be integrated, of course, into one coherent system capable of making the job of each Border Patrol agent a piece of cake.

ISIS was a dismal and expensive attempt at constructing a border fence based upon technological solutions to patrolling the line. Lessons to be learned from ISIS were plausibly denied by the DHS, the Border Patrol, defense contractors, and Congress. Too soon ISIS was completely forgotten.

Chapter 6
Dubuque

Congressman Frank James "Jim" Sensenbrenner, Jr., chair of the House Committee on the Judiciary, comfortably readjusts his large, tailored frame, then reaches for another piece of candy from the special stash by his right elbow. Exactly one day before President George W. Bush is to make his last defense of his immigration legislation before a crowd of supporters at Anzalduas County Park, Jim Sensenbrenner peels off the candy wrapper, casts it aside, then pops the sugar globe into his mouth. From behind a table less than three feet from the stage upon which the congressman and his committee are ensconced, I hear him sigh.

As the sluggish Mississippi River rolls by the Grand River Center in Dubuque, Iowa, Congressman Sensenbrenner is poised to chair the twenty-first, and last, chance for the public to voice its concern about immigration to its elected House representatives. The first of these field hearings was held in San Diego in June 2006, and this final one is three months later on September 1.

In accordance with the wishes of the conservative branch of the Republican leadership in the House, personified by Chairman Sensenbrenner, all across the nation, in cities and small towns in thirteen different states, immigration information, data, and perspectives have been presented before the committee members, each of whom professes a keen interest in public input on this wedge issue.[1] Dissatisfied with the core of President Bush's own immigration bill, only after the field hearings are completed will congressional Republicans, bolstered by conservative Democrats, offer their own legislation. Or at least that is what many in this Dubuque audience believe based upon the press releases from Sensenbrenner's Washington office.

At each stop on the tour the liberal Democrats on Sensenbrenner's committee also have been trying to get their message heard and documented for the public record. The minority party in Congress has been pushing compromise to their own party, President Bush, and those Republicans, like Sensenbrenner, to the right of the president on immigration issues. All this is happening just as incumbent congressional candidates and their colleagues prepare for the final stages of campaigning and the elections in November.

A career politician with eight terms as a representative from Wisconsin, Sensenbrenner has spent much of his adult life before audiences like the one now literally at his feet. While latecomers find their seats, the crowd of two hundred buzzes with excitement. No one in the audience can remember how long it has been since a Washington hearing was held in Dubuque. At the back of the auditorium the national media scurry around the room adjusting their cameras and sound equipment and, once finally settled, assume an attitude of perpetual boredom.[2] Next to Sensenbrenner's outsized wooden gavel lies a pile of candy wrappers. Only a few candies remain.

In a deep public voice, Congressman Sensenbrenner calls the House Committee on the Judiciary to order. All the members of the audience, not including the four undercover officers in jeans and running shoes, their handguns bulging from beneath Hawaiian T-shirts, fall silent. Gazing down over the audience from atop his perch on the raised platform, Sensenbrenner soaks in the warmth of the artificial silence he himself has manufactured. The congressman appears genuinely to enjoy both the place and the moment. Carelessly, as if swatting a fly at a Fourth of July picnic at his home in Menomonee Falls, Wisconsin—one of his three residences—he tests the microphone before he speaks.

Next to his microphone and candy wrappers, as much symbol of the chair's authority as the gavel, sits a black cube housing a digital clock. The clock, closely watched and controlled by a technician at the back of the auditorium, counts down by seconds from five minutes in dull red calligraphy. When sixty seconds remain, the clock's digits flash rigorously. At thirty seconds, the red digits became even more frantic. Only Rep. Sensenbrenner, as chairman, possesses the power to override the clock and speak, or let others speak, for as long as he permits.

Sensenbrenner first lays out the ground rules of his hearing. In a manner of his choosing, experts at the foot of the stage will give their invited testimony. His committee members will listen to this testimony and, when permitted by Sensenbrenner, will be allowed to ask the experts relevant questions. The questions and/or statements by the members of his committee are also carefully timed and controlled by the chairman. If there are disruptions of any kind in this procedure, Sensenbrenner warns the audience, those who break his rules will be summarily removed by federal law enforcement officers.

Speaking without notes, Sensenbrenner then discusses his own views on immigration issues. After three months and twenty hearings, he knows his speech by heart.

At first it is not clear whether the majority of those in the audience realize that only the invited experts are permitted to speak at this public hearing. Such has been the case in El Paso and all the other stops in border and nonborder states. Sensenbrenner has not allowed a single member of the public to speak before the committee. Before this hearing began, I talked with many in the crowd who patiently awaited their turn at the microphone. Many in the Dubuque audience still believe, for whatever reasons, they are going to be given an opportunity to share their experiences and viewpoints with the Washington politicians. Chairman Sensenbrenner has no way of knowing about all those who traveled from as far away as Minnesota and Missouri to speak at the public hearing in Dubuque. These individuals believe that, after the experts have testified, they will be given an open microphone, or at the very least will have the chance to chat about the issues with the politicians.

Their heads ankle-high to Sensenbrenner and the rest of the members of his committee, the five experts—three selected by the Republican majority, the other two by the minority Democrats—sit quietly at a table with their backs to the audience. All summer long the Republican witnesses, along with the Republican members of the committee, have been allowed more than their fair share of time to speak. In stark contrast, the experts invited by the Democrats, as well as the Democratic committee members themselves, have been kept strictly to the digital clock controlled by Chairman Sensenbrenner.[3] When committee Democrats repeatedly pleaded for additional seconds after their five minutes were expended, their pleas fell on deaf ears.

Democratic committee members have argued at each hearing for the creation of a joint committee of the House and Senate to resolve the impasse posed by pending immigration legislation. Sensenbrenner labels these requests as showboating, reiterating that he is always open to the formation of a joint committee but has never been approached by the Democratic leadership. In response, more and more of the Democratic committee members fail to show up at the hearings because they believe Sensenbrenner's unsubtle strategy is to block any attempts at negotiation or compromise between Republicans and Democrats on any immigration bills other than his own.

Other immigration bills are before the House besides those affirmed by President Bush and bipartisan supporters. Among them is H.R. 4437, the "Border Protection, Antiterrorism, and Illegal Immigration Control Act of 2005," which is commonly referred to as the Sensenbrenner Bill. Broadly speaking, this bill emphasizes the need for public funding for border security but avoids specific details. In addition, the Sensenbrenner Bill calls for the full enforcement of current immigration laws, including detention and deportation of illegal aliens.

President Bush supports "The Comprehensive Immigration and Reform Act of 2006," S. 2611, the so-called Reid-Kennedy Bill, already passed by the Senate. In general terms the Reid-Kennedy Bill differs from the Sensenbrenner Bill by stressing the need for a worker management program. This bill also calls for increased border security, but President Bush, a former governor of a border state, puts less emphasis on detention and the criminalization of offenders. Labeled as an "amnesty program" by critics of the bill, President Bush's bill offers illegal workers a stringent pathway to citizenship. President Bush has placed the prestige of his office behind the Senate's Reid-Kennedy Bill, one reason he so highly touts the benefits of his bill in his speech at Anzalduas County Park.[4]

Sensenbrenner and other Republicans to the right of President Bush on this issue vigorously criticize S. 2611 as being soft on illegal aliens. They believe that those who entered the country broke the law and, therefore, should not be rewarded with a pathway to citizenship that might encourage others to do likewise.

A joint committee of the House and Senate normally would be called by party leadership to work out, if possible, a political compromise between contending pieces of legislation, but in a Republican-led House and Senate with a sitting Republican president, no such effort is in the works. In his position as chair of the House Committee on the Judiciary, Rep. Sensenbrenner plays, in spite of denials to the contrary, a very strategic role in blocking even the slightest possibility of a legislative compromise. Without Sensenbrenner's support, along with the conservative Republican votes he musters, any so-called comprehensive immigration bill directly addressing other vital immigration issues in addition to border security has little chance of passing.

The ranking minority member on the House Committee on the Judiciary is Congresswoman Sheila Jackson Lee. She is the only Democrat present at this public hearing in Dubuque. Before Sensenbrenner fires up the hearing, one of the congressional staffers tells me bluntly, "The rest of the Democrats on this committee aren't wasting their time here in Dubuque. They're out right now on the campaign trail helping their friends get reelected." The pragmatic decision by the minority party committee members to skip the Dubuque hearing leaves Rep. Jackson Lee alone among the Republicans on the stage. There she sits, a smallish, stout woman dressed in a pale yellow business suit and a thick string of pearls. Pinned to her chest is a broach the size of a headlight.

After Sensenbrenner's opening remarks, it falls on Congresswoman Jackson Lee to present her party's case for its immigration legislation. She pokes fun at Sensenbrenner's notion that the House and the Senate cannot find time during the months of June, July, and August to negotiate any legislative compromises. After six years of the Bush administration, she says that she is frustrated by what she describes as the president's and the Republican Party's failure to secure the Mexican border. She cannot understand why the Sensenbrenner Bill, H.R. 4437, fails to consider a worker management program. In the last seconds of her five minutes, Sensenbrenner firmly admonishes her that her time is almost up. Then he cuts off her microphone while she's in midsentence. Since Jackson Lee has already experienced this twenty times before in as many cities, she does not look at all ruffled by the chairman's action.

Invited to speak as an expert on immigration by Rep. Jackson Lee, Dubuque City Council member Ann E. Michalski vigorously outlines her own position on immigration and compares it to the immigration bills before Congress. Her stance is based upon her lifetime experiences in Dubuque, including her involvement in municipal politics. Approaching seventy years of age, Councilwoman Michalski ignores the unfriendly Republican glares from the stage as she reads her testimony in a no-nonsense voice. Unfortunately, she goes a dangerous ten seconds beyond the clock's allotted five-minute time limit for Democrats, Chairman Sensenbrenner tapping loudly on his microphone as the clock's digits flash madly by. For her ten-second offense she is abruptly silenced by the chairman.

In point of fact, Ms. Michalski arguably is more knowledgeable of the impact of both legal and illegal immigration on Dubuque than any other individual sitting on stage or at the table of experts. The daughter of immigrants, she is old enough both to remember stories her parents told her about their personal joys and tragedies in this new country and to have experienced them for herself. She testifies that immigration "presented our community with both challenge and opportunity." Dubuque's immigrants at the turn of the twentieth century, the Irish and the Germans, "want[ed] a better life for themselves and their families." So too do today's Latinos in Dubuque. The Dubuque politician says, "Iowa needs better, productive citizens who desire to contribute to the life of the community."

She continues: "We must assume that some of our new inhabitants have illegally crossed our borders. We can tell this by the degrees of anxiety they express in certain situations and by their reluctance to participate in some aspects of city life. Even given this barrier, our Hispanic residents are becoming part of our community, and we find their presence enriching."[5]

On stage the Republican committee members are not pleased by the testimony from the Dubuque council member. She is quickly asked by one, as if her answer is a litmus test of her patriotism, "If Congress passed a law to deport every illegal immigrant in Dubuque, would you uphold this federal law?"

"No, I could not," Ms. Michalski honestly replies. She will not turn a single friend or neighbor over to federal authorities because a law made in Washington demands she do so. She also affirms she will be no less an American citizen or patriot for not having complied with a federal law based upon what she considers to be ignorance and foolishness.

Echoing much of the sentiment I have already heard in South Texas, the council member from Dubuque also does not believe her answer calls into question either the moral fiber of her patriotism or her unwillingness as an elected official to uphold the law. Instead, she attempts to insert both morality and pragmatism into the debate. The immigrants in Dubuque, old or brand new, legal or illegal, are a vital part of her community. How can Washington lawmakers expect Councilwoman Michalski to participate in deporting her neighbors and fellow congregants?

There it is once more: one of the immigration cats so quickly, so completely, out of the immigration bag on the Dubuque banks of the Mississippi River. Legal and illegal immigration are far too nuanced for beltway legislative platitudes—at least from Councilwoman Michalski's perspective as a lifetime resident of Dubuque, as a member of the Dubuque City Council, as the daughter of immigrants, and as good friend of old and new immigrants alike.

When the complexities of real human experience are contextualized within our own history, simplistic political solutions become self-evidently trivial. Sound bites are no match for Ms. Michalski's hardworking neighbors, churchgoing friends, and upstanding members of Dubuque, many of whom are immigrants just like her.

Sitting to one side of Councilwoman Michalski, Senator Charles "Chuck" Grassley, the senior Republican senator from Iowa, stresses some of the same concerns as Michalski about present and impending immigration legislation in Washington.[6] Invited to speak by the committee's Republican majority, Senator Grassley cautions that the emotional fervor and turmoil elicited by immigration in 2006 is not a new phenomenon. Senator Grassley was a very young senator in Washington when the Simpson-Mazzoli Bill, the Immigration Reform and Control Act (IRCA), was enacted by Congress in 1986. According to the senator from Iowa, IRCA was passed two decades earlier amid considerable controversy and debate. He also reminds the committee on stage of the importance of debate and the legitimacy of the diverse beliefs held by Americans. Says Grassley: "We continue to be a nation of immigrants. We have benefited and continue to benefit from the talents of diverse cultures coming to America."[7]

In spite of Sensenbrenner's hard eye on the digital clock and heavy hand on the gavel (one critic refers to it as an "iron gavel"), a variety of different viewpoints about immigration manage to emerge at the field hearings throughout the summer. Opposition comes not just from the experts called by the minority Democrats, but also from the Republicans' own experts, like Republican senator Grassley.[8]

Public frustration and anger concerning immigration, along with suggested policy reforms, boil over regardless of the limitations set by the chairman of the House Committee on the Judiciary at the summer hearings. For example, local border sheriffs invited by the Republican committee members to testify at the El Paso hearing had to slug it out with their own Republican hosts before being silenced for their testimony—but not until after the sheriffs presented their own immigration facts, their analysis of border immigration issues, and their proposed solutions.[9]

The entire fiasco in El Paso was recorded in front of C-Span cameras. But either the National Park Service, which hosted the event at the Chamizal venue, forgot to pay its utility bill, or the lighting technicians failed to report for work. In any case, only one Klieg light was fully operable, so at times the Republican experts were literally lost in dark shadows as they fended off a series of hostile questions and remarks from their congressional hosts.

After their sheriffs and other experts testified, residents of El Paso grew angry when they realized they were excluded from presenting their views at the field hearing, In part, this response was because many citizens of El Paso face multiple problems tied to national immigration and NAFTA policy, including rising unemployment in the maquiladoras of El Paso and its sister city, Juárez.[10]

Throughout the summer months similar eruptions occurred in immigration hearings in Laredo and other border cities, where history and emotions run deep. Even in states many miles from Mexico the immigration hearings generated strong responses from a public aching to voice their opinions before their elected congressional representatives.[11]

Despite all this, I am genuinely surprised when the little man sitting next to me suddenly becomes, once the media lights and cameras turn his way, an immigration firebrand. Director of the Center for American Common Culture at the Hudson Institute, John Fonte politely exchanged cards and copies of testimony with me before the hearing got underway, shaking my hand and welcoming me to the table in a quiet, reserved voice.

But in what can only be defined as a high-pitched yelp, in his testimony this same person now claims that an immigration apocalypse is on the horizon. He warns that new illegal immigrants do not meet the stringent standards of American patriots—standards that were met and exceeded by former immigrants and that facilitated their assimilation into American society. According to Mr. Fonte, the recent Latino immigration protests in Los Angeles, New York, Chicago, and other major cities clearly demonstrate the need for tighter border security. Immigrants who cannot be assimilated into our "common culture" must be separated out from those who can. In his third minute of testimony, Fonte suggests that only those immigrants who can easily "assimilate into mainstream America" should be allowed to cross our borders.[12]

I immediately wonder what these unnamed prequalifications for entry might be. What exactly is Fonte's definition of "mainstream America," including his notion of a "common culture"? I think of my paternal Jewish grandfather, Harry Aaron Maril, a legal immigrant who spoke English with a heavy accent until the day he died, an accent carried from his native Lithuanian shtetl to his new home in Oklahoma City. My grandfather fled to the United States to avoid family and religious issues. Entering the country legally at a very young age, he soon joined the army and honorably served during the aftermath of the Spanish-American War. An oddity in Oklahoma—he was a tailor by day and a painter in oils the rest of his waking hours—this legal Lithuanian immigrant eventually purchased a modest home three doors down from the neighborhood Baptist church. Over the years the congregation grew and grew until my grandfather's house and the few others remaining on the block were surrounded by church buildings and church parking lots. In spite of the economic benefits he might have received from selling out, my grandfather refused in unmannerly ways the repeated offers from the megachurch. Harry Aaron Maril could do this without fear of any kind of retribution, because he enjoyed the full rights of American citizenship.

Would the director of the Center for American Common Culture have judged my paternal grandfather worthy of legal entry into this country, especially after he unceremoniously vented his spleen upon the Southern Baptists in Oklahoma City? I fear that my grandfather's values and manners, at times anathema to his own family, fell far outside of Fonte's notions of "mainstream America" and "common culture."

The audience grown increasingly restive as each expert speaks in turn, Fonte receives a few spontaneous boos after his testimony. With his gavel Chairman Sensenbrenner quickly silences the response of some in the crowd to Fonte's point of view and solutions to current immigration problems.

Yet in spite of Sensenbrenner's heavy gavel, boos from the audience intensify, along with shouts of support when Michael Cutler, another expert called by the Republican committee members, describes his own doomsday immigration scenario. Hollywood moguls would relish the cinematic potential of Cutler's vision. A Border Patrol agent two decades in the past, and now a fellow at the Center of Immigration Studies, Cutler's testimony is far bleaker than that of Fonte. If, for example, border security continues to ignore international terrorists, then in Cutler's depiction of the near future terrorists will flood into the United States to wreak havoc upon the civilian population.[13]

Dramatically raising the gavel high above his right shoulder, pausing to make sure all eyes are upon him, Chairman Sensenbrenner slams it down on the table in front of him with all the power he can muster. Up until this special minute Sensenbrenner, not discounting his absolutist partisanship, arguably conducts himself within the range of the parliamentary process. One might dismiss much of his behavior at the hearing as merely rude or unbecoming of a congressperson. Certainly, at least before the hearing began, Sensenbrenner was cordial enough to all regardless of their assumed leanings. Working his way down the table of presenters, he shook my hand and said in a sincere voice, eyes to my eyes, "Thank you for coming, Professor." Then he was on to the next individual with a firm and practiced handshake.

But the gavel slamming is something different, an act suggesting there may be much more to this experienced politician than first meets the eye. A big, lumbering man, Sensenbrenner at all times seems very much at ease on stage at this hearing. In another two months this seemingly uncomplicated, plain-spoken politician will easily win reelection to his ninth congressional term. The gavel slamming appears totally inconsistent for a politician of this stature.

While rehearsing my presentation back at the Dubuque Holiday Inn, I consistently went thirty seconds over the allotted five minutes. In spite of reports I have been reading in the major newspapers, it never dawns on me, perhaps because of previous experience testifying before Congress, that Congressman Sensenbrenner will treat me any differently than he will the Republicans.[14]

So instead of editing my testimony for time, I walk the streets for signs of the impact of new and old immigrants upon Dubuque. Just across the parking lot from the Grand River Center, I stop at Catfish Planet. Outside this memorial to Mississippi catfish, housed in the National Mississippi River Museum and Aquarium, I find a first clue to the immigrant history of the region. To one side of the museum stands a huge paddle wheel extracted from the steamship *William S. Black*. The wood and steel wheel weighs a whopping thirty-two tons and measures twenty-five feet in diameter. The giant blades now turn slowly in a shallow brick basin of stale yellow water littered with plastic cups. Inside the museum, under a film noir detective hat, a slouching catfish tells his Chamber of Commerce–inspired story:

> I was traveling the mighty Mississippi, my destination . . . DUBUQUE.
> I had arrived just before lunch when I discovered a most peculiar place. Catfish Planet. The locals were quiet [*sic*] friendly. Sometimes one skips shaving. NO ONE should skip this.

I continue my tour of the tanks of colorful, exotic catfish, some from as far away as China, ignoring when possible the large, distracting banners, including one that reads, "Did you know that one out of every five fish on earth is a catfish?"

The Humphrey Bogart catfish, if garish, is somewhat on target. The locals are "quiet friendly," although not numerous. From the Blackwater Grill on the corner I count the cars motoring past down Main Street. My count comes to two cars every sixty seconds. Business is very slow in downtown Dubuque at 12:30 p.m. At the Blackwater Grill, The Mexican and The Laughing Ass top the list of local brews.

If Catfish Planet provides a hint of the historical and economic overview I am searching for, Dubuque's geography is undeniable. Just south of Lock Number 11, Dubuque sits precariously on the western side of the upper Mississippi. At the intersection of three states, Iowa, Wisconsin, and Illinois, the Mississippi River, in bewildering contrast to the Rio Grande, expands to an astounding width of one and one-half miles. Reflecting the wealth of previous centuries, proud Victorian houses stand high on the bluffs overlooking the river. Some of these structures, mirroring Dubuque's new economy, have morphed into bed and breakfasts. Not far from the former mansions are a convent and a Catholic liberal arts college.

Dubuque's economic future yet may hang in the balance, but the city has finally won its fight for survival against the forces of the Mississippi River. In 1973 the Army Corps of Engineers completed an impressive system of levees and dikes to protect the city from the river at flood stage. Since then Dubuque has not suffered through a single spring flood. When the massive gates to Ice Harbor and other vulnerable points in the city are closed, floodwaters are forced downriver, where other cities and towns must deal with them.

Trapper and trader Julien Dubuque claimed this site for the French in 1781. Today downtown Dubuque is a hodgepodge of upscale restaurants, modestly regentrified office buildings, parking structures, stores, and restaurants. Three hundred million dollars has been poured into the revitalization of this Historic Downtown, including the Grand River Center, the adjoining hotel and water park, and the national museum and aquarium housing Catfish Planet.

Given these investment numbers and new enterprises in place, most city planners would declare an economic victory in Dubuque. They would be wrong. There is telltale plywood in the windows of an abandoned restaurant on Main Street, and, a few blocks north of the Clock Tower, which serves as a focal point for weekend music concerts, downtown gentrification has devolved into a uniform shop, seedy bars, and a host of empty storefronts, including failed restaurants and stores.

Diamond Jo Casino, however, in contrast to major sections of the downtown, throbs with a certain vitality inside a simulated paddle wheeler bolted to pilings in Ice Harbor. Its three levels of claustrophobic decks attract busloads of senior citizens from the tri-state area to play the slots, gaming tables, and roulette wheels. The casino logo flies above photos of smiling winners in their retirement years receiving their lap-sized checks: "Don't be a watcher, be a winner." Next door, the Disneyesque environment spreads onto a spot of artificial wetlands where transplanted grasses form a minihabitat for a few struggling marsh birds and otters.

The real history of Dubuque, a blue-collar city built upon the backs of Irish and German ship workers, finally reveals itself at the humble Boatyard Museum. During the heyday of the mighty Mississippi steamers, boat manufacturers thrived in Dubuque. Immigrant laborers forged paddle wheelers for the Mississippi and beyond. When the paddle wheelers became dinosaurs, the factory workers transitioned to constructing steel barges and river tugs.

A labor force of skilled metal workers shaped enormous steel steam boilers and other metal forms from giant presses. In photos displayed in the Boatyard Museum, hundreds of these immigrants, roughly dressed men young and old, stand proudly by as their vessels are christened by dignitaries and launched down wooden ramps into the Mississippi River.

Behind the pervading catfish iconography, the theme park tourism, and recent attempts at gentrification of the Historic Downtown, Dubuque has a vibrant immigrant heart, a city once thriving upon the labors of Irish and Germans ship builders and their descendants. In addition to economic developers, today it is Latino workers and their families who attempt to fill the vacuum left by the demise of the city's industrial core. Latinos are not only employees, but also purveyors of new businesses in Dubuque. This trend among Latinos and other new immigrants is not unique to Dubuque; it has been widely observed and studied throughout the country.[15]

A vocal minority is frustrated and angry about Hispanic immigration to Dubuque and surrounding areas in Iowa, Illinois, and Wisconsin. Approaching a group of five men just ordered off the street by the Dubuque police because they are blocking a public access, I shake the hand of a Minuteman. He holds up a sign reading, "I support the Border Patrol."

"I support the Border Patrol, too," I say to him, smiling. But then he shows me the other side of his sign, which reads: "Mexicans Go Home."

"The Mexicans want to come here and take over our country," says the Minuteman, who refuses to give his name. In his thirties, dressed in jeans and a polo shirt, he seems very sincere about the Mexicans' intent to "turn it back to that history treaty in 1848 when California and Texas belonged to them."

"You mean the Treaty of Guadalupe Hidalgo?" I ask him.

"I guess so. Anyhow, they plan to take over the Southwest like it was theirs." This man says he lives in Dubuque and is sick to death of Mexicans taking American jobs. He came to the hearing to tell the Washington politicians what every American already knows, namely, that there are far too many Mexicans in the United States, and they should be sent back where they came from. The Mexicans cause all kinds of problems, do not pay taxes, expect Americans to foot the bill for their kids' educations, and commit violent crimes against American citizens.

Minutemen patrolling the Mexican borders make a very large splash in the spring, summer, and fall of 2006. Rising from political obscurity, these civilian patrols attract national interest and public sympathy and support. Looking for votes, elected politicians at all levels follow the lead of this emergent group in both border and many nonborder states.[16]

I follow the group of Minutemen through the security line at the Grand River Center, where they soon become part of the diverse audience at the hearing.

I've been invited by Congresswoman Sheila Jackson Lee to give my testimony, but my intent is very different from that of the other speakers. With the exception of Councilwoman Michalski, the majority of experts at the hearing are think tankers, politicians, and Washington consultants. I would seriously doubt that any of them, excluding Michael Cutler, who was an agent many years before, have ever visited the Mexican border or, if they have, took the time to learn much about it.[17] Their facts as I have heard them at the hearing do not match what I personally have observed, experienced, and documented along the U.S.-Mexico border.

I know my testimony is problematic, albeit for different reasons, for many Republicans, some Democrats, and various interest groups from the Minutemen to those representing immigrant rights. Some immigrant rights groups, for example, dislike my research because I insist on presenting an unromanticized portrait of border crossers.[18] At the other end of the political spectrum, law enforcers and their supporters, although they may have little or no data to support their assertions, take issue with my depiction of a dysfunctional Border Patrol led by petty managers and visionless political appointees. That said, conservative Republicans find more to dislike in my testimony than most. Since there is only one Democrat sitting on the stage, I expect an unfriendly reception.

All too briefly I discuss the problems with illegal immigration along the Mexican border as I have seen it, starting with the human suffering I personally witnessed beginning in 2000. At the same time, I also describe men and women in the Border Patrol who day after day, night after night put their lives at risk while relying on a sensor system that does not work. I state that, based upon what I have seen, those who believe all illegal immigrants are without fault are also gravely off the mark. Among those apprehended by the Border Patrol I have observed common criminals, drunks, individuals high on various drugs, and members of known gangs.

The vast majority who cross *sin papeles*, however, do so because they face very limited options and choices. There are too few legal visas available to citizens of Mexico, and those that are available are very expensive. The objective of the vast majority of these new immigrants is simply to find work and/or join or rejoin family members already employed.[19] Most who enter illegally and are apprehended by the Border Patrol are exhausted from their journey, already victims of some crime against them, and scared to death.

Congressman Sensenbrenner times my testimony to the millisecond. When the manic beams of the red digits flash before me, I am left with no alternative. Shifting into overdrive, as if my life depends on it, I speed read my way through the last paragraphs. Sucking air at the end of this verbal sprint, when I look up on stage I think I see the slightest grin cross Sensenbrenner's face.

Before I can catch my breath, the congressman has already gone on to the next expert at the table. Soon afterward, the Washington politicians on stage, cued by the chairman, begin their litany of rhetorical questions of the experts. While I wait out their attempts to score sound bites with their targeted demographics, I doodle in frustration on the sheets of my testimony, drink from my water glass, then write in the margins, again staring at the stage within arm's reach, "Sensenbrenner?"

A chink in Rep. Jim Sensenbrenner's armor appears in the land of blue-collar immigrants, steel barges, catfish, and casinos. Slumping back in his chair, the congressman unknowingly reveals a bit of his more human self. Unbeknownst to him, both legs of his tailored suit project from beneath the bottom of the starched linen covering the table before him, and as he fidgets, he crosses and recrosses his legs, betraying some anxiety and simultaneously exposing, above a dark sock, the ankle of his left leg.

Underneath the harsh camera lights the pale, pink skin, all too human, offers a backstage glimpse of the imposing personage. Behind the bravado and starch of this Washington politician are pale skin and bone, flesh and blood. From his body language below the table, Jim Sensenbrenner appears nervous about the outcome of the hearing. Or perhaps there are other, more serious matters awaiting him. This raises a crucial question: Rep. Sensenbrenner plays the role of the virtuoso politician in backwater towns like Dubuque, Iowa, but what are his accomplishments in Washington?

Frank James Sensenbrenner, Jr., was born rich, was educated in elite schools, and married well. His grandfather established the family's foundation of wealth and privilege after inventing the Kotex feminine napkin. Based upon the riches generated by that product, Sensenbrenner's grandfather invested heavily in the nascent Kimberly Clark Company shortly after World War I. Kimberly Clark is now a multinational corporation.[20]

Born in Chicago in 1943 but raised in Shorewood, Wisconsin, Sensenbrenner attended the prestigious and private Milwaukee Country Day School, then went on to Stanford University, where he majored in political science. While still in college, Sensenbrenner found time to serve as a staff assistant to California congressman J. Arthur Younger. Receiving his law degree in 1968 from the University of Wisconsin, young Sensenbrenner was elected by voters that very same year, at the tender age of twenty-five, to the Wisconsin State Assembly. A politically precocious Jim Sensenbrenner then spent four years in the assembly before winning a seat in the Wisconsin senate by the slim margin of 589 votes.

Along the way, before taking his Wisconsin State Senate seat in 1977, Jim Sensenbrenner married Cheryl Warren, the daughter of U.S. District Judge Robert Warren, a prominent state politician who was a former attorney general of Wisconsin. At the time of the hearing in Dubuque in 2006, Rep. Sensenbrenner's listed assets are worth more than $11.5 million.

For almost two decades faithful Wisconsin constituents elected and re-elected Sensenbrenner as their representative of the Fifth Congressional District. He successfully has managed to cultivate among his constituents a populist image despite his vast inherited wealth, his lifestyle, and his legislative leadership. Each election Sensenbrenner faced few serious challengers to his seat in Washington, either in his party primaries or against Democratic opponents. After winning eight congressional elections in a row—he would go on to win his ninth in November—one might reasonably expect Rep. Sensenbrenner's legislative legacy to be both long and notable.

Instead, Jim Sensenbrenner's legislative legacy in Washington is neither: after almost twenty years in Washington, even a generous appraisal of his record includes barely three pieces of legislation. The first legislation for which Sensenbrenner deserves some credit is the USA Patriot Act, signed by President Bush in 2001. Sensenbrenner actually did not author or provide ideas for the Patriot Act, which is generally attributed to former assistant attorney general Viet Dinh, but he was one of its strongest proponents. Sensenbrenner is considered the author of the Real ID Act of 2005, his second piece of legislation, which in part creates a federal database for state driver's licenses so that they may better serve as a security document for their holders. The Real ID Act continues to face strong resistance from an increasing number of states wrestling with the practicalities of the legislation, including its costs. Third, and last, Congressman Sensenbrenner was one of the House managers of proceedings in the impeachment of President Bill Clinton in 1998.

After almost twenty years, these three pieces of legislation form the sum total of Sensenbrenner's legislative legacy in Washington.

Based upon major donors to his election campaigns, Rep. Sensenbrenner is a lifetime advocate of reducing taxes. He is also a strong supporter of increasing prison terms for certain criminal acts. The congressman also is anti-abortion. Finally, again based upon his political contributors, Sensenbrenner fights in Congress to protect intellectual copyrights. Yet there is no legislation offered by Sensenbrenner directly addressing any of these positions.

After Sensenbrenner completed his six-year term as chairman of the

House Judiciary Committee in 2006, *Human Events*, a conservative, tax-rights publication, named him its man of the year. That same year *Rolling Stone Magazine*, on the liberal side of the political spectrum, counted Congressman Sensenbrenner as "the second worst member of the House," while dubbing him "the dictator."[21]

Sensenbrenner also has a history of petulance, even when it comes to his relations with his own party. Going against the wishes of conservatives in the Republican Party, he held hearings on the FBI raid of the offices of Rep. William J. Jefferson, Democrat from Mississippi.[22] Some House legislators call him a pit bull, while others praise his willingness, when committee room doors are closed, to negotiate. He is, at the same time, described as being the most mimicked member of the House. One side of his public persona, summarized by several critics as cantankerous, may in fact be rooted in issues of anger management.[23]

There is little disagreement among both political friends and enemies that Sensenbrenner possesses a volatile temper. While chairing the House Committee on the Judiciary, as members discussed the Patriot Act, Sensenbrenner had a major temper tantrum. The congressman threw out all pretenses of parliamentary procedure to exert his own personal will upon the committee, angering not only his adversaries but also his fellow Republicans.

While few question Rep. Sensenbrenner's hair-trigger temper or loyalty to a handful of issues, what seems most telling about his two decades in Congress is his unremarkable legislative legacy. Time and again this record suggests Sensenbrenner is at best a follower, never a leader.

In light of solid voter support back home in Wisconsin, including well-funded campaign chests and a family fortune, Sensenbrenner has been most content simply to block legislation. His congressional seniority and influence do not seem to have encouraged him to invest his time and talent, with the three exceptions noted, into innovative legislation addressing any number of national problems. Since his first election to Congress, Sensenbrenner only on the rarest of occasions has taken a position of leadership on contestable issues. His position as chairman of the House Committee on the Judiciary would have given most politicians a bully pulpit from which to endorse and/or influence any number of pieces of legislation. But that position, his facile campaigns for public office, and his personal safety net seem to have engendered nothing more than career mediocrity.

There is certainly no fault in a congressman's lack of higher political ambitions. There are more than enough members of the House with aspirations that exceed their talents and character. But for almost two decades Sensenbrenner's record in Congress is little more than that of a temperamental place holder.

One critic attempts to demonstrate the structural linkages between Sensenbrenner's immigration agenda and the actions of Grupo México, a large Mexican mining company connected to his family's multinational corporation. But the suggestion that his stance on immigration and his immigration legislation might benefit his own holdings in his grandfather's multinational, or that of other family members, seems in all fairness an assertion based upon theoretical supposition rather than documentation.[24]

With the full influence of a Republican administration at his back, along with a Republican-controlled House and Senate, Jim Sensenbrenner has demonstrated that he can push through legislation like the Patriot Act and the Real ID Act. But his congressional legacy is not in generating pragmatic and thoughtful solutions to difficult national issues but as a legislative obstructionist. Fueled by his out-of-control temper, one of the things Sensenbrenner is good at is dishing it out to his adversaries in a public setting in which he holds the parliamentary reins. But can he take it?

Giving himself all the time in the world, Congressman Sensenbrenner asks a series of questions to every expert on the Dubuque panel. We are directed by the chairman to answer only "yes" or "no." No explanations, qualifications, or details may be offered. Far from a true collection of information or perspective on immigration issues, Sensenbrenner's kindergarten exercise during the third act of his theatrical production is a final mockery of the proceedings.

Sensenbrenner goes up and down the line of experts repeating the same question to them one at a time: "Do you believe, yes or no, that we should have a fence along the border?" In this spelling bee atmosphere, those who slightly hesitate are defined as indecisive, even weak. I answer "yes." Given his rules, I am not allowed to elaborate, discuss, or ask for any clarification, and, unlike my Republican colleagues at the table, I have not seen the questions before or had time to prepare answers. What kind of border fence does the congressman have in mind? Is it a system of barriers? A virtual fence? Towers? Dogs? Sensors? Helicopters? All of the above? Does the Wisconsin politician refer to a fence along the entire border or only along certain parts? Is the border fence a standalone construction or part of a larger immigration policy that would include provisions such as a worker management program? This is not intellectual quibbling. Sensenbrenner eliminates political compromise by the debater's trick of establishing false dichotomies.

The next question is: "Do you believe the crime of human trafficking by *coyotes* should receive a stiffer sentence than they are now getting? Yes or no?" The question itself masks a gross ignorance of crime in the borderlands and the reality that human traffickers rarely are apprehended and even more rarely convicted. Court convictions remain unlikely because illegal aliens rarely will testify against their *coyotes*. Filling jails with *coyotes* makes even less sense, because for every *coyote* imprisoned there are thousands more waiting to take the job. On the south side of the border employment is rare: the going rate for a *coyote* is a hundred times the daily rate for Mexican factory workers lucky enough to find jobs. And on the north side of the impoverished borderline there also is no shortage of the unemployed or underemployed, some with long histories of smuggling.

Frustration peaking, when my turn comes before Congressman Pink Ankle, I answer differently than the others. Neither a sanctioned "yes" nor an official "no" comes from my lips. Instead, I belt out, with as much irony as I can attach to a small cluster of words, "They never catch the *coyotes* anyway, so it doesn't matter." Of course my words fail to register with the chairman as he moves on down the line of experts.

Steve King, a Republican congressperson from Iowa sitting at the far end of the table, is one of several committee members dissatisfied with my testimony. Based upon my research, I testified that the vast quantities of illegal drugs transported by criminal organizations into the United States demonstrate that, "The War on Drugs was over, and our side has lost."[25]

When Chairman Sensenbrenner finishes with his questions, Congressman King asks me if I truly feel that we have lost the drug war. I know that King, after receiving my unacceptable response, will then turn to his own expert among the witnesses for the response he really seeks.

"Yes," I say.

"Do you really believe that there is nothing that can be done at this point?" he continues.[26]

"If we had the political will, perhaps the incredible flow of illegal drugs could be lessened. Especially if we focused upon drug prevention and care of those who use them."

"Ah," he says, pouncing on my words with a zeal born of years of cross-examining witnesses during trial. "Then there is hope after all." As his words go into the public record, Congressman King does not allow me to respond.

This is not a public hearing whose mission is to gather facts about immigration; it is a mutant simulation created by the majority party. As such, the congressman from Wisconsin is going to have the final word. Sensenbrenner reads a summary of the information he asserts his witnesses have provided the House Committee on the Judiciary, testimony exactly matching his positions on immigration issues and policy. According to Sensenbrenner, the members of the committee will take this public testimony back Washington to formulate new immigration legislation.

At this point Congresswoman Jackson Lee exchanges a quick word with

Sensenbrenner. I lean forward to catch what she tells him, sure that those next to me at the table, not to mention the audience, cannot have heard what transpires on stage. Sensenbrenner, obviously rattled by what Jackson Lee tells him, then says irritably, "I would like nothing better than to send a letter over to the Senate." Jackson Lee immediately leaps into this small opening Sensenbrenner, because of his temperament, has allowed her.

"Oh," she says in mock dismay, "You are saying that you will write a letter right now to the Senate and the House so they can get together in Washington?"

In a voice channeling the late Congresswoman Barbara Jordan, Jackson Lee preaches to the congregation, voice rising a full octave as she highlights the second word of her response to the chairman: "I'll *sign* such a letter."

For a few slow seconds in Dubuque, Congressman Sensenbrenner is so angry he becomes speechless. Outwitted in his own scripted play as the moments pass by, he is left to sit there searching for words on stage before an audience grown restless and hostile. No words immediately come to him because Jackson Lee's lines are not in his play, and neither is his killer rejoinder.

Instead, Jackson Lee has a last chance to communicate her own partisan message. She chastises the chairman for a lack of leadership on the critical national issue of immigration, reminding him that compromise is the basis of democracy. She reminds him once again that the Republicans control the White House, the House of Representatives, and the Senate. If Congressman Sensenbrenner genuinely desires a deal on immigration with the Democrats, she intones from her temporary pulpit, then the chairman is the one to facilitate and lead it.

The chairman's jowls turn a ruddy red during Rep. Jackson Lee's speech. His composure returns from holiday as he argues back that any such meeting is unnecessary, because the Senate's immigration bill is so ill-founded it will never be seriously considered by the House.

Although Sensenbrenner regains his composure, he cannot regain control of his own field hearing. Realizing the hearing is almost over and there will be no opportunity to be heard, the unruly audience rushes forward at the sound of the final gavel. A small crowd spontaneously surrounds Jackson Lee to shake her hand and pat her awkwardly on the back. In the meantime, Sensenbrenner is left to make small talk within a tiny circle of the same Minutemen I'd met outside.

The twenty-first and last immigration field hearing in Dubuque is over.

Within fifteen minutes Rep. Sensenbrenner and his entourage shuttle to the airport. Still standing on stage, Rep. Jackson Lee remains surrounded by a group of fawning admirers. By increments she slowly works her way down to the auditorium floor, then along one aisle, to the door, to the lobby of the Grand River Center and, finally, to a car waiting to take her to the airport.

The large parking lot in front of the Grand River Center quickly clears. I spot the Minutemen with their protest signs, followed not far behind by the Hispanic family from Minnesota, who climb into a battered van. Each member of this family sports a button on their chest reading, "We're Americans." An Irish parish priest from Dubuque, who had approached me at the end of the hearing, also climbs into his car and motors off in the direction of the empty streets of historic downtown Dubuque.

Back in the lobby of the Dubuque Holiday Inn, I fall into a long conversation with four immigration lawyers who represent clients to the INS. The four, two men and two women, drove from Chicago the night before. Some of their clients are legal immigrants, some not. Frustrated by what they just witnessed as part of the audience at the field hearing, they are bursting with comments based upon their work experiences with the current immigration laws, policies, and rules. I ask them what they think of the INS. They all agree that the INS is grossly understaffed and underfunded. The attorneys work with INS managers, some of whom they say are both understanding and compassionate, willing when necessary to cut through massive red tape.

The voices of these four immigration lawyers, the Minutemen, the Hispanic family from Minnesota, the Irish priest, and the other diverse residents of Dubuque and the surrounding states regrettably never are heard before Chairman Sensenbrenner's House Committee on the Judiciary. Their relevant immigration experiences and perspectives never become part of the public record at the Dubuque field hearing. Nor do the statements of citizens in El Paso, San Diego, and the nineteen other towns and cities on this congressional road show. If different opinions and perspectives do manage to sneak into the public record at these summer hearings, it is in spite of Sensenbrenner's best efforts to exclude them. Regardless of one's political leanings, these twenty-one field hearings are not just a missed opportunity or blunder, but a tactical mockery of our political system.

One month after Sensenbrenner and his colleagues fly back from the immigration hearing in Dubuque to Washington; one month after President George W. Bush promotes his immigration legislation before a friendly audience at Anzalduas County Park, a Republican candidate for Congress from Pennsylvania, Raj Peter Bhakta, hires an elephant and mariachi band in Brownsville, Texas.[27] Two blocks from the campus of UTB-TSC, both the pachyderm and the musicians march back and forth across the Rio Grande. At no time during this rental charade from the United States to Mexico, then back again, does the Border Patrol or any other law enforcement officials deter either the rental elephant or the mariachis.

While state and national politicians in both parties begin to seize on immigration issues as so much campaign fodder, the Mexican border with the United States remains fundamentally unchanged: the border is a chaotic stew of illegal crossers, drug smugglers, common criminals, and others playing cat and mouse with a Border Patrol backed by an antiquated system of sensors. But in this borderlands game, violence and death pervade. Something needs to be done. Not surprisingly, the folks in Washington have answers.

Part Two

Crossing to Safety

Chapter 7

More Virtual Fences

I n search of semisecret Project 28, a prototype,
according to Boeing, Inc., for the virtual border fence, we leave the stifling heat and smog
of Tucson for Sasabe, Arizona. Sasabe, pronounced by locals with the emphasis on the first
syllable, is a very tiny and very remote border
community thirty miles west of Nogales.[1] Gaining
altitude as we head due south along Highway 19,
and as the broad sky temporarily clears and the
raw heat dissipates, my wife, Dindy Reich, who is
my research assistant on this trip to the border,
and I see up close the high desert basins bisected
by mountain ridges. Stately saguaro cactus, feath-
ery cholla, and prickly pear ready to blossom sur-
round us.[2] Between the turnoff to Arivaca and
Tucson upscale golf resorts dot both sides of the
four-lane highway, but West Arivaca Road, poorly
signed and hidden between a modest ranch house
and the only roadside restaurant for many miles,
quickly turns into two narrow lanes of meander-
ing asphalt.

Large ranches dominate this desolate border

place, but in the drought of 2009 cattle and hay fields thrive only where water wells have been drilled and crops irrigated. In late July random fields in a surreal green lie juxtaposed against the arid ridges of the Sierrita Mountains and the saguaro. Traces of undocumented workers are everywhere: plastic water bottles abandoned in dry washes, barbed wire fences pulled askew, random pieces of clothing blowing in a dry wind, and a slew of new No Trespassing signs affixed to aging fence posts. The closer we come to the Mexican border and to Sasabe, the more the isolated ranch houses with their outbuildings resemble fortifications in razor wire.

Before we reach Arivaca, an unincorporated desert community of 909 hardy souls, we drive past a lone tower under construction on the south side of the rural highway. I stop the rental car further down the narrow two lanes and carefully turn the car around, more concerned about running off the shoulderless road than bumping into any oncoming traffic; in the last twenty-five miles a total of four ranch trucks have passed us.

At this construction site sit three new white Ford trucks, all with identical logos on the driver's door. The steel tower rising out of the brush and cactus, with two large, asymmetrical shapes attached to its upper quadrant, is, according to a small sign stuck in the ground, "Construction Area Communication Tower Site 331945." While this tower closely resembles photos I have seen, I am not convinced I am actually looking out my car window at a piece of Boeing's Project 28.

Ten miles further west, just south of the intersection of West Arivaca Road and Highway 286, stand two more towers along with personnel and trucks identical to those at the first tower. Excited, I pull over to the west side of the road and get out of the car, digital camera in hand. A sign similar to that at the first site sticks out of the brush. As I stare at the towers, a white Ford truck like the ones at the first tower turns off the highway in front of me and rumbles through the entrance to the construction site. I glimpse two men with hard hats in the front seat; they, in turn, give me the once-over.

No more than five seconds later a new Ford truck appears, this one gray with windows up as it idles in the heat, no human life visible behind the darkly tinted glass. If I had any doubt about the security guards within, all I have to do is read the sign on the driver's door: EODT Security. (I learn later that EODT Security is a division of EOD Technology, Inc., with corporate headquarters in Lenoir, Tennessee, along with international offices in Baghdad and Kabul.)

Neither meaning nor wanting to break any laws of any kind, I take a few steps back onto the empty pavement of the public road to see what the individual(s) inside the EODT security truck plan to do. Said individual(s) make no movement I can detect. In turn I make none. From my perspective this is not a standoff but a further indicator of what rises before me into a desert sky.

I remember Honeywell's demonstration project three years earlier at their Florida plant, in which their virtual lab staff proudly demonstrated their latest security package designed to guard ICBM sites. According to Honeywell engineers, that state-of-the art software could separate local doofuses looking for rural beer barns from domestic or international terrorists. Did I set off just such an invisible sensor? Did a state-of-the-art software package just compare my facial imprint to those of known terrorists? Or did the two engineers in the white truck motor over to the on-duty security vehicle, buzz down the driver's-side window, and then point a finger at the doofus standing in the road?

Whatever the case, I walk slowly and carefully back to my rental car, climb innocently in, and continue due south down Highway 286 towards Sasabe. As I drive, I recite out loud a list of why these towers, based upon circumstantial evidence, must be a part of Boeing's Project 28. My list goes something like this: the second and third towers at the intersection of West Arivaca Road and Highway 286 are approximately ten to twelve miles directly north of the border on a high vantage point, perfect for a surface radar system to scan the border area; the signage at both construction sites is the same, looks new, and is intentionally vague; the towers resemble photographs I've seen of Project 28; and, most convincing, if these towers were really run-of-the-mill communications towers, why would there be such a rapid security response to my presence?

Continuing south on Highway 286, the Buenos Aires National Wildlife Reserve on our left, we pass by two more gates and cattle guards painted in the same colors as those at the previous communications towers. Behind the gates single-lane roads disappear into the brush and the cactus. The winding two-lane highway takes us by a small Border Patrol compound encircled by a bulky chain link fence. Topping the fence is a thick strand of razor wire that reflects the rays of the sun, soon to give way to a rare desert thunderstorm.

The town of Sasabe proper, which appears to be one-twentieth the size of Arivaca, is one short street of brightly painted abandoned stores and shops. The only exceptions are the post office, a general store, a cabin housing the chamber of commerce, and a brightly painted portable toilet. As we drive through the diminutive town, my eye catches a snakelike ridgeline connecting the town to the border port of entry. Off to the left, perched on a high point, a Border Patrol vehicle monitors our progress.

Sasabe's new port of entry, at least one-half the size of Sasabe's main street, resembles more a farmer's market in Tucson, Portland, or Austin than a border crossing in the middle of nowhere. Notwithstanding the barbed wire and the small tower that fronts it, one can easily imagine under the three rooflines festive booths, vendors, and the smell of exotic foods and fresh flowers. We turn around on the lone approach road to the port of entry—there is indeed nowhere else to go and nothing else to record—and slowly head back through the main street. Before we leave Sasabe, we stop off, after a brief hesitation, at the only store open for business at 3:00 p.m. on a weekday afternoon. Inside we are immediately greeted by a pert, blonde woman of a certain age, apparently the only employee overseeing the long aisles with well-stocked shelves. We are the only customers. I'm at the back of the store checking out the three different kinds of peanuts the store carries when the employee asks my wife, "Where are you all from?"

My wife replies, "We're from North Carolina."

"Really?" the saleswoman says with a big smile that sets off pleasant laugh lines. "There are engineers coming in here all the time from North Carolina and Virginia. They are all southern gentlemen. If they are not, I put them in their place."

"That's a coincidence," my wife says. Both states are the homes of a number of engineering firms connected to Boeing as well as security companies, including Xe, the reincarnation of Blackwater, Inc.[3]

"Yeah, they work at that secret Project 28 just outside of town. Those secret towers. They come in here all the time to buy stuff. You know. That virtual fence Boeing is building."

The Politics of Fence Building

The immigration field hearing in Dubuque in September 2006, along with the preceding twenty productions staged by Congressman James Sensenbrenner, serves to legitimize and provide credibility for his and other conservative Republican immigration legislation. In sharp contrast, President Bush's bill, supported by a bipartisan contingent in the Senate and the House, is dead in the water. In Washington, timing is everything.

Notwithstanding the failures of ISIS, the major argument for a border fence becomes increasingly justified for reasons of national security against international terrorists. Conservative Democrats and a group of vocal Republicans on the right, along with Minutemen, media pundits, and other interest groups, effectively argue from the same script that potential terrorists who might cross the Mexican border into the United States are a direct risk to national security. In one fell swoop, fear of international terrorists is wedded to immigration policy.[4]

At bottom, this tactic has strong political legs, because fear of another 9/11, when mixed with a fear that we are being overrun by undocumented workers, avoids charges of racism by attracting a sympathetic public response. According to this line of thinking, other hot immigration issues, including amnesty programs for undocumented workers, must be set aside until the Mexican border is secured. The only way to really secure the border is to build a border fence against the terrorists. Such a fence will also serve to stop undocumented workers in their tracks. A border fence thus becomes the simple sound bite solution to complex issues. Interestingly, illegal drugs are all but forgotten in this theory; the new border fence is only about terrorists and illegal immigration.

These untested assertions have become the new common sense. Any fundamental questions about how to construct a border fence are not raised, and the completion of the fence then frames and excludes the need for a national immigration policy or even the need to discuss such a policy.

What is lost in this rush to a simple solution is the fact that international terrorists can find any number of ways to enter this country other than by crossing the Mexican border. The terrorists involved in 9/11 in fact entered on legal visas.[5] The new border fence, backed by sophisticated technology for which this country is famous, is a juggernaut on which politicians of all persuasions find comfortable seats.

Few elected politicians who face debates over immigration in the late summer and fall of 2006 believe they can escape as winners in the November elections. A border fence bill demonstrates that incumbents are strong on national security, and at the same time it bypasses a no-win discussion of immigration policies. Political exigency trumps public debate over the complexities of Mexican border issues and national immigration policy. Politicians are simply unwilling to lose the Hispanic vote. Although the new border fence is in many ways nothing but a stop-gap measure, a delay of a public consideration of broader immigration legislation, it is quite appealing to members of both major political parties.

Any reservations about the efficacy of high-tech solutions to a permeable Mexican border, lessons that should have been learned from the virtual dreams, false claims, and absolute failures of ISIS, are set aside by the two branches of Congress and the administration during the feverish campaigns before the congressional elections of 2006. In place of legislation addressing a coherent national immigration policy, both the House, backed by Congress members including James Sensenbrenner, and the Senate instead pass tidbit legislation that incumbents hope demonstrates to their constituents their hard-line stance on both national security issues and illegal immigration. A product of political exigency, this piecemeal legislation includes the Secure Fence Act of 2006.

President Bush signs the Secure Fence Act of 2006 on October 26, just before voters cast their ballots for the congressperson of their choice. The bill authorizes construction of seven hundred miles of border fencing, to include sensors, cameras, lighting, and other appropriate technologies.

It is crucial to note that in the small print of this new bill the DHS is given full responsibility to decide all aspects of the new fence, including what the exact nature of the fence will be, its component parts, and its placement. President Bush declares at the signing of this legislation, "We're just going to make sure that we build it [the fence] in a spot where it works." Before signing the Secure Fence Act, President Bush also signs a spending bill that allocates $1.2 billion to building the new fence, including technologies such as surface radar.[6]

Institutional memory is in short supply in Chertoff's DHS. More than five years after 9/11, DHS is still plagued by internal woes caused by stuffing two hundred thousand employees from twenty-two different federal agencies under one very large umbrella, even though the department had reorganized itself yet again in 2005. Political ideologues, some with little administrative or management experience, riddle the organizational landscape.[7]

Secretary Chertoff, who takes the reins of DHS from Tom Ridge in 2005, is bolstered at DHS by a phalanx of advisors with little specific knowledge or understanding of the U.S.-Mexico borderlands. The firestorm of public concern leading to the marriage of international terrorism to immigration will soon dissipate before the national economy begins its free fall. But in the spring, summer, and fall of 2006, international terrorism and illegal immigration are preeminent concerns as the Minutemen in California and Arizona effectively kidnap the attention of the national media.[8] A border fence infused with sophisticated technology becomes a major metric by which Chertoff's DHS will be measured by both Congress and the public.

Secretary Chertoff is several steps ahead of this emerging political agenda. Former secretary Ridge, as if ISIS never existed, morphed the hopes and dreams of a virtual border fence into core parcels of the American Shield Initiative (ASI) in 2004. Chertoff then took the short-lived ASI and submerged it within the Secure Border Initiative (SBI) in 2005. Now, working within a more supportive political environment in 2006, he christens several new attempts at border security, eventually ending up with Project 28.

Following the congressional elections of 2006, the political posturing of presidential candidates of both major parties intensifies in the presidential campaigning towards 2008, and the candidates on both sides of the aisle ratchet up their national security rhetoric to expand their campaign war chests. The proclaimed righteousness of a new border fence provides room for all to position themselves as strong on national security while they ignore the wisdom of a fence as well as any detailed discussion of immigration issues.

The national push towards a fence becomes a search for not just any fence, but a perfect fence that will attract campaign dollars, score political points in public debates, and collar potential voters for the primaries. The perfect fence, absent other significant legislation to address major immigration issues, itself becomes a major public policy.[9]

The public's fear of another 9/11, which the Bush administration has successfully employed as a political tactic for some time, in part drives this search for a perfect border fence. At the same time, the far right is very successful in churning racist attitudes towards both illegal and legal immigrants. In general, Democrats do little but try to turn these tendencies to their own advantage at the polls. The ways in which national politics and politicians in the Bush administration, frequently with the full support of the Democrats, frame the search for a perfect fence also predisposes certain border fence models to be accepted pro forma while others are flung onto the scrap heap.[10]

A perfect fence, a tall, strong and impenetrable fence, will keep terrorists from crossing our southern border and, at the same time, once and for all stem the flow of illegal aliens. As the economy begins to worsen, these same illegal immigrants are increasingly blamed for various societal problems. This does nothing so much as hasten the need for such a border fence. What this border fence will actually be, in terms of nuts and bolts—not to mention the feasibility of such an effort along a two-thousand-mile border—is never seriously discussed. Indeed, the real cost for a border fence remains unknown. In the public sphere no voice expresses the slightest doubt that a perfect border fence can be built. Engineering expertise and American gumption will get the job done.

While politicians vying for credibility constantly mention national security and illegal immigration at the southern border, they largely ignore the vulnerability of the four-thousand-mile Canadian border, as well as the United States' extensive coastlines, bays, and inlets. When political ideologies are debated before the public, details are the first victims. There is little discussion during the presidential primaries, or afterward by the Obama and McCain campaigns, of the hard realities of constructing a Mexican border fence from Brownsville to San Diego. While the Obama campaign does suggest that as soon as their candidate takes the oath a host of immigration-related policies immediately will be addressed, it, like the rival McCain campaign, presumes the feasibility and efficacy of a Mexican border fence.

At a minimum, real debate between Senators McCain and Obama during their run for the presidency would have included how a Mexican border fence bolstered the larger strategy and specific tactical plans of DHS and the CBP in confronting international terrorism. Such a national conversation would have been forced to ground itself in deterrence theory, the only justification used by DHS and CBP for the frontal deployment of assets initiated in the early 1990s. How would the border fence, for example, deter the two very different categories of border crossers: international terrorists and undocumented workers?

Given the public firestorm regarding terrorism and illegal immigration, other basic questions that might have been debated are: What are the specific objectives of a border fence? How will these objectives be accomplished by a new border fence? What are the specific measurements by which the success of the fence will be determined? How, in addition, will the CBP patrol this new fence, and what new tactics will be required? Because of changes brought on by a new border fence, how will risk to CBP agents and workers crossing into the United States be minimized? What will be the economic, social, and psychological impacts of this new fence upon residents of border communities? Will the border fence increase the possibility of natural disasters, such as flooding, cross-border wildfires, or contagious diseases? What will be the effects of the fence on migrating wildlife? What kind of public oversight of contracts will ensure that another ISIS is avoided? Although crucial and obvious questions, these and others are never raised by any of the major presidential candidates.

Washington insiders insist a deal has been struck after the primaries between the Obama campaign and the McCain campaign. The McCain campaign and Republicans in Congress agree not to hammer the Obama campaign on security and immigration issues, including the Mexican border fence, as long as congressional Democrats in return continue funding allocations for the Secure Fence Act of 2006. If this quid pro quo is credible, then the compromise allows Obama the ability to claim he is a hardliner on national security issues, including the border fence, at the same time the Republicans are allowed, under the eye of Secretary Chertoff, to continue building the Mexican border fence. In fact, Democrats did allow allocations to continue to flow under the Secure Fence Act throughout the first year of the Obama presidency.[11]

A fundamental problem, of course, is the difficulty of discussing any of these border fence issues because they are pseudosecret, and even when aspects of them can be discussed, the language that is employed often obfuscates interpretations except by experts trained in security-military-engineering-corporate jargon.[12] If the new border fence's exact objectives, theoretical justifications, size, dimensions, materials, capabilities, and placement, among other things, are unknown or unclear to the general public, then openly discussing the topics becomes a betrayal of patriotism in a society in which fear of more 9/11-style attacks still prevails.

What is lost in this faux secrecy is the public's right to be informed—to hear candidates running for election at all levels of government debate their viewpoints and positions before open public forums. The public is effectively denied the opportunity to be informed before entering the voting booth.

In such a political climate defense contractors such as Honeywell are canny opportunists. For defense contractors the perfect border fence is, in the end, nothing more than a chance for outrageous profits, a cash cow that promises to sustain the winning general contractor and secondary contractors and subcontractors for years to come. The commodification of the events of 9/11 and its aftermath brings with it all the inherent contradictions between the vested interests of the defense contractors and the welfare of the general public.

The federal government's failure to take a position on immigration issues leaves border states and nonborder states alike holding the bag. Especially during the second term of President Bush, it became clear that a number of immigration-related problems and their social costs were going to be left to local municipalities, county governments, and state legislatures. To considerable fanfare, some of these entities generated their own immediate solutions to perceived problems caused by illegal aliens. Issues ranged from access to public education to driver's licenses, appropriate taxation, housing, social services, and a variety of other concerns. Solutions ranged from city to city, from state to state, and spanned the political spectrum from creating places of refuge for undocumented workers to sweeping local barrios with the assistance of armed civilians.[13]

DHS's 287(g) program encourages local police, county sheriffs, state police, and Immigration and Customs Enforcement (ICE) to work closely together on the enforcement of immigration laws. This means that law enforcement agencies in border and nonborder states are trained to check the immigration status of individuals (including those already incarcerated), arrest them as necessary, and place them in detention centers. Municipal and county jails become routine holding pens for undocumented workers waiting for adjudication, and local law enforcers work with DHS in the deportation of illegal aliens who are serving time for criminal offenses, including repeated illegal entry into the United States.

After 9/11 private corporations soon constructed a system of detention centers, which they own, operate, and maintain to house the growing number of detainees no longer bonded out under INS's former catch-and-release policy. The only semblance of any attempt at oversight of these detention centers is provided by a single corporate employee at each charged with making sure his company meets the requirements of its DHS contract so that it may be renewed. Staffed by poorly trained guards and other support personnel working at minimum wage, this new detention system soon had two hundred thousand detainees per year under its direct supervision.

CBP Agents Compean and Ramos

National media exposure, fired up by cable rants, blogs, and radio talk shows, is often used to exploit half-truths and fears about immigration policies along the Mexican border in order to divert public attention from other, more crucial immigration issues, including serious examination of the need for a border fence. The media's treatment of the case of El Paso Border Patrol agents Jose A. Compean and Ignacio Ramos is a prime example.

The controversial case, based upon events of February 17, 2005, thirty miles east of El Paso near the village of Fabens, resulted in a brouhaha that stirred a potent base of voters to demand congressional legislation, including the Secure Fence Act of 2006. After the trial, the case took on even greater import as the crucial details receded from the public's memory or were bent to exploit political agendas.

The two Border Patrol agents were patrolling the borderline when they confronted the driver of a van, Osvaldo Aldrete Davila (Aldrete). Aldrete fled, and as he did, Agent Compean fired his Beretta service weapon at him. The agents testified they believed the suspect was not wounded by these shots, but Aldrete did receive superficial wounds. Aldrete escaped to the Mexican side of the Rio Grande.

Agents Ramos and Compean were investigated by the Border Patrol after this incident, as required by Border Patrol policy, then based upon that evidence indicted by a U.S. district attorney, brought to trial, found guilty by a jury of their peers after all evidence was presented by attorneys representing both the prosecution and the defendants, and sentenced by a trial judge to mandated terms in federal penitentiaries. Ramos received an eleven-year sentence; Compean, twelve years.[14]

The case of Compean and Ramos quickly became a rallying point for the Minutemen, their supporters, and other interest groups to whom the conviction of these two CBP agents demonstrated that the rights of illegal immigrants supersede the enforcement of American laws and that criminals are defended while those assigned to uphold federal law are persecuted.[15] At first glance, because of the emphasis in the mass media and the ways in which special interest groups, including the Minutemen, interpreted the case, the reasonable conclusion is that the arrest and conviction of the agents is wrongheaded, counterintuitive, and even tragic.

Unfortunately the legal facts, rarely detailed by those who bemoan their definition of the issues the loudest, do not sustain assertions that the two Border Patrol agents are victims of an out-of-control national immigration policy. Nevertheless, the Compean-Ramos case becomes the poster child for tougher immigration policy among the cable media, Minutemen, bloggers, and a sympathetic portion of the American public from 2005 through 2008.

Supporters of Agents Compean and Ramos maintain that Aldrete was a known Mexican drug smuggler caught in the act. Furthermore, he was not seriously injured in the shooting incident. These two agents, therefore, should be applauded for their actions, and the smuggler, Aldrete, should be prose-cuted to the fullest extent of the law. Only in this way can our nation reaffirm its support for these upstanding agents as well as all the others patrolling the Mexican border. Following that story line, or similar versions repeated ad nauseam by media and others without fact checking, these same two agents then were unfairly tried by a jury and thrown into federal prison. The real criminal, Aldrete, was allowed to go free.[16]

The facts of the case substantially differ from this politicized script. Agents who discharge their weapon while on duty are required by agency policy immediately to report this occurrence to their shift supervisor. The agent involved then fills out a detailed report of the circumstances and ne-cessity for firing. In turn, this report becomes part of a full investigation by the Border Patrol. At the scene, Agents Compean and Ramos both were asked by a supervisor if an assault had occurred. Both agents lied to the supervisor about the assault and then lied again to their supervisor when they failed to tell him one of their service weapons had been discharged. These lies are not minor sins of omission but substantive lapses in formal law enforcement procedures, in which every CBP agent is thoroughly schooled.

These two experienced agents knew the standard procedures, clearly un-derstood why such policies were in place, but then chose to engage in a cover-up of their actions. A jury heard all the relevant legal evidence pre-sented at the trial of Agents Compean and Ramos, and, based upon that evi-dence, reached the verdict that the two were guilty as charged. All legal appeals of Agents Compean and Ramos were rejected by higher courts be-cause they were determined to have no legal merit.

A number of respected professional law enforcement officials I have in-terviewed emphasized that agents Compean and Ramos knew what correct agency procedures required and, nevertheless, willfully ignored those pro-cedures. Moreover, they contaminated the evidence of their actions by dis-posing of the cases of the rounds fired at Aldrete. Those interviewed also agreed that the agents should have been, and were, held to a higher standard than normal citizens because they were federal law enforcement officers.[17]

All Border Patrol agents sign an oath to uphold the agency rules, policies, and laws and spend academy classroom hours, probationary years of employment, and time in professional workshops learning the legal limits and boundaries of all their actions while on duty. But for whatever reasons, these two agents did everything in their power to cover up an investigation of their actions, including both a denial any shooting had occurred and contamination of the scene of the shooting. Therein lies the basis of their criminal offenses.

The often-raised issue of the character of Osvaldo Aldrete Davila has no legal bearing in this case. Border Patrol agents fully understand that his character cannot be used as a justification or rationalization by Compean and Ramos for the criminal behavior in which they engaged.[18]

In interviewing Border Patrol agents about this case, I found very little support for Agents Compean and Ramos among the rank and file or managers. Border Patrol agents readily admitted those two men were guilty as charged and that there is never a moral or legal excuse for an attempted cover-up by agents. They also generally agreed that both Compean and Ramos committed serious crimes by lying about the discharge of a service weapon and then attempting to cover up any evidence of the shooting. Agents who regularly patrol the line do not have to be reminded how difficult their jobs are. But those difficulties never justify, according to the CBP rank and file and supervisors, excusing the two agents for their criminal actions.

At the same time, Border Patrol employees I interviewed genuinely feared former agents Compean and Ramos would be attacked or killed in prison while serving out their terms. Prison officials soon reported, in fact, that both inmates were beaten by members of the general prison population. To prevent future attacks, both men eventually were placed in solitary confinement for their own safety.

Any number of acts of bravery by Border Patrol agents easily could have been highlighted by cable newscasters, the Minutemen, and others frustrated with immigration policy along the Mexican border instead of the sad case of Compean and Ramos. For example, Border Patrol agent Robert Rosas was killed July 23, 2009, while patrolling the line near San Diego.[19]

There are, indeed, many questionable immigration policies and procedures in place. As previously discussed, there is no question that the work of CBP agents patrolling the line is challenging, dangerous, and made more difficult by limitations set by a dysfunctional law enforcement agency. It is unfortunate, however, that none of the exemplary cases of the diligent work and bravery of CBP agents gained the same national attention as the criminal offenses of Agents Compean and Ramos.

In the last days before the inauguration of Barack Obama, President Bush pardoned Compean and Ramos from serving the remainder of their sentences. But the decision by Bush to pardon the two former agents did not exonerate them of their crimes. In fact, Bush chose to let stand their felony convictions. According to an anonymous White House official, President Bush felt that "they were fairly tried and received a just verdict."[20]

The Compean-Ramos case shows that when called upon the Border Patrol can summon the institutional fortitude to police its own organization by demanding every agent follow agency procedures, policies, and laws. Justice in the Compean-Ramos case was duly served. A single case, however, does not prove the agency is without systemic flaws. Instead, the Compean-Ramos case is a clear demonstration that critics on the right flogged the wrong immigration policy horse for three years before President Bush finally ended the controversy. Unfortunately, the case remains phoenixlike, still alluded to by media pundits, Minutemen, and others as part of a legacy of misdeeds sanctioned by the federal government. There is such a legacy, but the Compean-Ramos case is not a part of it.

The Compean and Ramos legal case reduced complex issues into talking points to the neglect of more informed, thoughtful public discussions centered on a number of pressing immigration issues. The political, social, and technological problems of constructing a fence in the U.S.-Mexico borderlands were complexities rarely discussed during that period either by politicians running for election, those already in office, the DHS, the CBP, or any other federal agency or program.

During the eight years of the Bush administration, including the elections of 2006 and 2008 in which Democrats vigorously participated, the absence of thoughtful and open debate about a range of related immigration policies and problems left a political vacuum. While national security and immigration shout fests ruled the blogosphere and the cable networks, most notably the programs of CNN's Lou Dobbs, Secretaries Ridge and Chertoff and their DHS rigorously enforced immigration tactics at least tacitly blessed by the Bush administration. The DHS became committed to building both a low-tech border fence and a high-tech virtual fence that would, it believed, once and for all bring the Mexican border under its control. Under a veil of bureaucratic semisecrecy DHS maintained very high hopes and expectations for two border fence projects.

The American Shield Initiative
Secretary Tom Ridge moved the failed ISIS program into the Department of Homeland Security after the department's creation in 2002.[21] Under the megalithic DHS the U.S. Border Patrol at the same time was merged with the

U.S. Customs Service, and the new bureaucracy was named Customs and Border Protection (CBP). Under Ridge the ISIS program was then moved into CBP.

In 2004 Secretary Ridge's DHS created the American Shields Initiative (ASI), "the goals of which were to address ISIS capability limitations and support the department's antiterrorism mission." DHS handed over the day-to-day management of ASI to the newly created CBP. Seven months later, Chertoff's DHS announced that "ISIS was subsumed within ASI."[22] Thus did Chertoff formally, by little more than a rearrangement of an organization chart, finally execute ISIS.

This paperwork beheading was timely because the victim was burdened by a long history of false claims, technological failures, and budgets for which there was no fiscal accountability. In executing ISIS, Secretary Chertoff and DHS offered up under the auspices of the newly formed CBP the promise of a brand new security program along the Mexican border without ever having to admit the grand disasters of its predecessor. The general public, the media, and even those in Congress who knew better about the disastrous ISIS program all took little note of this bureaucratic sleight of hand.[23]

Secretary Chertoff grossly underestimated CBP's ability to manage efficiently the rebranded ASI. A reshuffling of responsibilities on Chertoff's DHS spreadsheet could not mask, however, the long-standing structural and cultural problems inherited by Customs and Border Protection. Merging two poorly managed agencies premised upon political cronyism, U.S. Customs and the U.S. Border Patrol, into one new, rapidly expanding agency guaranteed that the bureaucratic offspring bore the malfunctioning genes of both parents. In this case the historically weaker agency, the Border Patrol, immediately lunged into turf wars with Customs over resources, each agency viewing the other's losses as its gains.

This zero-sum mentality benefited neither Customs nor the Border Patrol. Border Patrol agents, now CBP agents, had new titles, but their daily jobs patrolling the line changed little. Similarly, even though they were now also CBP agents, Customs agents continued to police the ports of entry as always, although new technologies of surveillance were beginning to filter their way. In practice, although wearing the same insignia on the sleeves of their uniform, these two agencies maintained separate institutional identities as they eyed their counterparts with suspicion.

In 2001 there were approximately 9,600 Border Patrol agents. By 2006 there were an additional 3,000. In December 2008, the Border Patrol announced it had reached its goal of 18,000 agents.[24] Given its fundamental flaws, a much larger Border Patrol, however, did not necessarily mean a more productive or more efficient Border Patrol. Border Patrol managers, for example, still lack basic skills and expertise in fiscal oversight and policy implementation. Moreover, the additional heft of the Border Patrol, now the largest federal law enforcement agency in the land, makes its pairing with Customs all the more tenuous. Border Patrol leadership is no longer willing to be treated as the lesser agency of the two and now possesses the budget, the employees, and the hardware to position the Border Patrol as the dominant agency within CBP.

Under Chertoff's DHS the Border Patrol is hobbled by the same fundamental problems that have dogged it since its inception in 1924; Customs is little better.[25] The Border Patrol remains a top-down hierarchy in which cronyism still rules the day, and it is no better equipped to manage the ASI program than it was ISIS.

The Border Patrol's antiquated organizational culture is still one in which harassment of female agents is symptomatic of significant deficiencies in leadership, management, and professional standards of law enforcement, and the agency continues to be run at the sector level by a generation of men with little formal education and limited experience within the Washington beltway.[26] Generations of Border Patrol supervisors have little or no formal management training beyond what any of them who were NCOs in the American military may have acquired. MBAs and attorneys remain anathema in this law enforcement agency, as do managers with military experience beyond the rank of lieutenant. Frequently when these professionals are hired by the Border Patrol, they are employed on a part-time or consultant basis.

When former military officers apply for Border Patrol jobs, for which they are more than qualified based upon their training and experience, they are told they must start at the bottom of the CBP ranks, at the GL-9 level, and work their way up. Experienced officers at the grade of O-3 or above go elsewhere.

At the top of the Border Patrol hierarchy are political appointees regularly installed by whichever party is in power. Under the Bush administration, these appointees possessed excellent ideological credentials, but as former political advisors, policy wonks, and party supporters they frequently lacked the professional law enforcement background and experience to make sound management decisions and to suggest policy-driven agendas.[27]

Expertise on the U.S.-Mexico borderlands is sorely lacking among BP executives. While some in the highest ranks certainly have served along the Mexican border, their experience is from the 1980s and 1990s. Occasional trips to the border provide them only a superficial familiarity with challenges in the new millennium. Following the administrative tenor established by Secretary Chertoff, these administrators demand rather than request, assume rather than ascertain, and are immune to feedback from those directly influenced by their decisions and policies. Their view from Washington is, in short, myopic, ill-informed, and reactive rather than proactive.

For DHS secretary Chertoff to have handed over the creation and management of the new ASI program to the CBP clearly demonstrates how unfamiliar he and his advisors were with the inadequacies of the newly named agency. One can only conclude that, at best, Chertoff kept believing in CBP because he had no other agency to which he could turn. DHS could never admit that the Border Patrol and Customs were totally incapable of implementing ASI. To do so would have revealed the fallibility and impotence of DHS. A part of Secretary Chertoff's hubris consisted in a total unwillingness to assume any responsibility for the failures of the CBP, even though Chertoff knew CBP could not succeed.

Constructed on the ruins of ISIS, ASI's stated goals are almost identical to those of the previously failed border fence program: "Maintain legacy systems operations; provide surveillance of the entire land border between ports of entry; integrate surveillance capabilities with agent operations; provide decision support capabilities; support rapid and flexible deployment of surveillance assets; provide reliable, all-environment, 24-hour surveillance capability; improve collaboration and interoperability with mission partners and state, local, tribal, and federal enforcements; use state-of-the-market technology to create a cost-effective system, and provide open architecture solutions."

Exact spending for these programs is unnecessarily difficult to pin down, as various numbers are paraded out at one time or the other as if to mask or hide specific allocations. INS and DHS secretaries Ridge and Chertoff spent approximately $340.3 million on ISIS and ASI from 1997 through 2005. As of September 2005, CBP still held on to an additional $112.1 million of unspent funds budgeted for ASI.[28]

The Secure Border Initiative

Barely a year after Secretary Chertoff created the American Shield Initiative, then handed off the program to CBP, he directed ASI to be "subsumed" under the auspices of yet another invented program, the Secure Border Initiative (SBI). SBI was initially described as a "broader border and interior enforcement strategy."[29]

In light of serious concerns with CBP's management of the ASI, the DHS had its own Investment Review Board examine the status of its brand new border security program. This investigation and report can be seen as a straightforward attempt by DHS to determine and document the failures of CBP in managing SBI. Or, given the reality of political institutions such as

DHS, this investigation may be viewed as DHS's last-minute attempt to protect its own best interests and image.

The second interpretation seems closer to the facts. In a separate study the U.S. Government Accountability Office (GAO) independently analyzed DHS's review of the American Shield Initiative under CBP and broadly concluded:

> The ASI program had not established the people and process capabilities required for effective program management. As of August 2005, it had filled 30 of its 47 office positions, and it had defined roles and responsibilities for only 3 of them. In addition, while the program had defined and begun implementing a plan to manage program risks, it had not yet defined key acquisition management processes, such as effective project planning, and contract tracking and oversight. *As a result, the program risked repeating the inadequate contract management oversight that led to a number of problems in deploying, and operating and maintaining ISIS technology.*"[30]

Equally alarming, the GAO found that DHS's Investment Review Board had not approved planning documents for the ASI, including operation needs that directly addressed "known limitations in ISIS capabilities and supporting CBP counter-terrorism efforts through enhanced border surveillance capabilities." The Investment Review Board had in fact turned down the ASI's "program management plan, acquisition plan, and a preliminary operational requirements document."[31]

The GAO report also discovered that the brand new ASI program was not efficiently tied to other programs and departments within DHS. Nor, and this is particularly noteworthy, had DHS's relationship with ASI ever been clearly delineated within DHS organizational architecture. Incredibly, fiscal oversight of the ASI acquisition management process, including oversight of contractors, contracts, and specific project plans, all under the direct supervision of CBP, was not yet in place. This lack of fiscal oversight of the brand new ASI, according to the GAO, was identical to the same acquisition problems with the earlier ISIS.[32]

After ASI had been ongoing for a year under the leadership of CBP, the one and only accolade thrown its way was that its program managers had initiated a risk management process that was defined as a basic requirement in assuring adequate fiscal oversight.[33] But this lone accolade was only a fundamental prerequisite of a viable program.

Secretary Chertoff's DHS fully accepted GAO's devastating analysis and critique of its new ASI program. Said Chertoff, "We agree with the overall thrust of the report," and, further, that the GAO report "identifies key issues regarding effective program management of ASI."[34] DHS then promptly divested itself of any blame for ASI, assigning all the program's failures to CBP, as if by doing so it somehow absolved itself of any and all management errors in judgment, expertise, or policy decisions.

For the exact same reasons DHS should never have handed over programmatic management of the ASI to CBP in the first place, CBP was the perfect DHS agency to take the fall. The ideologically correct and vetted political appointees heading CBP were not about to contradict or debate their boss in public, nor was anyone else who witnessed ASI sinking into the CBP management quagmire.[35] CBP was no more prepared to direct the ASI program than it had been to lead ISIS in the late 1990s, but Bush-appointed ideologues, along with career managers in CBP, would never join the ranks of federal whistleblowers.

Secretary Chertoff could not acknowledge that the new CBP was as incapable and inadequate an agency as it had proven itself to be. After all, any problems in the U.S. Border Patrol and U.S. Customs nominally had been erased by Chertoff's predecessor, Tom Ridge, and any minor issues finally eliminated by Chertoff when he reorganized DHS in 2005. The two agencies now merged into one much larger entity that was growing each day with new recruits from the Border Patrol academy in New Mexico. But Secretary Chertoff could and did blame CBP for any and all problems associated with the SBI. DHS named CBP as the fall guy for its toddler ASI, Chertoff spinning political gold from an otherwise wasted $340 million.

At this point, with the floodwaters at the door of his executive suite, Chertoff launched and marketed SBI. In effect, he asserted that since CBP had miserably failed its ASI assignment, DHS was picking up the fallen flag and marching bravely forward on the field of battle with a new super-widget, SBI, which would resolve all existing border issues in one fell swoop of the functionary's pen.

In Chertoff's bureaucratic discourse, failures of the two previous programs, ISIS and ASI, were sins of the past already long forgotten. ASI, the diseased program, was going to be incorporated into a healthy, squeaky clean, new SBI directly supervised by DHS.

Secretary Chertoff's DHS made no reference, of course, to the wasted $340 million spent on ISIS and ASI or the additional security risks presumably encountered by this country because of DHS's own ineptitude in assigning ASI to CBP. Nor did Chertoff point out the thousands of undocumented workers who continue to cross our international border with Mexico looking for jobs or joining or rejoining family members.

Said another way, after five years, several hundred million dollars, and two DHS major border initiatives since 9/11, conditions along the Mexican border are little changed.

Notwithstanding ISIS and ASI, Chertoff boldly asserted that the path to success was now finally assured, because SBI, DHS's newest attempt to bring order to the Mexican border, was "a comprehensive strategy to achieve border security and interior enforcement goals." Further, CBP could not repeat the failures of the recent past because DHS resolved all the problems outlined in the critical GAO report. Chief among these solutions to past failures was that "CBP has implemented an effective process for program management . . . that will provide a solid foundation as SBI proceeds toward achieving the goal of preventing illegal entry into the United States."[36]

This brand new, can't-fail CBP program management is worth detailing in full:

> CBP has created a SBI Program Management Office (PMO) in the Office of Policy and Planning, a component of the Commissioner's Office with direct reporting responsibility to the Commissioner. Secretary Chertoff's emphasis on the priority of SBI is reflected in the level of daily supervision of this effort by the CHP Acting Commissioner, and the direct management of the relevant activities by senior CBP leaders including the Chief of the Border Patrol, Assistant Commissioners for Information and Technology, Finance, Field Operations, CBP Air, Human Resources Management, Training and other offices. The Acting Commissioner and several of these senior managers attend the weekly "War Room" meetings, where the Secretary and other senior DHS leadership review the progress of the SBI. This same group of CBP senior managers are members of the SBI Executive Steering Committee, chaired by the Commissioner, which meets monthly or more if necessary, to discuss the overall SBI effort and issues of cross-agency concern.[37]

SBI is thus going to be successful, according to DHS, not only because CBP has new program management in place, but also because CBP will be more highly integrated into DHS. Bureaucratic jargon and management structures aside, DHS is saying it will no longer allow CBP to screw up. How? DHS will be constantly advising CBP to make sure that professional procedures are followed under the new SBI, most notably the "acquisition process," which includes fiscal oversight over contractors: "This organizational structure provides the SBI PMO [Program Management Office] with the advantage of drawing on the full range of relevant expertise and capabilities within the CBP to ensure successful management of the effort. Leaders from the operational side of the agency provide overall project management, while *the acquisition process for SBI technology and infrastructure is supervised by highly trained and certified program managers from the Office of Information and Technology with extensive experience implementing major federal systems.*" Eleven new specific measures are then outlined by DHS detailing how CBP cannot fail to ensure full accountability over all contracts and spending for the new SBI.[38]

If these DHS assurances are not enough, the building of a border fence will also be facilitated by Congressman Jim Sensenbrenner's Real ID Act of 2005. The very same politician who engineered the immigration field hearings also authored this relatively obscure piece of post-9/11 legislation, which received little attention. Upon a closer reading, that bill is not only about driver's licenses, but it also essentially gives to Chertoff's DHS the sweeping legal right to waive all laws and regulations governing the construction of the new border fence. SBI will not face any delays, because DHS can use the right of eminent domain to take land from private owners along the border, condemn the land, offer a fair market price, and purchase the land to build the fence.

Because of the Real ID Act and Rep. Sensenbrenner's rare legislative leadership, DHS can ignore all environmental laws or concerns that might delay the construction.[39] In the name of national security, Sensenbrenner's legislation circumvents the powers of the Environmental Protection Agency or any other federal, state, or local entity designed to protect the public's greater welfare.

By March 2006, less than a year after the initial launch of SBI, DHS had redefined the major purposes of SBI. In this newest manifestation it still is a "comprehensive approach of the Department of Homeland Security to secure the United States borders." The two major components of SBI are "border control" and "interior enforcement," but the ways in which these two objectives are to be met are now outlined in more detail. The strategic goals of the first component are "to detect and respond to all cross-border crime; to end 'catch and release' of non-Mexican illegal aliens; and to deter cross-border crime." This would be accomplished by the use of technologies including cameras, radar, and sensors. The second strategic goal of SBI, new on the menu, is to "identify and remove incarcerated aliens, immigration fugitives, and violators; to build strong compliance and enforcement programs for law-abiding employers; and to uproot the infrastructure of illegal immigration."[40]

To clarify, what we have here is a major change in Border Patrol and immigration policy under the guise of tweaking this third-generation border fence program. On the one hand, advanced technologies will be employed in SBI to both detect and deter "all cross-border crime," presumably including illegal immigration and illegal drugs. International terrorists are not specifically mentioned. Presumably "advanced technologies" refers to a border fence, including a virtual fence. Given this opaque federal jargon, the rest of the specific details of this first SBI objective are left to the reader's imagination. The deterrence assumption behind all previous border security, including all policing of the border by the Border Patrol, a theoretical assumption upon which all previous border security strategies have been premised, is left in place. But a new "detect" component is added by DHS to the mix. Just how the "detect" component will be achieved is not mentioned.

The second objective of SBI is to be met by another new strategy, that of "interior enforcement." This strategy, of course, is not new at all; in fact, it is a return to the 1990s and the days before El Paso Sector chief Silvestre Reyes and Operation Blockade. Only the exact details of this "interior enforcement" are new: the new strategies and tactics, including the "detention" and "removal" process, "employers programs," and the promised uprooting of the "infrastructure of illegal immigration."

Reliance solely on the frontal deployment of assets along the Mexican border has, according to the newest tenets of SBI, officially come to an end. There are no parades, no farewells, no retirement speeches, and no formal obituary for this defunct border strategy initiated by Reyes. Why? An announcement of the death of a major CBP policy in place since the early 1990s might require specific reasons and justifications for its replacement.

The explanations for a new strategy would have to include why the former can't-miss strategy failed, how much its failure cost, and who is responsible for the failure. And they would have to include how the third-generation strategy, SBI, is expected to work. In simple English, what is missing is: What are the objectives of SBI? What are the standards SBI is expected to meet? And how will SBI's successes be objectively measured?

SBI is the first new strategic overhaul of border security since the early 1990s. Although presented in oblique bureaucratese embedded in a terminology that assures institutional deniability, SBI, more than another bureaucratic reshuffling of the organizational architecture—although its ultimate successes are premised upon such a reshuffling—represents a significant turning point in Mexican border enforcement. Secretary Chertoff and his staff assure the public that DHS's Secure Border Initiative cannot fail.

Yet the invention of SBI more than five years after 9/11 amounts to little less than a Bush administration coverup of the failure of its Department of Homeland Security to control and secure the Mexican border. No one, least of all the public, seems to notice.

SBInet

The Department of Homeland Security bills SBI essentially as a grand program that will resolve all border security issues. But then DHS announces an add-on, the Secure Border Initiative Network (SBInet). SBInet "will support all components and strategic objectives of SBI by integrating technologies, infrastructure, rapid response capability and personnel into a comprehensive border protection system." Further, "The goal of SBInet is to provide the stakeholder, CBP inspectors and the Air and Marine interdiction agents tasked with securing the borders of the United States, with every advantage in denying the illegal entry of people and contraband into the country. . . . Through the right mix of personnel, rapid response capability, infrastructure and technology, SBInet will give our front line stakeholders the best possible environment to effectively detect, respond to, apprehend and remove individuals attempting illegal entry." Physical barriers, says DHS, will be used. Finally, "SBInet will serve to further the goals of the Secure Border Initiative" because "SBInet will steward investment in the SBI goals toward maximum effectiveness."[41]

While the SBI Program Executive Office in DHS directly administers SBI, the SBInet Program Management Office is going to administer SBInet. But who will monitor the new SBInet program management? None other than Customs and Border Protection. Lest there are concerns about the management skills of CBP, DHS managers will keep a watchful eye on both CBP and SBInet. At least that is how it is supposed to work in the new DHS organization chart.

DHS also announces at about this same time that it plans to add additional procurement staff to monitor all SBI and SBInet contracts to contractors.[42] GAO reports, as suggested, have repeatedly detailed a severe lack of contract oversight staff directly leading to the failures of ISIS and ASI. The same reports also have documented DHS and CBP inability to fill funded staff positions in a timely manner. DHS announces that after it has filled these new positions—it does not set a deadline—it will have a total of nine employees charged with fiscal oversight of SBI and SBInet.

SBI TI

In a matter of months DHS announces a second offshoot of SBI, the Secure Border Initiative Tactical Initiative, or just plain SBI TI. TI will focus upon "fencing, roads, and lighting intended to enhance U.S. Border Patrol agents' ability to respond to the area of the illegal entry and bring the situation to a law enforcement resolution." Fencing is divided into two kinds: pedestrian fencing, designed to keep border crossers from illegally entering the United

States on foot; and vehicle fencing, designed to discourage vehicles, primarily those driven by drug smugglers, from entering.[43]

Although crucial to a comprehensive border security program, SBInet and SBI TI appear to be DHS seat-of-the-pants afterthoughts to their already overly complex organizational architecture. At best these two new programs attempt to refine and tweak the specific responsibilities and duties of a bureaucracy that repeatedly has failed to achieve its objectives. But Secretary Chertoff's DHS saves the biggest bombshell for the very last.

The SBI Systems Integrator

Five and one-half years after 9/11, after ISIS, ASI, SBI, SBInet, and SBI TI— in short after years of DHS and CBP planning and spending—Chertoff's DHS admits it has no coherent plan for "gaining operational control of the border." Instead, DHS has yet another brand new plan: *it will hire a defense contractor to develop a new plan.*

Chertoff takes meticulous care to downplay the implications of this decision. Its substance is first outlined in early January 2006 in a DHS letter responding to the GAO report highly critical of ASI.[44] In this relatively obscure exchange between DHS and the GAO, DHS announces it henceforth will rely on the private sector "to provide the comprehensive solution to the challenge of gaining operational control of the border." DHS plans to publish a request for proposal (RFP), which will then be awarded in March 2006 "to the successful bidder, who will then be crowned the *SBI Systems Integrator.*"[45]

In Chertoff's program du jour a primary defense contractor, which in the best of organization jargon he names the SBI Systems Integrator, will take on all the responsibilities, planning, and design that DHS and CBP never accomplished. Through a federal contract bidding process, defense contractors will propose border security solutions to DHS. In turn, DHS will purportedly choose the border security vision, design, and supporting hardware it most admires.

America's private defense contractors are asked to do what Chertoff's DHS and CBP could never do. In best face-saving fashion, DHS makes no mention of previous failed programs or cost to taxpayers quickly approaching one-half billion dollars. Our country's private sector will ride to the rescue. The cowboy who dismounts will, after receiving fair payment for his or her services, presumably wave a magic wand over the Mexican border, and the borderlands miraculously will be transformed by "comprehensive solutions," which include the integration of a low-tech fence with a high-tech virtual fence.

It is worth detailing the list of solutions that the DHS cannot accomplish but the SBI Systems Integrator will now provide . The SBI Systems Integrator:

> Fully integrates and balances the tradeoffs of personnel, technology and infrastructure requirements. Addresses the need to coordinate operations and share information among all relevant DHS agencies and other federal, state, local and tribal law enforcement, defense, legal and intelligence agencies. Evaluates the illegal entry threat against the current level of resources, prioritizes the shortfalls based on areas of greatest operational need, and provides a comprehensive road map for achieving full operational control of the border in the shortest possible time. Includes a detailed and comprehensive set of performance measures to ensure we have a robust ability to view and understand the impact of adding resources to ensure that the expected improvement in operational capabilities actually are occurring.[46]

Just two months later, by March 2006, DHS restates, arguably redefines, its motives for asking the defense industry to save the day by creating real and pragmatic solutions leading to control of the Mexican border. CBP emphasizes that SBInet will be based upon "best practices, rigorous governance, and accountable management." In addition the ruins of ISIS and ASI, obliquely referred to as "existing assets and lessons learned," are also added to this narrative. DHS also states that the new SBI Systems Integrator, the defense contractor who wins the contract bid, will be a full partner in SBI.[47]

Notably absent from the original justifications for involvement of the private sector is the need for DHS to secure full control of the border in the shortest time possible. To admit time is a vital factor in securing the border draws unwanted attention to DHS's previous failures. Also missing in this latest redefinition is reference to the need to share all relevant intelligence to other DHS agencies and federal, state, and local entities.

Hiring a private SBI Systems Integrator immediately after the congressional elections of 2006 and before the primaries and presidential election of 2008 conveniently supports the deal made by Democrats and Republicans to downplay immigration issues and policies. DHS is in effect telling the public that it no longer must worry, because all of our needless worries are soon going to be in the hands of the new SBI Systems Integrator.

Concerns about the American defense industry aside, Chertoff's DHS hands over the nuts and bolts of a major immigration strategy, the border fence, to a private contractor. This is undeniably a smart political move for DHS, because from this day forth it can blame the SBI Systems Integrator for any subsequent programmatic failures while taking credit for all successes. The border fence in all its as yet unspecified shapes, forms, and contortions is nevertheless the key component in border security, which, in turn, is defined by both political parties as a necessity for all future immigration reform.

In this political context the line between strategy and policy is thin. In the absence of viable policies in place, the border fence security strategy becomes a de facto major immigration policy in and of itself. The border fence is bound to have an impact upon immigration flows of illegal workers, illegal drugs, the public safety of agents and illegal crossers, and border communities, among others.

Regardless of their business acumen, private defense contractors must never be allowed to develop or formulate key strategic components of immigration policy. In our democracy we have an elected Congress, an elected president, and an appointed secretary of state to develop and put into place immigration policies and laws and, as well, to take responsibility for them.

While hiring a defense contractor provides DHS another political buffer when things go wrong, it still leaves the actual operation of the new security infrastructure to Customs and Border Protection. By hiring an SBI Systems Integrator, Chertoff's DHS finally concludes that CBP is incapable of envisioning, designing, and planning a border fence. Ironically enough, DHS, by eliminating the role of CBP as programmatic leader, then loses out on all of CBP's experience and knowledge, which might have been incorporated in the construction of the fence. And when the fence is finished, it is this same CBP that will be expected to police the borderline.

But even as DHS excludes any significant input by CBP agents into the border fence, the department does not remove CBP from a role in the general oversight of the new SBI Systems Integrator. While the vision for border security, design, planning, and construction belongs to the new SBI Systems Integrator, CBP, under DHS's careful management eye, is still responsible for major oversight of the project. Even after CBP has continually failed miserably as program manager, it is once again called upon by DHS to play a role. CBP is always a convenient fall guy when things go wrong.

Very few in Washington are alarmed by the announcement of an SBI Systems Integrator. A bill at $429 million for ISIS and ASI, however, is not acceptable to a very small handful of congresspersons from both parties along with a few agency officials with good memories. One among them is Rep. Bennie Thompson (D-Mississippi), who has not forgotten DHS's exaggerated promises or its previous spending.[48] That spending, of course, does not count the cost of the new SBI and its mutated siblings or the newly announced SBI Systems Integrator. The first virtual fence contract is estimated at $20 million, but subsequent contracts may be much higher.

A small group of administrators and politicians, buttressed by DHS's own internal reports, no longer believe that the SBI program, including SBInet, SBI TI, and the SBI Systems Integrator, could be properly managed and held accountable. Instead, a fistful of informed critics believe that fundamental management and procurement programs within DHS, for all the organizational reshuffling instigated by Secretary Chertoff, fail adequately to guard against programmatic failures and wasteful spending.

As early as July 2005 DHS's own inspector general, Richard L. Skinner, expressed grave concerns over operations within his own very large bureaucracy. In his study Skinner found that there was a lack of certified program managers in place throughout DHS and that no standardized department code or procedures for program management existed in the department. He reported that DHS placed a higher organization value upon the expedition of contracts to private industry than upon an accurate and cautious auditing process. Further, Skinner reported that DHS lacked, in spite of protests to the contrary, adequate numbers of contract procurement managers. Workloads among managers, for example, were unequally distributed to the point that one manager might oversee $3 million in contracts, and another, $30 million. Proper oversight of contracts was also deficient. Management and procurement oversight practices required major changes in DHS staffing and resources—changes that could not be rectified by another change of DHS's organization chart. DHS's own inspector general then made five detailed recommendations to remedy these systemic problems.[49]

Rep. Harold Rogers (R-Ky.) is one of a tiny number of senior members of the Homeland Security Appropriations Subcommittee in the House who expresses grave concerns about SBI and SBInet. Says Rogers: "We've been at this juncture before. We have been presented with expensive proposals for elaborate border technology that have eventually proved to be ineffective and wasteful systems, such as the Integrated Surveillance Intelligence System and America's Shield Initiative." Rogers insists DHS develop a comprehensive strategic plan for SBI. Another congressman, Martin Olva Sabo (D-Minn.), questions the fundamental role of the private sector as SBI Systems Integrator. Says Sabo, "I'm worried that DHS thinks that the solution is to hire a private technology company to run the SBI, and then sit back and watch."[50]

More than a year after DHS announces it will hire an SBI Systems Integrator, Inspector General Richard Skinner again reports to Congress that DHS is still not ready to provide adequate program management and fiscal oversight over SBI, SBInet, or an SBInet Systems Integrator. Skinner testifies that "the department [DHS] hasn't yet laid the foundation" for these new programs. Again, Skinner states that DHS had not hired enough staff to oversee the procurement contracts with the private sector.

Rep. Mike Rogers (R-Ala.), in direct response to the testimony of DHS's inspector general, declares, "This is now too cloudy for comfort." Another DHS official responding to these accusations by the DHS inspector general admits there is a problem. However, he tells Congress that DHS will have an adequate number of procurement staff by the summer of 2007.[51]

Industry Day

In late January 2006, DHS secretary Chertoff holds Industry Day at the Reagan Building. More than four hundred representatives of the private sector attend the affair. Attendees are treated to a selection of session speakers, including Michael P. Jackson, DHS deputy secretary; Deborah Spero, acting commissioner of CBP; Gregory Giddens, director of the Executive Office, DHS; Kevin Stevens, acting director of CBP's SBI Program Management Office; and representatives from CBP's SBInet project office and procurement office.[52]

The list of four hundred representatives reads like a Who's Who of national and international defense contractors. At the top of the official list of contractors is 3001, Inc., an entity with an address in Fairfax Virginia. Last on the list is Zenyon, Inc., in Maple Lawn, Maryland. Honeywell, Inc., representatives attend Industry Day even though the multinational decides not to compete as a prime contractor for the SBI Systems Integrator.

Also on the list are executives from industry giants Ericsson, Boeing, Lockheed Martin, Northrop Grumman, and Raytheon. These five international corporations eventually become the prime contract bidders in the race to win the general contract as the SBI Systems Integrator. Seven representatives from L-3 Communications, the defense contractor that played such an instrumental role in the failures of the ISIS program, also attend Industry Day.[53]

Deputy Secretary Michael Jackson, leaving no question that after six years his agency possesses any comprehensive border security strategy, urges the crowd of contractors "to come back and tell us how to do our business."

In turn, Lockheed spokesman Jeff Adams, reflecting the general perspective of the defense contractors present at Industry Day, promises to "propose a solution that will enable our government to obtain operational control of our borders."[54]

The five primary defense contractors, their engineering teams, like Honeywell's, at work on their border proposals long before DHS officially announces the RFP, submit their RFPs to secure the Mexican border. None of these proposals are burdened by the historical failures and lessons to be learned from ISIS or the ASI. Nor are these proposals tainted by the crash and total destruction of Predator 2, the Border Patrol's $6.5 million drone selected to serve as a prototype for border surveillance in unpopulated border areas. The aircraft goes down in April 2006 near Tubac, Arizona.[55]

Northrop Grumman submits a proposal relying heavily on unmanned drones to patrol and surveil the border region. Lockheed Martin, in contrast, proposes blimps to accomplish the same task. Tethered blimps have already been used with some success along the border to provide surveillance in the remotest of border locations. Raytheon's proposal, in contrast to Grumman's and Lockheed's, envisions "letting agents watch incidents unfold on Google Earth."[56] The proposal of industry giant Boeing details a series of eighteen hundred permanent towers along the border, each of which will support sophisticated surveillance equipment.

One can naively argue that DHS's contract process allows the best ideas of these multinationals to rise to the top—or one can accept the fact that each of these multinationals, as in the case of Honeywell, holds a corporate vision and business plan of Mexican border security long before its engineers ever sit down at the planning table. In every case this overriding corporate vision is predicated by existing product or supply lines that require little, if any, new research and development. In each corporation's proposal, the vital parts of the security technology are already gathering dust in their own warehouses or the warehouses of second-tier suppliers.

There is, therefore, absolutely no need to waste valuable time learning about the uniqueness of the U.S.-Mexico borderlands as it might impact any attempts to bring it under full operational control. There is no need to waste time in discussions of the demonstrated ability of undocumented workers and drug traffickers to respond rapidly to changing Border Patrol tactics. Nor is it necessary to waste time discussing the potential impact of new security technologies on resident American and Mexican populations along both sides of the border. Under the dominant corporate paradigm, the history, culture, social problems, topographies, and populations of border communities are all irrelevant in developing border security based upon a virtual border fence.[57]

Thus, all of these talented executives cum engineers seated around the corporate planning tables do not have to wrestle with the hard facts that millions of illegal aliens have crossed and recrossed the Mexican border, frequently supported by networks of criminals whose economic livelihoods depend on the status quo, and that Mexican drug cartels are heavily invested in this same status quo, bringing with them the leverage of billions in assets and an experienced labor force of violent criminals, savvy lawyers, and corrupt government officials reaching into the highest echelons of the Mexican federal government and to the lowest levels in counties like Hidalgo and Cameron in South Texas.[58] Then there are the international terrorists, terrorists highly trained and adept at crossing national borders.

These considerations aside, each defense contractor looks at its product inventory languishing on the shelves, or at its supply chain capable of manufacturing and delivering existing products on an on-time basis. These security products are the foundation upon which each contractor develops its comprehensive security strategy in a bid to become SBInet Systems Integrator.

What we have in Grumman, Boeing, and the others is less the creation of innovative and practical border security systems by the best minds money can buy than a fire sale on last year's damper flapper. The most challenging task, given their business approach to becoming SBI Systems Integrator, is to transform the company's damper flapper into a sophisticated, cutting-edge security technology worthy of being bragged about by Secretary Chertoff. The marketing departments of all these primary bidders possess talented personnel who are more than qualified to accomplish this product rebranding.

How can last year's hodgepodge of old security gizmos be rebranded to justify the big federal dollars future contracts may soon demand? Chertoff's DHS needs a high-profile winner. Pushed and pulled by an aroused public bedazzled by immigration fire and brimstone preached by the Minutemen and media pundits, along with other special interest groups, the DHS decision makers are highly motivated to find a comprehensive solution to border security, or, at the very least, to pick an SBI Systems Integrator that will become DHS's next excuse for failure.[59]

The multinationals have no difficulty in placing a price tag on their respective damper flappers. The defense contractors, like Honeywell, spend a great amount of time and expertise determining the value of the product. In this process they are not burdened by the same rules of the free market that govern smaller businesses. Instead, they base that value on a certain set of assumptions that exclude the actual cost of the item. In the case of DHS's SBI Systems Integrator, their guiding principle in determining the value of their product is very easy: How much is the federal government willing to pay? DHS is willing to pay a modest amount for an initial strategic plan and prototype, in the range of $20 million. Overall, DHS believes that a virtual fence all along the Mexican border may cost in the range of $2 billion.[60]

These days a $20 million federal contract is considered small potatoes. The primary defense contractors have their eye on the total price tag of a virtual fence spanning the entire border. They well know that once projects are underway, exploding budgets and cost overruns are more common than not. Drones, computers, satellite uplinks, and any and all sophisticated technological solutions, in addition to the cost of inflation during construction, could shoot potential budgets into the $30 billion range—or, since no price tag for the virtual border fence or its brethren has been floated, much higher. All these technological gadgets, of course, require training and retraining of personnel to properly operate them, along with maintenance contracts and replacement contracts as the equipment ages.

Further down the line after construction comes the "tweaking" of the technology, a fundamental engineering assumption to bringing the system into full operation. Like Honeywell, all these corporations assume their products will be tweaked while in use. This practice, as discussed earlier, discounts any impact upon the safety of human lives while the system is brought up to standards. There is, as suggested earlier, an inherent and unrealized risk in the tweaking process when the well-being of illegal aliens, border agents, and members of communities on both sides of the borderline is considered. Little consideration, if any, is given to the effect of failures upon human lives or their cost in human suffering. If you are a defense contractor, your first and only concern is winning the business.

When DHS hands over Mexican border security to the private sector in the form of the SBI Systems Integrator, national security becomes another sorry example of commodification. It becomes another product, bringing into play the same economic dynamics as the buying and selling of the most mundane of services. Only in this case the welfare of the American public is at stake.

On September 21, 2006, Chertoff's DHS announces that Boeing, Inc., is the winning bidder for SBI Systems Integrator. Secretary Chertoff tells the press, "SBInet will integrate the latest technology and infrastructure to interdict illegal immigration and stop threats attempting to cross borders. This strategic partnership allows the department to exploit private sector ingenuity and expertise to *quickly* secure our nation's borders." The press release further outlines DHS's future hopes and dreams of its anointed defense contractor: "SBInet will provide frontline personnel advantages in securing the nation's land borders by fielding the most effective mix of current and next generation technology, infrastructure, and response platforms."[61]

Boeing explains its success in the bidding process by suggesting that its technological strategy for control of the Mexican border is in fact low risk, that all its sophisticated technology along the border, "has been proven to work." This brag is better interpreted as Boeing engineers reaching back into their old inventory (or the inventory of their suppliers), wiping off the dust, and rebranding these security products.

According to Boeing, Inc., their new virtual fence will be fully deployed all along the border in three years' time.[62] Then the Mexican border will, at long last, be operationally secured.

Project 28

Soon after DHS awards its contract for SBI Systems Integrator to Boeing, Inc., the defense contractor announces that its design for a virtual border fence is predicated upon permanent towers on which sophisticated surveillance equipment will be mounted. Boeing plans to build, as a working prototype system, nine towers on the Mexico-Arizona border south of Tucson. The towers will be able to completely surveil, according to Boeing, 90 percent to 95 percent of a twenty-eight-mile swath of the border. Boeing names this working prototype Project 28, or P-28.[63]

Few question DHS's selection of Boeing as SBI Systems Integrator. In spite of Secretary Chertoff's public confidence in handing over the design, planning, and construction of the virtual wall to Boeing, its record is in truth a mixed bag. For example, Boeing was quick to praise itself for promptly delivering baggage screening devices to airports after 9/11, but critics pointed out that the Boeing machines had unusually high false alarm rates. Major defense contractor Boeing has, in fact, a track record of significant problems in delivering its products in a timely and cost-effective manner.[64]

Few dispute, however, that Boeing is capable of exerting an unusually powerful influence on politicians. The corporation's lobbyists are numerous, experienced, and talented, giving Boeing a very strong presence in Washington. In 2008 the company would demonstrate its raw political power by successfully pressuring Congress to overturn a $40 billion jet tanker fleet contract for which it bid unsuccessfully. The contract was originally awarded to Northrop Grumman and European contractor Airbus, but as a result of Boeing's lobbying, Congress made the unusual decision to nullify the original contract award.[65]

Not a single voice of objection is heard when it becomes clear that Boeing has selected L-3 Communications to play an as yet undetermined role in Project 28. L-3, now a major defense contractor in its own right by virtue of its contracts related to the Iraq War, is the very same corporation that blundered its way through the ISIS project. L-3's documented wasteful practices and managerial incompetence directly contributed to the failure of ISIS, yet, all evidence to the contrary, the CEO of L-3 consistently denied before Congress any responsibility for the failure of ISIS.[66]

Since the days of ISIS, L-3 has grown and prospered, with fourth-quarter 2008 net sales of $4.011 billion. L-3 describes itself as a "prime contractor in Command, Control and Communications, Intelligence, Surveillance and Reconnaissance, Government Services, Aircraft Modernization and Maintenance and has the broadest base of Specialized Products in the industry. L-3 is also a major provider of homeland defense products and services for a variety of emerging markets."[67]

If Border Patrol leadership is in the least bit wary of the track records of either Boeing, Inc., or L-3 Communications, it does not demonstrate its concerns. While for one of first times alluding in public to the history of the BP's failures, David Aguilar, chief of the Border Patrol, is enthusiastic about Boeing and Project 28: "Too often in the past, we tried for one magical piece of equipment, one solution to take care of the problem of our borders. The difference today is, this is going to be an integrated system that links several pieces of technology—rudimentary and 21st century."

In fact, Project 28, according to the BP chief, will succeed because instead of all the other previous DHS and CBP unnamed and failed strategies of "one magical piece of equipment," Boeing will seamlessly meld both old and new technologies into an "integrated system."[68]

According to Boeing, these low-tech and high-tech tools, which will finally provide control of the border, will rely on a platform that is going to be both mobile and tower-based. The details of the mobile platforms are not specified. Boeing, as first ever SBInet Systems Integrator, will construct towers that will support sensors and cameras with special surveillance capabilities. The exact nature of these capabilities also is ambiguous, if not secret, and equally opaque are the exact details of the Boeing's "21st century" technologies to be employed.[69]

Boeing's original plan also calls for a small number of unarmed drones, launched from the backs of CBP trucks by CBP agents, to patrol the border from the air. But drones are old hat. Drones have been successfully field tested, and thousands of them have been operated in the Iraq and Afghanistan wars and other areas by the U.S. military. Oddly, any direct mention of drones as integral to Project 28 or the virtual wall quickly disappears, falling out of the original plan as if they never existed.[70]

By April 2007 Boeing engineers complete tests in Fort Walton Beach, Florida, of what they call the first mobile tower. Their engineers report that the tower's infrastructure meets "established technical criteria, such as for the interfaces between power, data, cameras, radar, and the tower's security system." These ninety-eight-foot towers are now defined as the key component in the SBInet system.

In perhaps the most detailed explanation to date of how the system functions, Boeing states that its tower provides

the relocatable version of the platform for SBInet's main sensing capability that will deliver the ability to detect and identify entries into the U.S. when they occur (who they are, how many, etc.), allowing the Border Patrol to effectively and efficiently respond to the entry and resolve the situation with appropriate law enforcement. The tower houses cameras and radars, wireless data access points, communications and computer equipment, and a tower security system to prevent tampering with its operations. When combined with Border Patrol agent vehicle modifications, the mobile sensor towers will provide surveillance data to the Common Operating Picture (COP) as a critical component of CBP's comprehensive border security solution.[71]

While Project 28 costs a modest $20 million, estimates for a security network of eighteen hundred towers are now raised to $8 billion, up from an initial estimate of $2 billion. An emerging group of critics of SBInet and the virtual fence, however, disagree with this assessment of Boeing's budget. The DHS's own inspector general suggests that the actual cost of placing the towers is more likely to be in the range of $30 billion.[72]

Boeing, with the help of CBP agents, plans to test Project 28 for one to two months at the Tucson site. Engineers will then tweak the prototype, working out all the operating bugs. Beginning in the fall of 2007, Boeing will then deploy large numbers of completed towers to one region that spans 262 miles of Mexican border near Tucson, and another, 126 miles of border near Yuma.[73]

At about this time, Chertoff's DHS quietly contracts with Boeing to build a computer command center to coordinate data generated by Project 28. The cost of the computer command center is $47 million.

According to Gregory Giddens, executive director of SBI, Boeing will complete construction of the eighteen hundred towers in 2013.[74] Originally, DHS announced the date of completion as 2009, three years after Boeing was awarded the contract. No reason is given by Giddens for the necessity of an additional four years of construction time for the fence.

The National Hot Rod Association

The garage door is already raised when I reach Tom Cleary's suburban residence in Edinburg, Texas, ten miles north of the Mexican border. I walk past a black Chrysler Ram pickup that looks like it's never been driven. Out front is an equally pristine black Chrysler 300 that Tom informs me can do 160 miles per hour on State Highway 281 north of town—if Tom were so inclined.

Since his accident in the Corvette four months before, Tom has been confined to a motorized wheelchair, and he has never looked worse than when I visit him in November 2008. But he is still a fireball of energy. A bulky man with multiple medical issues, in between bathroom pit stops he zooms around his kitchen and den, then speeds down the hallway to retrieve documents from his home office.

"I float to the top of my damn pool like I was filled with nothing but air. Like a raft," he tells me, shouting from the bathroom. "It's the meds I'm taking." He motors back into the kitchen where we've been talking for an hour about Project 28. As we talk, his two mongrel chihuahuas lick my shoes for a scrap of attention. I look over just in time to see Tom's oversized cat climbing into my backpack, where I meticulously store my laptop, field notes, cameras, and other gear.

Before his most recent accident, Tom drove a black Corvette. Now his new pickup has a special hydraulic attachment to raise and lower his wheelchair. Tom hates with a passion this constraint on his mobility and has been unleashing his frustrations on the Internet for the last five days. He flings down in front of me several different photos of Project 28 available on the Internet. While Project 28 remains a pseudosecret, reporters and members of the public have managed to snap many different shots of it. Comparing what he knows about Project 28 to his own military experience, Tom is puzzled. Then he is flabbergasted.

"Look, I was an enlisted man in the navy before I retired. Went down to their office when I was eighteen and signed up. It was only later I graduated college and started grad school. I was in intelligence the whole time I was in the navy. Just a technician, but I went to navy school and I learned what they taught me as good as anyone else in those classes. Probably better, because I took it seriously and I wanted to succeed. This surface radar on these towers is a joke. What the hell does Boeing think it's doing?"

Part of the pseudosecret technology Boeing chooses to use in Project 28 is revealed when, by the fall of 2008, Project 28 experiences several serious setbacks. The bugs in the Tucson prototype appear to have eluded Boeing's finest engineering talents. As a result, Project 28 is months behind schedule, Congress is grumbling, and CBP agents and other intelligence sources with whom I've spoken are referring to Project 28 as "a big joke."

"This surface radar has been around for decades," says Tom. "It's no big deal. They [the American military] had surface radar at Pearl Harbor. It was December 7th, 1941. They watched the Jap planes coming in to attack. Followed them all the way in and then out when they left. Surface radar is not a new technology. That's my point. And it has its limitations. Look, radar is just microwaves. You send them out, they reflect off a surface, then they bounce back. The English had it in World War II, then the Germans got it from them.

"But this is surface radar on these towers. It's limited by its nature. What I'm telling you is that it will only go as far as the horizon. So Boeing says it's got these ninety-eight-foot towers. Radar from a ninety-eight-foot tower will go exactly fourteen miles. No less, no more. It's a mathematical formula. I know the Border Patrol says it will only go ten miles, but that's pure hogwash. Believe me, it'll go fourteen miles, and any expert worth his salt knows its fourteen miles. The higher the tower, the further the radar goes. The further it can see. So if they had balloons, say, tethered balloons, then that's just like having a higher tower than ninety-eight feet. You change the formula with the height. But ninety-eight feet is going to get you fourteen miles.

"But look, if it rains or snows, then forget it," Tom yells at me from his wheelchair five feet away. "I mean, just forget it. You know what you are going to see if it rains?"

I tell him I have no idea.

"Raindrops." Tom is laughing now, his bulk shaking the frame of the wheelchair.

"Raindrops, I'm telling you. That's all you are going to see." Tom repeats his words to make sure I understand his point.

"I don't care what bullshit Boeing is saying about its surface radar, if it starts to rain, it's not going to work. I've operated surface radar systems a thousand times and that's what you are going to get. Damn raindrops. Sand is going to be a problem. If it blows, sand is going to be a problem. Any disturbance in the weather."

Tom adds, "That's not the only problem with this. Surface radar was invented to identify large tactical forces in the field. Like tanks. But it's not so hot with individuals. Especially ones moving around a lot. Surface radar was developed to track troop movements on the battlefield, not illegal aliens scrambling over the border. It can spot a platoon of soldiers with some artillery. That's what it has been used for by the military for years. But not to identify one guy running around in circles."[75]

What Boeing is saying about its surface radar, a crucial component that it now publicly admits is an integral part of Project 28, is that it has not completely worked out all the operational bugs. Boeing's problems with surface radar have placed Project 28 far behind schedule. Other problems have also emerged, according to informants, including difficulties integrating the computer system.

The GAO is now investigating Boeing's virtual border fence, which appears to be, full denials by DHS, CBP, and Boeing to the contrary, at a virtual standstill.

I ask Tom about the high-definition cameras Boeing is employing on the towers. Are these state-of-the-art cameras up to the rigors demanded of them?

"Give me a break," Tom tells me. "High-definition my ass! Of course they have high-definition cameras. Everybody has those things. You want to know how difficult it is to deploy high-definition cameras? The NHRA has been using high-definition cameras for three years. You know what the NHRA is?"

"No."

"The National Hot Rod Association. They're on the cable sports channel. The NHRA has had them on TV for three years. They can shoot up to six hundred frames per second. Look, what I'm telling you is that all these cameras, all this Project 28 technology, comes directly from the military. And they get it from the defense contractors. We've had that stuff for decades. Remember the U-2? The pilot, what was his name, Gary something, well, anyway, he could shoot those spy photographs from a hundred thousand feet.

"This Project 28 is kind of a hoax it seems to me. No, I take that back, it is a hoax, because they keep making it seem like something it isn't. Because what they're saying about the technology, like the surface radar, is dead wrong. Boeing knows that if it rains, then all their surface radar shuts down. Everybody knows that. So all our enemies have to do with this system is just wait until it rains, then come on over. Easy as pie.

"What about the new magnetic sensors?" I ask Tom. Plans for Project 28 call for state-of-the art unattended ground sensors to replace the Vietnam-era ones CBP agents have been complaining about for more than two decades. But now Tom has his back to me at the granite kitchen counter while he's grinding some coffee beans, telling me about how he gets his beans in the mail from a friend. He's also boiling water for the espresso he knows I need to stay awake. He swivels in his wheelchair just as I finally swat at one of the chihuahuas chomping on my ankle. If Tom notices, he doesn't say a thing. Instead, he arranges his wire bifocals on his nose, rubs his hand over the heavy wrinkles on his forehead, then wags his finger at me.

"Do you think that any so-called new sensor is really new? After what I've been telling you? I'm telling you what I know after more than twenty-five years of serving my country with pride. I know surface radar. I know high-definition cameras. Do you really think any sensor Boeing comes up with is going to be anything more than old military hardware?"

"So how do you think Project 28 is designed to operate?" I ask him.

Tom zooms out of the room on his wheelchair. I hear noise again in his home office as his printer rolls out sheet after sheet of paper. Tom is back in five minutes handing me more photographs of Project 28's towers.

"Found these on line just this morning. Lots of photographs taken by reporters, and they are all showing the same thing. Listen, this Project 28 is very basic. You've got towers spaced out that are ninety-eight feet tall. On each tower are high-definition cameras that can rotate on a base, video cameras, and antennas to make contact with a satellite. At the base of the tower you see what has got to be the power source and a satellite dish to keep in touch with central control. Then presumably you've got an agent in his truck with a laptop. And then there are these so-called new sensors planted in strategic places they think people are going to walk.

"This is how Project 28 works. An illegal immigrant or drug smuggler or whatever is spotted by the surface radar—of course it can't be raining when this happens, or the surface radar won't see him—and a high-definition camera pans towards him, or maybe just a plain old video camera. Or an operator trains the cameras or radar on a specific area because one of the sensors goes off. Then the image from the tower is sent out from its satellite dish to the satellite and then on to the central control. Central control alerts the agent in the field, who gets the GPS coordinates of the sighting. Plus on his laptop maybe he also gets a real-time image of the illegal. The agent also has a hand-held GPS. The control operator directs the agent in the field to the illegal, using GPS coordinates. The agent can also use his laptop to get the image that the tower is seeing to make his own judgments. Then, if they need to, the agent or the control operator can call in a plane or helicopter to the exact location using the GPS coordinates being relayed in real time. The agent makes contact with the illegal because the radar and cameras on the tower are locked onto the target or another tower picks up the image if and when the target gets out of range. If you add drones, they work just like another camera. It should be very simple for them to set this up.

"What I'm telling you is, the military has been doing this kind of thing for decades. This is not a big deal. But look, the surface radar is best with groups of people and big hardware like tanks or artillery. But really, integrating all these components is not a big problem. They should be able to do it easily. I mean, we had mobile systems forty-five years ago that could do more than this stationary system is being asked to do. Think about all the computer advances in that span of time. Boeing should be able to this with no sweat.

"But here's something you should think about. Operator error. I saw it every day when I was in the navy. The system is only as good as the people running it. The Border Patrol has got to train the right kind of people to run this thing. Especially at their central control. Man, I'm telling you, it's all about operator error."

I immediately think of ISIS and its reliance on LECAs, law enforcement communications assistants charged with operating the data entry and the computers integrating the system. The linchpin of ISIS, LECAs were never given the proper training, data, or reliable computer power to do their jobs properly.[76]

I thank Tom for his time and begin to pack up my gear. As I leave, the chihuahuas bark as Tom follows me out to the driveway. I ask him if I should use his real name.

Tom snorts. "Don't worry about it. Look at me. What can they do to me at this point?"

Boeing's Project 28 Does Not Work

In the fall of 2008 the GAO testifies before the Committee on Homeland Security about growing concerns with Boeing's Project 28. In spite of multiple assurances by Boeing, Inc., and Chertoff's DHS that Project 28 is on schedule, the GAO reports that the program has not been "effectively managed."[77]

Although in May 2008 CBP, under the direction of DHS, finally drafted a test management strategy for SBInet to guide it in providing oversight of Project 28, this management strategy was never finalized or approved. That unapproved management strategy lacks a "high-level master schedule of SBInet test activities, metrics for measuring testing progress, and a clear definition of testing roles and responsibilities. Further, the program office has not tested the individual system components to be deployed to the initial deployment locations, even though the contractor initiated testing of these components and other system components and subsystems in June 2008."

Equally damning, GAO testifies that the program requirements for SBInet "have not been effectively defined." GAO also reports that "several requirements including definition and management limitations exist. . . . Having set no measurable standards for SBInet, it was impossible to measure whether Boeing, Inc., had met those standards." The GAO report summarizes: *"Important aspects of SBInet remain ambiguous and in a continued state of flux, making it unclear and uncertain what technology capabilities will be delivered and when, where, and how they will be delivered."*[78]

GAO recommends eight solutions to DHS and CBP, which involve "reassessing its approach to and plans for the program, including its associated exposure to cost, schedule and performance risks, and disclosing these risks and alternative courses of action to DHS and congressional decision makers."

Most important, the GAO report states that its "recommendations also provide for correcting *the weaknesses surrounding the program's unclear and constantly changing commitments and its life cycle management approach and processes, as well as implementing key requirements development and management and testing practices."*[79]

Shortly thereafter, amid little public fanfare, Chertoff's DHS suddenly fires Boeing as its SBI Systems Integrator and terminates Boeing's fixed contract of $20 million to build a prototype virtual border fence. During roughly this same time period Chertoff's DHS, however, continues to pay Boeing for its $47 million contract to develop an operating picture software system for CBP command centers.

Until the very day it is fired, Boeing denies any problems with Project 28 that are not imminently resolvable. In fact, Project 28 was, according to DHS, "conditionally approved" on December 7, 2007. At that time Border Patrol agents were given a free trial run of Project 28 in Arizona which lasted from forty-five to sixty days.[80] During that time rumors begin to spread from one station of the Border Patrol to the next that Project 28 is a big failure in spite of all the denials by Boeing and DHS.

Somewhat confusing is the fact that at this same time DHS demands and receives a $2 million refund on Project 28 from Boeing. On closer inspection, however, what really occurs is that Boeing gave DHS a $2 million discount against further work it would accomplish in order to receive the remaining $1.5 million DHS was holding until Project 28 was successfully completed. This additional work was the remaining contract of approximately $47 million to build the software for the computer command center for CBP.

In sharp contrast to the Boeing disclaimers, GAO reports that it is still a fact that in 2008, as a result of all the problems associated with the SBI Systems Integrator "*Border Patrol agents have to rely upon existing limited technological capabilities to help achieve control of the border.*"[81]

Secretary Chertoff then announces that the new SBInet technologies to be deployed along the Mexican border cannot be deployed by the end of 2008. Instead, the newest deployment target date for the border virtual fence is set at 2011, a three-year delay. (Secretary Chertoff's announcement directly contradicts a previous one giving the date of completion as 2013.) The GAO then lists a number of reasons for these delays by DHS, including SBInet program uncertainties, changes in scheduling, and legal battles over environmental permits.[82]

Then, on May 7, 2009, Chertoff's DHS just as suddenly rehires Boeing as the SBI Systems Integrator. Project 28 is once again declared viable and on target.

SBI executive director Mark Borkowski announces that Boeing will soon work all of the bugs out of Project 28. Then working models of Project 28 will be built along the Arizona border by the end of the summer of 2009. Named Tucson-1 and Ajo-1, these newest projects each will cover about thirty miles of the border.

Borkowski's SBInet budget for the border fencing in 2009 is $770 million. The Obama administration's stimulus package, under new DHS secretary Napolitano, is estimated to provide an additional $200 million.[83]

Project 28, and now its derivatives, Tucson-1 and Ajo-1, remain under the watchful eye of CBP and DHS, although those agencies still do not have in place an approved management plan for it.

The Low-Tech Border Fence

Meanwhile, DHS construction of the low-tech fence makes some progress along the Mexican border, only not the progress planned by DHS. By August 2008 DHS reports that it has completed 341 miles of low-tech border fence against a statutory goal of 670 miles by the end of the year.

The SBI TI, in charge of the construction, faces numerous setbacks. The Consolidated Appropriations Act of 2008 requires DHS to complete fencing construction along the border as Secretary Chertoff judges appropriate. Chertoff is given a deadline of December 31, 2008, to complete some combination of pedestrian and vehicle fencing totaling 670 miles. In September 2008 DHS reports that it will complete 670 miles "either built, under construction, or under contract by December, 31, 2008." Then, in December, the department reports it cannot reach these border fencing goals and will, instead, complete the 670 miles of fencing by March 2009.[84]

Equally troubling, SBI TI fence construction costs skyrocket, doubling in one year alone. Originally DHS announced that pedestrian fencing would cost $4 million a mile and vehicle fencing $2 million a mile. But by 2008 the costs rise to $7.5 million a mile for pedestrian fencing and $4 million for vehicle fencing. DHS blames the exploding budget on labor costs and "land acquisition issues."[85]

In March 2009 CBP announces it is going to begin to bury a new generation of high-tech sensors along a twenty-three-mile stretch of Arizona border. Completion along Arizona's share of the Mexican border is scheduled for 2011.[86]

It is only about this same time, spring of 2009, that CBP managers and Boeing's SBInet project manager, Jack Chenevey, finally admit that Project 28 is riddled with problems. They reveal that Boeing engineers patched together commercially available cameras, radar systems, and sensors to create Project 28.[87] Although Boeing is paid $20 million for Project 28, this virtual border fence does not function properly.

Boeing's engineers, under the flawed supervision of CBP contract managers and DHS, have put together a ragtag array of damper flappers. But the parts are not from Boeing's own warehouses. After all, Boeing builds big planes. Boeing admits it shopped sneaky cheap, purchasing components from Radio Shack and other commercial retailers. In so doing, Boeing maximized its profits on its modest $20 million contract

The off-the-shelf Radio Shack parts, according to Boeing's own spokesperson, identified border cactus and other underbrush as illegal border crossers. Project 28 also could not identify images along the border when it rained, and the satellite up-links intended to deliver real-time data to agents in the field were totally useless.[88] As a result of this weekend hobbyist business plan, Boeing's Project 28 failed.

Furthermore, Mark Borkowski, executive director of SBI, is quoted as saying that when the contract for the SBI Systems Integrator was awarded to Boeing in 2006, CBP was still coming together and didn't have the staff or the skills to handle such a complex project. According to Borkowski, CBP could not detail for Boeing exactly what they wanted the system (Project 28) to do.[89]

Borkowski apparently is unaware of the history of his own agency. By 2006 CBP was four years old and already had demonstrated remarkable incompetence in the program management of the ASI. The Border Patrol before becoming the CBP, starting in 1998, had also learned nothing in its oversight and leadership of ISIS. Chertoff's DHS had, in fact, promised that by reshuffling a bureaucratic chart DHS would closely monitor CBP to assure its success in managing Project 28.

Boeing's spokesperson also forgets to mention that there had been major management changes within Boeing since the inception of Project 28. Boeing managers directly accountable for the failures of the project were replaced midstream by new ones. None of the nameless executives who were replaced were in any way held accountable for the Radio Shack business plan for Project 28. Nor were any Boeing executives ever held accountable for the total failure of Project 28.

Borkowski also fails to mention the inherent weaknesses in using a surface radar system as an integral part of Project 28. No mention is made of the new towers of Project 28 serving as stationary targets for those smuggling illegal goods or as geographic markers for illegal border crossers. However, success, according to CBP's Mr. Borkowski, is just around the next corner. CBP plans to hire one hundred new oversight managers over the course of the next several years.[90]

In the meantime, Borkowski does not explain how CBP intends to provide oversight over Boeing and the Project 28 juggernaut that is still rolling. Again, Borkowski, executive director of CBP's SBI, seems strategically to disremember the promises made by Chertoff's DHS several years earlier with regard to oversight of CBP, along with all of the claims for Project 28.

CBP is a complete loser when it comes to program management of the virtual fence, but its agents do know more than a thing or two about the proper positioning and placement of the low-tech version of the fence. Increasingly, however, DHS, feeling the political heat from the failure of

Project 28 along with increased pressure from Congress to complete the low-tech portion as scheduled, grows testy. DHS officials tell some CBP managers, who believe that the low-tech border fence is not being built in the correct border areas where its impact will be maximized: "We build the fence, you patrol it."[91]

What Does All This Mean?
The Integrated Surveillance Intelligence System, initiated by the INS in 1998, was a total and costly failure. Secretary of the DHS Ridge then begat the American Shield Initiative in 2004. The ASI failed in less than a year's time. Chertoff's DHS then begat the Secure Border Initiative in 2006. Then they begat SBInet and SBI TI. None of these programs developed either under the Clinton or the George W. Bush administration placed any comprehensive and operable security system along the Mexican border. Since Mexican border security became a political prerequisite for a national discussion of immigration policy during the approach to the presidential elections of 2008, major immigration policies were nominally put on hold.

Chertoff's DHS then begat the SBI Systems Integrator. Handing the moniker to Boeing, Inc., a private defense contractor, did not solve much except increase Boeing's profits. Boeing then begat Project 28, for $20 million, along with a project to develop command center software, the same project attempted during ISIS, for another $47 million. In spite of claims to the contrary by Boeing and DHS, Project 28, under the program management of CBP, also failed miserably. Secretary Chertoff fired Boeing, then rehired the company in 2009 to continue its development of Project 28.

But the begetting was not over. A revived Project 28 mysteriously begat Tucson-1 and Ajo-1 in 2009. At this writing, Boeing's vice president for global security, Timothy Peters, the third Boeing vice president to be in charge of Boeing's contract with DHS and CBP, declared Project 28 "an experiment."[92] Peters also stated to Congress that Project 28 was "overly ambitious."[93]

With almost no public outcry, Boeing completely changes its technological objectives and strategies in building Tucson-1 and Ajo-1, both a system of towers varying in height from Project 28's standard ninety-eight feet. The multinational now declares that its touted virtual surveillance system will rely henceforth on microwave transmissions from one fixed tower to the next as its main system of communications. Satellite uplinks in Project 28 have been jettisoned, along with a number of other systems. Also tossed into the dumpster is real-time transmission of images to CBP agents sitting in their vehicles.

According to DHS's Mark Borkowski, Tucson-1 is "the installation of the no-kidding real SBI-net system."[94]

Border Patrol agents asked to test Tucson-1 find, according to the GAO's Richard M. Stana, that there are significant problems with the system that make it inoperable in the field. The first derivative begat from Project 28 is to date of no practical use. This is all the more alarming because Boeing's metric standard for this newest project is 70 percent; if and when the new derivative can spy illegal border crossers seven out of ten times, it will be declared a success. Retesting by the CBP is scheduled for January 1, 2010, and deployment to the Texas border is now projected by Boeing to be completed by 2014. Complete deployment of the virtual border fence is currently scheduled for 2016. Total cost to date since 2004 is, according to GAO's Stana, at $7.6 billion and rising.

In spite of all this begetting, GAO's Stana reports that Border Patrol agents still rely on legacy hardware, the old sensor system, to patrol the border. Stana reports that the border is not at this time under operational control.

During the first year of the Obama administration, Border Patrol agents police the Mexican border in significantly larger numbers, about eighteen thousand, than ever before. They are better equipped and have more adequate interagency intelligence data supporting their efforts. Agents also have newer and improved vehicles, patrol boats, scope trucks, planes, helicopters, and facilities, including new sector headquarters and stations along with new ports of entry. Certain policies were changed during the Bush administration—for example, catch-and-release—and a complex system of privately owned and operated detention centers has been established. DHS under the previous administration engaged in a number of highly publicized programs to deter crime along the border and to discourage employers from hiring undocumented workers by instigating employee raids, most notably on Iowa meat packers. While the Obama administration put a halt to some of the Bush administration initiatives, money continues to flow from Washington to construct both low-tech and virtual border fences.

These substantive changes along the border acknowledged, the primary technology upon which Border Patrol agents patrol the line, Vietnam-era ground sensors, remain largely inoperative and of little practical utility to agents. The low-tech fence is about one-third completed. In Texas, including the Valley, ninety-two miles of monumental fencing have been completed, and twenty-three miles remain. Inoperable sensors, partial and incomplete border fencing, and a few low-tech cameras and other unsophisticated technology remain the sole barriers against illegal immigrants, drug traffickers, and other illegal border crossers.

If immigration policy is not to be publicly discussed until the borderlands are secure, until it is operationally controlled, then such a discussion can begin no earlier than 2016.

The new border fence in all its various forms is ephemeral, a failed symbol of public security and safety. After all the begetting of highly publicized border security initiatives at a price tag of hundreds of millions of dollars, Border Patrol agents who know the borderline, who risk their lives day in and out doing their job, repeatedly acknowledge that crucial problems prevail in this region. One of these problems is the border fence.

Undoubtedly it is more difficult to cross and recross the Mexican border because of the increased number of CBP agents, the nascent fence, and other tactics employed by law enforcers at various different levels who now possess new resources and act on new strategies in nonborder states. At the same time, drug-related violence has escalated on the Mexican side of the border and in the Mexican interior as drug cartels shoot it out over turf; more than six thousand Mexican citizens were murdered in 2008, and the numbers grew higher in 2009 and 2010.

The challenges in the Mexican borderlands are complex, interrelated, and in major ways grounded in the history of border communities and longstanding binational relations. The inability of various entities to recognize or allow for this complexity—institutions including Secretary Chertoff's DHS (and more recently, Secretary Napolitano's DHS), Boeing, an antiquated CBP, and a Congress asleep at the wheel—guarantees major programmatic failures in the future. These institutions, among others, play undeniably crucial roles in Mexican border security, but they also constitute part of the problem.

There remains an overriding political miscalculation among the public and at various levels of government that sophisticated technology fueled by federal dollars can resolve intricate international issues and domestic immigration policies. The Mexican border fence, whether the low-tech version, virtual Project 28, Tucson-1, Ajo-1, or whatever new forms it might morph into, is seriously flawed. This fence, far from completed along the Mexican border, is already badly broken. Only no one will admit it.

Chapter 8
CBP Agent Nora Muñoz

CBP agent Nora Muñoz always wanted to be in law enforcement. Since she was a little girl, she wanted to be a beat cop in her own hometown. But it was not her mother, father, or her eventual husband who helped make up her mind about her life's work.[1]

"It was when I first saw *Chips* on TV," she tells me.

"The show with the two cops?" I ask her. She nods in agreement. After spending a few moments in silence, neither of us can remember the names of the actors or the characters they played on *Chips*.

Long, blonde bangs framing her pleasant, sun-worn face, the person across from me does not resemble the stereotype of a CBP agent with more than ten years on the line. At first glance Agent Muñoz easily passes as a soccer mom. But when she entered the door at Starbucks, customers unconsciously stood aside as she walked over to my table to introduce herself.

Dressed in slacks and a plaid top, Nora Muñoz conveys a military bearing incompatible with the outward image of a stereotypical Tucson housewife. Underneath the quiet inflections of voice and manner, Agent Muñoz has weathered tough experiences while on the job—not just from patrolling the line day in and day out, but also from the treatment she has received while attempting to perform her duties as a federal law enforcement officer. No Hollywood ending guaranteed, these experiences have exacted palpable scars.

The Starbucks buzz around us, creating a wall of immediate privacy, is broken by shrieks from a teenage girl at the table immediately to our left. I flinch, but Nora Muñoz never looks up. The shrill voice reverberates off the Mexican floor tile, countertops, and walls, a perfect sounding board for the semihysterics of a sixteen-year-old with too much caffeine pulsing through her veins. Perhaps realizing her audience is not just the boyfriend sitting next to her, the drama queen falls silent.

"Where were you born?" I ask as the routine noise resumes. Outside, a rare desert rain temporarily flattens the dust on the Tucson pavement.

"Not far from here. Born and raised near Tucson, but in high school my father moved us around with his jobs. Then we moved back to the Tucson area. I met my husband here in college. Got married after two years. I've got two teenagers at home. Both girls."

After my book on the Border Patrol was published, a number of agents, both male and female, contacted me about the challenges they faced in sectors all along the Mexican border. Agent Muñoz wrote, "My experience . . . is that I have had many, many difficulties related to my gender. I actually fear retaliation. . . ." I contacted her, talked to her at length, and eventually arranged to fly to Arizona to meet with her.

I was interested in Agent Muñoz's struggle against gender discrimination because her personal narrative brought into focus issues the Border Patrol will not acknowledge. Only about 5 percent of all working agents in the Border Patrol are women. In station management, the percentages are far less. Although it is unacknowledged by the CBP, a major cause of this dismal percentage of female agents is pervasive gender discrimination in the workplace.[2]

This gender discrimination plays out in a variety of ways and contexts, including overt actions and behaviors of coworkers along with inappropriate remarks and "jokes." It also can include Border Patrol management decisions that systematically discriminate against female agents in daily shift assignments, merit pay increases, and promotions, among others things.

All Border Patrol agents, federal enforcers of the law, are themselves protected from gender discrimination in the workplace by the Equal Employment Opportunity Commission (EEOC). Words, actions, and behavior of agents, supes, field operation supervisors, deputy sector chiefs, sector chiefs, and other managers, as well as all other employees of the CBP, fall under the jurisdiction of the EEOC.

In July 2005 the Border Patrol "launched a national recruiting campaign to increase its ranks by an additional six thousand new Border Patrol agents by the end of December 2008."[3] In order to meet the number of Border Patrol agents mandated by the Bush administration and Congress as necessary to secure the Mexican border, thousands of men and women were recruited and then trained at the Border Patrol academy at Artesia, New Mexico. By the winter of 2007 there were eleven thousand agents in the Border Patrol. Still thousands of recruits more were needed, and eventually the total number of agents approached twenty thousand, making the Border Patrol the largest federal law enforcement agency in the land. This recruitment and training effort, however, would have failed if new female agents could not have been successfully recruited, trained and, most importantly, retained in their jobs.[4]

Female Border Patrol agents on a daily basis demonstrate they are as capable of patrolling the line as male agents. Yet the Border Patrol remains steeped in a male culture that, at worst, trivializes the competencies and work of female agents. The Border Patrol, in fact, refuses to acknowledge that gender discrimination exists in the workplace. Yet gender discrimination against female agents is pervasive in Border Patrol stations all along the Mexican border and a major reason why the number of female agents remains a small fraction of the number of male agents. The managers at stations and sector headquarters, almost entirely male, deny that their masculinist culture is a serious issue worthy of discussion.

Unlike many other work environments that may be viewed as hostile because of gender discrimination, in the Border Patrol the daily safety of all agents is closely entwined with how male agents view female agents. Any values and attitudes embedded in discrimination can potentially question the essential relationship between shift partners and between agents on the line and any backup agents who may arrive to aid them. All agents on the line must firmly believe that, regardless of gender, their fellow agents have their back in high-risk confrontations, apprehensions, and drug busts.

As suggested earlier, by its nature the work of Border Patrol agents is increasingly dangerous as violence against agents escalates. Assaults against agents along the border rose from 384 in 2004 to 987 in 2007. In 2007 more than 600 physical assaults were reported against agents.[5] There is every reason to believe that as the number of agents increases, and as it becomes harder to cross illegally, violence directed against agents will increase. It can also be argued that the rise in violence against agents is one measure of the effectiveness of their work in securing the border.

Gender discrimination in the Border Patrol, therefore, has severe implications for the safety and welfare of agents in the field. It can destroy trust between agents, thereby undermining an agent's ability to make sound decisions in the field based upon professional training. Gender discrimination puts both male and female Border Patrol agents at greater risk while performing their jobs along the line.

Although highly motivated to become a municipal police officer like her husband, Cesar, or even a county deputy sheriff like her father-in-law, Israel, Nora Muñoz never seriously considered a career as a federal law enforcement agent. Soon a mother of two young children, Nora looked for work that would keep her close to her family. At the time, a job as a bank teller was the best employment Nora could find. For eight years she worked at a small, family-owned bank as she climbed the modest employment ladder. Eventually she found herself in charge of the bank's escrow department.

Soon after that promotion Nora realized that "sitting behind a desk was not something I was made to do." Her dream job, she now acknowledges, was to work in the same police department as her husband. She applied for a position, any position, at her local police department, but to her dismay, every time Nora applied for an opening, she "never made it past the oral interview." Not discouraged by this turn of events, she decided, now that her two girls were older and child-care issues were less demanding, to apply to other police departments in nearby Tucson suburbs.

But to Nora's astonishment, the results of her job search were always the same. "They don't have to tell you what you did wrong at the interview," she tells me. But word gets around fast in a small town. Nora learned that less qualified male applicants were getting hired instead of her—individuals who possessed less education, less job experience, and fewer other job qualifications.

"What did your husband say about all this?" I ask. After all, Cesar was a cop, who had to know and understand how the local police departments functioned. He must have heard something through the cop rumor mill.

"Cesar was supportive. He knew what was going on. So did Israel. He's been in law enforcement with the county for more than thirty years." Cesar and Israel told her the same thing: she was not getting hired because she was a woman. They both told her that her chances were very slim, in spite of her qualifications, that she would ever get hired by local law enforcement agencies.

"Eventually, when I didn't get into any of the departments around here, I applied to the Border Patrol. But you need to understand it was never my first choice. I just believed that with a federal agency I'd get treated better. So did my family. I was accepted after all the paperwork and went off to the academy. It was in Charleston [South Carolina] then."

For more than five long months at the Charleston training academy, Nora Muñoz wrestled with the tough physical fitness standards, practiced her Spanish, and learned the often counterintuitive immigration laws and their history. Although born and raised in the borderlands and married to a Latino, Spanish never came easy to Nora.[6] She spent hour after hour at her desk memorizing the vocabulary lists and studying grammar in order to pass the required language tests.

But Spanish was not her biggest hurdle at the academy. As the days and weeks went by, Nora terribly missed her family back home in Tucson. For more than five months she did not see her children or her husband.

"How many female instructors were there at the Border Patrol academy in 1997?" I ask.

"None," says Agent Muñoz.

I ask her how many other female recruits were in her academy class.

"Maybe eight or nine. I can't remember the exact number. There were total about four hundred of us, I'd guess." In 1997 only about 2 percent of the academy recruits were female.

Nora Muñoz stuck out the academy to the bitter end. Before she stood in line to receive her diploma, she estimated that about a third or more of her fellow recruits had either dropped out or were sent home.

Upon graduation from the Border Patrol academy, Agent Nora Muñoz was posted back to the Tucson area. She felt very lucky to be back in Tucson. Under a Border Patrol policy only recently amended, she might have been posted to any station from Brownsville to San Diego. If that had happened, Cesar would have been forced to resign his job, and the family would have had to find new housing and schools for the girls and contend with a multitude of changes brought on by a major move far from home.

The Border Patrol justified this long-standing policy on several counts. The most substantive was for reasons of security. A Border Patrol agent returning to his/her home town might be, according to Border Patrol reasoning, more easily corrupted by local criminals. According to this rationale, former friends, acquaintances, or even family members might prove successful in bribing a new agent assigned to their home town.

This former policy created a number of unintended consequences for agents, their families, their friends, and the residents of border communities. For male agents who were born or raised along the Mexican border, the mandatory move uprooted them from their hometowns and jettisoned them into other border communities about which they knew little and had few, if any, significant social ties. All border communities are not the same. In a new community, male agents gravitated towards the friendship and support of other male agents both in the workplace and outside it. In short order the policy could lead to the social isolation of agents who were insulated from the communities in which they resided.

At the same time, there were also no social support networks for spouses of male agents, many of whom gave up jobs to move with their husbands. Unlike the American military, the families of agents were totally on their own. Divorces were common after the first posting.[7]

For new female agents, both married and single, there were often very few, if any, female agents in their new communities upon whom they could rely. Married female agents had their families, of course, but single female agents faced new communities with few social networks or institutions in place.[8] For example, when Nora returned to Arizona after her training at the academy, she joined eighty other agents at her station. At the time, there was only one other female agent working at Nora's station, but Nora rarely saw her because they were seldom assigned to the same shifts. Including Nora, the female agents at her station constituted less than 2 percent of the total number of agents employed.

"I felt lucky," says Nora. "I already had my kids. They [the male Border Patrol managers] looked down on agents who got pregnant. They made that very clear. Before I came, you had to take a leave of absence without pay to have your baby."

From the very start Agent Muñoz loved her work in the Border Patrol. In spite of the hardships at the academy, she never once thought about return-ing to her desk job in the escrow department at the bank. One of the aspects of her job she especially appreciated was working under the broad Arizona sky with no bank manager looking over her shoulder. Managers at her sta-tion, as at most others, rarely left the confines of their offices.[9] During Agent Muñoz's first year, her probationary year, she spent the majority of shift hours chasing and apprehending undocumented workers in the nearby des-ert and mountains. Because drug loads along this section of the border were at the time relatively unusual, only occasionally did she directly participate in a drug bust.

Like most agents, Nora Muñoz quickly learned that certain policies, such as catch-and-release and VRing Mexican nationals, were both counterpro-ductive and mindless. Nevertheless, although she repeatedly arrested illegal aliens only to see them apprehended again a few days or a week later, she followed every order, regulation, and policy. Whether it was a day shift or night shift, Agent Muñoz enjoyed her work in spite of its frustrations. At the end of the long shifts in "mountain and desert work," Nora felt a genuine sense of accomplishment and professional worth.

From the very first Nora hated the "city duty," shifts spent patrolling the small communities adjacent to the border. In the rough terrain she felt much more at ease, freer to rely on her own professional judgment when outguessing undocumented workers. At the same time, she was far from the supervisors back at the station drinking their coffee and soaking in the air conditioning. When assigned city duty, she had to not only check out every off-the-wall hunch sent to her over the radio by her supe, but also pay close attention to the useless tips handed out at each muster before the shift started. These tips, often in the form of an anonymous phone call, always proved a big waste of time.

On the job she learned the Border Patrol has little if any intelligence on which an agent in the field can consistently rely and operate. Or, as one supervisor recently told me, "Intel in the Border Patrol? You got to be kidding. We have none. If we had real intel about what these guys [human traffickers and drug cartels] are doing, don't you think we'd make better decisions?"

Following random information from the dispatcher while on city duty, occasionally sprinkled in with armchair directions from a shift supe, Nora searched for illegal aliens hiding under "houses, buses, and in basements." She found city duty far less personally rewarding than trekking through the desert, but she always followed the orders of her supes, and she never complained.

In fact, Agent Muñoz always made a point of keeping her mouth shut. She always did what she was asked to do whether she agreed with it or not. In the Border Patrol she quickly learned she must never be critical of management decisions or actions of her fellow agents. She watched as other agents who committed such acts were told to keep their mouths shut or face being ostracized. Instead, Nora focused upon performing her job, whatever the assignment, to the best of her abilities. In turn, she always received positive evaluations from her supes, successfully completing her probationary year of employment as a Border Patrol agent.

As the years began to roll by, Nora increasingly observed that she and the only other female agent at her station were much more likely than the male agents to be assigned to city duty. While the male agents at the station were routinely rotated through mountain, desert, and city duties, Nora and her female colleague were left to patrol streets.

When not assigning her to city duty, a group of shift supes also routinely assigned Nora to the midnight shift on the scope truck. Border Patrol agents all along the Mexican border consider scope truck assignments as one of the most onerous and boring jobs. This is the case, in part, because scope truck duty makes it much more difficult to raise a family and lead a normal life, especially if you have children.

Assigned to the scope truck for eight to ten hours at a time, an agent must scrutinize a small, green screen within the confines of the front seat of a truck cab. The only breaks in this routine are a possible meet with other agents to discuss strategies, but the agent never leaves the truck because he or she might miss seeing an illegal crosser. Once in position and aimed, a procedure that must be accomplished with some care, the scope truck mechanism collects and measures infrared heat from living objects by turning that energy into screen images. Set up by the agent so that it can take advantage of the terrain, the scope truck holds the same position for the duration of the shift or for nights at a time. The scope truck becomes an anchor to which an agent is chained.

From one long hour to the next, an agent in the scope truck observes the screen images of dogs, cats, livestock, and wild animals. Very occasionally, and sometimes not once during a ten-hour shift, a human shape may appear on the screen. These human shapes may or may not be undocumented workers or others involved in criminal activity. If the human shapes appear to an experienced scope truck operator to be undocumented workers or drug mules, then the agent immediately calls in other agents in vehicles to apprehend the suspects.

Most of the time the agent in the scope truck drinks coffee and tries not to fall asleep; there is nothing to do for ten hours except look at the small screen and communicate with other agents on the radio or cell phone. Scope truck routines get old very fast. After you look at the small green screen for many hours, you begin to see after-images. Headaches and other side effects can soon follow this tedium. While no Border Patrol agent would deny that the scope truck is crucial to apprehensions, no agent ever volunteers for it. Scope truck duty falls to those with the least seniority. And the nature of the work on scope truck duty, since it is tedious and unrewarding, is commonly used as a form of punishment by supes. In the idiom of Border Patrol culture, if you keep getting scope truck duty, you are on a supe's shit list. Once the scope truck duty is announced at muster, the agent who is selected may be razzed by other agents, and many other agents visibly relax in their chairs because they have been spared the tedium.

By its very nature, scope truck duty is socially isolating; only rarely are two agents assigned to the truck. The scope truck operator's only guaranteed human contact is with the dispatcher by radio or other agents who might call or be called. Occasionally other agents may randomly stop by to pass the time. Supes rarely leave the station, so they almost never stop by. In practice, a scope truck operator may not see another agent from the time he or she leaves the station until the time she or he returns to the station motor pool.

Agent Nora Muñoz, finding herself assigned night after night to the scope truck, was marginalized and isolated by her shift assignment from the rest of her fellow agents at the station. At the same time, her opportunities to apprehend undocumented workers and participate in drug busts were eliminated. Agents establish their reputations for competency and efficiency based upon how other agents, and their supes, perceive their rates of apprehension of illegals and illegal drugs. In turn, these perceptions can directly affect their chances for pay increases, promotions, and personal references leading to other federal law enforcement jobs.

Scope truck duty, as a common informal punishment meted out to agents who do not meet official or unofficial expectations, carries with it deniability by supes, deniability that an agent is in fact being punished. But all agents within Border Patrol culture understand the message of repeated scope duty assignments and quickly endeavor to discover, if they already do not know, the reason why they are being punished by the supe or the field operations supervisor (FOS). Agents may quickly acknowledge and apologize for their perceived error to avoid additional scope truck duty.

However, Agent Nora Muñoz did not know why or what she had done to be repeatedly assigned scope truck duty and the repeated city duty. But she tried to make the best of a bad situation. The late-night hours in the scope truck at least gave her time to see her kids off to school the next morning, grab some sleep, then be up and moving when the school bus arrived at the end of the day. She could make dinner for her family, get the girls off to bed, and spend time with Cesar before heading out the door for the midnight shift. But the regular night schedule on the scope truck left Nora little time to do much else, including seeing other family and friends, keeping up with the housework, and all the other family chores, responsibilities, and activities.

As the months of scope truck duty and city duty slogged on, Agent Muñoz finally decided enough was enough. Never one to make waves, always an agent who kept silent and never criticized the actions of her fellow workers or Border Patrol policies, Nora was very hesitant about talking with one of her shift supes. But in early 2001 she finally went to a supe to explain her concerns. She asked her male boss why she and her fellow female agent did not have the same shift rotation as all the other male agents. She also asked him why, unlike all the other agents, she was continually assigned to the scope truck.

Immediately following this conversation with this shift supervisor, Nora was once again given the same shift rotations as all the male agents at the station. For exactly one month she was treated by all her shift supes, a group of five men, in a fair and equitable manner. Then, for no reason that Nora could discern, this same group of supes once more placed her routinely on city duty and, soon after, on the midnight shift in the scope truck.

A few months later a thief broke into Nora's own truck, which was parked in her driveway, and burgled four other vehicles in her neighborhood as well. As always, Nora had locked her truck, but this time, perhaps because of fatigue brought on by yet another midnight shift in the scope truck, she left her "tricky bag" in the front seat. A tricky bag is a gym bag filled with an agent's personal gear needed for a shift, including maps, binoculars, first aid kit, snacks, and anything else required. Unfortunately, Agent Muñoz also left her copy of the code book in her tricky bag. This slim volume contained maps pinpointing the location of all the ground sensors in her sector.

While the loss of the code book to a thief at first might seem a serious threat to border security, the hard reality is that smugglers and *narcotraffi- cantes* already know where all the sensors are buried along the border. The professional criminals avoid the buried sensors like the plague; only the rank amateurs may be foiled by ground sensors, and then only if the sensors happen to be in working order. It is widely known in the Border Patrol that criminals and others already have copies of the code book. Such copies, or pages torn from the copies, are frequently found in the possession of those who, often by luck, are apprehended.[10]

At Nora's station several male agents admitted that within the last six months they had lost their code books, too. None of them were in any way punished—not even given scope truck duty—for losing their code books.

Not so with Agent Muñoz. Nora's shift supe told her she would receive a letter of reprimand to be placed in her permanent personnel file. As an additional punishment for the theft, Nora would be forced to take an undisclosed number of annual leave days without pay.

Feeling that she was yet again being treated far differently than male agents at the station, Agent Muñoz finally went to her union representative, a member of the National Border Patrol Council, for help and advice.[11] The two scheduled a meeting with Agent Muñoz's shift supe, arguing before him that the punishments Agent Muñoz received did not meet the alleged offense. While agreeing that Agent Muñoz should not have left a code book in her locked truck, they also pointed out to the male supe that male agents who had recently lost their code books were not reprimanded in a similar manner. Nora's punishment, they reasoned, was clearly a case of unequal treatment based upon gender when considered within the historical context of the extra scope truck duty and city duty Nora had been assigned. Agent Muñoz and her union rep also discussed a number of inappropriate remarks and "jokes" made to Nora by her shift supervisors and other agents while on the job, along with other documented gender-based actions and policies at the Border Patrol station.

The supe refused to change his decision. Fed up, Nora appealed to the deputy sector chief. The deputy sector chief responded in a letter that Agent Nora Muñoz had demonstrated poor professional judgment by leaving her code book in her truck. In Nora's own words, the deputy sector chief cited her as being "careless" and "not protecting the code [book]." He rejected Nora's appeal to reverse the punishment given her.

Both the letter of reprimand and the rejection of her appeal by the deputy sector chief were career-busting actions for Nora. Not only did these two decisions potentially embolden the group of male supes and other male agents to continue to discriminate against her, but the documents in her file might limit all opportunities for Nora to transfer to another law enforcement agency.

Nora's father-in-law Israel, with more than thirty years of law enforcement experience as a county sheriff, was dumbfounded by the Border Patrol's response to Nora's appeal. He expected his daughter-in-law, as a federal law enforcement officer, would be treated far better than if she worked in a local or county law enforcement agency. He was wrong.

Never one to make waves, Nora now believed her career in law enforcement was in grave jeopardy. She felt, given the gender discrimination she had endured already, she was left no other choice but to appeal the decision by the deputy sector chief to the U.S. Equal Employment Opportunity Commission (EEOC). This was absolutely the last thing Agent Muñoz wanted to do, but she felt her job, and her future jobs in law enforcement, along with the economic security of her family, were threatened.

In her appeal to the EEOC, Agent Muñoz documented the circumstances surrounding the loss of the code book, the letter of reprimand, the loss of leave without pay, her years of disproportional assignments to the scope truck and to city duty, and a detailed list of other discriminatory actions by a group of male Border Patrol supervisors and agents at her station. She named each one of these supervisors. Agent Muñoz's legal appeal, based upon the documentation of these facts, presented a very strong case of systematic and repeated discrimination by the Border Patrol over a period of years based solely upon her gender.

The EEOC immediately recommended arbitration. In response to the EEOC's request, Agent Muñoz's sector chief, taking the full and legal limit of one year to make his decision, rejected the EEOC's recommendation for arbitration. By taking the full year, he was stalling, hoping Agent Muñoz would withdraw her complaint under continued peer pressure, stress, and concern for her career.[12]

Finally, a full three years after Nora Muñoz originally filed her EEOC complaint of gender discrimination against the Border Patrol, a federal district judge found in her favor. After reviewing all the evidence presented by both Agent Muñoz and the Border Patrol, the federal district judge ruled that "this sector was found to have discriminated against an agent based upon gender."[13]

The judge further wrote in the bench decision: "Complainant [Agent Muñoz] did point to [names a supervisor] as someone whom she believed would turn around if he saw her coming down the hallway just to avoid her," and, "Complainant also no longer felt a part of the group and believed that the rules that applied to others did not apply to her." The EEOC judge additionally agreed that the complainant legitimately felt "under stress" because of the direct actions of her male supervisors and others based upon gender. Agent Muñoz, according to the judge's written decision, also legitimately feared, based upon the evidence presented, that these same supervisors might retaliate against her because she had appealed the decision of one of their group to the EEOC.[14]

The EEOC judge awarded Agent Muñoz a modest damage settlement of three thousand dollars, but it was never about the money for Agent Muñoz; it was about the principle of equal treatment in the workplace. She resented the Border Patrol supe's attempt to destroy her dream and the dreams of other women who sought meaningful careers in the Border Patrol. And, said Nora, it was also about the threat to her family, about not being allowed to provide economic security for her children when performing her job as Border Patrol agent to the same level of professionalism as her male counterparts.

This was not all Agent Muñoz won from the EEOC judge. The federal district judge demanded that the individuals who discriminated against Agent Muñoz, not just her shift supes but also the deputy sector chief and sector chief who supported the supes by their actions, confront the seriousness of their gender discrimination. In part this would be accomplished by an unusual legal order to this Border Patrol sector. The judge's decision read: "I am also ordering the Agency [the Border Patrol] to post a notice which I will attach to my written bench decision in public places at the [named] Station and at sector headquarters. The Agency shall maintain the Notices for twelve consecutive months in conspicuous places, including places where notices to employees and applicants for employment are customarily posted."[15]

Any members of the general public could thus read the judge's finding that the Border Patrol had discriminated against one of their own agents based upon gender. As well, all other employees at both Nora's station and sector headquarters would see this same decision and know that Agent Muñoz had been unfairly treated by the Border Patrol management based upon gender.

The judge's verdict in Agent Muñoz's case was clear and unambiguous. A group of Border Patrol supes had selected her for workplace discrimination based upon her gender. Over a period of years, they repeatedly treated her differently from her male counterparts, thus creating a hostile work environment. The letter of reprimand and unpaid leave were an inequitable punishment for Nora's alleged offense, solely a part of the systematic gender discrimination against Agent Muñoz. This same group of supes attempted to make Agent Muñoz's job so intolerable she would quit. In spite of her satisfactory annual performance evaluations, it was evident by their actions that these supes believed that since Agent Muñoz was female, she should not be allowed to function as a Border Patrol agent. The sector chief and his deputy sector chief, by their actions, defended, protected, and thus enabled this group of supes, thereby sanctioning those who broke federal laws.

The day after I first met Agent Nora Muñoz at the local Starbucks, I interviewed two Border Patrol public affairs officers (PAOs) at sector headquarters. When I originally contacted the PAOs, they were very hesitant about meeting with me. Clearly stating my reasons for interviewing them and referencing my credentials, I first emailed them in advance of my visit to Arizona. Upon their additional request, I provided them supplementary information. There were minor negotiations about time and place which finally led to their agreement to meet with me.

After a fifteen-minute wait in a small lobby at sector headquarters, I was ushered past the metal detector and into a large, formal room complete with brightly polished conference table, executive chairs, and computers and media technology. Across from me at the end of the long conference table sat Charles Herbwell, a former newscaster for the local network affiliate. Herbwell says he has been working for twenty years for the Border Patrol.[16] Never actually a Border Patrol agent, this PAO holds a civilian position at sector headquarters. Indeed, Charles possesses that superficial ruggedness and demeanor that seem a requirement in all television markets.

Next to him in a practiced military pose is Agent Ricardo Rojo, his uniform ironed and spotless. Unlike Charles, Ricardo knows by rote all the routines, rules, policies, and procedures of patrolling the line, because he served for many years in the field. His days patrolling the line long since past, Ricardo's loyalties now reside within the management ranks. Agent Rojo soon reveals in the course of our cordial conversation that he works, and has worked, at the same station as Agent Muñoz. He also resides in the same community outside Tucson as Muñoz.

I ask these two PAOs about a variety of topics, including sector trends in the apprehension of undocumented workers and drug interdictions. Other than expressing excitement over the new border fence construction, their answers are not particularly helpful or insightful. But both men are always courteous. Toward the end of our meeting, I raise the issue of the recruitment of thousands of new agents to the Border Patrol and the possible problems associated with such a massive effort. Both PAOs assure me that there are no recruitment issues worth my consideration.

I add at this point, "Have you had any problems with gender discrimination in this sector?"

"It is not an issue," says PAO Ricardo Rojo. This PAO, of course, knows Agent Muñoz personally, knows the details of her appeal to the sector deputy chief, and knows that the sector chief refused arbitration as requested by EEOC. He also knows the judge's final legal decision in favor of Agent Muñoz because, if for no other reason, the judge ordered the Border Patrol to post it in multiple locations for one year at his own station and at sector headquarters. PAO Ricardo Rojo has seen the judge's letter many times while it was posted at his station.

A final time I ask both PAOs, "So you are saying there are no legal problems with gender discrimination in this sector?"

"Absolutely none," they both tell me.

Two hours later I sit across the table from Agent Nora Muñoz at the same noisy Starbucks. I tell her that the PAOs at her sector headquarters deny any knowledge of gender discrimination at her station. They also told me, I relate to Agent Muñoz, that they are not familiar with any problems with gender discrimination in her sector.

In a calm voice Agent Muñoz says, "I have known Agent Rojo for many years. He knows all about me."

Two months after the EEOC judgment in favor of complainant Nora Muñoz against the Border Patrol, two months after the judge orders the bench's decision posted at sector headquarters and all stations within the sector so that, along with the public, all Border Patrol personnel know that a group of male Border Patrol supervisors repeatedly discriminated against Agent Muñoz over the course of several years, the gender discrimination against Agent Muñoz resumes. It is, once more, the same group of Border Patrol managers who consistently treat Agent Nora Muñoz differently than they treat all male agents at the station.

Once more at musters the shift supes regularly assign Agent Muñoz the worst shift duty. When not relegated to night duty on the scope truck, she is given city duty. Nora also notices that when she does not spend the shift in the scope truck, she is regularly assigned Border Patrol vehicles that are among the worst in the motor pool. On one rare occasion when she is assigned desert duty, her supe prohibits her from signing out a new Hummer, which she is certified to operate, in favor of a ten-year-old vehicle.

Seemingly a petty slight, this action masks a fundamental safety issue: vehicular accidents on patrol are a common risk to agents as they pursue undocumented workers and others.[17] In order to work safely and effectively, all Border Patrol agents require the best, and newest, vehicles available.

"It was the stress that was getting to me," Nora tells me. The last thing any Border Patrol agent needs, male or female, is turmoil on the job along with the knowledge he or she may not be able to rely on fellow officers.

"I don't have problems with most of the agents," Nora says. "Only a few of them. Hostile remarks, that kind of thing. It's that group of supes that are the real problem. Not everybody. But you know, I'll be talking with another agent and he'll say something like, 'I got nothing personal against you, but I just don't want to be collateral damage.'"

"What does that mean?"

"That just being my partner for a shift can put them in the wrong place at the wrong time. When a supe is trying to get at me, they don't care who else they get."

Vindicated by the judge and tolerated, if not respected, by at least some male agents at the station, Agent Nora Muñoz still is a pariah because on a daily basis she is stigmatized by a group of managers who do not treat her in a fair and equitable way. Other agents in this organizational culture are encouraged to perpetuate the gender-based hostility because they know management has their backs. And these managers know they can count on those at the top when legal push comes to shove, thus perpetuating the masculinist bureaucracy.

Agent Muñoz has been told by several male agents with whom she is friends, "They're out to get you. They're out to find something wrong with you." Another agent directly tells her, "I don't want to ride with you because you bring too much trouble."

Muñoz has never been a quitter. She intends to remain in the Border Patrol in spite of the gender discrimination. She tells me if she ever leaves the Border Patrol, it will be on her terms and not because the managers force her out. But now she is very worried that even the most insignificant error or mistake on her part will provide grounds for her dismissal.

Several weeks after one of the agents tells Muñoz he does not want to be "collateral damage," she forgets to inspect her assigned vehicle from the motor pool before departing. Standard operating procedure requires a quick eyeballing and hands-on inspection to reduce vehicular failures and accidents. Agents routinely thump the tires, check under the hood, test the lights and sirens, and so on. Nora and her male shift partner motor less than a mile from the station before she remembers to check their vehicle. A fair supe would normally discount Nora's minor infraction. However, Nora tells me she was worried one of the managers would blow her minor error out of proportion in an attempt to get her fired. Luckily for Nora the shift supe was drinking coffee at his desk and never noticed her gaffe.

Agent Muñoz, however, could see the handwriting on the wall. Knowing the legal system cannot protect her from the Border Patrol supes determined to get her, Nora decides to go back to college to finish her degree. A college degree may open up new opportunities within and outside of law enforcement. She enrolls at the local university and begins taking courses in criminal justice. Because she is working full time and also raising a family, her progress towards college graduation is slow. Fearing she will lose her job if she does not keep her mouth shut, Nora works her shifts on the scope truck and city duty and does not complain. She never considers filing another complaint with the EEOC because winning her grievance against her supes did not stop the gender discrimination.

For two more years Agent Muñoz endures the discrimination from her managers. Then one night on scope truck duty, when Nora is drinking coffee at three a.m. to keep herself awake, she suddenly notices a vehicle slowly approaching her. It is evident to Nora the driver is trying to sneak up on her. Agent Muñoz knows that backup, should she require it, might take thirty minutes or more to reach her. Anxiety mounting, Nora watches a male figure slowly exit the unknown vehicle and approach her under cover of darkness. Agent Muñoz still cannot see the face of the approaching figure or how he is dressed, but she finally recognizes his vehicle. It is a Border Patrol truck. The supervisor for her shift, one of the same men whom she named in her legal appeal to the EEOC, knocks on the window of Nora's scope truck.

"Why would he sneak up on you?" I ask her, not understanding.

"He was trying to catch me sleeping. Which makes no sense at all. When you are on the scope truck, you've got to call in regularly to the dispatcher at the station. The supe would know about those calls [which he should be monitoring]. If you are sleeping on duty, those calls don't get made."

"So what did he say?"

"He said, 'I just thought I'd see if you needed anything.' Really, actually, he didn't know what to say. He was speechless because he thought he'd catch me sleeping. He's the kind of person who has to think what to say before he talks. He didn't have anything thought out to say to me because I wasn't sleeping on the job. So that was the best he could come up with."

"That's pretty lame," I tell Agent Muñoz.

"That's not the end. Along comes four a.m., and I look in my rearview and there's another vehicle sneaking up on me from the back. The driver gets out, tries to come up so I can't see him in my rearview. This time I roll down the window and ask, 'What's up?' It's another supe. One of that same group. He tells me that I didn't check in with the dispatcher like I was supposed to, so he drove all the way out from the station to see if I was okay. Now you know as well as I do that it takes a whole lot to get a supe out in the field. But he told me, 'You didn't check in.' That was a lie, and we both knew it. They record everything that goes over the radio between the dispatcher and the agents. So I knew he had heard me check in, and he was just trying to catch me doing something."

"Did you ever hear of the supes checking on male agents in the scope truck?"

"No."

Dead tired of the discrimination, Agent Muñoz finally hires a private attorney. Nora's lawyer, after meeting with her and reading the EEOC case file and the bench decision, writes a letter to Border Patrol sector headquarters documenting the ways in which his client has been unfairly treated since the EEOC judgment against the Border Patrol. In the letter Nora's lawyer cites a list of specific examples of gender discrimination against his client by the same group of male shift supervisors.

In response, the Border Patrol sector chief opens an investigation by his Office of Internal Affairs (OIA). Agent Nora Muñoz is subsequently interviewed by a team of two investigators from OIA. During this interview, Agent Muñoz says, she was interrogated as if she were a suspect in a crime, not the victim of a crime reporting it to the Border Patrol. Refusing to lose her composure, Agent Muñoz answers a series of hostile and, at times, humiliating questions to the best of her abilities.[18]

Five new female recruits recently joined Agent Muñoz and her other female colleague. In a matter of several months four of these five women, rather than continue to patrol the line, voluntarily took desk jobs at Nora's station. Only one of the new female agents now patrols in the field. Nora tells me she is convinced gender discrimination is the major reason most of the new female agents turned to desk jobs as an alternative to field duty. Desk jobs at the Border Patrol station minimize the possibilities for discrimination and harassment. Those who discriminate, including the group of male managers, feel that female Border Patrol agents belong behind a desk and not patrolling the line. The former they consider proper female work; the latter they consider proper male work. However, these same desk jobs automatically limit female agents' opportunity for the same professional development, career promotions, and salary increases as male agents patrolling the line.

For her own sanity and personal welfare, and the welfare of her family, Agent Nora Muñoz decides that, like the new female recruits to the station, she would volunteer for desk duty. This is a decision she hates to make, because she joined the Border Patrol to escape the doldrums of a relatively meaningless desk job. But she feels that she has run out of job options. By taking a desk job, she at least temporarily avoids the most blatant gender harassment. She also does not have to face midnight shift on the scope truck and city duty. Time off from the worst of the gender discrimination gives her the opportunity to reconsider her career options in law enforcement, including what is best for her family.

Agent Nora Muñoz estimates that with the most recent addition of female agents to her station, figuring in at the same time the growing number of male agents assigned there, in 2008 approximately 5 percent of all agents at her station are female.[19] When the number of female agents who patrol the line is counted, however, the percentage of female agents drops to 2 percent. Since discrimination based on gender has not ceased at her station, female agents continue to choose desk jobs as the best strategy to dampen its personal impact. This is the same percentage of female agents in the field, 2 percent, as when Nora first joined the station in 1997.

While the discrimination diminishes when Agent Nora Muñoz works at a desk job, it does not disappear. "It keeps getting back to the stress of it," Nora says.

Recently she was harangued by one of the supervisors about her annual leave. "They kept calling me up way ahead of the time they needed to know, asking me again and again when I planned to take my leave." Since Nora's husband is a cop, and his vacation time is limited, scheduling family vacation time for two working parents is not as easy as it sounds. The managers know that, of course, and chose to nag her about it for no other reason than entitlement.

"They just keep bugging me," she says.

Discrimination at Nora's Border Patrol Station still runs the gamut from the relatively mundane and irritating, for instance the petty haranguing, to the potentially life-threatening situations when male and female shift partners in the field may feel, as a result of discord sowed and heightened by the sanctioned gender discrimination, that they may not be able to rely on each other. The gender discrimination at Agent Muñoz's station takes the form not only of undeniable concrete actions and behaviors towards female agents, such as dead-end job assignments, but also overt, gendered symbolic statements.

When an agent dies, the American flag in front of Nora's Border Patrol station is immediately lowered to half mast to show respect for the agent and remains at half mast up to, and after, the funeral services and graveside ceremonies, a symbolic recognition of the personal contributions of the agent to the overall mission of the U.S. Border Patrol. The lowering of the flag is a long-standing tradition. One of the female agents recently assigned to Agent Muñoz's station died of natural causes. Shortly thereafter, one of only a small handful of retired female Border Patrol agents who served at this same station died after twenty years of service. After the deaths of both these female agents the station flag was lowered to half mast—but only on the days the agents were buried.

Whatever the various forms and shapes gender discrimination assumes in the U.S. Border Patrol, there are significant real costs to the taxpayer for each female agent who quits her job because she cannot tolerate the abuse. There are costs also to the general public because gender discrimination in many different ways obstructs the Border Patrol from its stated mission. Beyond this waste of fiscal and human resources, there is an equally pernicious personal cost to every individual female Border Patrol agent who daily faces job harassment. There are, too, the subsequent emotional and financial costs to the families of these dedicated female agents.

"You know," Agent Nora Muñoz says, "it just doesn't seem right. All that time I was out there facing all that risk with my life, they were causing stress within the job. I mean, it just seems like every agent already has all the stress they can manage outside of the job to not need it from the inside. They should be protecting you. You should feel safe from inside the job. But I never did. I never felt really safe."

CBP Agent Nora Muñoz

Chapter 9

Juliet Garcia's Fence and
Michael Chertoff's Wall

You've noticed the unique campus we
have here," David Pearson tells me,
"the palm forests, the Spanish tiles,
the historical restorations, the conversation areas where learning and education are encouraged to take place in informal and formal
surroundings. With President Garcia's full backing, the University Planning Committee has their
hand on every inch of space on this campus. We
have provided the infrastructure for real education to take place here. As a result, our campus is
unique. Students can see and feel the difference.
So can the faculty. Our challenge is we have to get
the students here first to see what we have to offer
them. Once they see our campus, they know they
want to be a part of what we have to offer."

Dr. David Pearson, vice president of partnership affairs, is in charge of marketing the University of Texas at Brownsville and Texas Southmost
College to the community and the region. He is
also in charge of all new construction on campus,

which means he is in charge of building the new border fence separating the campus from Matamoros, Tamaulipas, Mexico.

While her boss waits patiently for my full attention, the administrative assistant hands me a mug of hot coffee. Eyeing me from behind an impressively outsized desk in what was once the Fort Brown army infirmary that housed officers dying from malaria, Pearson resumes his well-rehearsed presentation as soon as I am ready. Never to be mistaken for a faculty member at UTB-TSC, at 8:30 in the morning Pearson, a tall, persuasive-looking individual, dresses in a dark suit, white shirt, and distinctive power tie.

Outside the thick brick-and-mortar office walls, under a restored loggia of the old fort, college students drift by on their way to classes. Before this same building was restored to its present pristine condition, less than fifty feet from where we sit in Pearson's generous surroundings Antonio Zavaleta, Olga Rivera Garcia, and I officed in cubicles paneled by Walmart.

It is the second week of October 2008. The campus fuss started eighteen months earlier when a group of campus administrators Googled the DHS website to locate exactly where the new border fence would be sited in Brownsville. The administrators stared at the map in front of them in amazement, then stared some more, because they could not believe their eyes: the line representing Secretary Chertoff's new border fence ran smack through the middle of their campus.

Along with community residents all along the border, these university administrators realized something the functionaries in Washington did not seem to understand. All land and people who end up on the south side of the new border fence, between the proposed new border fence and the Rio Grande, will no longer be in Brownsville. For all practical purposes, those located between the new border fence and the river at best will be in a no-man's land fully controlled by neither one country nor the other. Dividing the university with a new border fence automatically places the south side of the university in the existing transnational space between Mexico and the United States—a space most visible from the air as being marked by trash, river vegetation, and the absence of buildings.[1] The last thing the administrators wanted was pieces of UTB-TSC in border limbo.

For its part, DHS suggested that there was no reason to get excited about the impact of an eighteen-foot fence crossing the Brownsville university campus. They insisted that students, faculty, and anyone else who needs to get from point A to point B will still be able to do so with little difficulty. The DHS vaguely mentioned, for example, gates manned by Border Patrol agents. University students armed with special IDs issued by the Border Patrol would be granted passage from one side of the border fence to the other. No other information was forthcoming. Secretary Chertoff's posture, as filtered through the DHS staff and CBP officials in contact with the university, was bluntly dismissive of any concerns about the new border fence and its impact on campus life.

The Department of Homeland Security treated all landowners along the Rio Grande in exactly the same thoughtless manner. To DHS a university campus of twelve thousand students and seven hundred faculty and staff was no different than Baldomero Muñiz, a U.S. citizen and longtime Cameron County migrant farmworker who raises goats upriver from UTB-TSC. Both this minority public university and Baldomero Muñiz, who does not read English, got virtually the same letter from DHS demanding they immediately sign away their legal rights to their land bordering the Rio Grande so that DHS could survey it for a new border fence. In the same letter DHS threatened a lawsuit against any landowner, whether minority public university or Pamela Rivas, another citizen and owner of a few acres on the Rio Grande, who hesitated to sign.[2]

"I was one of the first people at the university to sit down at the table with them," Dr. Pearson continues. "You know, they just don't want to bargain. It was DHS and representatives from the Border Patrol. They were . . . ," Dr. Pearson now pauses to search for the exact word to describe these federal officials without seeming to offend them. His pause continuing to linger uncomfortably in the air, I offer up one among many possibilities.

"Intractable?" I say.

"Intractable," Dr. Pearson continues, very satisfied with my suggestion. "But you have to negotiate with them, and it was obvious from the first we were not going to get everything we wanted. You know," he adds in what seems a well-rehearsed aphorism, "that's kind of how it is in life. To some extent you wouldn't want to completely win the war, because then you have banished them, and there can be hard feelings about that."

University vice president Pearson was in on the first meetings with DHS officials flanked by CBP managers, but not before federal district judge Hanem ordered Chertoff's DHS and CBP to reach a settlement with President Garcia and her university. To get that order, Garcia took DHS and CBP to a hearing before the judge. The judge was not pleased by either the attitude or the behavior of DHS and its lawyers, and ordered both sides, the feds and the university, to the negotiating table with a deadline for a settlement amendable to both.

DHS's die-hard refusal to negotiate a single comma in their demands of President Garcia, or with any of the other border landowners in Cameron County, including those represented by Texas RioGrande Legal Aid's David Hall, genuinely displeased Judge Hanem. Since the full weight of the law was behind DHS and CBP, there was little question about the eventual out-come of this legal conflict between DHS and the university. But by DHS's underestimation of the power and influence of Cameron County politics upon the judicial system, a lesson long since learned by major Dallas and Houston legal firms with criminal or civil cases before Valley courts, DHS forfeited its overwhelming legal advantage by annoying the judge.[3] As a result, valuable construction time for the new border fence was irretriev-ably lost.

DHS also failed to appreciate the local, state, and national leverage of President Garcia as chief administrator of a Latino public university in an impoverished border region. And Judge Hanem did not tolerate DHS's bul-lying in his courtroom.

In short, there would have been far fewer time delays in the construction of this portion of the border fence in Cameron County, and others all along the borderlands, if DHS and CBP had approached landowners, including this public university, with a modicum of respect, empathy, and willingness to discuss mutual needs and objectives. In the total absence of any DHS and CBP planning or marketing of the border fence to community residents, the general public in many border communities sensed they were once more being trod upon by federal outsiders.[4] The citizens of Cameron County, and their elected representatives, were more than willing to fight back when DHS and CBP threw the first set of legal punches.[5]

To the U.S. Congress, DHS officials described the resulting time delays in fence construction along the border as unavoidable problems in "land acqui-sitions."[6] But the majority of the land acquisition delays in Cameron County, which cost DHS additional millions of dollars, could have been at least partly avoided if Chertoff's DHS had relinquished its steamroller tactics. While that approach may have worked in some border areas, it failed miser-ably in others.

Valley property owners strongly resisted DHS's bullying, which was pre-mised upon threats of condemnation proceedings and a stance of nonnego-tiation. Of the 122 Texas property owners who refused to sell their land to DHS, 97 owned land in the Valley. These Valley landowners continued to hold out against DHS through the fall of 2008. The direct result of this strat-egy by Valley landowners and others in the Texas borderlands is that while DHS was able to start four border fence projects in adjacent Hidalgo County, seventeen other Valley fence projects had not moved beyond the initial plan-ning stages by the same time.[7]

The DHS officials, along with the CBP, filled the preliminary UTB-TSC meetings with big-city bravado, legal obfuscation, and Washingtonian chat-ter designed to intimidate the local border yokels. But their steely-eyed squints and bad manners failed miserably in Brownsville. The university administrators, armed with professional legal counsel and local heavyweights such as Michael Putegnat, a former university board member and successful entrepreneur, had seen this federal dog-and-pony show before.

For many years the citizens of Brownsville and their elected and appointed representatives, as is the case throughout the Valley and along the borderlands, fought hard for their fair share of funding from the state and the feds for regional infrastructure, health care clinics for migrant farmworkers, secondary school facilities, bilingual education, higher education, and basic necessities for low-income Latino residents living in border *colonias*. From the perspective of many residents of the borderlands, little distinction exists between federal and state governments, agencies, and programs. Brownsville and Cameron County, like many of the other municipalities and counties in the borderlands, have been historically shortchanged, ignored, and manipulated by state and federal officials, agencies, and programs, often in favor of more affluent Anglo districts or regions with stronger political representation in Austin and Washington.

One particularly egregious example of the long-term neglect of the impoverished borderlands, including the Valley, is a Mexican American Legal Defense and Education Fund (MALDEF) class action lawsuit, *LULAC et al. v. Richards et al.*, against the State of Texas and the University of Texas System. The lawsuit, filed in 1987 for the historical failure to adequately fund border universities and colleges, was finally settled after a long litigation process. One result of the settlement was new construction with a price tag of $500 million at Texas border campuses. These border institutions, all with predominantly Hispanic student bodies, included UTB-TSC in Brownsville, University of Texas–Pan American in Hidalgo County, and other state universities in Laredo and El Paso.[8]

President Garcia wisely hired a nationally known security expert to aid her university in their negotiations with DHS and CBP. University officials at the negotiating table were, as the days, weeks, and months passed by, far from intimidated by the gyrations of the federal representatives. Even though DHS had the full weight of federal law squarely on its side, its legal shell games and swagger simply did not sway these university officials. As these perambulations dragged on and on, DHS continued day by day to lose irretrievable construction time on the border fence. Finally, DHS agreed to a settlement with the university. Then, at the very last minute, DHS summarily reneged on the negotiated agreement, and the two sides were back at square one.

Judge Hanem was not amused by DHS's arrogance at the bargaining table. Nor was he pleased with DHS's lack of information, including information on the design and planning of the proposed border fence to be constructed in Cameron County. Months rolling by, representatives for DHS and CBP, chastised by the judge, returned to the bargaining table yet again and eventually reached a second agreement with the university that was identical to the first. Embedded in this final negotiated agreement between the two parties, an agreement approved by Judge Hanem, is a rather offbeat, quirky grenade of a concept, a border fence never before remotely considered by DHS, CBP, Boeing, or any other public entity.

In return for the concessions that the University of Texas Brownsville–Texas Southmost College by law had to cede to DHS and CBP—these laws the result of Rep. Sensenbrenner's Real ID Act of 2005—the university negotiated a repositioned border fence on its campus. This new border fence was much better suited to the needs of the university community and Brownsville. The real bombshell in the final settlement, however, was that the university's portion of the border fence would, to a degree never before imagined by federal officials, accommodate the aesthetics of the university's longstanding planning committee, which is responsible for the overall design of the campus. According to the agreement between DHS and the university, the university border fence would be pleasing and as inoffensive to the university community and border residents as possible.

A significant portion of the university's student population, faculty, staff, and administration, like that of the University of Texas at El Paso and other institutions along or near the Mexican border, are Hispanic by birth and culture. Many resident Anglos also share a regional heritage with the Hispanic population. President Garcia believed that the border fence must not, under any circumstances, send the wrong message to either this constituency, the city, or the county, the majority of whom are Americans of Hispanic descent, or to the residents of Matamoros, Brownsville's twin city for more than one and one-half centuries.

To President Juliet Garcia, staff member Olga Garcia, administrators David Pearson and Antonio Zavaleta, longtime Brownsville resident and former board member Michael Putegnat, and many other residents of Brownsville and Cameron County, Matamoros in the state of Tamaulipas is not a foreign city in a distant land. This border region is, contrary to what DHS and CBP imagine it, one people breathing the same air, drinking water from the same river, and enjoying many of the same values and aspirations. Although this shared heritage has been stained by centuries of bloody conflicts, it posits DHS and CBP less as friends and protectors than as remote slumlords periodically appearing with lists of nonnegotiable demands.

In effect, President Garcia and her administrators insisted that DHS and CBP agree that UTB-TSC is and should be treated as a binational institution of public learning. The university is not, as DHS would have it, another anonymous landowner along the Rio Grande who DHS can bully into submission.

President Juliet Garcia's border fence in Brownsville is as different from Boeing's Project 28 as a slingshot is from a rocket propelled grenade. Juliet Garcia's border fence is a mesh, chain-link affair not uncommon to many American backyards. Carefully attended to by university groundskeepers, this fence is taller by a few feet than backyard fences, but unobtrusive; one sees through the green mesh. Human-sized, Juliet Garcia's green mesh border fence is the epitome of low tech, even though it is backed by visually unobtrusive cameras and other security devices. But the modest dimensions of the university fence do not compromise its security purpose. This is a border fence that would have kept the two undocumented workers who crossed the running path of Antonio Zavaleta and me, so many years ago, from disappearing into the nearby streets of downtown Brownsville.

This barrier falls within what most Americans envision when they hear the words *border fence* pronounced by the DHS, CBP, and elected politicians when referencing the new construction in the U.S.-Mexico borderlands. While it fits well within CBP's category of primary fencing to prohibit pedestrians from crossing into the United States, the university fence is uniquely different.

Simplicity at its core, this university border fence is the antithesis of low-tech fence construction and virtual Project 28.

At $1.04 million a mile, Dr. Juliet Garcia's fence is also much less expensive than all other border fences to date. It is, in fact, four to seven times cheaper in 2009 dollars than any of its counterparts. One way the university saved money was by hiring a local contractor rather than outside regional or national contractors. According to David Pearson, the primary contractor for the university border fence was Thrall Construction *Rent-A-Fence*. Emphasis added.

That's right. Thrall Construction *Rent-A-Fence*.

Pearson tells me, "It's going to be ten feet tall with nine-inch chain mesh. It sits on a concrete foundation, and the mesh is anchored to it below the ground. It's going to have posts every fifteen feet or so that are plastered over in an earth-tone color. It will fit aesthetically with our educational mission.

"We've got to clear four feet on either side of it from any vegetation, but the president [Juliet Garcia] is hoping that after a while the Border Patrol will forget about it and then we can plant bougainvillea."

"When do you start?"

"Very soon. By the end of this month. We've got to keep to the schedule that we agreed upon with DHS. So we start in three weeks, maybe less."

Fig. 9.1 University of Texas at Brownsville–Texas Southmost College border fence, Brownsville, Texas, 2009.

While DHS and CBP wasted valuable time attempting to intimidate the university at the negotiating table in Brownsville, the Hidalgo County Commissioners' Court next door to Cameron County commenced border fence construction. In some sections along the Rio Grande, the fence is very near completion.

Swiveling in his chair, Pearson asks me, "You want to see some photos of the fence construction in Hidalgo County?" He scans through a list of files on his desktop computer and then turns back to me in frustration.

"Sorry about this. As you can imagine, I have so many documents about the fence that I can't find the photo files right now. I was going to print them for you. We got many photos of the construction after we were given a tour by the Border Patrol."

Then he adds as an afterthought, "You can see the poor quality of the construction in the photos. It's very clear."

"Oh?" I say.

"Well, you can tell it is being built too fast. They are rushing it. So that's what you get when you try to rush things. You know, lack of craftsmanship, that sort of thing."

Then Pearson, a careful professional who perhaps realizes he may have spoken out of turn, recites a list of the construction projects he has overseen or currently oversees for the university. The price tag for these projects exceeds $150 million. There is the new university library, the student recreational and wellness center, the university day care center, the student health center, and major conversions of student dormitories. Pearson is naturally very proud of this list of accomplishments that he has supervised and signed off on. In the process he has followed the new construction from the planning stages to ribbon cutting while daily overseeing all of the contractors and subcontractors.

As trained, I remain silent, waiting for Pearson to add any additional observations about the quality of the border fence that he personally observed under construction in Hidalgo County. Hearing no new information about this topic, I carefully probe the subject further, but he is unwilling to say much more.[9] He gives me a list of names of some of the others who were on this same tour of the border fence construction in Hidalgo County.

After being pleasantly ushered out of Dr. Pearson's office, I walk over to Olin Library to find Olga Rivera Garcia. I have not seen Olga for six months. Following her directions, I climb the lobby stairs but then search in vain for her office. Circling the entire second floor of the library, I finally stop to ask directions at one of the student reading labs.

"Olga Rivera Garcia," repeats a friendly woman seated just inside the door of the lab.

"She moved here a few months ago. She's in Information Technology on this floor."

The bespectacled woman looks through a hard copy of the campus phone directory, goes online, shakes her head, then gets up and walks out the door. She returns five minutes later.

"She's in room 203," she tells me.

"I know that. But I can't find the room."

Again the woman, now deeply sighing, disappears. After she returns, she tells me to follow her. We walk around the stacks and soon stand at the top of the main staircase.

"Right here," she says, pointing at a door. Someone has covered the glass windows of the office with an opaque material that looks like cloth. The office door is closed and locked. A sign on the door reads, "Secure Area." The number on the office door is not in sequence with any of the other doors along the corridor, but that matters little because the numbers are too faded to read.

After trying the door, I knock loudly. Surprised to see a visitor, a middle-aged man opens the door. Several computers fill the tops of four ancient wooden desks jammed into the small, dark room. I ask to see Olga, but I hear a coworker behind the door say she is not there and he does not know where she is. I leave her a written message.

More than twenty years after leaving UTB-TSC for another university position, I climb the stairs leading to the offices of my former colleague and running partner, Antonio Zavaleta, now vice president for external affairs. One of Antonio's administrative assistants announces my presence, and Antonio comes striding out of his office with a stack of books under his arm.

A large man, even without benefit of his cowboy boots, Tony immediately fills the waiting room with his girth and his personality. After the traditional *abrazo*, he proudly hands me a book on the history of Brownsville that he edited. Only then do I notice his face creased from sun, wind, and too many hours spent in university committee meetings. With gusto Antonio tells me about his newest book.

"You know those brown bags I was always collecting back in the day?"

I nod my head.

"I went around to all the *farmacias*, pharmacies, and *yerberias*, stores selling medicinal herbs, in Matamoros to collect them. The *curanderos*, folk healers, told me where to go and what to buy. Do you really remember all that stuff in my book cases?"

I nod again because I can still clearly see the small brown bags stuffed with hundreds of samples of herbs for a variety of ailments ranging from diarrhea to lost love. By the time I left Brownsville, many of those brown bags literally had begun to deteriorate, the leaves and stems of their dusty contents falling to the floor whenever a breeze wafted through an open window.

"My book is finally about to come out. It turns out that no one has studied this since Trotter and Chavira's work on alcoholism and *curanderismo*, folk healing."[10] With pride Antonio hands me a page of the forthcoming manuscript that includes a partial list of natural remedies in Spanish and English alongside their medicinal uses. All are neatly categorized and enumerated on a spreadsheet.

"I thought I'd never see the day I would get this put together," he tells me. "It's the first medicinal dictionary of its kind."

I congratulate Antonio on his academic accomplishments as he shows me the most recent pictures of his eleven-month-old son. Wonder and amazement in his voice, he tells me, "I'm going to be eighty years old when he graduates from high school. So I'm taking care of myself more than I used to."

That gives me the opportunity, as we finally sit down in Antonio's cluttered corner office, to ask if he remembers the time we were running around the golf course when two undocumented workers came out of the river weeds. Antonio says he remembers, although the incident clearly made a much stronger impression on me than him. We talk about those days and how the new border fence may change the borderlands. Then he tells me he owns ten acres along the Rio Grande.

"Did you get a letter from DHS?"

"Damn right I did. I'm doing everything I can to comply with them. I'm not trying to cause any problems. But did you hear what DHS is doing to the Sabal Palm grove? The Sabal Palm Grove Sanctuary is a national treasure. You've been there, right? They've fenced it off from the public. Makes no sense. Remember the wild parrots? The wildlife? There's a caretaker who lives out there, and the sanctuary is now separated from his house by the fence. This is no joke. I can't believe it."

I ask him about Olga Rivera Garcia. "There are some people on campus who don't realize what an asset to this community she is," Antonio tells me. "She is a whirlwind of activity." I remind him of the days when Olga mustered our teenage surveyors, pushing them by her own example to work up to their potential.

"She was something," Antonio agrees.

Although Antonio complains about the major aches and pains of years gone by, he has a life as full as that of any three individuals. He's a larger-than-life personality always in motion. The late Brownsville artist George Truan once dropped as an aside that he regularly saw auras framing the heads of those he encountered. For George Truan it was clearly not a startling announcement or claim, simply a statement of *lo que pasa*, what happens to him when he looks at others. At the time, Antonio and I were standing in the street in front of George's house drinking beer out of cans and talking about contemporary Chicano art and how best to restore old pickup trucks. Given hindsight, I am sure George must have witnessed Antonio's brightly colored aura on repeated occasions.

Making a sweeping gesture around his office, a space filled to every nook and cranny with Chicano art, enlarged photos of local saints and *curanderos*, home altars of patron saints, and hundreds of other mementos of his border research, Antonio Zavaleta gets to the point. "This fence has taken a major portion of our time as an institution. You would not believe those DHS guys. It's been a mess."

Although border fence construction has not commenced in Cameron County because of the legal delays brought by the UTB-TSC case as well as cases filed by Executive Director David Hall at Texas RioGrande Legal Aid and lawyers representing the owners of large ranches and farms bordering the river, the Hidalgo County Commissioners' Court has been supervising fence planning and construction for more than a year. Once more I set up a tour with the Weslaco Border Patrol, which polices a major section of the Mexican border in Hidalgo County. But first I want to get my own view of construction sites without the Border Patrol entourage in tow. The day after seeing David Pearson, Antonio Zavaleta, and other university officials, I once more drive out Old Military Highway to Anzalduas County Park.

The drive to Anzalduas takes much longer than usual because heavy construction equipment blocks the narrow highway, along with road workers holding signs cautioning drivers to reduce their speed. When I finally round the corner of the road leading into Anzalduas County Park, I see to the east, set back half a mile from the Rio Grande, a two-mile stretch of the earthen levee built by the Army Corps of Engineers after Hurricane Beulah hit this region in 1967. Now out-of-scale earth moving equipment has bulldozed and dumped an additional three feet of material atop this old levee, bringing it to a standard height of ten feet. To reach this new height, the base of the levee also has been substantially broadened to bear the extra load.

An extra three feet seems insignificant, but it noticeably raises the new levee on which I stand above the stunted mesquite and other vegetation covering the flat Valley delta lands. Only the palm trees along the river loom higher. After knowing this same view for three decades, I try to imagine the completed structure when an additional eight feet in steel tubes are set in place by the giant cranes. The project engineers refer to the steel tubes as bollards. With the bollards in place, the border fence facing the Rio Grande will stand a full eighteen feet high and twenty-five feet or more thick at its base. I try to imagine a completed concrete and steel structure three times my height stretching in either direction to the horizon.

Unlike either the university border fence or the border fence to be built in the rest of Cameron County, this stretch of Hidalgo County fence is a unique result of direct negotiations between a Hidalgo County judge, J. D. Salinas, and Secretary Chertoff's DHS. Again looking at the partially completed levee, I try to imagine what the new spatial environment created between the new border fence and the Rio Grande, a corridor of riparian farmland from a quarter to more than half a mile in width, will become six months into the future. For more than two and one-half centuries this same area has been ranchland and farmland. My attempt to envision this

Fig. 9.2 Workers pouring concrete in front of old levee for Hidalgo County hydraulic wall. View from south side of levee, 2008. (Courtesy Cari Lambrecht and Hidalgo County Drainage District)

new rural landscape falls short, because I am overwhelmed by the changes that already have taken place since my last visit.

Although it is in transition, what I see before me now is much more than a new corridor defined by the growing border fence on one side and the Rio Grande on the other. This rural landscape a not yet a no-man's land. While owned by American farmers and ranchers, this unfinished, new space at this time seems entirely defined by its vulnerability to Mexico.

The new border fence in Hidalgo County is stuck for the present in the process of becoming. In full-throttle change, it is temporarily neither fish nor fowl. But this becoming fence emphasizes how open the international border was and still is between the two countries—how much the bends and twists of the Rio Grande/Río Bravo are both American and Mexican and neither. If you build a border fence of the proportions I now see between Mexico and the United States where there was no fence before, then the

Fig. 9.3 Construction of hydraulic wall at Anzalduas County Park, Hidalgo County, Texas, 2009. View from the south.

partial construction of the fence highlights its prior absence. Now the necessity to complete the border fence to protect the homeland appears at least visually compelling.

I am staggered by both the visual changes and implications for the future brought about by the contractors hired by the Hidalgo County Commissioners' Court. What sticks with me most throughout the rest of the day is both the immense size of this project in progress and, too, the substantive human changes that must logically follow. It is one thing to see the border fence drawn out on Google maps and quite another to observe its dominating presence and to consider its future impacts.

From a road atop the old levee I motor down into the seeming quiet of Anzalduas County Park. At the park entrance I am surprised to find two Hidalgo County deputy sheriffs waiting for me. Following their hand motions, I pull over in my rental and lower my window. The full heat of the day comes flooding into the car. It is the first time in thirty years I have encountered Hidalgo County deputy sheriffs at Anzalduas.

At the park entrance there is normally a nondescript county employee sitting in dark blue pants and pale blue shirt inside a small butler building. This employee always waves visitors on into the park environs, then returns to whatever business with which he was engaged. These two Hidalgo County deputies are an anomaly. They return my greeting and then give me and my rental a quick professional once-over. Then the one closest to me says, as if employed by the Hidalgo County Chamber of Commerce, "Enjoy your visit." Except this ambassador of goodwill has a gun on his hip, handcuffs and extra bullet clips on his tool belt, and a shotgun visible in the front seat of his patrol car.

This time driving into Anzalduas I feel the same as when I clear a Border Patrol checkpoint on the main highways heading north out of the Valley—one on the south side of Falfurrias, and the other on the south side of Kingsville. Like everyone else at those checkpoints I am methodically scrutinized by law enforcement officers for possibly smuggling humans, drugs, or otherwise being a person of interest. For five seconds I am a suspect, then, after the visual check and, on occasion, a run-by from the sniffer dog, I am directed through and past the checkpoint to continue on my trip to Houston or Austin.

But there is a substantive difference between the encounter with law enforcers at Anzalduas and that at Valley CBP checkpoints. At Anzalduas I am doing nothing more than entering a recreational park owned by the general public. I remain, in fact, at least a quarter of a mile from the Rio Grande.

As soon as the new border fence is completed, Anzalduas County Park effectively will be between countries in a land squeezed between an eighteen-foot-tall imposing construction and the Rio Grande. As you enter the park to kick back and relax after a hard week's work, you will be greeted by friendly hosts who are heavily armed. The human and drug smugglers, as suggested earlier, will no longer take over Anzalduas from dusk to dawn; they will simply move up or down river to quieter landings where the new border fence does not interfere with their business.

After the events of 9/11, there has been a slow but steady move by DHS to employ various law enforcement agencies to increase border security. At the time of 9/11, CBP agents possessed limited legal authority to stop or arrest suspects at a certain distance from the border. Forced at times to depend on local law enforcement, the CBP rarely put much trust in them, because historically local law enforcers, including the most recent sheriffs of Hidalgo and Cameron Counties, worked for the Mexican drug cartels. The county governments, as discussed earlier, have also been riddled with graft and corruption at every elected and appointed level, including law enforcement.

Nevertheless, the DHS has developed a number of joint programs with municipal, county, and state law enforcement agencies, referred to as the ICE 287(g) programs, designed to assist DHS and CBP along the border and in the interior with broadly defined security and immigration issues. DHS cannot rely directly on the American military for this assistance, because the Posse Comitatus Act of 1878 prevents the military from policing civilians except when authorized by Congress. Participation in these joint DHS-funded programs is voluntary, although substantial federal grants were offered to cash-strapped police and sheriff's departments in the impoverished borderlands and nonborder states. Fiscal oversight of these interagency programs is tepid, as are program performance evaluations and accountability.[11]

On this October afternoon there is only one other vehicle visiting Anzalduas County Park. A pickup with Texas plates pulls up about fifty yards from where I stand staring across the river at Mexico. A young Latino couple climbs out of the truck cab, looks briefly around, then just as quickly climbs back in and drives off. I hear the echo of the exhaust as the truck leaves the park. Other than the couple, the only other individuals I see throughout my visit are a handful of Hidalgo County groundskeepers.

New concrete barriers block off all side roads in and out of Anzalduas. New steel cables border the main park road that ambles among the stately mesquites. New chain link fence covers the crumbling dock along the river. A half-hearted attempt has been made to paint the rotting wood of the old pier. On the Mexican banks of the Río Bravo young boys swim leisurely in the river water, and to their right, upriver, three male adults fish, with the bobbers on their lines lazily drifting in the slow current. Several other men on the Mexican banks drink beer as they light up their portable grills.

On my way out of Anzalduas I check the park fences and the thick brush for any telltale signs of smuggling. I find human tracks in the dust, new cuts in the barbed wire fencing, empty green garbage bags and discarded cans of food, empty plastic water bottles, and other signs of human smuggling within the boundaries of the park.

The old walls of La Lomita Chapel, long a landmark for drug smugglers and human traffickers, is covered in new gang graffiti. In front of the former Oblate place of worship, the parking lot is cordoned off by a makeshift barbed wire fence. At Pepe's River Side Fiesta Club, a stone's throw upriver from Anzalduas, the parking lot is empty. Several other nearby businesses look empty or closed.

Later in the day, again at the Blue Onion Restaurant in Weslaco, David

Hall tells me, "We got them temporarily on what you might call a legal technicality," this with a sly arch of the eyebrow. Dressed in the same suit as he was the last time I saw him, this time the executive director of Texas RioGrande Legal Aid is without his Yale lawyer. He looks wearier than usual, more restrained, but explains it away as having some "health issues."

"I've got those property owners with the letters from DHS," David continues. "When stalling didn't work, we went to Plan B. The bill that Congress passed allows them to build a fence 'along the river.' But somewhere, as these things often do, the wording got changed to 'vicinity of the river.'

"DHS is trying to get access to land owned by one of my Cameron County clients that is at least one-half mile from the river. Not 'along the river,' but in the 'vicinity of the river.' I've got the issue before Judge Hanem. He hasn't ruled on it yet, but, until he does, they [DHS and CBP] are dead in the water in Cameron County. They can't build until he gives a ruling. I have no idea what else Judge Hanem has before him, but I'm guessing maybe some concerns put out by the attorneys for the big ranchers and farmers in the area. Who knows what else.

"Here's the thing. Even if the judge throws out my piece of paper, it's going to take DHS at least three to four months to start building something. I mean, they're going to turn around and give the Army Corps of Engineers the go-ahead, but that in itself is going to take some time." When David mentions the Army Corps of Engineers, he visibly grimaces.

"Then the Corps—what a bunch of incompetents they are—is going to start hiring the subcontractors to actually do the work. Some from in-state, some from far away. Do you know why the construction is really slowed down with the fence in Hidalgo County?"

"No."

"Can't find enough legal workers. Imagine that. Can't find enough legal workers. You know the feds want to stay squeaky clean on this one or they will get egg on their face. Just imagine what would happen if they got caught using illegal workers to build a fence to keep out illegal workers."

For the first time David chuckles, a cynical guffaw based on forty years of litigating against employers in South Texas who won't pay farmworkers after they pick their harvest, or fairly compensate crews on shrimp boats the same as their American counterparts. Then there are the national insurance companies that arbitrarily raised the premiums on the trucks of farmworkers just before they are ready to migrate up north to work the fields. And the greedy Valley developers who foreclose on *colonia* residents after they miss just one payment on their house, built with their own hands, because they are working the crops in Missouri, Iowa, or Wisconsin.[12] David has a long list.

One result of this kind of history of employment abuse in the Valley and elsewhere is that citizens are hesitant to work jobs that pay minimum wage and are also burdened with safety abuses. One such American industry is the construction industry. In North Carolina, for example, the rate of serious injuries and deaths has been rising in the last decade; the majority of these construction workers are Hispanic and undocumented.[13] Even in the Valley, notorious for its high rates of poverty, unemployed workers who are legal residents stay away from any industry in which serious injuries and deaths are common.

We talk about the presidential elections fast approaching, David saying finally, "I don't know if this country can take another four years like the last eight we had. I don't know if Legal Aid can take it. I'm not sure I can. Might have to ship out. You know, fill up the boat with food, tequila, and all the other necessities, then head for Mexico."

"You're telling me you are going to retire if McCain wins the election?" I can't believe that after all these years David Hall may call it quits.

"I came down here in 1965 and became the executive director in 1969," David says, not answering my question.

"That's a long time."

"You know, even if Barack wins, it's going to take a year, maybe eighteen months, for the bozos to stop building the fence here. Congress appropriated the money, and they're just going to keep building it. Let's just say for the hell of it Barack wins. He'll make his political appointments, they'll meet, task forces will be formed, that kind of thing. But it won't happen overnight. It'll take them a while to figure out what they want to do [with the border fence]."

Later, heading towards Weslaco on Highway 83, I reconsider what I've just seen earlier at Anzalduas. I cannot get the images of the eighteen-foot fence out of my head. How can you consider an unfinished eighteen-foot-tall structure, a massive structure already dwarfing the landscape before its completion, a mere fence?

Up until this point I always try to call the border structure what others call it. They say fence, I say fence. They say wall, I say wall. But naming and identifying what I've just seen at Anzalduas a border fence makes little rational sense. Certainly the Anzalduas structure is not comparable to the barrier I observed in Belfast separating Protestant and Catholic neighborhoods. Although covering a distance of not more than ten miles, the Belfast wall was solid, much taller, and topped with chain link nets to catch bombs hurled from one side to the other. Nor does the Anzalduas fence exactly compare to the former Berlin Wall, which I also observed from both sides of the divided city. While taller and longer than the wall that divided Berlin, the Anzalduas fence will not have machine gun emplacements, orders to shoot on sight, or mine fields. However different, both the constructions in Belfast and Berlin were clearly walls.

Language is crucial and persuasive in and of itself. Ultimately, the use of certain terms instead of others can have political and social consequences. If DHS and CBP, along with their public supporters and the media, call this construction a border fence, then that connotes to those who have not actually seen it a meaning and definition that is, for all practical purposes, totally deceptive. These new sections of the border fence are not *fence* in any sense of the word as commonly understood or meant. Already before completion, these constructions are nothing more or less than imposing and massive border walls.

Omar Sanchez, Weslaco Station field operation supervisor (FOS), and I drive silently along the same route as the last time. The FOS stops once more to show me the new border construction at the Progreso bridge, the port of entry near Donna, and at Cage Boulevard. Nuevo Progreso is a tiny sister community to Progreso. Winter tourists are attracted to Nuevo Progreso by the inexpensive Mexican prescription drugs, liquor, leather jackets, pottery, household items in volume, such as toothpaste, soap, and dish cleaner, and the usual assortment of Mexican trinkets. This Mexican border community is best known for Arturo's Restaurant, where rag-tag cover bands play "I Can't Get No Satisfaction" and "Let it Be" to customers gorging on "game dinners" and *cervezas*.

Nuevo Progreso's most recent claim to fame is that part of it blew up. A leak in a gas line at the Red Snapper Restaurant damaged a few blocks of Nuevo Progreso tourist curio shops along the main thoroughfare, including *farmacias*, *dentisterias*, and *restaurantes*. Six Mexicans were killed, and another fourteen injured.[14] For many years Nuevo Progreso also has been a hot spot for human smugglers and drug traffickers.

What I see before me now is not a fence, as the case at Anzalduas, but a full-blown border wall. But the wall facing Nuevo Progreso is further along towards completion and, in ways not yet evident at Anzalduas, substantively and permanently changes the rural landscape. Sculptured by a fleet of giant earth movers, road graders, and cranes, this new border wall captures, separates, and totally isolates the farmlands bordering the Rio Grande. In so doing, the wall creates new vistas and boundaries shaped in parallelograms and rhomboids filled with fields of sugarcane and orchards not yet in seasonal bloom.

FOS Sanchez, in contrast to my earlier visit, no longer refers to the new construction as a fence. It is now, perhaps in partial deference to the obvious, a "border barrier." But this man-made construction before us is no more a barrier than the mighty Mississippi at Dubuque, Iowa, is a stream. Facing Nuevo Progreso and its surroundings, the wall I see before me is monumental in size and scale. It stretches to the east and west as far as the eye can see. Outsized cranes move concrete forms around like Tinkertoys as newly poured concrete cures under the heat of a tropical sun.

At once both friendly and brisk, but always an exemplar of the professional CBP agent, FOS Sanchez tells me that the recent rains from Hurricane Dolly slowed barrier construction to a standstill, but now it has resumed. We trek through the mud to get to the wall, FOS Sanchez in full uniform, including body armor and service weapon. In many places a foot or more of water covers the foundation footings of the border wall, causing the sides of the sandy trenches to cave in. The water table this near the Rio Grande must be very close to the surface. Pumps work hard to empty the water from the trenches. I have no way to tell if the water is from Hurricane Dolly or seepage from the groundwater.

In the unfinished sections the exposed concrete foundations bearing the full weight of the wall cut five to eight feet into the ground below the old levees. Extending ten feet above ground level, solid concrete forms, perhaps two feet or more thick, front the old earthen levees. In theory, although untested, this concrete buffer in front of the levees protects the structural integrity of the old levee from potential flooding. Atop the ten feet of concrete are steel bollards rising an additional eight feet. Perhaps eight to ten inches or more in diameter, the bollards are spaced so that no individual can squeeze between them even if he or she may manage to climb to the summit of the concrete portion of the wall.

I walk up to the wall, gazing upward at an angle to see the clear blue sky between the steel beams. This steel cannot be cut with wire cutters. Instead, these bollards require a welder, a torch, and a tank of acetylene. I am reminded of the welding shops in Matamoros typical along the border—an industry renowned for inexpensive car and truck repairs. The Mexican tube wranglers near Anzalduas also come to mind.[15]

Drug smugglers have already built specially designed portable steel ramps across the border wall in the desert south of Tucson. After crossing loaded vans, cars, and trucks over the border wall by way of the ramp, they then dismantle it before CBP agents can arrive.[16] Could I be witnessing the birth of a new occupation and industry along the Mexican border, that of welders harvesting bollards bundled like sugarcane? Then en el otro lado the bollard harvesters would resell the scarce steel to construct casas y tiendas, homes and stores.

The new monolith rising up in Hidalgo County is a part of the old levee system designed to control the floodwaters of the Rio Grande.[17] Where the new border wall under construction follows the line of the existing old levee, there is a narrow gap between the two of five feet or less, presumably waiting to be filled in after the concrete cures.

On the south side of this immense concrete and steel wall there is also a drag road for Border Patrol vehicles. A quarter to half a mile straight south—distances are difficult to gauge in this flat land—lies a twisting line of palms and vegetation marking the banks of the Rio Grande. Unfenced farmland surrounds the construction site, miles and miles of flat fields on both sides of the new wall, fields fallow but for some knee-high sugarcane and occasional citrus orchards bare of fruit. Between this new wall and the Rio Grande, three irrigation workers dressed in traditional white move slowly from the field to their truck, then back again to the field, as they manipulate sections of plastic pipe in anticipation of the next season's plantings.

FOS Sanchez continues to refer to the new wall as a "barrier." I do not contradict him, although I am growing irritated by what I see before me and the terminology he and the rest of the CBP agents I have met that day insist upon using.

I ask permission to take photographs of the border wall. Sanchez brakes his truck, and I stiffly climb out of the front passenger seat to shoot the wall with a disposable camera purchased from Rite Aid. I snap several photographs before scraping the mud from my boots and climbing back into the cab.

At last the image pops into my head of what, at least in terms of scale, my optical nerve has recorded at Anzalduas, Nuevo Progreso, and the Donna port of entry. This border wall in scale, size, and location matches some of the photographs I have seen of WPA projects during the Great Depression, including construction projects in many national and state parks in mountain valleys and deserts far from urban populations. Only the border wall here in South Texas is without the phalanxes of workers; they have been replaced by giant cranes and road plows. During the entire afternoon I see, in fact, no more than ten to fifteen construction workers tending to the wall. Only in the earlier stages of construction, when the concrete is poured onto the forms, are workers required in greater numbers. The majority of workers I do observe sit behind the wheels of heavy equipment excavating dirt, positioning bollards, and moving concrete forms about. Another difference from the WPA projects is the antiseptic character of this wall, which is purely functional in design. It is like an out-of-scale prison wall situated in a game preserve. In fact, this portion of the border wall is only a few miles upriver of the Santa Ana National Wildlife Refuge.

To get a better look at the border wall at the Donna port of entry, the FOS and I again step into thick mud that later threatens to capture our vehicle. There, only a few bollards are in place atop the wall.

I am somewhat surprised there is a wall being built here, but say nothing to FOS Sanchez. While Nuevo Progreso has been a hot spot for illegal crossers for years, Donna has rarely been a locus for human or drug trafficking.

The final portion of the border wall FOS Sanchez shows me is straight south of McAllen near Cage Boulevard. Six months earlier I watched a city crew complete work on a nearby culvert in preparation for the wall construction. Today I find no recognizable landmarks around the wall save for the street; the landscape has been created anew. Again the massive construction project stretches eastward to the horizon. I ask FOS Sanchez, as I did on my last visit, how the farmers, ranchers, and other field workers are going to gain access to the lands lying between the new wall and the Rio Grande. His answer is the same as before.

"We honestly don't know yet. Gates, I think."

"Where will the gates go?" I ask.

"DHS is running this." Irritation is evident in his tone of voice. "They haven't told us anything. Look, this is not a Border Patrol fence, this is strictly DHS. They have not asked us for input. When we raise questions, they tell us, 'This is our fence, not yours.'"

"How is the wall going to change the ways in which you pursue illegal workers or drug traffickers?"

"I don't know," FOS Sanchez tells me. "I really haven't given it much thought. I guess it should make it easier. But as far as tactics and management strategies of personnel, I really haven't thought about it.

"What I can tell you is I'm pleased there were no protests to talk about. We were very concerned about it. But there were no protests out here. I think people started seeing that it [the barrier] was a good thing. They're pretty conservative around here, like those big houses over there you see in that development. Those are houses of the rich. I'd say that Judge Salinas was a smart politician to bring all this together. I never paid him much attention. I mean, the way he got them [DHS] to build on the levees and got them moving on it. It was him that put it all together. Not like down in Cameron County, where there has been no progress.

"But I'm a little worried about the flooding. We had a bunch of water coming out of Amistad [Lake Amistad Dam] upstream. Not just flooding the Mexican side, but our side. We had to suspend patrolling of certain sections of the river because our men were getting stuck in the mud. You know, we got all that rain from the hurricanes plus that runoff from the Mexican mountains. It's been a very wet year for them [Mexico]."

I ask the FOS about David Hall's concern that the new levee and wall system in Hidalgo County might contribute to flooding on the south side of the Río Bravo.

"Let me put it this way. If there was a rain again like we had the last few months, well, this new wall going up could flood Cameron County real bad. That's just common sense. Of course, that was the kind of rain we don't get much around here."

"What about the Mexican side?"

"You can figure that one out for yourself." FOS Sanchez knows that Mexicans always suffer tenfold from flooding compared to those on the north side of the river. That is because the Mexican side is much more densely populated, the poor live in low-lying areas in structures that cannot withstand rising waters, and the Mexican levee and drainage system is inferior.

This FOS is, on the one hand, unwilling to speak his mind about the new border wall but does voice his concerns over new Border Patrol agents graduating from the academy. He tells me that 76 percent of all his agents at the Weslaco Border Patrol station are recruits fresh from the training academy in New Mexico. The ratio of new agents to experienced agents is so one-sided that second-year CBP agents, still completing the last year of their "internship," must out of necessity serve as mentors for first-year agents. It is a case of the inexperienced leading novices.

"They're not teaching them real Spanish anymore the way they used to," he says as we follow a road atop an uncompleted levee wall. "They're teaching them phrases at the academy, but not the whole language." Under a new policy recruits who do not speak Spanish must take an additional forty days of Spanish classes at the academy, bringing their total language exposure to ninety-five classroom days. Agents who flunk the Spanish test after the classes are given forty more days, then are allowed to take the test as necessary until they pass it.

"The new guys are telling me that real lawyers are teaching the immigration law to them now. Now, I'm sure those lawyers know the law, but should they be the ones to teach these recruits?" Or, I wonder, can these lawyers necessarily be good teachers of relatively complex concepts only because they are legal experts? Knowing specialized material such as immigration laws is not the same as being a good classroom teacher. Most practicing lawyers, regardless of their legal expertise and subspecialties, are not prepared to teach in a classroom setting just because they wax eloquent before a jury.

FOS Sanchez always accentuates, however, the positive changes he witnesses and supervises. There are now more than enough agents to work "soft bubbles." Agents are now encouraged to get out of their vehicles, to pursue possible smugglers when necessary, and to track sign. Since there are more agents than ever before at the Weslaco station, the border areas patrolled are smaller and more manageable. This is a distinct advantage to the Border Patrol that should result in more apprehensions of human traffickers and drug smugglers or at least, according to their point of view, more deterrence. Now the issue, says FOS Sanchez, is that there are not enough operable vehicles for all the new agents to patrol the line.

This FOS seems particularly pleased that his stretch of the border wall is low-tech—that the wall in South Texas has not been tainted by Boeing's virtual Project 28. There are going to be cameras and other security devices supporting this wall-levee system in Hidalgo County, but the virtual fairy dust is not soon in the offing. FOS Sanchez has heard firsthand from CBP agents in Arizona that the virtual system does not work. He seriously doubts, in his personal opinion, it will ever work.

"Will this barrier stop everyone from crossing here? No it won't," he cautions me. "But it will force most people to go somewhere else. That way we can control it better. It will force people to go to places where we have more control and a better chance of catching them. You've got to look at all this as making it harder for them to cross at this place."

"Will it be safer for Border Patrol agents?" I ask.

"Yes, definitely."

"How?"

"I'm not sure."

"What about for undocumented workers?" I also ask.

"I haven't thought about it that way," Sanchez tells me honestly.

FOS Omar Sanchez has faith that the new border wall in Hidalgo County is going to work. Much more of a headache, according to Sanchez, are the daily turf wars within DHS. "Look, remember there are no more customs agents. There are only CBP agents." But the agencies and departments now under CBP, including the Border Patrol, Customs, and Air and Marine "speak a different language." Based on their backgrounds, job training, and specific job assignments, Customs and the Border Patrol did not always understand each other before 9/11. That meant, on a pragmatic level, that they were less productive than they otherwise might have been. After 9/11, problems remain.

"What I'm saying is, let's just say a Border Patrol agent spots some OTMs sneaking across. He calls in air support. The pilot shows up, and he's speaking a different language. He's calling out GPS coordinates when the agent on the ground is saying, 'I got a group of ten running across farmer Brown's onions.' You know we got all of our places named around here. We have always called them that.

"I see it every day when I call up Customs and need to talk to them about a problem I've got. I can tell they are not in the Border Patrol because we don't always speak the same language.

"It's the same thing in DHS. There are real problems in ICE versus the others. Nobody is talking about it, but it's a problem I see. It's too centralized. You've got to remember that everything changed for us in March 2003 [when twenty-one agencies were incorporated into the Department of Homeland Security].

"But the bigger problem I'm seeing, like I told you, is the one between the legacies and the new guys coming in now. We're talking apples and oranges here. It's not just experience and not having it. These new guys are different. They are just thinking about themselves and what they can get out of the Border Patrol. You can tell a legacy from the others because it's not just a job for him. He's got pride in what he's doing every day. I'm not seeing it in the new recruits the same as in the legacies."

But then FOS Sanchez tells me, "Look, it's a great time to be in the Border Patrol." By that he means the new border wall, new equipment, support from other law enforcement agencies, and a state-of-the-art station. A new Weslaco station will soon replace the original located on International Boulevard, providing the extra room the additional recruits require as well as space for the intelligence computers upon which the CBP is increasingly relying.

"We're becoming," says FOS Sanchez, "a paramilitary organization modeled after the military. It's taking time. We're becoming more professional."

Driving back slowly and carefully to the old Weslaco station, Sanchez compares illegal immigration to the problem his wife, an elementary schoolteacher, faces every day in her classroom. "You've got the ones in the middle, the 75 percent, who are good kids, then the ones at either end, and the ones that cause the problems. But who is she supposed to teach to? Just the smart ones? She's got to jam them all up, teach to the middle, the average students. What else can she do?"

It's been a long day. I do not agree with the comparison between how to teach public school elementary students and how we treat undocumented workers at the border. I tell him so.

Instead of listening to the FOS express himself further, then writing it down in a nonjudgmental fashion as I have been trained to do, I grow more irritated with him. Frustration getting the best of me, my voice rises when I ask the FOS about the four hundred or more undocumented workers who die every year while illegally entering the United States. What about the daily suffering of women and children abused and exploited long before they reach the Rio Grande? What about the new detention centers we put the kids in for unreasonable amounts of time, underaged children separated from their families and who do not speak English? Most of these children, until recently outfitted in prison uniforms, are eventually deported after waiting for months for a hearing before an INS judge.[18] In the cab of the Border Patrol truck on our way back to the motor pool we, the FOS and I, both lose our tempers. Maybe Omar Sanchez had a long day too.

"Look," he tells me, angered by my questions, "I'm a Mexican American. A U.S. citizen. Not a Mexican citizen. I work for the Border Patrol, and I like what I do. I'm not responsible for what the Mexicans do to illegals. I don't like it, but I'm not responsible for it. What kind of parents would bring their baby or their five-year-old kid with them on a trip where they know they can get hurt? I can't help what the Mexicans do to each other. I'm not responsible for their actions. Or the El Sals [El Salvadorians] and the rest of them. The way I see it, it's Hispanics hurting other Hispanics. What can I do about it? There are always going to be victims."

FOS Sanchez drops me off in the parking lot in front of the Weslaco Station. I'm still steaming. We both forgo the usual pleasantries and go our separate ways.

An hour later, my temper cooled, I meet with CBP agent Sparrow at our usual cantina in McAllen. Today, however, there are few patrons and no music from the jukebox. Agent Sparrow asks about my tour with the FOS along the new barrier. I tell him I'm surprised that, along with Anzalduas, Nuevo Progreso, and Cage Boulevard, the new Donna port of entry was chosen as a construction site for the border wall in Hidalgo County. As I remember it, the area never was a hot spot.

Agent Sparrow smiles, then orders a beer and cheese fries from a hovering server. Last time it was an onion blossom. "You got to remember that CBP is not calling the shots on the barrier. You and I and the agents at the Weslaco station know Donna is not a hot spot. But DHS is under the gun from Washington. They have to build so many miles of fence by such and such a date. The rumor at sector is the barrier at Donna is supposed to cost $50 million. They have the money. DHS says build the barrier, they build the barrier."

I grimace.

"It's a rumor about President Bush's State of the Union Address. He said he was going to build sixty miles of border fence by such and such a date. DHS did not plan for sixty miles. But the president says it to a national audience, so DHS has to get it done. What I hear is that it was a mistake. Shit happens. We really don't need it [the wall] at Donna, but DHS builds it so the naysayers can't call the president a liar. I do know for a fact they never asked CBP about it."

"Let me get this straight. You are saying that the Donna portion of the barrier is not needed, but they built it anyway at a cost of $50 million?" I ask Agent Sparrow to make sure I understand exactly what he is telling me.

"You could say it was politics," he replies.

"Is this happening in other parts of the border?" I ask him. Agent Sparrow's draft beer arrives, but not the cheese fries. Agent Sparrow takes a long, cold swallow.

"I don't know," he says, putting down his beer mug. "But I'll tell you this. Our job is to provide security. That's what CBP and DHS are supposed to do. We want Americans to feel more secure. Make people feel better. That's what security is about. So people can live their lives and not have to worry about the terrorists here."

I wait for Agent Sparrow to continue. The cheese fries have not arrived and he is growing uneasy. So while waiting for his cheese fries in McAllen, Texas, Agent Sparrow tells me terrorist sleeper cells with international connections are already embedded in different cities in the United States. The terrorists are in some cases tied to Muslim enclaves in several cities large and small. DHS is denying it so the average American will feel more secure, according to Agent Sparrow. He tells me the average American needs to believe, must believe, there are no terrorists within our national boundaries so he and his family can sleep at night. A big part of terrorism is psychological warfare. If DHS admits international terrorists are already embedded in American cities and suburbs, then the public will panic.

In other words, DHS and the Bush administration firmly believe the public is not capable of handling the truth. If we know terrorists are already hiding out on our soil in sleeper cells, then we won't want to get up each morning and go to work. The international terrorists, given this scenario, will have won.

"Who told you this?" I ask.

"Some guys I trust at DHS. They know. They have no reason to jack me around. Some other guys told me the same thing."

"What about the wall?" I ask Agent Sparrow, using my own terminology for what I observed. If the terrorists are already here, why are we being told that a border wall will stop international terrorists from sneaking into the United States? Agent Sparrow orders another beer.

"Politics," he tells me. "The border barrier can't keep them [international terrorists] out. Anybody who knows about this will tell you the same thing. What it [the border wall] will do is make it harder for them to get in. But I'm saying they are already here. Legally on visas. Some of them are citizens. Or faked documents. We're keeping an eye on them. Look, the thing about the barrier is, it's worth it because we're going to catch some of the Mexican gangs now that other agencies are sharing their intel with us. Already have. And it's slowing down the illegals. *Coyote* prices are way up."

"What about the terrorists?" I ask Agent Sparrow.

"No reason for them to do it [enter by way of the Mexican border]." His cheese fries arriving, Agent Sparrow falls silent and, when he resumes, quickly changes the conversation to the Dallas Cowboys and the on-the-field and off-the-field exploits of Terrell Owens.

On my flight back home the next day, I meet former DHS analyst Patricia Wells at Bubba's Restaurant at the George Bush International Airport in Houston. Ms. Wells agreed to speak with me when she heard I was writing a book about the border wall.

"I worked for several years as an intelligence analyst," she says without my having to ask. Drinking bad coffee, we are sitting at the far end of Bubba's, nearest the windows overlooking the gates and with a view of the runways. Completely ignoring us, passengers come and go.

"What did you actually do?" I quiz her.

"I worked to connect DHS with CBP, state, and local law enforcement. I worked closely with our Mexican specialists, plus I traveled to Mexico on a regular basis."

"You mean passing intel from DHS agencies down to the locals?" I ask, not quite understanding her DHS job.

"No, it was value-added intel."

"What is that?" I ask her.

"I analyzed the data we had at DHS, along with our other analysts, then met with the locals at the border and shared it. They told me what the trends were they were seeing, and I carried it back to DHS."

"What border states?" I say.

Wells adjusts herself in her chair, looks over my shoulder at the rest of the room, then takes a sip of her bad coffee. Dressed in an off-the-rack business suit and white blouse, she looks more like a book rep on her way to hock her catalog, or maybe a supervisor of a small work team at FedEx's corporate campus in Memphis. Her retro wire-frame glasses give her an academic look, but her blonde hair and heavy makeup don't match the rest of her appearance.

Wells avoids answering my question, instead saying, "If you are going to write a book about the wall and the Mexican border, you've got to take a larger perspective. You've got to have a broader theoretical perspective. You're an academic. I know DHS is not known for its innovative theoretical models, but we have people who specialize in failed states. We bring in scholars from the best universities, have seminars, that kind of thing. We talk them up and listen to what they have to say. Sometimes we hire them as consultants or commission papers from them. We like review papers best and finding out what the latest thinking is about certain regional locations."

My plane not boarding for another two hours, I wait her out.

"I've traveled all over the world on various projects," Ms. Wells continues. "We see failed states in a variety of places now. Afghanistan and Somalia, to name the obvious ones."

"So you are saying Mexico is a failed state?" I ask her. The notion of Mexico as a failed state is not a new one, but it certainly serves the best interests of some of those in the American intelligence community. There are those in federal agencies and other entities whose careers, if such a public perception becomes part of the lexicon of foreign policy, would blossom. So the more this notion is suggested as a given, the more Wells and others may directly benefit.

"No. I'm saying I think it is headed in that direction very soon. Calderón did not expect the pushback he is getting from the drug cartels when he campaigned on getting rid of them. He was not prepared for it. The Mexican military is critical in the next several years to the future of Mexico. The military is the most important stabilizing institution in Mexico. They come from the best families, are well educated, and trained to do their job. They should be because we help train them. But they are starting to get impatient with Calderón. These Mexican criminal organizations are highly organized. They have vertically integrated their industry from growing the product, to sophisticated transportation systems using various policing agencies, to cross-border smuggling into the U.S., distribution to urban and rural areas, money laundering, investments in legitimate businesses, and corruption of elected officials. They are using American gangs to get some of this done.

"I'm telling you these Mexican criminal organizations are something new. Something we don't have an answer for at this time. They have gone international. They're not just moving product into the U.S. They are bankrolling other criminal organizations in third-world countries and exploiting new markets for their product. They are doing more than that; they are corrupting legitimate foreign governments and destabilizing certain regions. That's part of what's new in this. What I'm saying is that they are creating new forms of global criminal networks financed by drugs. DHS has not come up with answers."

"Mexico is already corrupt," I tell her. "Everybody knows that. From the bottom to the top."

"I'm not talking about what Mexico was like even ten years ago. Even five years ago. Mexico has fundamentally changed. There was corruption, but what I'm telling you is that there is now much greater corruption than ever before involving all levels of society. You are missing the key point here. They don't want to bring down Calderón or whoever replaces him or his party. Doesn't matter if it's the PRI [Partido Revolucionario Institucional] or PAN [Partido Acción Nacional]. They want a weakened nation state they can control. A failed state is not what they want at all."

I tell Wells that the PRI ran the country from the Mexican Revolution up to the 2000 elections. I can't see that the PAN has done much better with the corruption issue since then, although they've tried. Vicente Fox (PAN) did not have much more success than Zedillo (PRI). While Fox made some concrete motions to clean up the graft and corruption in Mexican law enforcement, he only scratched the surface. As far as I can understand it, Mexico is still an oligarchy under Calderón. I tell her that I've seen some of those superrich Mexican families up close. They act and live like royalty.

"I know all that. But what I'm telling you is that Mexico is changing very rapidly, transforming because of these criminal organizations and their global networks. The criminal organizations are investing their profits into all levels of the *policía judicial*, judicial police, and the *policía preventiva*, preventive police. At both the municipal, state, and federal levels. They are buying up the court judges, the state governors, and the elected national representatives in Mexico City. They are politically able to tie up legislation that Calderón wants passed. The military keeps pushing Calderón to hit them regardless of any negative publicity from collateral damage. Calderón is getting squeezed. The military is only going to wait so long, only going to allow a certain number of casualties among its ranks, before it acts. The criminal organizations are walking a very tight line."

"So what are you telling me?" I say.

"That we are seeing new forms of global criminal organizations. That the Mexican criminal organizations do not want to destroy Calderón and his party, or the PRI. They certainly don't want to take on the Mexican military directly, although some of them, the Zetas, come directly from the military. By the way, they are very afraid of our military and what it can do. What they really want is to continue to infiltrate all levels of Mexican society and put their people in key decision-making positions. They don't want to destroy Mexico, and they certainly don't want the Mexican military to come in and put one of their generals in charge. They want to keep it going, but on their terms."

"Let's say you are right. What does that mean for us?"

"Right now Mexico is our buffer between us and the rest of Latin America. It means that the U.S. may very soon have a weakened buffer between our border and the rest of Latin America. Because of these criminal organizations, Mexico could become a neighbor we cannot trust. They are hiring our barrio gangs to work for them. Border gangs know how to go back and forth from one border city to another, and they don't attract attention in their neighborhoods. The day may come when we are forced to partition off Mexico into two regions, north and south. We support and control the northern region, let the criminal organizations do their thing in the south.

"Are you kidding me?"

"I'm trying to tell you what I saw and what they're thinking. I'm offering you a possible scenario and a time frame. We are facing a new enemy now, one that has mutated and is nothing like we have ever seen before. We have to be strategically and tactically ready for it."

"Where does the border wall fit in?"

"I can't comment on that."

"Can't or won't?"

"I'm not qualified to answer that kind of question. I have my opinions, but that's not what I did when I was in DHS. But I can tell you that no international terrorists are going to risk coming in through the Mexican border. Not when they can enter legally."

"How?"

"Forged documents. Terrorists are not going to risk losing their human assets when they can enter legally. It takes time to train them. And money. What the fence is doing is intensifying the violence against the Border Patrol because with the fence you are giving traffickers fewer choices. The border fence is going to create more contact between them and the CBP. Not less. So you're seeing an escalation of the violence against CBP. The fence is not finished. When it is, the violence on this side is going to increase like we've never seen it before.

"But remember, the criminal organizations want to avoid violence on this side of the border. El Paso is a safe place to live, but Ciudad Juárez is becoming a war zone. The criminal organizations do not want the violence to cross over to our side, because they are afraid of the consequences. But the more we tighten up the border, the more we're going to create scenarios where they are forced to confront the CBP.

"Why build the border wall when most of the drugs are still coming across at the ports of entry?" I ask Wells.

"Because we are developing more sophisticated technology that really works at the POEs. We're putting it in place. Slowly, I admit. But we're going to get it done. It's going to be there and we're going to be confiscating more and more of their product. But the criminal organizations will adapt. That's what they do. When we complete the border fence, we're going to make it even harder for them to do their business. Look at the submersibles they have had some success with. And the tunnels in Nogales. But here's one of the contradictions in all this. We lose our force multipliers."

I had not heard the term *force multipliers* since ISIS in 1999, when INS falsely claimed ISIS would make force multipliers out of our undermanned Border Patrol agents. With ISIS in place, the Border Patrol would, it was argued in 1999, take complete control of the U.S.-Mexico border.

"The force multipliers are the residents and citizens of border towns. We know their potential. When the violence at the border really increases between the criminal organizations and the CBP, when it overflows into the communities and citizens are getting shot on the streets like in Ciudad Juárez, public opinion along the border is going to turn completely around. We're going to lose a lot, maybe all, of our community support. The local residents are going to get sick of the shootouts and the rest of the violence in their neighborhoods from local gangs paid by the Mexicans. So we are going to lose our force multipliers, and I don't see any other way around it.

"You know the bottom line problem with this?" Wells leans forward to tell me in a softened voice that no one can overhear at Bubba's.

I shake my head.

"You can't shoot illegal border crossers. If we could just shoot them, like they did with the Berlin Wall, then there would be no problem, and we wouldn't be sitting here discussing it. But most Americans will not stand for that. It's the weak side of being a democracy. We can't do what totalitarian countries do. This all would be a lot easier if we could shoot them."

Chapter 10
Three Different Walls

We wrote it down on a napkin. Remember that?" Judge J. D. Salinas III says to Godfrey Garza, Jr., sitting to his left at a long conference table. The border wall in Hidalgo County, according to Judge Salinas, is the brainchild of their joint doodling. Judge Salinas handled the political deal making, and Mr. Garza, district manager of Hidalgo County Drainage District Number One, provided the technological expertise. The other person in the room in the spring of 2009, to the left of Judge Salinas, is Cari Lambrecht, public information officer for the Hidalgo County Commissioners' Court.

"We were talking with [Senator John] Cornyn. It was a fundraiser for him given by the Hunt family out at their ranch north of here." Now the handsome judge is turning towards Godfrey once more, intentionally including him in the credit for the original idea of a border wall tied to a system of aging levees. "We'd been thinking about the fence out loud. Then we started drawing what it would look like on a napkin. We showed Cornyn the napkin and explained to him what the idea was about."

Senator Cornyn was getting his first look at their new concept for a border wall while they were driving him back to the Miller International Airport in McAllen. It was the night of October 10, 2007. The drive gave Judge Salinas valuable face time with Senator Cornyn. The judge could already see then that the toughest part of the deal was to secure funding for their project when so many different levels of government were going to be directly involved.

"How did it go over with the senator?" I ask. As the stylishly dressed judge talks on, I listen and also sift through the stack of materials one of his assistants brings me. As the judge explains the politics behind the construction of Hidalgo County's unique border wall system, the stack of materials grows.

Meanwhile, a floor below us, the different Hidalgo County courts at law are in full session: groups of inmates dressed in jail-orange jumpsuits shuffle in their shackles from the main holding cell to the courtrooms' wooden pews, hobbling past crowds of loved ones, their friends, and supporters. The inmates' hands are stuffed into large mittens resembling kitchen hot pads, contrivances designed both to make difficult their escape from their restraints and muffle punches they might feel like throwing. The oversized mittens also make impossible any gestures between inmates and family members as each inmate in turn is whisked before the presiding judge. Then through the glass walls I can see the inmates slowly paraded back down a hallway to their holding cell before being transported back to the county jail.

"Cornyn liked it," says Judge Salinas. If he is aware of what goes on behind the glass walls below us, he gives no clue. "But naturally the senator wanted to see more. You know, see what the details were going to be. But he liked the concept. It was a win-win for everybody." Godfrey nods in agreement and Cari, who must have heard the same story countless times before, remains silent.

The doodle Judge Salinas and Godfrey Garza, Jr., concocted on the napkin depicted in pencil how to combine the old levee system in Hidalgo County with the border fence DHS was mandated by Congress to build.

Judge Salinas repeats his litany once more: "It was a win-win for everybody."

Judge Salinas officially refers to this new wall-levee in his county as a "hydraulic wall." At the same time, he soon falls back into calling it, at one time or another, the "fence," the "wall," the "barrier," and the "new levee system." But when not forgetting its exact nomenclature, Judge Salinas calls his creation a hydraulic wall.

"At first, you know, I was antifence," the judge tells me as an aside. "Did you know that? You probably didn't know that, but yes, I was antifence. But after I got elected in early 2007, I was looking through the pile of mail. Over in the corner there." Judge Salinas swivels in his chair and points at the exact spot he discovered his predecessor's mail. "The other judge just left it behind. It was a big pile. And right in the middle was a letter from FEMA.[1] The FEMA letter stated they were going to 'decertify' the entire levee system in Hidalgo County because it failed to meet standards. Hidalgo County was at the top of FEMA's list for decertification."

If the levees in Hidalgo County were decertified, premiums on home insurance for Hidalgo County residents, the judge's constituents, would substantially rise, because a large number of county dwellings were redefined as standing directly in the Rio Grande floodplain. One Valley economist estimated a total premium increase of $40 million for fifty-eight thousand Hidalgo County homeowners. That figure did not include premium increases for an additional three thousand small business owners in Hidalgo County who also were, under the decertification of the Hidalgo levees by FEMA, lying squarely in a floodplain.[2]

Some of the same Valley homeowners and businesspersons who voted Judge Salinas into office were now, because of FEMA, going to get a big bill in their mailboxes as a result of the FEMA directive. Or, worse still, their properties would be inundated by floodwaters from the next hurricane.

Judge Salinas and Godfrey Garza did their homework. They found that the Hidalgo County levee system was originally constructed in the 1930s. After a new analysis of the levees by FEMA, the materials with which the levees were originally constructed were determined under standards in place in 2007 to be a poor barrier against rising waters from the Rio Grande. Neglected by the local water district for decades, the county levees received only minor repairs after Hurricane Beulah blew through the Valley in the 1960s. Now, more than forty-five years since these last superficial repairs, FEMA engineers deemed these aging earthen mounds no longer capable of protecting the lives and the homes of Hidalgo County residents from a rampaging Rio Grande.

"Not on my watch," says Judge Salinas in a forceful voice from the end of the table. Meaning no federal agency from Washington was going to get away with charging his constituents, a majority of whom were in or close to poverty, a sum of money that they could not afford.

From the Valley perspective, it looked like another attempt by a federal agency to interfere, this time in the form of an added tax on homeowners who least could afford it.

"It was not going to happen while I was county judge. But the biggest problem was the IBWC [International Boundary and Water Commission]. It had to be a win-win situation for them." Where other less astute Valley politicians saw another example of federal intervention, Judge Salinas envisioned a rare political opportunity.

An experienced Valley politician, the astute judge fails to mention that the opportunity was, in his favorite phrase, "a win-win" for Hidalgo County residents and his political ambitions as well.

The local Hidalgo County water district, Drainage District Number 1, already had requested annual funding for levee repairs from the IBWC at a modest $2 million. Their request to repair Hidalgo levees fell far short of an estimated $150 million required to meet the new FEMA standards. Judge Salinas knew his county, one of the poorest in the country, would be hard pressed to support a bond issue upgrading the decaying levee system. By the time a campaign came to fruition to bring the bond issue to a vote, if indeed he could persuade voters it was in their best interests, the DHS border fence would already be built and the insurance bills already in his constituents' mailboxes.

Any solution to this dilemma was complicated by both the usual array of governmental entities involved and the binational aspects of levee construction along an international border. Established in 1889, the IBWC maintained a long-standing international treaty with Mexico that specifically restrained its actions in regard to the construction and maintenance of levees on the north side of the Río Bravo. Falling under the U.S. Department of State, the IBWC communicated daily with the Mexican Ministry of Foreign Affairs, headquartered in Ciudad Juárez across from El Paso.[3]

Judge Salinas faced the daunting task of enlisting the support of the binational IBWC, including the concerns of the Mexican Ministry of Foreign Affairs, and, if that were not enough, organizing all the elected officials in the towns and communities situated along the Rio Grande in his county. It was also necessary for the judge to keep the local water district on board while, at the same time, gaining the support of the Environmental Protection Agency and the necessary elected officials in Washington, a list of which began with Senator John Cornyn and Congressman Henry Cuellar (D-Texas). If that were not enough, Judge Salinas also had to find a way to work directly and efficiently with DHS. The judge would have to contend not only with DHS's myriad agencies, but also its dismissive attitude towards the residents of South Texas.

Born and raised in nearby La Joya, Judge Salinas knows the intricacies of Hidalgo County politics. The judge graduated from La Joya High School, then traveled to College Station to earn a bachelor of science degree from Texas A&M University. Returning to the Valley soon after, Salinas was first elected a municipal judge in his hometown of La Joya, then afterwards served as an administrative assistant to the Hidalgo County Commissioners' Court from 1991 to 1996. The county voters then elected him to two sequential terms as Hidalgo County clerk.[4] Along the way, Judge Salinas picked up a master's degree in public administration from the University of Texas–Pan American.

While educated in Hidalgo County politics, Judge Salinas was still faced with the rather daunting task of uniting county politicos, each with his or her individual aspirations and interests, then somehow bringing on board the state, the feds, and a binational agency. This was a gargantuan effort few other politicians would have attempted.

After President Bush signed off on the Secure Border Fence Act in late October 2006, local opposition in Hidalgo County quickly came together. A coalition of property owners, environmentalists, public interest groups, and individual citizens voiced strong opposition to the proposed DHS fence.[5] Within a matter of months, in spite of this opposition by his constituents, Judge Salinas had gathered resolutions from seventeen Hidalgo County municipalities supporting his innovative concept of combining a border fence with renovation of the aging Hidalgo levee system. Soon after, he received the full backing of the influential Texas Border Coalition.[6]

Although the exact details of the fence-levee went through several different major transformations, according to Judge Salinas, Senator Cornyn was from day one the staunchest of supporters. In part this was because Salinas, before he pitched the idea to the senator on the ride back to the McAllen airport, had the political acumen first to establish successful ties with DHS. Meeting with Secretary of Homeland Security Chertoff in Laredo in late February 2007, Judge Salinas says, "We told him firsthand what we thought of the border fence and we told him it was not necessary. And he [Chertoff] answers and says, 'You're right. We may need it in Arizona and New Mexico, but the Rio Grande River is a structure we need to work with.'"

As Valley opposition to the border fence grew more heated, community leaders aimed their frustration at representatives from DHS and the CBP in a public meeting at the Brownsville Convention Center on June 1. Similar emotions were aired by the general public in Hidalgo County soon after. Those against the Valley border fence coordinated a media campaign even as larger Valley property owners threatened to take DHS to court.

On November 17, less than a month after showing their napkin sketch to Senator Cornyn, Judge Salinas wangled a meeting in Washington which all the major players promised to attend. At the same Washington table Salinas put together officials from the IBWC, the DHS, the CBP, and the EPA and staff from the offices of Senator Cornyn and Congressman Cuellar. In hindsight it is unprecedented for a Texas county judge, virtually unknown outside the Valley, to exert such Machiavellian diplomacy inside the far-off Beltway.

Judge Salinas modestly gives due credit to the senator and the congressman, but this Valley politico is clearly the project kingmaker. Once the key players were at the same table, Salinas elicited a stunning promise from the IBWC, an agency known for making decisions at glacier speed. According to Judge Salinas, one of the IBWC representatives told the other officials at the meeting, "I don't see why this won't work."[7] Coming from the IBWC, that modest statement was interpreted as its rare blessing on the Valley project, a blessing guaranteeing the safe and quick passage of Judge Salinas's hydro-wall through a maze of red tape.

While Judge Salinas scored in Washington, his deal-making in Hidalgo County was in many ways equally challenging. Fueled by an intractable DHS capable by its statements and attitude of setting off a storm of protest, Valley opposition against the border fence coalesced. Against charges by those against the border fence of historical racism, federal intrusion into local Valley affairs, and irrevocable environmental impacts, Judge Salinas played the money card. His deal with the bureaucratic devils, he argued, would give Hidalgo County taxpayers a hundred million federal dollars towards a new levee system—a levee system that Hidalgo County was going to be forced to build and pay for anyway. If that were not enough to turn the political tide, homeowners, of whom many could not afford to pay the extra flood insurance premium, would be let off the financial hook. So too would thousands of Hidalgo County business owners otherwise defined as lying in the floodplain.

In Hidalgo County big money gets big attention from impoverished voters. Residents can do their own math. The feds, and all the agencies were the feds, were going to give them a new levee system for next to nothing. Plus, Judge Salinas fixed it so they would not be charged an extra dollar on their annual insurance premiums. It was a no-brainer.

Judge Salinas became an instant hero, the Hidalgo County politician who tricked the feds into giving something, the new levee system, for next to nothing—a modest match by the county. The average citizen in Hidalgo County always believed, one way or the other, that the feds were going to get their way on the border fence in the long run. There was going to be a border fence whether the majority of Hidalgo County citizens wanted it or not. So why not benefit from the inevitable?

Only a year later, warp speed measured in bureaucratic time, 95 percent of the levee fence has been completed in Hidalgo County. The Department of Homeland Security agreed to pay 76 percent of the cost for the 21.9 miles of new fence-levee at approximately $145 million, according to Judge Salinas.

Fig. 10.1 Workers constructing hydraulic wall in front of old levee in Hidalgo County, near McAllen, Texas, 2008. (Courtesy Cari Lambrecht and Hidalgo County Drainage District)

Hidalgo County picked up the remaining 24 percent, or $45 million. The cost of border fence construction in Hidalgo County was, according to the judge, $5.1 million a mile. While this still leaves a remaining twenty miles of decertified levees along the Rio Grande in Hidalgo County, in addition to ninety miles of interior levees, most of the judge's constituents did not seem to care, because Judge Salinas had put one over on the feds. A political hero to men like FOS Omar Sanchez, Judge J. D. Salinas could do no wrong.

While Judge Salinas is in the middle of telling me his plans, a staffer for Secretary of Homeland Security Napolitano, the Arizona governor who replaced Chertoff under the new Obama administration, calls the judge to discuss personally the details of the border fence. IBWC has just received $220 million through the Obama stimulus plan, plus another promised $13 million. Judge Salinas's immediate political ploy is to apply for a chunk of these stimulus monies to complete the old levee repair, declaring to the Washington staffer that Hidalgo County is "shovel ready to do this thing."

The judge apologizes as he leaves the room to speak with the staffer from Napolitano's DHS. I cannot help but hear him through the doorway of the other room. He is on a speaker phone to Washington.

"What do we need?" he asks the DHS staffer. "Why, we need money down here. We need money to finish this thing off. Please send us money." This appeal, although serious in message, is followed by hearty laughter from the judge, but the judge wants DHS to know he means business. He expects DHS to hold up their end of the bargain even though DHS secretary Chertoff, as well as many of his Republican appointees in DHS, have been replaced by Obama appointees.

In fact, in Chertoff's last year the Hidalgo border fence became a poster child, one of DHS's few border success stories. Judge Salinas is determined his hydro-wall be treated in a similar fashion under Napolitano's new reign. After so many failures with the Mexican border fence under the Bush administration, the astute judge knows that Napolitano's DHS needs demonstrable political victories. Congress must get the message that DHS is not squandering taxpayer funds as border fence construction continues into 2009, 2010, and beyond.

What exactly are the specifics of this hydraulic wall that Judge Salinas almost single-handedly willed into being? On the napkin Judge Salinas and Mr. Garza handed Senator Cornyn was a pencil sketch of an old levee combined with a fortified wall. In theory, this hydraulic wall is the unlikely offspring of a 1930s-model levee built on top of a new twenty-seven-foot-wide concrete base. The dirt is fronted by a twelve to fifteen-inch concrete exterior on the side of the wall facing the border. Eight-foot-tall bollards are then placed on top of this construction, bringing it to a height of eighteen feet or more, depending on its specific location.

Since DHS required the border fence be no shorter than eighteen feet in height, and since the old Hidalgo levee varies in certain segments from ten feet to more than fourteen feet, the bollards make up the height difference. In some places along the old levee system the earthen mounds already reached eighteen feet in height, so the bollards serve as safety guards for CBP vehicles traveling on paved road atop the levee structure. The height of the hydraulic wall and its exact form differ depending on the varying dimensions of the old levee system.

In the western part of Hidalgo County the hydraulic wall stretches from the tiny communities of Hidalgo to Penitas. Smaller sections have been constructed in the eastern part of the county. Together there are ten different hydraulic walls built by six different contractors.

The hydraulic wall under construction at Anzalduas County Park forms a crucial piece of the entire Valley flood control system because it is the site of a river dam that siphons off a majority of the Rio Grande water for irrigation purposes to the more northern parts of the county.[8] If the Rio Grande floods and the Anzalduas hydraulic wall fails, the entire structural integrity of the hydraulic wall will be threatened, because floodwaters would freely flow behind it, on the side not protected by the new concrete fronting.

Gates are also a part of the hydraulic wall approved by DHS—gates wide enough to allow landowners to move their bulky farm machinery from the north side of the hydraulic wall to rich farmland on the south side bordering the Rio Grande. Earth movers already have built earthen ramps to ascend to these gates at the top of the old levees. Here, at these open gate entrances to the hydraulic wall, in order to maintain a consistent height of eighteen feet or more there are progressively lengthier bollards atop the wall as the ramps ascend higher and higher to reach the gates. It is not clear how these gates will stem the flow of rising floodwaters. Neither is it clear how these gates will be operated.

I ask Judge Salinas about the gates, spaces through which hundreds of undocumented workers now can enter this country any day or night of the week.

"That's up to DHS," the judge tells me. "Not our problem. And it's not in our budget. I hear through the grapevine that DHS is designing something."

Then the judge looks a little peeved. "You know what DHS calls the farmers and the other residents who need to get access to their land between the hydraulic wall and the river? They call them 'friendlies.'"

Sitting on my left, the public information officer turns noticeably uncomfortable in her chair as she nods her head in agreement with the judge. Neither Judge Salinas nor Ms. Lambrecht like this term, because it is usually reserved for a war zone. For the judge and the PIO, there is no conflict between neighboring Mexican communities and the Valley that would warrant the use of such language. That DHS uses *friendlies* also suggests that everyone else in the Valley and Mexico who DHS or CBP dislikes is by extension a "hostile."

There are many potential problems created by the hydraulic wall in Hidalgo County, some more obvious than others. One of the obvious, as suggested, is the environmental impact. Texas RioGrande Legal Aid's David Hall, for example, is one among many who points out that when the levees are raised in Hidalgo County the risk of flooding will increase in the more densely populated areas on the south side of the river, including the city of Reynosa, home to more than half a million residents—not to mention downstream in Cameron County. Certainly this is the case in Dubuque, Iowa, where the levee system on the Mississippi has saved their city from flooding since the 1970s but done nothing for the communities downstream.

When I raise this issue, Judge Salinas is suddenly very defensive, even bordering on the illogical: "The IBWC is only responsible for water to the middle of the river. All our new levee system is doing is keeping floodwater in the river." In other words, the IBWC and all the other relevant agencies gave Hidalgo County legal permission to build the new levees. What happens as the result of the new hydraulic wall is "Mexico's problem, not mine."

What about downstream on the American side? If rising floodwaters are channeled south to Cameron County by a more efficient Hidalgo hydraulic wall, doesn't that put the residents of Cameron County in greater potential danger? Judge Salinas says in response that, "They have a problem with their levees. They haven't received their letter from FEMA, but they will. We got decertified first. Hidalgo County was in the first tier. But Cameron County is on the list, and they are going to get decertified. We're doing the right thing here for the residents of Hidalgo County. It's a win-win for my constituents. Cameron County is not my problem."

"We know exactly what happens when the levee system doesn't work here," the judge tells me between rushing back and forth from one office to the next as he continues his conversation by speaker phone with DHS staffers in Washington. He shows me a map outlining the flooding caused by Hurricane Dolly, a modest storm that hit the Valley in the fall of 2008. The floodwaters of the Rio Grande reached beyond Highway 283, the main corridor connecting McAllen to Brownsville. Highway 283 is in some spots up to ten miles from the banks of the Rio Grande. "This won't happen," the judge tells me, "once the new construction is finished."[9]

Judge Salinas then explains how all the contractors and subcontractors maintain quality control, the same quality control questioned by Vice President Pearson at UTB-TSC, during construction of the hydraulic wall. There are six different contractors, two local and four regional, employing six hundred workers. The locals are Ballenger Construction and McAllen Construction; the outsiders, Zachry, Williams Brothers, SER, and Longhorn. All of the work by these contractors, according to Judge Salinas, is regularly inspected by representatives from DHS, CBP, the EPA, the Texas Fish and Wildlife Department, and the IBWC. Various officials from Hidalgo County also ensure that the construction meets the required specs. In addition, each of the six contractors hires an independent inspector to monitor the quality of its work.

Kickbacks and local corruption in this elaborate system of inspection are, implies the judge, impossible. All the federal and county dollars, Judge Salinas assures me, have been meticulously accounted for by multiple agency auditors.

While I have no reason to doubt Judge Salinas's sincerity, I remain highly skeptical of the quality control and fiscal oversight of the Hidalgo County hydraulic wall. It eerily reminds me, albeit at the local level, of the hodge-podge of DHS assurances, flow charts, graphs, tables, and other bureaucratic paraphernalia delineating DHS oversight of CBP's program planning of ASI, SBI, and all the rest. A fundamental principle of effective management remains: if too many bureaucracies are in charge, no one is in charge. This is, too, Hidalgo County, Texas, a county burdened by a long history of corruption and graft.

Even as the hydraulic wall in Hidalgo County reaches completion, the judge's own constituents raise concerns about, in addition to flooding, the quality of construction and fiscal oversight. Protests against the wall have by no means disappeared. Constituent opposition against Judge Salinas's hydraulic wall in Hidalgo County falls into three general categories. One group of voters questions whether the new levees will in fact do the job for which they were constructed. At the same time, since the hydraulic wall has been constructed in segments, gaps between the walls could cause serious erosion of the earthen levees. No engineering reports or independent research have been offered by Judge Salinas or Mr. Garza to substantiate the efficacy of their hydraulic wall. There have been no engineering studies completed that demonstrate "the safety and the efficacy of the untried idea of integrating walls into existing earthen levees, many of which already have problems with their structural integrity."[10]

Hidalgo County environmentalists are also strongly opposed to the new hydraulic wall. They point out that for the last quarter-century the Rio Grande Valley National Wildlife Refuge has been purchasing land to create a wildlife corridor along the river. The separate parcels of land already purchased cannot in and of themselves support the wildlife, including rare and endangered species such as jaguarundi. The hydraulic wall, they maintain, cuts off wildlife from direct access to the river, the only reliable source of water, thus guaranteeing the demise of various endangered species.[11] This same group also points to the State of Texas environmental draft document, a study that rejected the wall construction because of light pollution, increased vehicle strikes of wildlife, and the impact on nesting sites of birds.[12]

A third and final constituent concern is for the safety of U.S. Fish and Wildlife Service (USFWS) employees working in the area between the hydraulic wall and the Rio Grande. Constituents note that the new wall will block the escape of USFWS workers from "wildfires, criminal activities, and medical emergencies."[13] Other than the objections of those representing the rights of undocumented workers, this remains the sole and only public recognition that the new border wall may directly affect the safety and welfare of those working in the borderlands.

As I shake Judge Salinas's hand as I leave his offices at the Hidalgo County courthouse, he promises to send me more documents than the pile his staff has duplicated for me. The judge also mentions a video his staff is preparing that documents the hydraulic wall construction from start to finish.[14] "I'm still educating people here in Hidalgo County," he tells me with a patient smile.

Judge J. D. Salinas has succeeded as the grand deal maker in Hidalgo County—as the political glue binding local, state, federal, and binational agencies in a common cause. He comes across as remarkably competent, smooth, and positive but remains modest in spite of his successes.[15] But the truest test of this Valley politician rests less in the quality of his deal making than in whether his hydraulic wall fulfills its expectations.

It is long past five o'clock closing time at the Hidalgo County Commissioners' Court. The inmates in jail orange no longer spill over into the corridors outside the courtrooms, and their families have long since emptied the building. A security guard nods in my direction as I head for the parking lot with a bundle of documents under my arm.

At two in the afternoon a few months after meeting Judge J. D. Salinas, I wait patiently for more than thirty minutes for my appointment with Brownsville county commissioner John Wood. Commissioner Wood is variously having a late lunch at a nearby restaurant, on his way back to the office, caught in traffic, in the building somewhere talking to someone, etc.

I remind myself I am in Brownsville, Texas, and not on big-city time. Eventually Commissioner Wood appears in the doorway in cowboy boots, khaki trousers, and a pressed sports shirt, as contrary an image as possible to that of Judge Salinas. We share an *abrazo*; I have known John Wood for more than twenty-five years. He leads me back into his comfortable, disorganized office decorated with antiques.

For many years County Commissioner Wood was a local businessman, at first a manager for his father-in-law's fish house and shrimp boats at Port Brownsville. After the commercial fishing industry took a nosedive in the 1980s from which it never fully recovered, John Wood jumped into Brownsville politics.[16] Today, Commissioner Wood is a well-versed South Texas politician representing the western part of Cameron County. His constituents, some of whom reside in barrios contiguous to Brownsville, are identical to those of J. D. Salinas's Hidalgo County; the majority are Latino and very poor. Directly involved with developing infrastructure in *colonias* in Cameron County, including water and drainage projects, Commissioner Wood also heads the Cameron County Mental Health Task Force.[17]

In a university ceremony two days before I arrive back in town, President

Juliet Garcia and the administrators at the University of Texas Brownsville–Texas Southmost College commemorate the completion of the construction of their section of the border fence by planting rows of brightly colored flowers. The fence now stands ten feet tall with plastered white pillars supporting green chain-link fencing. The pillars are spaced about every fifteen feet and separate the Scorpions baseball field from the university-owned campus golf course. There are no gates in place yet, and it is unclear where the gates eventually will be located so that students and the public can cross from one side of the border fence to the other. But for now it does not matter, because university construction necessitates keeping feeder streets open from the campus to the golf course. As a result, the university border fence, at least for now, is a very minor inconvenience.

The new UTB-TSC fence will soon meld at its western end into the nexus of CBP security measures buttressing the port of entry at Brownsville's international bridge. The CBP border fence is made of a much tougher mesh, stands several feet taller than the university's border fence, and is topped with razor wire sparkling under a steaming sun.

From the very first news of a border fence, residents of Brownsville and throughout Cameron County were, as suggested, very strident in their opposition. Politicians, including Commissioner Wood, joined with Brownsville's mayor, Pat Ahumada, a former shrimper, to protest loudly against DHS's border wall.[18] The statement by Mayor Ahumada in early 2008 is typical of the sentiment felt by many in Brownsville:

> DHS' refusal to work with local leaders along the border goes to show how our federal government can turn against its own people and suspend our rights and liberties as they did to the Japanese in World War Two. . . . No one is against enforcing our laws against illegal immigration, drug trafficking and fighting terrorism, but it does not make sense to force a fence no one wants in this region and by the Department of Homeland Security's own admission can be breached in 3 to 7 minutes. . . . Our heritage, culture, traditions, commerce and good neighbor policy will be affected in an adverse way. Already the resentment by our neighbors is becoming evident and those of us with a Mexican heritage are resentful towards those who are promoting what we believe to be a racial divide under the pretext of securing our border.[19]

John Wood is as circumspect and cautious as Mayor Ahumada is bluntly outspoken. Other than at the university, fence construction has only recently commenced in Cameron County, and, while Commissioner Wood is strongly against it, he seems resigned to its eventual completion, which he believes will bring with it certain political and social consequences: "I sat in on one or two of those meetings with the DHS officials. When it was my turn to talk, I asked them about problems I thought the fence would create. They looked uncomfortable about my questions and didn't answer them directly."

Commissioner Wood took the same tour of the new hydraulic wall in Hidalgo County as did David Pearson at UTB-TSC. An experienced businessman, Wood raised the issue of DHS's track record of overpayment to contractors for services rendered. Wood believes that the CBP, in contrast to DHS, will be more frugal with taxpayers' dollars spent on the border wall. "From what I hear," he tells me, "that fence over at UTB has a bunch of cameras that watch everybody. It has the kind of high-tech cameras that can focus on one face, then follow that person around in a crowd. DHS would pay thirty thousand dollars for a camera like that, but I hear the Border Patrol got the same thing for three thousand."

In this Texas county there are no deal makers forging a broad coalition of all levels of elected government with federal law enforcement agencies and binational bureaucracies. By late February 2009 there are still only two sections under construction in Cameron County. A total of seven miles in length, these segments of the border wall both lie between the small river communities of La Paloma and Los Indios.

Commissioner Wood, in sharp contrast to Judge Salinas in neighboring Hidalgo County, shows absolutely no concern about the possibility of a faltering levee system in his district. "We just got our certification for our levees in Cameron County last month for 2008," the commissioner tells me.

Napolitano's DHS in Hidalgo County feeds all federal dollars through the Hidalgo County Commissioners' Court. In Cameron County, in contrast, officials have absolutely no contact with border wall federal dollars. At the same time, Cameron County officials also bypass any oversight or construction duties and responsibilities regarding the new border wall.

There are other differences between the two adjacent counties with a shared cultural heritage. The DHS wall in Cameron County stands alone, separate and distinct from its antiquated levee system, which was originally built at the same time as Hidalgo County's. In fact, DHS's border wall in Cameron County is separate and distinct from the levee system because it is constructed and positioned directly *behind* the old Cameron County levees.

Commissioner Wood and the other elected officials in Cameron County have totally rejected the notion that their levees are inadequate and soon must be replaced. They do not fear that their constituents will have to suffer the price of higher flood insurance premiums because they firmly believe their levees will not be decertified by FEMA. Although Judge Salinas says that the FEMA letter "decertifying" Cameron County levees is just a matter of time, Cameron County officials deny this premise.

Instead, officials in Cameron County have spent the majority of their political capital fighting DHS and CBP every step of the bitter way. While they eventually lost the legal battle, their efforts delayed fence construction by at least eighteen months. As a result of this politically orchestrated delay, in which the Cameron County commissioners are one player among others, Hidalgo County is wrapping up construction of its hydraulic wall just as, with the notable exception of the major section of the university fence, construction is just getting started throughout the rest of Cameron County.

According to Commissioner Wood, the thirty-two miles of border wall in his county will cover about 60 percent of the frontage along the Rio Grande. All of the new wall is planned to stand behind the old earthen levee, which will continue to serve as a buffer against floodwaters. With the border wall eventually in place, the old levee system will function as an additional barrier that illegal border crossers must surmount then cross before confronting the border wall.

"Did you know they want to fence the Sabal Palm Grove?" I ask Commissioner Wood.

"Yeah, there's a guy that lives out there in a little house, and DHS has put a fence right through the middle of it so the house is on one side of the fence and the palms on the other."

"We're doing it differently here," he continues with pride. "In Hidalgo I know the DHS money is going through the commissioners' court, then to the contractors. But here we have nothing to do with the contracting part of it. There are two contractors I know about, one local, one not. We never see the money, because it goes directly from DHS to those contractors."

What Commissioner Wood implies is that the possibilities for local graft and corruption associated with the new border wall are considerably less in Cameron County compared to those in Hidalgo County. The way in which the border wall monies are channeled and structured does not automatically rule out more Cameron County graft and corruption, but it does make it much more difficult, at least in theory, for any public officials in the county to break the law. Commissioner Wood knows that the fiscal burden now rests with DHS and its contractors, not on the shoulders of the Cameron County commissioners. He also knows the same is true in terms of oversight and management of the actual construction of the border wall in his county.

It is my best guess that Commissioner Wood is relieved not to have to share this responsibility because he knows firsthand the volatility and history of Cameron County politics. He has himself, in fact, recently weathered accusations of improperly supervising one of his county employees. A local scandal simmered and burned in the local newspaper for a few weeks, then flamed out for lack of evidence.[20]

I ask Commissioner Wood if he has kept an eye on DHS wall construction in his district.

"Sure. I've been out there. There are No Trespassing signs, but I just ignore them and drive around to see what is going on. The worst thing they can do is kick you out," says the commissioner as he smiles at the thought.

Following Commissioner Wood's directions an hour later, I drive out Old Military Highway and turn left when I reach Cantu Road. To the south towards the river I see the large cranes, the earthmovers, and the other signs of border wall construction. Taking to the dirt roads, I roam around while taking photos of the construction sites marked by the No Trespassing signs posted by Kiewit Construction. I note, as Commissioner Wood had described to me in his office, the pallets of bollards stacked neatly behind the chain-link fence, the concrete forms, and the other building materials piled high.

Two days later I once more get a detailed inspection of the border wall in Hidalgo County from FOS Omar Sanchez at the Weslaco Border Patrol Station. Our differences resolved since my last tour of the border wall, the FOS first shows me the progress in wall construction at the Progreso bridge and at the new Donna port of entry. Crossing down an earthen ramp on the south side of the new wall near the new Donna bridge, I get my first view of how the wall will appear to illegal border crossers entering the United States.

The view of the south side of the hydraulic wall is entirely different than from that of the north side. From the north one sees the back of the retrofitted levee, with bollards rising out of the concrete wall. There are no gates in place, just large, gaping holes. But from the south, from the viewpoint of an illegal crosser, the brute size of the wall is more than impressive, with the south side of the levee covered in concrete to a height of ten to twelve feet. The eight-foot steel bollards at the top of the concrete wall bring the wall to a total height of eighteen feet or more, an imposing structure that dwarfs the surrounding flat landscape. Stretching for miles as far as the eye can see in either direction, this completed hydraulic wall appears not only monumental in size, but also impenetrable.

I move one hundred yards south of the hydraulic wall for a different visual perspective. Looking at what confronts me, then eyeballing this same imposing barrier as I turn my head left and right to see the wall disappearing to the horizon, I am left with only one reasonable conclusion: only fools and those with no better choices will attempt to illegally cross into the United States at this point along the Mexico-U.S. border. The majority will enter elsewhere. First an illegal crosser must traverse the Río Bravo. Then he must

Fig. 10.2 Workers on concrete forms fronting old levee in Hidalgo County, near Weslaco, Texas, 2008. (Courtesy Cari Lambrecht and Hidalgo County Drainage District)

cross a virtual no-man's land between the river and the hydraulic wall. Then he must somehow climb over the wall while having no way to know what he must face on the other side. It is too much for the average crosser—too dangerous, too many unknown risks, and too high a probability of being caught.

At the same time, I realize the resiliency of illegal border crossers, their motivations, and their limited options. Highly motivated illegal crossers will find ways to circumvent this hydraulic wall, but the majority of illegal crossers will go somewhere else to cross.

Fig. 10.3 View from north side of Hidalgo County hydraulic wall with bollards in place, 2009. Hydraulic wall gate is not constructed.

Off in the distance I see an open space between two sections of the hydraulic wall.

"That's where there's going to be a gate so the landowners have access," FOS Sanchez tells me.

"What kind of gate?"

"I don't know. Nobody has told me anything about it. In the meantime, we are going to have to post an agent there 24/7." They are still waiting on the gates promised by DHS.

"How are your tactics and strategies going to change because of the wall?" I ask him.

"I don't know yet. It's not something we have talked about. But the wall is going to make a big difference in how we do things. For one thing, it's going to be a hell of a lot easier to apprehend illegals. Would you try crossing here?"

"No."

"It's going to force them to try somewhere else. The public thinks the barrier is solid all along the river, but that's not true, as you can see. We built it at the hot spots, the places where we have traffic. Now the bad guys will have to go somewhere else, and that somewhere else is where we will have a tactical advantage."

We drive along the levee construction until we reach a small farm fronting the Rio Grande a quarter of a mile to the south. It's the Brewster Farm, recognized for many years as a locus for human and drug smuggling.[21] On it sits a dilapidated house with a sagging porch on one side along with several outbuildings and sheds. Generations of junked farm equipment and other vehicles slowly rust in the salt-laden air, while a string of laundry on a line dries in a mild breeze.

"This family is just white trash," FOS Sanchez tells me, shaking his finger at them from the cab of his Border Patrol truck. "They have been trafficking in drugs and illegals for generations. I mean generations. Father, sons, and then some. You can see the river is over there at that tree line. This used to be one of the busiest spots in our sector. Now it has all stopped. You can see where the barrier is going up. It'll separate those buildings over there where they used to hide the contraband and the human traffic. Business is over for the Brewsters."

"What are they going to do?" I ask him.

"I couldn't care less. All I know is that we have shut them down. They were smuggling for generations. That's all they did. Now they are officially out of business. And it's because of the barrier."

I ask FOS Sanchez about how CBP recruitment is coming along. Because of the sinking economy, I know the CBP, in contrast to recent years, is presently having no trouble meeting its quotas for new academy recruits.

"The ones graduating from the academy, like I told you before, are just not the same as they used to be. It's the lower standards and training, I know that, but I also think it's a generational thing. This generation is just too lazy and selfish compared to previous academy graduates. It's true anywhere you want to look."

FOS Sanchez admits that female graduates are scarce and that only a tiny minority of all CBP agents are women.

"Look, I know what is going on. Part of it is that the ones attracted to this job like to be working outside. They like their independence. Lots of them have a military background and we've recruited them there. So right away there are going to be more males than females. The Border Patrol is not where it should be on this. It's not only about gender. Gender is a problem. But it's also about race. We are not where we should be compared to the FBI or the DEA. We've got a hierarchy when it comes to gender and race. At the bottom are Mexican American females. Mexican American males, and I'm one of them, are not helping ourselves or the females.

"I've got an example for you. One of the new agents, very sharp guy, is a gringo from North Carolina. Where you live. He is getting his share of discrimination from Latino agents. That has got to change. Latinos are the majority, but we can't seem to get it together to help ourselves. To help the Border Patrol be a better place. It's a bad situation."

"If the Border Patrol was better at politics, then we'd be better off," he continues. "We just aren't as strong as we should be in Washington. We get pushed around by DHS and everybody else. We have to be politically stronger."

FOS Sanchez gives me a personal tour of the new Weslaco Border Patrol Station. Formerly a beer warehouse, the building has been gutted and, at a cost of $14 million, is now a state-of-the-art law enforcement facility. The new home for three hundred Border Patrol agents, now officed in a facility designed for fifty agents on International Boulevard in Weslaco, boasts a central command center that monitors all security at the station from processing of those apprehended to observation cameras in holding cells. It contains a special room for agents to access their computers, male and female locker rooms with showers, a gym, and a conference room.

Unlike conditions in some of the older stations still in use, professional safety standards for agents and those detained have been met and exceeded in the new Weslaco facility. For example, there are gun lockers for agents so that, when they transport illegal crossers from vans to the internal station entrance, times when agents frequently are outnumbered, the risk of having their service weapon taken from them has been minimized.

The FOS is proud of this new facility and excited about it. Sanchez and the other agents move into their new digs in less than a week. At the level of an agent patrolling the line, the Border Patrol is no longer poor in either facilities or equipment. Now its fundamental problems are less the result of inadequate congressional budgets than agency culture and organization: racism, gender discrimination, planning and fiscal oversight, professional development and training, identity, leadership, and vision. From an agent's perspective, all these institutional issues are geometrically magnified by a reliance on a system of old, dysfunctional border sensors mixed in with the hoopla and promises of a virtual wall.

The other uninvited guest now sitting at the immigration table, similar to the rental elephant marched back and forth across the Rio Grande at Brownsville to demonstrate the porousness of the international border, is increased violence and death. The border wall is slowly but surely concentrating violence as it becomes more difficult to cross drugs and humans. Drug traffickers and illegal crossers of all persuasions are forced by portions of the new wall into closer proximity with law enforcement agents. The closer the proximity, the greater the risk and danger to CBP agents.

The short- and long-term safety and welfare of CBP agents, legal and illegal border crossers, and border community residents meanwhile hang in the balance. As the border wall continues segment by segment to be constructed in South Texas and all along the border, most indicators suggest patrolling the line is getting more dangerous. There is always the possibility that this violence will spread into borderlands communities on this side of the new wall.

The American public and its leaders continue to believe that the new border wall is relatively fool-proof and uniform and that, when completed, it will solve the issues of illegal border crossers, illegal drugs, and international terrorists. At the time of its completion the borderline will be, according to promises of politicians, DHS, and Boeing, under so-called operational control. The public in 2009 has repeatedly been promised, most recently by Napolitano's DHS, that a high-tech solution, Project 28 and its offspring, will soon save the day.

While the new border wall may resolve some problems along the border, it seems to be creating new, unanticipated problems of even greater import.

Issues of human safety are rarely discussed in the public realm except as a fear of international terrorists. Concern for violence inspired by the *narcotrafficantes* in American border communities is high, but to date there is little to suggest that crime rates actually have risen. That is not the case in Mexican border cities and towns. But the residents of the Valley, as is true of the rest of the borderlands, understand the potential of unanticipated consequences. On a daily basis they must confront the human cost of illegal entry into the borderlands. While Judge J. D. Salinas and the Hidalgo County Commissioners' Court cut their deal with the DHS and elected officials like John Wood and others fought the border wall every step of the bitter way in Cameron County, ninety-seven men, women, and children died while illegally crossing into South Texas in 2008.[22] These deaths in the CBP's McAllen Sector accounted for approximately a quarter of documented illegal crossing deaths along the U.S.-Mexico border in that year.

Because CBP agents share their stories and experiences from one sector to another, a larger perspective local border community residents lack, CBP agents know that the number of deaths of illegal border crossers dramatically varies by region. CBP agents know, for example, the McAllen Sector has the second highest number of border deaths of any area along the two thousand miles separating Mexico from the United States.

In CBP reports, the choice of terminology to describe deaths from dehydration, the most common reason border crossers die, is "environmental exposure—heat."[23] This linguistic choice serves to sanitize the actual death of each of these individual border crossers, who suffer miserably in the border deserts and mountains. The use of this terminology also diverts responsibility for the deaths of these human beings to the natural elements and topography of the region. It is, in other words, weather and the geography that callously killed these individuals. Or the other rationale that excuses any responsibility is that illegal border crossers are too stupid to heed the obvious dangers facing them.

CBP agents in Nogales, Arizona, also know that their sector, the Tucson Sector, has the highest number of migrant deaths of any CBP sector along the Mexican border. During 2008, 171 migrant deaths were reported by the Border Patrol in the Tucson Sector, almost double the rate of the McAllen Sector.[24] The Tucson Sector accounted for about 43 percent of all migrant deaths along the U.S.-Mexico border. Together, the two sectors included approximately two-thirds of all border deaths of illegal crossers.

"It never storms from the southwest in July," a CBP agent astride a bike tells me with confidence as we both eye the first few drops of rain hitting the Nogales pavement. Just having been chased away from taking photographs of the wall, then followed by the Nogales police, I'm standing three blocks from the Nogales port of entry. The other CBP agent, also astride his bike, outfitted with a large assortment of policing aids, nods in a friendly manner as the rain picks up a notch, followed by a feisty border wind. The three of us sought shelter under the brightly striped awning of a *tienda*, store—one of many lining the downtown Nogales streets leading directly to the border bridge.

I'm searching for an eatery where my wife and I can ride out the storm, drink some coffee, then perhaps take more photographs of the Nogales border wall. When I earlier approached a parking lot attendant for restaurant information, he told me right off, "Burger King bad. McDonald good." But both restaurants are four blocks distant, and in the worsening storm, the rain now coming down in horizontal sheets as the streets begin to flood, four blocks is out of the question. As the unusual Mexican storm begins to pelt the dry-as-bones Nogales pavement, I keep dry by ducking behind a rack of clothes.

The two Nogales city police officers stationed near the border wall, one tall and thin, the other just the opposite, apparently took offense as I was shooting photos of the steel-plated border wall. I was standing, however, on a public sidewalk and only aiming my camera at the wall and the Mexican neighborhood behind it. I also went out of my way to show I was not taking any photos of the bridge or of any security-sensitive buildings or devices. No signs were clearly visible or posted to suggest that photos should not be taken. I know, regardless of the two local cops, that I was well within my

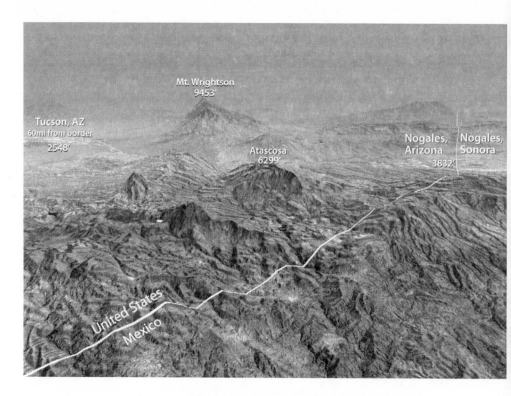

Map 3. Terrain near Nogales, Arizona, and Nogales, Sonora. (Map by Margret Mulcahy, East Carolina University Center for Geographic Information Science)

legal rights. But the two went out of their way to make it very clear that they did not want me to take any photographs of the border wall.

Before driving to Nogales that morning I intentionally dressed so I could be easily spotted and identified in my bright red polo shirt, khaki shorts, and white baseball cap. I walked slowly and obviously up and down the Nogales streets taking photos of the wall. I engaged in no suspicious behavior, did not hide my actions, and did not otherwise provoke in any way, shape, or form the CBP agents and other law enforcement agents around me. Nor did I distract them from their serious duties.

I had no intention of, nor did I at any time, break any laws. In fact, as I moved slowly about I smiled and waved in a friendly manner at all law enforcers if they looked my way.

Comparing the very modest shops of downtown Nogales, Arizona, from the barrios of its sister city, Nogales, Sonora, Mexico, one immediately recognizes that there are few other locales along the border, with the possible exception of El Paso/Juárez, where the stark differences between the two neighboring countries so literally collide one against the other. It is these differences between first-world retail stores and third-world slums, between economic opportunity and life lived in relative poverty, that are fundamental to an understanding of why Mexican citizens are willing to take risks to illegally enter our country to work or to join or rejoin their families.

Every fifteen feet, haphazard steel buttresses, appearing as if they are a construction afterthought, support the Nogales wall as it perilously clings to a hillside. On steep land subject to water and wind erosion, the wall looks as if at any moment it will slide down the hillside into oblivion. When it does, the twin border communities once more will be rejoined.

Up close, the rusting wall is a metal patchwork of welds covering holes punched into it from the other side. Some of the holes are small, some the size of a car tire. The Nogales border wall looks as if it is built of the same materials as the iconic border wall separating San Diego and Tijuana. As such, it requires constant maintenance and, in spite of attempts to retrofit it, is relatively easy to breach. To boot, it is an eyesore, a mud-colored, Rube Goldberg affair that, for all its excessive rusting steel and barbed wire, appears remarkably fragile and weak.

Up close to the Nogales wall, the sounds of everyday Mexico reverberate. Doors slam, car exhausts sputter, windows open and shut, residents gossip about the news of the day as they shout from one dilapidated building to the next. Toilets flush and dishes rattle in kitchen sinks. Babies cry, dogs bark.

From where I take my photos, I also can see Mexicans sitting at their windows and, from the height of crumbling second- and third-floor windows, looking down upon street life in another country, although in this particular case they are gazing down upon their compatriots as they legally shop the downtown stores in Nogales, Arizona. At a little before noon in July, nine out of every ten shoppers in the American *tiendas* are Mexican families with children in tow.

Never before have I observed so many law enforcement officers concentrated in one border community. In addition to the numerous CBP agents stationed at the border wall, or patrolling the perimeters of the Nogales port of entry, I counted several two-person CBP bike patrols in the nearby streets, including the ones I talked to, as well as CBP agents in marked green and white jeeps and trucks patrolling the small business district. I also observed CBP agents or Nogales municipal police on four-wheel ATVs, municipal police on three-wheel vehicles similar to Segways, and foot patrols.

Fig. 10.4 Border wall separating Nogales, Arizona, from Nogales, Mexico, 2009.

As I walked around the area before and after the storm, never more than three blocks distant from the POE, I also observed several county sheriffs in their patrol cars. In addition, I also saw law enforcement officials in unmarked cars. On this quiet morning in July, I counted at least thirty CBP, municipal, and county law enforcement officials patrolling this one small downtown area. This count does not include those law enforcement personnel I undoubtedly missed, including any hidden surveillance, and all law enforcement officers inside or near the POE. Given those I observed, I would guess there were at least forty to sixty law enforcement officers in downtown Nogales alone.

Less than five minutes after starting to take photos of the border wall that separates by a few feet the residents of Nogales, Sonora, Mexico, from Nogales, Arizona, the two policemen began to follow me. One is initially on a Segway clone, but he leaves it on the street when he joins his partner on foot. My wife, who is busy shopping in several of the *tiendas*, and I slowly make our way back to our parked rental car behind McDonald's. Periodically we enter the little stores to view their merchandise as possible presents for various family members. Each time we emerge, the same two city policemen are behind us, one of them talking on his radio. Irritated by what I interpret as an attempt at intimidation, I take photos of the two policemen as they follow us down the Nogales streets.

My wife and I stop in a small public park to use the rest room. Three blocks from the POE, one of the policemen who is following us crosses the street to where I am standing, then walks directly towards me with his regulation steel baton clearly visible in his right hand. His face stern, eyes on me alone, he never says a word as he approaches. His partner, meanwhile, remains across the street giving me a hard look. I smile at the officer with the steel baton as he approaches me. He walks up to me, passes by, then turns quickly and walks slowly by me once again. Speechless, his face is passive and unreadable.

A grey-haired, sixty-two-year-old man in khaki shorts, a red polo shirt, and a white baseball cap, I smile at the Nogales police officer every step he takes.

The Nogales policeman returns to his partner, they talk it over, and one of them gets on the radio yet again. Then they stare at us some more. When I begin talking with the two CBP agents on bike patrol, the two policemen once and for all disappear.

I chat amicably with the two agents as the desert storm descends on Nogales. Soon they seek, like me, a dryer place as the summer storm intensifies. I tell one of them as he pedals away, "Have a safe shift."

He responds over his shoulder, "Bro, take care."

It is not only the presence of an oversized contingent of law enforcers, it is their actions: in Nogales nonmilitary law enforcers mimic and mirror traditional military police tactics and strategies. They also appear to be equipped at the same levels of armament as our military police.

Two weeks after I leave Nogales, a judge in a Tucson courtroom sentences Walt Staton, a volunteer for the migrant advocacy group No More Deaths, to a year of probation and three hundred hours of community service for littering on the Buenos Aires National Wildlife Refuge, the site of many of the migrant deaths from "environmental exposure—heat" in the Tucson Sector. What Mr. Staton and three others with him say they were really doing, according to testimony, is placing plastic water bottles along trails to keep illegal crossers from dying. For years Staton and his group have been picking up litter in the refuge. Upon arresting them, an officer of the Fish and Wildlife Service and CBP agent Collins seized fourteen sealed gallon jugs of water from the four community volunteers. A dozen empty bottles this same group picked up to recycle were also confiscated by the agents.[25]

The same week that Staton is sentenced for littering in the Buenos Aires National Wildlife Refuge in the CBP's Tucson Sector, CBP agent Robert Rosas is shot and killed along the border near the San Diego wall. According to investigators, Agent Rosas was shot several times in the head and the body. At the time, Agent Rosas was attempting by himself to "catch a group of people who had crossed the border illegally." In response to this homicide of a federal law enforcement agent, CBP public information officer Lloyd Easterling tells a reporter that CBP is "constantly evaluating ways to make our job safer."[26]

This is the first murder of a CBP agent since the double homicide in 1998 of two Border Patrol agents, Ricardo Salinas and Susan Rodriguez, in Cameron County, Texas.[27] According to T. J. Bonner, president of the National Border Patrol Council, fifty CBP agents were fired upon in 2007; one CBP agent was killed when he was run over by a suspect fleeing in his vehicle.[28] While CBP data are notably unreliable and frequently not in the public domain, clearly violence directed towards agents patrolling the line is on the rise.

The Nogales border wall, augmented by the large number of CBP agents, local police, and county sheriffs, forces many border crossers to enter the United States illegally miles to the west or east of this city in terrain that is more remote and more hostile. The week I was in Nogales, the Tucson thermometer reached 112 degrees; it was undoubtedly several degrees higher in the Sonoran desert surrounding Nogales. At these extreme temperatures, illegal crossers are at risk of dehydration and death within forty-eight hours even if they carry water with them.

If Nogales, Arizona, is DHS secretary Napolitano's prototype for all border communities, then community residents all along the border soon will live like no other citizens of the United States. Even in the absence of the American military, Nogales, Arizona, is a fortified community. Because of the wall, the sheer number of law enforcers, patrolling tactics, and pervasive surveillance, it verges in part on a militarized community. Although clumsy, perhaps the best comparison to Nogales is a military base.

As Secretary Napolitano's border wall slouches towards 33 percent completion from Brownsville, Texas, to San Diego, California, there is a powerful, undeniable relationship between the border wall's increasing presence, violence directed at the CBP, rising migrant deaths, illegal drugs, and the short- and long-term safety of border residents. In constructing the new border wall, no American agency or institution appears to have planned for these very real consequences, some of which are undoubtedly unintended. At the same time, few in positions of authority or leadership seem interested in publicly discussing either how construction of the monumental border wall is changing the borderlands or the implications of these changes for all Americans.

Chapter 11

It's Getting Crowded along the Border

"The meaning of politics? Poli means more than
one. And ticks are bloodsucking parasites."

Kinky Friedman

A
s I approach the gated entrance to Peterson Air Force Base outside of Colorado Springs, armed sentries direct me
into the far right lane of traffic. I park
at the visitor's center then, feeling the altitude but
enjoying the bright sunshine, lazily walk across
the asphalt to have my documents checked. Not a
complete stranger to the ways of the military, a
month earlier I had contacted military officers at
the U.S. Northern Command (USNORTHCOM),
who agreed to meet with me.[1]

USNORTHCOM "anticipates and conducts
Homeland Defense and Civil Support operations
within the assigned areas of responsibility to defend, protect, and secure the United States and its
interests."[2] A relatively unknown entity to the
general public outside the military community,
USNORTHCOM is the military power behind the
Department of Homeland Security. As such, US-
NORTHCOM is the ultimate might and force to
resolve any and all border events and conflicts
DHS cannot handle. USNORTHCOM directs an

army battalion at Fort Bliss, outside of El Paso, Texas, as well as other military units stationed along the border.

In coming to USNORTHCOM my intention is to learn more from military experts about their perspective of the border wall. As well, very little is known about what the U.S. Army actually does on a day-by-day basis at the Mexican border. At the same time, I want to speak directly with the men and women at USNORTHCOM who are responsible for collecting data and information about the Mexican border, working with their Mexican counterparts, and sharing their border expertise with policy makers. If possible I also want to obtain their formal permission to interview soldiers at Fort Bliss and other border bases to gain a better understanding of their role, mission, and perspective.

Joining one of two designated lines at the visitor's center, both monitored by the watchful eyes of uniformed airmen, I observe that gaining access to USNORTHCOM is not unlike queuing up at the local post office. Only in this case the clerk behind the counter is barely nineteen years old and, like his fellow employees, in peak physical condition and armed to the teeth.

After showing ID I sign two more forms, one for myself and the other for my rental Malibu. The airman behind the counter asks me where I am headed. I tell him Building C and ask about the parking.

"Parking is kinda hard around here," he offers. "You're going to have to park in that big lot over there, then hike it." With a sweep of his arm, he motions over his shoulder in the general direction of the parking lot he has in mind.

All I can see of Peterson Air Force Base from the visitors center is three large glass office buildings typical of any urban office park. The only difference, upon closer inspection, is that the exteriors of these cubes are completely devoid of landscaping. Lined up along a broad street as if ready to salute, the buildings are identical in every respect except the alphabet letter assigned to them. At the entrance to Building C I am motioned by a uniformed airman to the front desk, where I show my various base passes, fill out another form, and in return receive a visitor's badge, which I clip to my suit lapel.

As the minutes pass while waiting for my first appointment with Col. Houston Polson, I watch uniformed men and women walk smartly by. After twenty minutes a short, plump man in his fifties approaches. Dressed in a rumpled white shirt, dark tie, and suit pants, Colonel Polson introduces himself, shakes my hand, then motions me down a long hallway to a multilevel cafeteria. "This will work better than my office," Colonel Polson tells me as he sits down at the nearest table. "How was your trip?" he adds hurriedly.

Col. Houston Polson (Ret.) is the deputy chief for the Education and

Training Division, J-7. In this capacity at USNORTHCOM one of the colonel's duties is to lead the Homeland Security Defense Education Consortium (HSDEC). To that end he helped organize a conference in San Antonio, Texas, at which I am soon to be giving a presentation. The title of the San Antonio conference is "Preparing and Responding to Disasters in North America." That is the sum total I know about Colonel Polson, but I hope to learn much more about him, his research on security, HSDEC, and his perspective on the border wall.

Only a few minutes into what quickly proves to be an awkward, one-sided conversation with Colonel Polson, Colonel McMann appears at our cafeteria table. Colonel McMann, also one of the conference organizers, and also dressed in civilian clothes, works in the Planning and Strategy Division, J-5. As if on cue, Colonel Polson excuses himself, but not before informing me that Sylvia Crocker will be meeting us in an hour. Ms. Crocker is in Interagency Coordination. While I corresponded with the two colonels and several others, I have no idea who and what Ms. Crocker and her Interagency Coordination are.

After grabbing coffee at the cafeteria counter, Colonel McMann and I find a secluded table. As we sit down, Colonel McMann hands me a three-ring binder filled with thirty pages of PowerPoint bullets, charts, and diagrams. Without a moment's hesitation, even though his audience of one sits just two feet from him, Colonel McMann launches into formal briefing mode. His topic, as well as I can decipher it, is the history of U.S.-Mexico relations since 1848.

I really had not traveled to Building C at USNORTHCOM in Colorado Springs to be needlessly briefed on a subject with which I was already familiar. After three long and excruciating minutes, it is clear, at least for me, that this briefing consists of an endless list of treaties, diplomatic events, and conflicts without benefit of historical context and interpretation. Just a list. This pretend overview of diplomatic and military relations with Mexico is not only superficial, but also could have been lifted directly out of a number of freshman college textbooks. Assuming Colonel McMann was ordered to give me this useless briefing, and still after five minutes not yet having reached the Mexican Revolution, I interrupt the colonel as he reads from Point 4, Item C, on page 5.

"How did you first get involved in this kind of job?" I ask.

The colonel suddenly stops briefing mode and looks up from the notebook without seeming the least bit offended. "It was almost by accident. I happened to be at the right place at the right time. I'd had a little Spanish in high school and junior college, so really I was the only one here that had much preparation. They needed someone right away and I applied."

University classes, certificates, and academic degrees are certainly no guarantee of expertise, but they do demonstrate a minimum level of competency in a specific area of study. Without some knowledge of the history, economics, and culture of Mexico, all that remains is a set of disconnected battles, wars, speeches, treaties, and foreign policies—not unlike this briefing. But self-education and experience should never be discounted.

"I don't have the training or the degrees," Colonel McMann readily admits. "I just was at the right place at the right time. I had Beginning Spanish, so I had an advantage over everyone else here. What I've been doing is reading everything I can get my hands on for the last four years. To educate myself. I was hoping you could give me some suggestions for reading."

"What exactly is your job, Colonel?" I ask, pursuing my question.

"I'm in charge of a staff of ten in J-5, Planning and Strategy. One of our specific tasks is to facilitate and promote relations between the Mexican military, the Canadian military, and us. The Canadians, of course, are no problem. They've been a part of NORAD [North American Aerospace Defense Command] for many years, so we know them. They're pretty much just like us. They've been right across the hall for a long time. We're used to them, you might say. But the Mexican military, well, I have to tell you that they are another deal."

I nod my head.

The colonel mistakes my nod as a signal to continue the briefing. He relaunches before I interrupt him for a second time.

"What do you mean by saying the Mexicans are 'another deal'?" I ask him.

"We have a long way to go with them. Bottom line, we don't have a lot of trust there. You know, because of the corruption issues they've had. The generals. But it is to our benefit to try to work with them on security issues along our border. We know that. There have been some cultural misunderstandings."

I share with the colonel some of my own cultural miscues and blunders over the course of a professional career spent along the Mexican border. Even as the colonel eyes his briefing book, his eyes noticeably brighten with interest.

"Same thing here," he concludes after listening to one of my stories. Colonel McMann was placed in charge of planning several visits by Mexican generals to USNORTHCOM—with mixed results. Each time the Mexican military flew in with their entourages, however, Colonel McMann learned more about Mexican mores, customs, and social expectations.

"I think it's all about size, isn't it?" the Colonel observes with a laugh. "They like big presents. Big things to remember when they get back to Mexico that they can show their friends. After one visit here, you know, we gave them the usual dinner, round of golf, social stuff, then some mementoes of their visit. It was small stuff. You could hold the gifts in your hand. It was regular Chamber of Commerce stuff, that kind of thing. Right away I could tell they were very disappointed. So the next time they came, I went out and bought the biggest stuff I could find. Big and heavy. They like presents with lots of colors.

"I have resistance at this end. Still do. Some, not all, of my superiors are reluctant. The trust thing. We just are not familiar with their culture. But we're getting better. It's different with the Canadians, because they are just like us."

Colonel McMann is not going to say much more. He returns to his briefing cant, but we never get much past World War II. When Sylvia Crocker from Interagency Coordination approaches, the colonel seems peeved but quickly recovers. Ms. Crocker introduces herself with a firm handshake, then sits down across from the colonel and me. Dressed in a dark business suit, she immediately asks me a series of questions. I cannot help but think she is on an assigned mission.

"Tell me why you are visiting us, Dr. Maril," she orders. I have several questions I would like to ask her, but it looks like I will never get the chance. I started making my list immediately after Colonel McMann limped through World War I. As expected in this kind of ritual, I recite my academic credentials and scholarly publications, then briefly explain to her my background in border research, work with the Border Patrol, and current project studying the border wall. I tell her I particularly want to understand the challenges our army and National Guard, assigned to the border by President Bush, face from one day to the next.

"You can't do that," Ms. Crocker corrects me right off. "We can't have you asking our men and women in uniform about those kinds of things. First of all, you would get in their way. Second, you would need permission. What I can do is give you the name of the public information officer in El Paso. You can talk directly with him. I'm sure he will get you everything you need to know."

I tell her that I appreciate her concerns, but military PIOs are notoriously of little help because they only deliver the official line.

"No way," she again replies. Crocker then lectures me for several minutes on why my research is impossible to conduct.

A week later, when I describe this same conversation to another US-NORTHCOM employee, he tells me, "She saw you as a target." Crocker serves as gatekeeper. At the time I assume she is sent by Colonel Polson or those above him to discourage me from my border research. Certainly she offers little real "interagency coordination" in my direct appeal for her help.

With Colonel McMann squirming in his chair, our conversation then turns a little nasty. Sylvia Crocker seems accustomed to having underlings, perhaps especially academics, always agree with her. I, in turn, am accustomed to finding some sort of bureaucratic accommodation that will allow me to conduct my research. When Crocker falls back upon the age-old academic tradition of declaring her educational institution superior to mine and thus, by implication, her present directives not to be questioned, I do not back down. It soon becomes a standoff, with Crocker growing increasingly uncomfortable with my failure to beat a hasty verbal retreat. The colonel continues to squirm.

Finally, Ms. Crocker stands to leave, attempting to assume a position of final authority by leaning her two elbows on the table between us, then staring me straight in the eyes. It is, however, a very uncomfortable position for her to hold because the total weight of her body rests on her forearms. She is left to speak very rapidly because her forearms are trembling with the effort it takes leaning on them. As forcefully as she can, she says, "I hope you have a great visit here. I'm sure I will see you someday on Fox News." Then she strides across the cafeteria and disappears around a hallway corner.

Feeling as if a fairy-tale curse has just been tossed my way, I finally say to Colonel McMann, "She seems a little angry."

"Yes," the colonel replies. Then, "Do you want to see Colonel Polson?"

As we get up to leave, I tell Colonel McMann I look forward to seeing him again at the San Antonio military conference. The colonel grimaces. "I'm not sure about that. I haven't been invited yet."

"But wasn't the conference mostly your idea?"

"Yes. But I'm not sure I'm going. There might not be enough money. I don't know. No one has said anything about it yet to me. Maybe I will be there."

We leave the cafeteria, find an elevator, then walk down long corridors lined with cubicles. We turn, then walk down more long corridors lined with cubicles. We stop in front of a doorless cubicle belonging to Colonel Polson. At the moment, Colonel Polson is not in the small space crammed to capacity with stacks of military manuals, reports, electronic gizmos, and their parts. Lounging about are two Air Force officers in flight suits waiting to see Colonel Polson. As I start up a conversation with the Air Force officers—my brother was an Air Force colonel—Colonel McMann slips away without a word.

Colonel Polson returns in a few minutes. After clearing the paper clutter from a chair, during which the officers drift off, he invites me to sit. I thank him for the opportunity to meet with Colonel McMann and Ms. Crocker, then tell him I need clarification on my role at the upcoming conference in San Antonio.

"What is it exactly you want me to talk about?" I ask the colonel.

"Just, well, just talk about your research. Try to make friends with the Mexicans. Try to think of something we can do with them."

"You mean," I say in some confusion, "develop research collaborations with Mexican scholars?"

"I don't know. Just something we can get started with."

I am still confused. Colonel Polson is the head of HSDEC, so I look to him for guidance. It strikes me, the longer I talk with him, that he does not have the foggiest idea what he wants me to do or say at the San Antonio conference. In its own right, this is somewhat alarming. Colonel Polson is the titular head of programs for more than one hundred universities and colleges that offer degrees in security studies. It is the colonel's responsibility to set professional standards for these programs and to assure curriculum quality. In this way the federal dollars spent underwriting HSDEC are well spent. I assume, given these circumstances, that Colonel Polson will be a reservoir of clearly stated tasks, goals, and objectives.

Now the colonel says, "Just talk with them during the social hour and see what you can start up."

Off the top of my head I venture, "Are you thinking about possible scenarios, maybe future exercises so that the Mexicans can interact with our military? Maybe you could have a joint exercise in response to an international health problem?"

"Sure, that would be great."

"I guess I still need some direction," I finally say to him. "As I understand it, one of J-7's goals, one of your goals as head of HSDEC, is to support research at the university level on national security and the border." The colonel nods his head. I continue: "I'm a researcher with experience in this topic. Can you provide me with some professional contacts? I'm not asking for research funds, I'm asking for the names of some colleagues at other universities I can contact who are involved in similar kinds of research."

Colonel Polson looks puzzled. "We have a number of research issues we've been thinking about. More than fifty topics."

I am genuinely surprised by this pronouncement and ask the colonel how I can find out more about the fifty research topics.

"We've had a few problems with this. The details are on our website, but it's currently under construction. It should be up and available in a few weeks." Later I learn from a USNORTHCOM employee that Colonel Polson's HSDEC webmaster quit. When the webmaster walked off Peterson Air Force

Base, he took all the website passwords with him. While it is technically true that Colonel Polson and HSDEC do have a website, there is no public access to it. It is, in fact, many more months after my visit to Peterson Air Force Base before the website was finally completed and accessible to the public, and by that time research funds are not available.

What bothers me about all of this is that Colonel Polson, in charge of the HSDEC security studies program for a hundred universities around the nation, has been locked out of his own website.

A few minutes later I meet Colonel Polson's immediate supervisor, Colonel Spellman. I ask Colonel Spellman for military contacts and references for my research, and he directs Colonel Polson to give them to me.

"He's my boss," Colonel Polson tells me after Colonel Spellman leaves. "I'll email you the names." Colonel Polson leads me back to the entrance of Building C. Exiting past the guards, I feel much the same as I did leaving Nogales, Arizona.

Hearing nothing from Colonel Polson for four weeks, I remind him by email of the contacts promised by Colonel Spellman. Several more weeks pass. Colonel Polson finally emails me that he has forgotten what it is I want. Would I mind, he writes, sending him the objectives of my visit and my credentials? For a second time I send him this same information. In spite of additional requests, I never receive another response from Colonel Polson.

The conference planned by Colonel McMann and Colonel Polson, designed to bring American generals together with their Mexican counterparts, begins on a Friday morning in early October in downtown San Antonio.[3] Funded by Colonel Polson's HSDEC, and cosponsored by the University of Texas San Antonio (UTSA) and my home institution of East Carolina University (ECU), both of which feature popular security studies programs, the conference commences with conferees sitting at fifteen round tables sipping coffee and downing donuts and *empanadas* from a local bakery. Of the seventy or so in attendance, approximately two-thirds wear military uniforms, the remainder suits and ties. Sprinkled among the latter group are a small number of academics.

Sitting across from me is Captain James W. Terbush, the command surgeon for USNORTHCOM at Peterson Air Force Base. When asked if Colonel Polson is in attendance, Captain Terbush says, "Apparently Houston was on his way to the airport in Colorado Springs when he had some sort of memory loss. He couldn't remember where he was or what he was doing. He pulled over to the side of the road and called his wife. She came and got him and took him to the ER. That's all I know at this point."

Colonel McMann, the co-organizer of the conference, is also not in attendance.

The conference begins with a prayer from a military chaplain. Standing at the podium the chaplain in his Air Force uniform reads from a scrap of paper in his hand, "Lord, help us today to plan for disasters."

The first hour of the conference consists of a ritualistic gift exchange between the military contingent and the academic ranks. Swapped are engraved plaques, San Antonio mementoes, wrapped university alumni trivia emblazoned with logos, formal handshakes, manly embraces, gratuitous praise for services rendered, and multitudinous promises of grander conferences in the near future. By the end of it all, everyone in the room is holding a gift of some kind except for me and the waiters. The way things are going, I fully expect ECU's mascot, Petey the Pirate, to parachute from the Texas sky, land at the podium, then hand out plastic swords to all the conferees.

During this treacly first hour, the only conference participants obviously enjoying the festivities are the Canadian military sitting at a table at the back of the room. These out-of-towners may have opened the cash bar earlier than announced on the conference schedule, because they seem to have the best of times throughout the conference, regardless of who is standing behind the podium.

The stultifying speeches provide an opportunity to scan for the Mexican generals in attendance. Table by table I cover every group present but see no one who remotely qualifies. Where are the Mexican generals?

At exactly nine o'clock—this conference is nothing if not a slave to the clock—Lieutenant General Charles G. Rodriguez, the adjutant general of the Texas National Guard, takes the podium. Lieutenant General Rodriguez is the keynote speaker.

The general's topic, at least as far as I can interpret it, is how well prepared the Texas National Guard is to kick the ass of any enemies of this nation foolish enough to cross the Mexican border into Texas. President Bush assigned six thousand National Guard to the Mexican border in the summer of 2006 on a temporary basis. Under the Obama administration, they remain in place and have been supplemented by additional Guardsmen. Down to the platoon level, the general describes the capabilities of the Texas National Guard, including a rambling history that loses its way at the turn of the last century. General Rodriguez uses many visual aids in his keynote address, including colorful PowerPoint pie charts, graphs, tables, diagrams, and photographs of different weapons.

At the end of this keynote address, General Rodriguez, in spite of having stated several times that his Texas National Guard will quickly decimate any enemy crossing into Texas from Mexico, proudly proclaims a "great relationship" with the Mexican military. The general goes on to say that he looks forward in the future to strengthening his relationship with the Mexican military.

Not to be outdone, Lieutenant General Robert T. Clark, commanding general at Fort Sam Houston of ARNORTH (United States Army North) and the Fifth Army, takes the podium. He then slogs through more than enough organizational charts, maps, and random bits of unrelated data to prevail in a small war. During General Clark's presentation we are shown the following slides, among others: "US Army North," "US Northern Command Joint Command All Services," "Spectrum of Operations," "Operational Area," "ARNORTH Operational Organization," "US ARNORTH C2 Vehicles," and "Regional Defense Coordinating Officer & Element (DCOE/E)."

Alone the slide titled "ARNORTH Operational Organization" boasts seventeen levels of command enclosed in a colorful box with red arrows, yellow stars, and fonts in purple, red, yellow, and black. The general speed-reads his presentation in twelve breathtaking minutes. As the Canadians heartily applaud the general's speech, I look again in vain for the whereabouts of the Mexican generals.

The remainder of the morning we hear from the director of Interagency Coordination (boss of Sylvia Crocker at USNORTHCOM in Colorado Springs), FEMA's deputy director of response, the director of programs at the Canadian Forces College (who receives prolonged applause from the back of the room both before and after he speaks), and the health director of the City of Laredo.

FEMA's deputy director of response, Michael W. Lowder, is deserving of his own special award, Greatest Obfuscation of a Bureaucratic Decision Making Structure. His eye-popping presentation includes multiple graphs and charts so microdetailed as to be utterly indecipherable. Even those military personnel closest to the screen at the front of the room cannot decipher the meaningless subcategories of endless duties and responsibilities of local, state, and national agencies and programs.

Almost all of these presentations have one commonality. Near the end of the speech, the speaker describes at some lengths the special role of his respective agency or institution in facilitating the Mexican army's humanitarian visit to our country to provide medical aid to victims of Hurricane Katrina. Various speakers tell us that after Hurricane Katrina, a Mexican convoy was cleared by American authorities at the Laredo port of entry, then rolled onto Texas highways on its way to Dallas to provide basic medical care and supplies to victims evacuated from disaster sites along the Gulf coast. Since this is the first time since the Treaty of Guadalupe Hidalgo in 1848 that Mexican soldiers have been welcomed onto American soil, the Mexican medical convoy is virtually unprecedented.

As this narrative unfolds, it also seems that before this convoy of Mexican doctors and nurses can reach its destination of Dallas, it is diverted to Kelly Air Force Base, only a few miles from the site of our conference. During this unscheduled stopover, according to various conference speechmakers heard at the podium, a partnership based upon understanding and mutual respect is founded between the Mexican army and the American military. This nascent partnership will soon blossom, according to speakers, into a strong and viable cross-border military collaboration focusing upon the shared concerns of national security.

Several speakers also refer to the annual commanders' conference, at which American generals meet with their Mexican counterparts to "discuss issues, embrace cooperation, and exchange experiences." It is this very same set of meetings that Colonel McMann at USNORTHCOM described to me; the self-taught colonel claimed to have learned much about Mexican culture from his experiences with visiting Mexican dignitaries.

One ray of hope emanates from Dr. Waldo Lopez, chief of disease control and epidemiology in Laredo and one of the only civilians to give a presentation at the morning conference session. Dr. Lopez describes the existing binational cooperation between medical communities in Laredo and Nuevo Laredo, detailing how each community over years of cooperation has strengthened the other. Dr. Lopez's binational health model reflects my own experiences of living in the border cities of Brownsville and McAllen. In those two communities, as is true all along the borderlands, local fire departments, police departments, health departments, and social services, among others, regularly cooperate and aid their counterparts on the other side of the border.

As the morning presentations unrelentingly seep into the afternoon, I have an opportunity during the brief lunch break to search once more for the Mexican generals—or, as time passes, the Mexican colonels, majors, captains, lieutenants, sergeants, or privates. Despite the fact that the stated purpose of this conference is to bring together ranking members of the Mexican military, American military, and academics to discuss binational disaster response, that is, binational security issues, I find not a single Mexican military officer or enlisted person in attendance.

Professor Abelardo Rodriguez Sumano, a researcher at Mexico's Center for North American Strategic Studies, is the only individual at the conference capable of viewing binational security issues from a Mexican perspective.[4] Maybe Professor Sumano may even know where the Mexican generals are hiding.

"They're not here," Professor Sumano tells me between bites of his sandwich. "None of them came."

"Why not?"

Professor Sumano sits comfortably at a table surrounded by American military officers. Smiling as he shrugs his shoulders, diplomacy exuding from every word, he tells me in a reserved voice, "They weren't given enough time. They only were told about this conference a month or two ago. That's not enough time in Mexico. Plus that's not really the problem. The problem is the fence. The fence in Mexico is considered a national insult."

According to Professor Sumano, the Mexican press, politicians at all levels, and the general public were greatly displeased when the fence between the two countries was first proposed and touted by the Americans. Mexicans did not comprehend why the United States would build a barrier to keep Mexican workers out of their country when for so many years American employers had welcomed them and profited greatly from their labor.

"But you know," continues Dr. Sumano, "even if the generals decided to come to this conference, who would you really get? Just those, as you should know, who are owed favors. Not the generals at the very top, not after the insult of the fence. No, the trip to this conference would be payback to lower-level officers who would treat it as a short vacation. Those that came would have no authority to make decisions. They would just be tourists here to enjoy the restaurants and entertainments of San Antonio. Of course, you would expect the conference planners to know this." Saying this, the professor again shrugs his shoulders.

Unfortunately, when Colonel McMann and Colonel Polson planned this conference six months earlier, they were still jousting with the perceived cultural perception that to please Mexican generals it is only necessary to offer them big, colorful, and weighty mementoes. It is my turn to shrug.

Professor Sumano goes on, "So if they really came, you'd get the middle-level guys who are owed favors for various reasons. You won't get the top ones now."

"What about the great relationship between the Mexican military and American military we heard so much about this morning? You know, all about that Mexican medical convoy helping out the Katrina survivors at Kelly?"

Professor Sumano's eyes twinkle, but the man remains silent.

Later, when it is finally Sumano's turn to take the microphone at the podium, he reads from handwritten notes he has been working on throughout the morning session. Many of the military are telling me they must leave in order to avoid the San Antonio Friday afternoon rush hour, and the audience is half the size it was before lunch. In his brief presentation without PowerPoint, Professor Sumano reminds the reduced audience Mexico and the United States have been political partners and allies since joining forces against the Nazis and fascists in World War II. But, he suggests, their relationship began to sour after Mexican president Miguel Alemán was elected in 1946, and in spite of the Bracero Program, which was in place from 1942 to 1965.

Professor Sumano admits in his presentation to the profound corruption among the highest levels of Mexican government and military, an embarrassing set of events exposed at about the same time Mexico joined NAFTA in 1994. Even by then, he reminds us, the Mexican *narcotrafficantes* were emboldened by their wealth and the political influence it purchased. For its part, Mexico expected to be treated as a partner in NAFTA, believing the international trade agreement would benefit all nations equally. But unfortunately it was also at this very same time that the Mexican economy seriously foundered, and his country found itself on the embarrassing end of an American economic bailout.

Mexican president Vicente Fox sought at the beginning of his term in 2000 to resurrect strong and equal ties between the two countries. Indeed, before 9/11 President Bush, a friend of Fox's before both men were elected to their nations' highest offices, also supported a closer, stronger relationship with Mexico. This relationship, Professor Sumano reminds his audience, included a new labor management plan modeled on the Bracero Program.

When American security along the border was handed over to US-NORTHCOM after 9/11, however, the Mexican military felt both intimidated by its next-door neighbor and also abandoned. The same Mexican military feared, says Professor Sumano, "being subordinated to USNORTHCOM." Sumano paints the Mexican military, including the army and, to a lesser degree, the navy, as one of the fundamental mainstays of Mexican society, providing both political and social stability since the PRI took over in the early twentieth century.

Wary of USNORTHCOM, the Mexican military nevertheless attempted, in the days after Hurricane Katrina, to demonstrate international goodwill and explore the possibilities of a renewed relationship with its powerful northern neighbor by offering direct medical aid along with expertise gained from similar efforts inside its own borders. After the Mexican medical caravan crossed the Río Bravo at Nuevo Laredo, it was, according to Sumano, dissuaded by the American government from motoring to its Dallas destination. Instead, the convoy was sidetracked to Kelly Air Force Base, where the feds swung into action.

According to Mexican military officials, the convoy was confronted at Kelly with mounds of American paperwork and red tape that hampered its medical mission. The American military would not allow experienced Mexican physicians, for example, to care for storm victims unless they were partnered with American personnel. The Mexican military doctors felt they were in effect being "shadowed." Never allowed to reach Dallas, the Mexican military were, from their perspective, professionally humiliated, and their gesture of international goodwill completely discounted. In short, major cultural misunderstandings between the Mexican military and the American military had serious implications for binational planning and policy, including security issues.

In this historical and political context, the professor summarizes, the building of a border fence between the two nations is a particularly insensitive symbolic act on the part of the United States, an impediment to real cooperation. Given this current situation, Professor Sumano calls for, once again, falling back on the language of diplomacy, the "construction of instruments and mechanisms of mutual confidence" that would be a part of a "new doctrine of foreign policy" and "a new generation of reforms."

To mediocre applause, Professor Sumano returns to his table. Lieutenant General Rodriguez, the conference keynote speaker, sits not more than five feet from the podium. Presumably General Rodriguez has listened carefully to the sole representative from Mexico at a conference designed to create stronger ties between the United States and Mexico.

Later in the evening at a bistro on San Antonio's River Walk I ask Professor Sumano if he feels his message reached General Rodriguez or any of the other ranking American military leaders at the conference. Again, Professor Sumano smiles, shrugs, but remains silent.

Cultural misunderstanding and opacity are not unique to the American military. In large part because of the semisecrecy surrounding the border wall, created and nourished by the Department of Homeland Security, the public is ill-informed or misinformed. This dearth of information about the border wall effectively limits and curtails productive public dialogue and discussion. Similarly, although for different reasons, there is also limited public knowledge about the status of illegal immigration during the major recession that began in 2008 along with a host of related immigration issues and policies; there is little agreement on policy solutions. Few public forums, in short, are not burdened by the paucity of concrete data. At the same time, media pundits and others with political agendas are quick to provide comments and solutions to data-poor audiences.

In my hometown of Greenville, North Carolina, I am roped into just such a community public forum on immigration issues. I am also forced quickly to confront the hard realities of discussing these issues when there are those who do not want American immigration history along with relevant data to displace their ideological rants.

On the same stage at East Carolina University are Adelcio Lugo, Hispanic local banker with the program Self-Help, Jeremy L. McKinney, a private immigration and naturalization attorney, Leticia Zavala, a legal immigrant from Mexico and organizer representing the Farm Labor Organizing Committee in nearby Raleigh, and William Gheen, president of the political action committee Americans for Legal Immigration. Moderator for this public forum, sponsored by the Pitt County chapter of the League of Women Voters, is Annette Newell, a news anchor at the local NBC affiliate WNCT-TV.[5]

After brief introductory statements by each individual, Mr. Gheen seizes the opportunity to dominate the microphone and all discussion thenceforth from the audience and other participants on stage by advocating at length for the political agenda of his PAC. Unfortunately, the moderator makes no attempt to reign in this one panelist out of five. Discounting any place for a discussion of the history of immigration in the United States, or the importance of fact-based policy, Gheen leaves no chance for response to his baseless assertions about immigration trends and public policy. His strident tone and insulting comments are very effective in intimidating those who may disagree with him. At one point a member of the audience asks the sources of Gheen's immigration "facts."

Mr. Gheen says, "I think these figures are from a magazine from last year. But I'm not sure." Gheen then announces he is a proud member of the Minutemen.[6]

The Minutemen were successful under the leadership of Jim Gilchrist in forcing illegal immigration along the Mexican border to the forefront of the national immigration debate in the spring of 2006. Spurred on by Lou Dobbs and other media pundits, small numbers of Minutemen demonstrated in dramatic fashion for the media the Border Patrol's inability to stem the flow of undocumented workers along the Mexican border. While their armed patrols of segments of the Mexican border did little but distract Border Patrol agents from their jobs, the Minutemen drew the public's attention to border issues. At the same time, the Minutemen crystallized public frustration with immigration policy under the Bush administration. Politicians of all persuasions jumped on the bandwagon built by the Minutemen.[7]

The Minutemen proved in the end to be little more than a one-trick pony, a single-issue social movement incapable of maintaining the attention of the American polity. Disorganized, underfinanced, and led by political novices, a handful of Minutemen ran for local and state office in several border states but garnered few votes in the fall of 2006.[8] After losing by significant margins, the Minutemen factionalized, splintered, then imploded. Scattered and discounted groups endure to this day, each charging the other with malfeasance and filing lawsuits against their fellow members.[9] But the Minutemen never were able to build a serious national movement before internal bickering led to their self-imposed demise. In the first year of Obama's administration there was a resurgence of the Minutemen in Arizona, but on the national level the Minutemen remain discredited and without an electoral base.

The various speakers on the ECU stage attempt through their own personal and professional experience to question Mr. Gheen's facts and assertions about immigrants and immigration policy in the United States. Gheen is very successful at not only reducing this public forum at times to a shouting match, but also diverting attention from a genuine discussion of the issues. In the local paper the next day Gheen is the centerpiece of the reportorial coverage.

My personal experiences with a range of broadcast media tell me there is a barrier to thoughtful discussion of the border wall and immigration issues. For perhaps very different reasons, both the Fox network and National Public Radio stations ask very one-sided questions pertaining to immigration issues and the Mexican border.

Soon after my strained conversation with Sylvia Crocker at USNORTHCOM, a Fox producer from *Fox and Friends* contacts me. After being "preinterviewed" on the phone by this producer, the two hosts of a live segment of *Fox and Friends* ask me to comment on topics of which I have no knowledge or expertise. At first they ask me to comment on research I have conducted, including the risks faced by CBP agents patrolling the line. Then they ask how a Mexican presidential election will affect events in the United States. While they are asking me additional questions about which I have no specific knowledge, the television screen is split into two halves; one half shows my profile answering the questions I am unqualified to answer, the other half, the iconic, dated footage of undocumented workers madly running across the port of entry at San Diego. My segment is followed by an interview with a musician who just won a national kazoo contest.

While my several interviews with local public radio stations around the country certainly allow for more depth and information, because they are longer than Fox's four-minute segment, the interviewers are always interested in only one major issue: the hardships faced by undocumented workers crossing the Mexican border. The single-mindedness of focus disallows discussion of any other related immigration issues and policies, including the border wall, which may in fact lead to a broader understanding of border deaths. NPR and Fox are both heavily biased, only in different ways.

I certainly should have checked the Chicago broadcast of the *Mancow Show* before agreeing to be on it. Hindsight never errs. My after-the-fact Googling of the show reveals colorful images of the host, Mancow, surrounded by midgets and dwarfs in wrestling garb challenging listeners to a round in the ring. But instead I took the producer at his word when he described the show as "news oriented and targeting the early morning commuter."

I stagger out of bed at 5:30 a.m. on a Tuesday morning, put water on to heat for tea, let the dog out, let the dog back in, and take a seat in my La-Z-Boy by the phone. Gulping down the hot tea, I remember my pound puppy will certainly bark during air time, so I jump up from the recliner, remove her to another room, then return just in time for the Chicago call. The voice on the other end of the line identifies itself as the studio engineer for the *Mancow Show*. We exchange pleasantries, then he says, "Okay, Professor Maril, I'm going to put you on hold so you can hear the show. Mancow will get you on in a minute or two."

After five minutes, ten minutes, then fifteen minutes and more, I am still waiting for my chance to be on the *Mancow Show* from Chicago. In the meantime, I am not sure whether Mancow is human, animal, or somewhere in between. What I hear on air is a cacophony of cartoon characters, flatulence, quotations attributed to famous Americans, random grunting, heavy metal bands, and more grunting. Suddenly, a male voice asks out of nowhere, "Turd, what do you think of this news story? A Mexican illegal shot a cop in Phoenix. I think it was Phoenix. Anyway, what do you think?"

A voice responds—I assume it belongs to Turd—with an affirmative groan.

Commercials suddenly flow hot and heavy: ads promoting college degrees by mail, medications for facial blemishes, more mail-order degrees and certificates, high-paying jobs in the comfort of your own home, diet plans, and rent-to-own furniture deals.

Twenty minutes and counting, after a commercial promoting a local junior college offering on-line courses in medical technology, Mancow says, "We have a special guest this morning who's written a book. How ya doing, Doc?"

Fed up, I say, "Not so good. I'm hanging up." I slam the phone down with as much force as, given the hour, I can muster.

Three weeks later I find a message on my phone machine. The producer for the *Mancow Show* called. The producer begins, "We enjoyed you so much last time on the show, we really want to have you back again. . . ."

Book signings in major border state cities fare little better, although they provide a greater opportunity to listen to the public and determine its understanding of immigration issues. In Houston, Dallas, and Austin I find highly opinionated voters who, at the same time, seem to know very little about the Mexican borderlands and the border wall. Admittedly selective, these experiences with broadcast media and the public emphasize a much broader trend among Americans, who increasingly distrust all media and/or only listen to media that support their political perspectives.[10]

For its part, the major media report almost exclusively on immigration news and happenings in San Diego/Tijuana, just a short drive from the media capital of Los Angeles. Much less often, until fall 2010, they fly into El Paso/Juárez, ignoring in this mediacentric coverage all the rest of the two-thousand-mile borderlands. When reporters do venture off the beaten media path, even if it is the Juárez–El Paso metroplex, they tend to act and dress before the cameras and microphones as if they are broadcasting from a Middle Eastern or African hinterland.

Americans are for many good reasons strongly divided about immigration issues and policies. In general, the data show there are real concerns that "immigrants are a burden to the country, taking jobs and housing and creating strains on the health care system." Many Americans "also worry about the cultural impact of the expanding numbers of newcomers in the U.S." An equal number of citizens, however, believe these same immigrants have a more positive effect on the country than a negative one.[11]

When Americans are asked about the best policy solutions to reducing illegal immigration, opinions vary. Nationally, 49 percent of all Americans believe penalizing employers of illegal workers is the best policy, while 33 percent believe that increasing the number of CBP agents is the best solution. Only 9 percent believe building more border fences is the best solution.[12]

Continued attempts by DHS secretaries Chertoff and Napolitano to keep the border wall wrapped in a shroud of pseudosecrecy may have backfired in the short term, at least as regards the support of the American public. Nevertheless, President Obama and a Democratic majority in Congress continue to pass legislation to finance construction of a border fence.

The drive back from Sasabe, situated in southern Pima County, to Tucson is a straight shot north up Highway 286. About twelve miles outside of the tiny community, we again see four of Boeing, Inc.'s Project 28 towers. They carry on them a variety of surveillance gizmos to monitor the area for illegal crossers between the border and the towers. As I catch the last of the towers in my rearview, I consider whether DHS's ongoing technological dream, defined as the final solution to operational control of the U.S.-Mexico border since its inception as ISIS in 1998, is reaching completion. Or is it slowly circling the drain?

Long before we reach the orderly, broad thoroughfares of Tucson, we pass by the mile fifteen sign on Highway 286, a marker signifying we are fifteen miles north of the Mexican border. Off to the side of a dry and wide wash a large bus, its windows blackened and its diesel engine rumbling while its driver naps at the wheel, sits among the saguaros. Lettered on the

Fig. 11.1 Project 28 towers outside of Sasabe, Arizona, 2009.

side of the bus is "Wackenhut Transportation." This vehicle belongs to Wackenhut Corporation, "the leading provider of quality, customer focused security solutions in the United States."[13] Wackenhut has the national contract to transport illegal border crossers apprehended by the CBP to station processing and then to the nearest detention centers.

In the drive back to Tucson, we also pass by one portable CBP checkpoint attended by six CBP vehicles. Further on, in succession, are one Border Patrol scope truck, four CBP vehicles at the side of highway, and two county sheriff's vehicles hiding behind inanimate objects. As we motor north we are also passed by twenty to twenty-five white Ford trucks, all the same model and year, each filled with engineers working on Project 28. Now, at the end of the workday, they are headed back to Tucson. We also observe eight grey security trucks headed south. In each security truck sit two uniformed security guards. For another thirty miles we drive through rolling desert basins surrounded by rugged mountains before the two-lane road gradually descends into the gridded outskirts of the Tucson suburbs.

According to one Tucson source, there are five hundred CBP agents currently stationed in the area. That number, however large it sounds, does not count, as is the case in Nogales, all the additional municipal, county, and state law enforcement officials assisting the Border Patrol in patrolling the line and the area between the line and Tucson.

There is a crowd near the Mexican border. Nogales is one thing, but this is quite another. As we leave behind the fortified Sasabe port of entry, along with the community's Border Patrol station encircled by razor wire, then the line of Boeing towers composing Project 28, the Wackenhut Corporation bus, the portable CBP checkpoint, the patrolling CBP in trucks and desert vehicles, the county sheriffs, as well as all the other security personnel I observed (and those I undoubtedly did not see, including the patrol helicopters and planes), it is finally clear that I have been distracted by the border wall.

What is under construction is not a border wall at all. A border wall, regardless of how imposing, suggests a single line or barrier. Cross over this wall, even if it consists of multiple barriers including a primary fence and a secondary fence with a drag road between, and you are done with it. What I'm seeing in Arizona is something very different than a border wall, or even the fortified wall at Nogales surrounded by a heavy contingent of guards patrolling the streets.

The area surrounding Sasabe is a highly controlled geographic space extending all the way north to Tucson and as many miles east to Nogales.[14] This is a militarized border zone—a broad swath of isolated, dangerous landscape from the border wall to the outskirts of Tucson. Portable highway and back road checkpoints that vary by day of the week dot the landscape, and many armed personnel in various types of vehicles designed for the rough terrain patrol the vast area.[15] This surveillance network, in the process of being integrated, is intentionally placed within a geographical area of high-plains desert and rugged mountains that boasts extreme temperatures fatal to border crossers.

To reach Tucson strip malls and concrete grid, I must first pass through a developing militarized border zone between Mexico and the United States staffed by nonmilitary personnel employing military tactics and using comparable military equipment. Nearby at the ready are fully equipped and battle-tested USNORTHCOM troops, many of whom served tours in Iraq. These lands south of Tucson to the border compose a burgeoning militarized zone in which the new border wall, including Project 28, is one of many system components.

I do not see the forest because I focus upon the tree; I do not see the militarized border zone because I am studying the Department of Homeland Security's fence.

Fence?

Chapter 12
Crossing to Safety

I t is a long, circuitous path from Honeywell engineers gathered around a conference table in Clearwater, Florida, to the towers of Boeing's Project 28 in the remote Chihuahuan desert outside of Sasabe, Arizona. Scattered all along the way are a number of individuals and institutions with a variety of perspectives, motivations, and objectives.

A short list includes Brownsville border resident Olga Rivera Garcia and her family; U.S. Congressman Frank James "Jim" Sensenbrenner, Jr.; Rio Grande Valley property owner and goatkeeper Baldomero Muñiz; Department of Homeland Security secretaries Michael Chertoff and Janet Napolitano; university president Dr. Juliet Garcia; Lieutenant General Charles Rodriguez, adjutant general of the Texas National Guard; border scholar Dr. Antonio Zavaleta; Boeing's vice president of global security, Timothy Peters; USNORTHCOM's Colonel Houston Polson; Mr. John Fonte of the Hudson Institute; Secure Border Initiative executive director Mark Borkowski; Congresswoman

Sheila Jackson Lee; Professor Abelardo Rodriguez Sumano of Mexico's Center for North American Strategic Studies; Texas RioGrande Legal Aid director David Hall; Hidalgo County judge J. D. Salinas; former CBP agents Jose A. Compean and Ignacio Ramos; Congressman Silvestre "Silver" Reyes; CBP field operations supervisor Omar Sanchez; ISIS director Walt Drabik; Walt Stanton of No More Deaths; and Americans for Legal Immigration's William Gheen. There are many others, each with a unique perspective and voice.

All of these individuals and more, along with the governmental institutions, corporations, law enforcement agencies, political parties, citizenry, militaries, think tanks, universities, and other public and private entities to which they belong, are in one way or another connected to the ongoing construction of the border wall between Mexico and the United States. Each in turn deserves scrutiny along with a healthy skepticism.

However imperfect and cumbersome, the insights and benefits of Time allow broad themes to emerge inductively from this exploratory overview of the border wall and nascent militarized border zone. These themes emerge when those who participate in the decision making, along with those directly or indirectly affected by these same decisions, are given a human voice and placed within a historical, political, and economic context. It is then that disparities in power among individual citizens, various levels of government, multinationals, the military, law enforcement, undocumented workers, the media, various interest groups, and other bureaucratic hierarchies are clearly revealed.[1]

It is when we peel away the layers of jargon from the speech of those who are elected or appointed to represent us, when we seriously question the motivations of very large federal bureaucracies such as the Department of Homeland Security and other entities claiming to act in the public's best interest, that we begin to approach the complexity of American immigration policy. It is when we consider the diverse voices of the general public, when we hear not only the usual talking heads but also those who are not paid to stand in front of the camera or microphone, that the opacity surrounding the Mexican border wall finally can be penetrated.

A transparent democracy requires sweeping aside various veils of pseudosecrecy, misinformation, bureaucratic jargon, and media hyperbole. The public always must be informed. This is not to argue that frequently unheard voices have exact answers to complex questions; rather, it is to assert that all perspectives must be heard lest we fall prey to the rhetoric of big law enforcement, big government, big business, big military, big politicians and their respective big parties, and big media, among others.

My objective has been to shove aside political bias—both Democrats and Republicans are given no special favors here—to uncover hard truths about the border wall and new military zones. The initial virtual wall project under the Clinton administration, ISIS, was carried to border-wide construction under the Bush administration. Now the border wall and military zones, both low- and high-tech components, are supported and funded by the Obama presidency.

Immigration is at the heart and core of our nation and its history, and that is no more evident than in the U.S.-Mexico borderlands. Immigration affects every one of us, although often in very different ways. Talk of immigration, especially illegal immigration, arouses deep emotions in times of serious economic recession. At its worst, immigration policies can embody excuses and justifications for systematic racism and acts of violence. Nowhere is this more evident than in the bloody and violent history of the U.S.-Mexico borderlands.

It is, therefore, as vital to understand the ongoing life and challenges faced by U.S. citizen and immigrant Olga Rivera Garcia and her family in Brownsville, Texas, as it is to understand the immigration machinations of Washington politicians Sensenbrenner, Jackson Lee, and Reyes. It is equally vital to document and understand the reasons why Secretaries Ridge, Chertoff, and Napolitano of the Department of Homeland Security build a borderlands wall, and to consider the implications and consequences of their decision upon the life and welfare of Baldomero Muñiz and other community residents on the banks of the Rio Grande or in the new militarized zone surrounding Nogales, Arizona.

By focusing on the new border zone separating Mexico from the United States, by paying closer attention to history, culture, geography, binational relations, and the perspective of border residents, the complex immigration issues can be more clearly delineated and judged. So, too, can the technological fixes to these complex issues. In and of itself, this process does not guarantee resolution of the many policy questions that finally must be decided by our elected representatives, but it is a major step toward discarding misleading information disguised as fact, deconstructing common labels and myths, revealing compelling motives and alliances, parsing the intricacies of binational issues, and avoiding the repeated failures of the recent past. Such an exercise can also highlight commonalities that provide the foundation for shared understanding and political compromise.

When I began this study I did not, indeed could not, know where it might lead. I was not aware of ISIS and the other attempts by the federal government to build a Mexican border wall, nor was I aware of all of the major participants, players, and enablers who eventually emerged. Nor was I prepared for, in spite of my previous research, the massive incompetency that was revealed.

It would be an act of personal hubris to offer a comprehensive list of immigration reforms based solely upon this exploratory study of the Mexican border wall and military zone; I leave that to others with far greater expertise and insights.[2] Instead, I offer a brief overview of how the construction of the border wall as an integral part of our system of national security fails to achieve its stated objectives and, at the same time, places the public in jeopardy. I also suggest several reforms that fall far outside of the traditional law enforcement paradigm. These reforms are informed and highlighted by the relationship between the new border wall and its various impacts upon federal law enforcement officers, undocumented workers, border residents and their communities, and the welfare of all Americans.

National Security and Public Safety

Attempts by our federal government to enhance national security do not automatically ensure a safer public. Law enforcement agencies and those that boost them can and do make mistakes. A case in point, one among many, is that of former Border Patrol sector chief Silvestre Reyes. As early as 2002 CBP, under the direction of DHS, began unceremoniously discarding Reyes's security strategy, which had first been employed in El Paso in the early 1990s. That borderlands strategy, touted by all agencies and programs after its initial successes, had one major flaw: it did not work. Agents in the field in many sectors grew increasingly dissatisfied with its repeated failures, and at least in one sector, possibly more, agents abandoned the system of fixed, visible positions predicated on unreliable sensors even though they faced reprimands by their supervisors. In that sector agents replaced Reyes's system with their own tactics based upon their professional expertise in patrolling the line.

During the more than ten years that Silvestre Reyes's strategy was employed, hundreds of thousands of undocumented border crossers entered this country, and hundreds of tons of illegal drugs passed by law enforcers poised at the border. Clearly, that strategy based upon deterrence theory, in spite of the rhetoric employed to defend it, did not benefit the welfare of the general public. No law enforcers or federal agencies ever shouldered any responsibility or blame for the multiple failures of the Reyes strategy. In a similar fashion, the Clinton administration's ISIS program was declared successful until it failed miserably and disappeared into a string of newly named federal programs under DHS secretaries Ridge and Chertoff.

Never looking back on these failed border strategies, the Department of Homeland Security under the Bush administration launched itself upon an identical course of deterrence after the events of 9/11. The rationalization for the U.S.-Mexico border fence was predicated upon three politically expedient premises: international terrorists threatened, undocumented workers crossing the border had to be controlled, and the flow of illegal drugs had to be stemmed. Completion of the border fence was thenceforth referred to by DHS and CBP officials as the major method of gaining operational control of the Mexican borderline.

Operational control was posited by both political parties as a prerequisite for a new national immigration policy to be addressed by a new administration after the elections of 2008. The understanding between Democratic and Republican leadership before the election, given the failure of the Bush administration and Congress to pass any kind of comprehensive immigration legislation, was based upon a shared belief that immigration issues were a political quagmire for both parties. Piecemeal legislation was offered up by Rep. James Sensenbrenner and others after the summer immigration field hearings in 2006, passed, and was signed by President Bush, and funds for it were allocated by Congress before the national elections. This legislative process, agreed to by both Democrats and Republicans, facilitated the continued construction of the border fence through the first year of the Obama administration.

The Mexican border fence was, in effect, a new immigration policy in and of itself, although it was never touted as such. It was offered as the primary reason why no other national immigration policies could be discussed until the project was finally completed and operational control of the border was achieved. The border fence was described as merely a predecessor to immigration reforms in the near offing.

A feature of the hastily passed legislation less clearly understood by the public is that this concrete-and-steel, low-tech border fence was to be complemented, according to Chertoff's DHS, by whiz-bang technological solutions to international terrorists, illegal aliens, and illegal drugs. This additional supplementary solution, the "virtual fence," would resolve any and all problems not handled by the low-tech fence, making the border impenetrable by any who might in whatever way threaten our public safety.

In part by lowering recruiting and training standards, large numbers of CBP agents were hired to patrol the line; a severe economic downturn also facilitated this process. Within a relatively short span of time almost twenty thousand Border Patrol agents, professionally equipped for the first time in their history but schooled for less than two months, patrolled the nation's borderline, with the vast majority of them stationed along the U.S.-Mexico border. CBP is now the largest federal law enforcement agency in the land. Congress also allocated funds for weaponry, vehicles, aircraft, and facilities. New apprehension policies also required a burgeoning and unregulated private detention system.

The new border fence, which is not a fence at all in many areas but is, in fact, a monumental wall, now covers a little less than one-third of the border. This new wall has increasingly forced illegal border crossers, both undocumented workers and drug smugglers, to make rational decisions in their own best interest about where to cross. With money no object, criminal organizations have many more rational choices and options at their disposal than do illegal workers with very limited financial resources, who often must rely on *coyotes*.

Border deaths of migrant workers are greatest in a handful of Border Patrol sectors. The data suggest that these deaths, the majority from dehydration in desert areas, are on the rise. Because these deaths are counted by the same agency that is invested in outcomes that demonstrate its efficiency and competence, it is highly questionable that the number of deaths reported represents the actual number. Given CBP's previous record of providing misleading statistics and interpreting those statistics to support its own best interests, there is every reason to believe that the actual number of illegal border crossers who die each year is higher than reported.

The U.S.-Mexico border wall, both the low- and high-tech versions, in all its shapes and forms, has proven, in conjunction with larger and larger numbers of border agents, to be more effective than previous failed and abandoned CBP and DHS strategies. Claims of the wall's effectiveness, however, must be interpreted within the context of the most serious national recession in modern times.

What is not in question is that the new border wall and the increase in agents patrolling the line has dramatically changed where illegal border crossers choose to enter the United States. There is every reason to believe that the locations they now choose are more likely to lead directly to increased numbers of deaths. As the arrest and conviction of activist Walt Staton suggest, it is a crime to attempt to save the lives of undocumented workers—at least in Arizona. Since shooting illegal border crossers is not an option in our democracy, the bureaucratic solution reached by Chertoff's DHS, and now Napolitano's DHS, is to push them into locales where nature pulls the trigger.

While on the one hand the CBP believes the new border wall will bring the border into operational control, the CBP has developed no new plans or tactics to protect the safety and welfare of its own agents patrolling the line. For example, how will agents who are injured between the borderline and the wall, an area from one-quarter to one-half mile or more wide in South Texas, quickly receive aid and medical care? What tactics will keep this newly created space from becoming a no-man's land, a free-fire zone rife with criminals preying upon border crossers? What are the risks to agents of a no-man's land, and how can those risks, if any, be avoided? How will the absence of gates in the border wall—or coherent policies where there are functioning gates—delay backup or medical attention? What kinds of new tactics can effectively be used between the Rio Grande and the wall to increase apprehensions and, at the same time, reduce risk to agents?

These same safety concerns should be raised in regard to illegal crossers. Namely, how will undocumented workers who are injured or otherwise in need of immediate medical aid receive it safely and quickly? What kinds of injuries are most likely to occur, given this monumental new wall? How can these new types of injuries be safely and quickly treated by professional medical personnel? As illegal workers develop new methods to circumvent the border wall, as they will do, how will their actions result in new kinds of risks and injuries?

The safety and welfare of federal agents and illegal border crossers should be addressed before more lives are lost. A Honeywell, Inc., or Boeing, Inc., engineering solution would be to tweak the new hardware or project after it is up and running. Retroactive tweaking, however, is the least responsible or morally acceptable solution when human lives are at risk.

The entire DHS strategy behind the construction of the border fence and wall can and should be reexamined in light of the number of deaths of illegal crossers. Undocumented workers could be funneled, for example, into geographic locations in which the terrain does not kill them in forty-eight hours. If funneled into relatively flat, forgiving terrain where drinking water is readily available, far fewer illegal crossers who successfully evade the wall and other barriers will suffer and die wretched deaths simply because they sought jobs in the United States.

CBP is, when directed and motivated, excellent at saving human lives. Almost every week of the year CBP protects and saves the lives of its own agents, illegal crossers, and members of the public. Agents patrolling the line regularly protect and safe lives: they rescue individuals from the Rio Grande and from the desert, they keep on the lookout for criminals who could do harm to border crossers, they offer medical assistance, they report crimes in progress in border communities, they fight fires, and they assist other law enforcers in apprehensions and arrests. These and other acts of bravery by the Border Patrol to protect the general welfare of fellow agents, illegal crossers, and the general public are rarely reported in the media.

CBP's Border Patrol Search, Trauma, and Rescue (BORSTAR) is a special unit officially commissioned in 1998 to provide aid to border patrol agents on the line, undocumented workers, and border residents. The problem with BORSTAR is not its mission, but its overall vision and budget. It is a fair and obvious question to ask why BORSTAR does not have a hundred times the personnel and matching budget to truly accomplish its public safety mission. If CBP's BORSTAR did have the personnel and the budget, a modest sum by federal standards, then the number of those who die each year along the Mexican border could be significantly reduced.

BORSTAR could employ any number of different kinds of training, equipment, and technology to aid in its search and rescue tactics. Regular satellite surveillance and saturation flyovers by CBP aircraft along known trails are effective in locating border crossers. The same kinds of surveillance systems that Boeing and other defense contractors manufacture for the military can be used to help save lives in the U.S.-Mexico borderlands. If federal RFPs did not attract primary contractors, then there are a host of smaller security firms with the expertise to develop these same kinds of systems based upon existing computer software. Such efforts would make it far safer for agents who suffer injuries while patrolling the line and require rapid extrication. Similar kinds of surveillance systems also would make it safer for the general public. Such efforts could simultaneously reduce the number of deaths of migrant workers and increase the number of undocumented workers apprehended.

Threat of death by drowning, dehydration from extreme heat, and other causes has been shown since statistics were first collected in 1994 to be ineffective in discouraging illegal border crossers. Deterrence theory, in fact, has never worked along the Mexican border. That theory of human behavior does not take into account the overwhelming social and economic motivations of those considering illegal entry. The policy of death by deterrence theory should be brought to a shameful conclusion.

Volunteers who reside in border communities are an unused resource who can supplement and aid BORSTAR in many different ways. They could include people with a variety of political persuasions and beliefs, from Minutemen to members of the immigrant rights groups, who might serve as force multipliers for the CBP. Instead of arresting these force multipliers and charging them with trespassing, littering, or other trumped-up crimes, why not enlist their aid, energy, and expertise? Properly vetted and trained, border residents can help BORSTAR make the borderline a safer place for all.

The rising violence directed towards the Border Patrol should be examined with great care. To what degree is this violence the result of border wall construction? How can it be mitigated? What kinds of professional training will aid agents in minimizing this violence? Rather than ignore them, as the CBP is wont to do, these and related issues should be addressed expeditiously.

There are undoubtedly many other ideas and strategies that CBP, DHS, security consultants, and corporate executives can never envision because of their ethnocentric perspectives. Residents of border communities are a rich, underutilized resource for pragmatic solutions. So, too, are the Border Patrol agents who daily patrol the line.

The second justification for building the wall in the U.S.-Mexico borderlands is to keep international terrorists from doing harm to the homeland. This essential rationalization for the border fence is demonstratively false and misleading and has broader consequences for public safety. Informed sources have repeatedly suggested that international terrorists will not enter our country from Mexico. There are strong indications that international terrorists, or those closely associated with them, are already embedded in the United States.[3] Several terrorist cells with international connections already have been discovered, including one located in Durham, North Carolina, sixty miles from where I reside.

Such a rationalization for the border wall deemphasizes the real risks from domestic terrorists, including white supremacist groups who are American born, the likes of Timothy McVeigh. The border wall should no longer be justified on the false grounds that it will stop international terrorists from entering this country. Neither is it in the best interests of public safety to believe terrorists may not live next door. They may. But that is not reason for national leaders to believe Americans will panic; rather, it is cause for Americans to be alert. An awareness of the real dangers facing the public will not destabilize our national psychology.

DHS's third justification for the border wall is to stem the flow of illegal drugs. There is no indication that the wall under construction has any major impact on the availability of illegal drugs in the United States. The single most important indicator of availability is not the increase in the amount of drugs confiscated by the CBP or other federal agencies, it is the street price for illegal drugs. This is a vital distinction that federal agencies, including DHS, obfuscate in their own best interests. The Mexican drug cartels may simply increase the amount of drugs they attempt to smuggle across the Mexican border to make up for the drugs interdicted by the CBP and other federal agencies. Price on the streets is the truest indicator of supply. The Mexican cartels may accept increased drug interdictions caused by the border wall simply as the cost of doing business. Their profits may subsequently decline, but not enough to keep illegal drugs from bringing them billions of dollars.

It is also important to remember that at the Mexican border the majority of illegal drugs enter at the ports of entry, and construction of the border wall will not affect this passageway. The *narcotrafficantes* are very good at changing transportation tactics of their product into the United States. While it might prove more costly, there is nothing to restrain the Mexican criminal organizations from employing a variety of other means and ways to move their product. These new tactics may totally circumvent the new, stationary border wall.

Throughout its institutional history the Border Patrol has repeatedly demonstrated in a variety of different contexts its stark inability to plan. CBP and DHS also seem incapable of bearing the slightest responsibility for unintended consequences resulting from new tactics, strategies, or policing actions. This is never more true than in the construction of the border wall. By making it more difficult for Mexican drug smugglers along the border to cross their illegal goods, the wall is increasingly forcing them to devise new ways and methods to outsmart the Border Patrol. Drug smugglers at a local level frequently change their tactics, develop new methods of smuggling, and constantly replace jailed employees with an unending supply of unemployed Mexican workers. The border wall may raise the criminal organizations' cost of doing business, but it also has the unintended consequence of bringing armed drug smugglers in closer and closer spatial contact with Border Patrol agents. This fact is, of course, exacerbated by the increase in the number of agents patrolling the line.

One of the real challenges faced by Border Patrol agents every day and night is to make quick professional judgments regarding the risk and danger facing them. In short, are the group of individuals they come across honest immigrant workers looking for jobs, or armed mules or scouts exploring new routes? Since 1924 there has been a set of informal rules in place held to by both illegal crossers and the Border Patrol. Historically, when agents, often alone, arrested illegal workers, they would yell at them in Spanish to halt. Frequently, but certainly not all the time, illegal workers submissively dropped to the ground. Then, again often alone, the agent marched his/her captives in single file to a waiting van.

Drug mules interdicted in this same manner were more likely to scatter and run, struggling to hide their loads or carry them back across the borderline. Or if the chase was in a van, the driver would bail out, leaving the vehicle loaded with drugs in the hands of the arresting Border Patrol agents. There are, of course, other scenarios, but my point is that there are informal rules in place governing acceptable behavior of both criminal border crossers and law enforcers. If illegal workers ran or protested, for example, they risked a punch or a beating from Border Patrol agents. In the case of drug smugglers, informal rules, although not necessarily acknowledged, were in force. For example, an armed drug smuggler confronted by a Border Patrol agent did not immediately pull out his weapon. Neither did an armed Border Patrol agent ambush armed drug smugglers. Mexican criminals who broke these taken-for-granted rules might in return expect harsh and exceptional punishment from Mexican law enforcers and/or their own criminal organizations themselves. Once drug smugglers dropped their loads and ran, they were not shot in the back by Border Patrol agents, even though the agents, as long ago as the 1990s, feared that the smugglers, after swimming the Rio Grande and returning to *el otro lado*, might fire at the agents from across the river. Gun violence, in short, had rules, and these rules are rapidly changing.

One recent adaptation by Mexican criminal organizations is to subcontract their smuggling and distribution to American gangs already embedded in border communities. From the perspective of these Mexican criminal organizations, this is a desirable solution; these organizations do not want to create the public perception in this country of increased drug-related violence on the American side of the border. The *narcotrafficantes* recognize that such attention might mean the likelihood of a stronger American military presence, which could fundamentally change their business model. To date these criminal organizations have been raking in tremendous profits at the same time their American subcontractors, local American gangs, take the heat and the prison time. In general, El Paso, for example, remains at this time a relatively safe border city, as do most American border communities and towns.

Under changing conditions exacerbated by the construction of the new border wall and increased numbers of CBP agents, gun violence between American-based gangs and local law enforcement could quickly spread throughout many American border communities. This gun violence potentially can threaten the public safety of all members of the border communities not bunkered behind private gated developments monitored by private security guards. Increased drive-by killings, shootouts between gang members, increasingly violent conflict between law enforcers and gangs, and other acts of violence centered on illegal drugs are possibilities at the heart of every border community.

A fundamental issue that Mexican officials have emphasized for decades is only beginning to be addressed in this country: there would be no illegal drug trade if Americans did not demand and pay for drugs. Public funds for the treatment of drug addiction as a public health issue have been scarce in proportion to law enforcement and security measures. A public policy decision that forced judges to hand out mandated sentences to drug users has resulted in our nation's expanding prison population, now the largest in the world in proportion to our national population. It has, at the same time, forced the construction of new and costly prisons throughout the nation. Of even greater concern is the decay of our neighborhoods and communities swamped by illegal drugs, the gun violence that accompanies them, and the criminal values that support them.

The CBP and DHS continue to ignore the efficacy of community policing tactics using community residents as force multipliers. Instead of using community residents as a resource, the agencies rely on increased military tactics involving heavy concentrations of law enforcement officers to the point of saturation, on surveillance technology, and on fortification of the wall and the ports of entry. In downtown Nogales, for example, patrolling law enforcement officials seemingly make no distinction between community residents, tourists like myself and my wife, and professional criminals. In the militarized vocabulary of the DHS in South Texas, for example, the DHS refers to border ranchers and farmers as war zone "friendlies." Everyone else, including other community residents and all border crossers, becomes by definition "hostiles."

It remains to be seen what impact military border zones may have upon the quality of life and social fabric of American border communities, but it is not too soon to limit the unintended consequences of this military strategy carried out by civilian law enforcers. If the Nogales area is indeed a CBP and DHS prototype for other American border communities, then a number of questions naturally arise. How does the presence of so many law enforcement personnel irreversibly change the quality of life in these border communities? How does it impact local businesses and the local economy? How does it affect the willingness of tourists, for example, to visit these areas? Will border residents choose to remain in communities that have such high concentrations of law enforcement?

The undeniable elephant still sits at the negotiating table, although DHS and CBP would prefer to deny there is either an uninvited guest or any table at which to sit: What kind of border wall is necessary from Brownsville to San Diego? Congress and the president have decided a border wall is the primary solution to achieve operational control of the Mexican border. While it is undeniable that nations require fixed and clear boundaries, this begs the question of what kind of border wall is appropriate between our homeland and Mexico. DHS's answer under Secretary Chertoff, and now Secretary Napolitano, is a one-size-fits-all policy, a low-tech wall and a virtual wall designed by engineers motivated by profit. What worked in one border community or geographic region, according to DHS and CBP, should automatically work in all areas along the border because the U.S.-Mexico border is, from this institutional perspective, homogeneous.

However small in scale it may be, President Juliet Garcia's cheap fence suggests DHS's solutions may have little merit along some parts of the Mexican border. There may be a variety of alternatives other than those proposed by a politicized, out-of-touch DHS and CBP buttressed by engineers motivated only by corporate profits. By emphasizing security measures predicated by a military model, sociocultural factors, history, economic forces, and even geography are conveniently devalued and ignored in favor of a model burdened by untested security assumptions.

Dr. Garcia's border fence, although the antithesis of the military model, could serve just as well as a prototype for a border barrier as the steel walls of the Nogales militarized zone. A very modest ten-foot-high, landscaped chain-link fence may be more appropriate in some areas along the borderlands than a monumental, and astronomically costly, concrete and steel construction. One can only hope that the efficacy and utility of this alternative border university fence will be tested and judged fairly by outside experts who have no ties to the vested interests of defense contractors.

Hidalgo County's hydraulic wall, the singular vision of Judge J. D. Salinas, also calls into question in its own way the notion of the monolithic paradigm promoted by DHS and CBP. Within the context of microlevel border politics, the hydraulic wall has been specifically construed, defined, and tinkered with. Putting aside for the moment the problems with Salinas's wall that we have already examined, his hydraulic wall calls into question, yet again, the efficacy of DHS's military model.

Both Garcia's university fence and Salinas's hydraulic wall are two examples of alternative models that preempt DHS's massive wall, virtual wall, and adjacent military zone as the only possible solution to national security along the border. Undoubtedly, other prototypes could be examined.

In spite of the best efforts of federal government under the three administrations of Clinton, Bush, and Obama to impose a monolithic low- and high-tech wall on the Mexican border, border residents in Cameron County and Hidalgo County have provided *sui generis* alternatives. It is not too late to reconsider the burden of the DHS and CBP militarized, massive model— to question not only its rationalizations, but also its motives and its unintended consequences.

Commodification

One of the most significant moments in the construction of the new border wall transpired when DHS handed over full responsibility for the virtual wall to the Secure Border Initiative Systems Integrator. From that point in 2006 to the present, Boeing engineers have designed and created a virtual border wall that provides the highest profits possible to their employer.

Although Boeing repeatedly failed to meet its contract objectives with Project 28, Congress has not sanctioned this major defense contractor. Indeed,

Boeing has been given directions, warnings, and second chances; has been fired by Secretary Chertoff; then has been given a third chance to build a dumbed-down virtual wall. To date the virtual wall does not function as planned and designed by Boeing engineers. Yet DHS continues to award contracts to Boeing, and Congress pretends Boeing, DHS, and CBP are doing what they are supposed to. At this point there are very few members of Congress who remember the hoopla proclaimed by ISIS cheerleaders in 1998. Congressional institutional memory, along with congressional fiscal oversight of these contracts to Boeing, has lapsed. A handful of congresspersons remind their fellow committee members of the tortuous path Boeing follows, but to no substantive avail.

In return, Boeing, DHS, and CBP continue to testify before Congress in a language few elected officials seem to comprehend. Even fewer members of the public can make sense of the pseudomilitary mumbo jumbo in which Boeing executives and bureaucrats obfuscate their acts of gross mismanagement, incompetence, and cost overruns. At the same time, they wave the banner of national security before these committees as if they are the only patriots in the room. Behind Boeing's patriotic façade is an indisputable economic motive to increase its bottom line at the expense of completing Project 28 and its derivatives. The longer it takes Boeing to complete these alleged prototypes, the higher the profit margin as construction costs continue to skyrocket. When the virtual border fence was auctioned off to a systems integrator, it became another security product designed to generate the greatest profits possible. In this fashion Boeing placed national safety and public safety as secondary to the corporate bottom line.

The process of commodification is also evident in the construction and operation of detention centers for detainees, the construction of ports of entry along the Mexican border, transportation and deportation of detainees, and all other private-sector services provided to the CBP. Boeing and likeminded corporations have successfully turned national security and safety into public largesse with scant oversight or accountability demanded either by DHS, CBP, or Congress.

Proper oversight of defense contractors is a prerequisite for the designing, planning, construction, and maintenance of the virtual border fence and the low-tech border wall. These multinationals not only deliver outrageous products and service, but also produce products that do not function as designed or promised. Simultaneously, they waste limited fiscal resources and place federal law enforcement officers and the public at risk because of endless delays and/or the failure of their products to meet professional standards.

Illegal border crossers are another victim of the commodification of border security. Only recently has the Obama administration initiated a review of the efficacy and professional standards of the extensive system of private, for-profit detention centers. This unregulated detention system may prove to be the locus for the widespread abuse of detainees.

When DHS handed Boeing the job as SBI Systems Integrator, Secretary Chertoff's DHS also sloughed off all blame and institutional responsibility. From the day Boeing was awarded Project 28, Boeing became not only DHS's sidekick and buddy, but also its corporate whipping boy before Congress. Now Napolitano's DHS, as was the case with her predecessor, stands to the side when members of Congress lob a few hardball questions at Boeing. Or in other cases DHS officials help Boeing create mind-numbing responses to specific questions from congresspersons, then play the role of arbitrator between Boeing and testy members of Congress. DHS's self-serving political strategy serves to spare itself while damaging our national security agenda and placing the general public in harm's way.

CBP

The construction of the border wall reveals in detail the structural and cultural failures within CBP. The Border Patrol was burdened with a variety of dysfunctions long before the events of 9/11, but this federal law enforcement agency now faces new sets of problems created by its rapid growth compounded by a fundamental lack of organizational leadership, planning, expertise, and political savvy. Although CBP no longer suffers from a lack of fiscal resources to accomplish its objectives, it still has not confronted its old-boy system that produces a corps of unskilled managers at all levels. These untrained and undereducated managers cannot uphold professional standards and policies in the workplace or provide leadership to agents patrolling the line. A formidable, competent cohort of CBP leaders has not emerged that can provide institutional vision along with organizational pathways to accomplish goals and objectives. CBP's institutional research skills do not meet the standards of other federal law enforcement agencies, while data collection and analysis are highly politicized. The CBP cultural climate is reminiscent of a federal law enforcement agency mired in the 1950s.

Time and again CBP failed to respond to DHS's expectations and demands from 1998 to the present in the planning, designing, and contract oversight of the construction of the new border wall. The CBP is simply incapable of these kinds of tasks at this time.

At the foundation of CBP's dysfunctions is a fundamental distrust of those with special skills, training, and education beyond the high school level or beyond military training at the level of enlisted personnel. Supervisors at the station level are reminiscent of staff sergeants who require their private enlistees, CBP agents, to keep their mouths shut and follow all orders without question. Those agents with special skills in language, management, accounting, and security exit the CBP because their expertise is discounted and disparaged. If those with expertise remain in the CBP, they are frequently marginalized, discredited, and not promoted to their true level of competence. At this point in its history, CBP leadership would rather fail at its assigned tasks under DHS than provide its own personnel with the education, professional development, and training to succeed. Similarly, CBP is hesitant to hire outsiders with expertise that exceeds its own for fear of revealing its institutional inadequacies.

If it would, CBP leadership can do much to address these issues and improve its efficiency and performance. For example, CBP could support and reward agents who enter with special skills, provide educational opportunities to those seeking expertise in demand by CBP, and promote competent managers and leaders. CBP leadership could begin to understand that while the heart of their law enforcement agency is CBP agents patrolling the line, those agents require a core of trained managers and law enforcement professionals to lead them into the world of modern law enforcement technologies, strategies, and institutional planning.

CBP could be instrumental in designing its own best practices to patrol the line while ensuring the safety of its own agents, illegal border crossers, and the general public. However, as long as CBP views the general public in exclusionary terms, as civilians who do not wear the CBP uniform and can in no other way really understand or support the CBP, it is doomed to lag behind other federal law enforcement agencies. In short, CBP requires much more than budget increases to become a federal agency of professional law enforcers.

A case in point is gender discrimination, the organizational belief held by some male CBP managers and some CBP male agents that female agents do not belong in the CBP except behind a desk. This is a societal artifact whose time has long since passed. Gender discrimination in the CBP is not only illegal, but it is also harmful to all agents patrolling the line. First and foremost, CBP leadership must radically change its agency culture to include female agents. In order to do that, CBP must throw aside its denial of this core problem. CBP can fairly enforce existing policies and standards in all sectors. Where necessary it can create new institutional policies and standards that support a safe workplace for all its employees, regardless of gender. CBP can also create and support policies that allow female CBP agents to give birth to, raise, educate, and parent their children while fulfilling all CBP's job expectations and standards. This is not currently the case. CBP can also fairly and equitably reward and promote female agents who excel in their work. It can provide statistics to the public that measure its efforts towards equity.

While the CBP is good at recruiting female agents, it cannot expect to retain them in a hostile work environment based upon gender discrimination. CBP can initiate this transformative process by bringing in outside, independent consultants to conduct scientifically based surveys detailing the issues and suggesting remedies. It is then up to CBP to begin systematically and aggressively to address the findings of these studies and begin to make the CBP as safe a place to work for women as it is for men. These are some of the initial steps necessary in transforming CBP's predominantly masculinist culture into the professional culture of a modern federal law enforcement agency.

CBP also faces a number of external challenges if it is to become an exemplary federal law enforcement agency. This is particularly true with regard to the consequences of CBP's new academy training. While shortening academy training of new CBP recruits to less than two months undoubtedly raised passing rates of new recruits, such training makes them less skillful. CBP agents do not need fewer professional skills; they need more lest they become little more than correctional guards.

Just what CBP will resemble in the next decade is a matter of conjecture. But one thing is certain: CBP is such a poor planner it has not even considered these challenges. In short, CBP can never hope to be an equal and respected partner within DHS if its new agents, now the majority of the workforce, meet minimal educational and training requirements, are supervised by managers who barely know how to operate a computer, and are led by individuals who do not comprehend, among other issues, the importance of gender equity in the workplace.

DHS

Napolitano's DHS confronts a confounding legacy in the new border wall. DHS must certainly take a much closer look at the various contractors and subcontractors building the wall in its name. While Hidalgo County judge J. D. Salinas is confident that an army of auditors is keeping an eye on the money as it passes through county government to contractors and their employees, the truth of the matter is that Hidalgo County and other border counties have a long history of graft and corruption. There is a long list of agencies providing oversight, but the bureaucratic lesson DHS should have learned by now is that if everyone is in charge, no one is in charge. The same holds true, of course, for the construction and operation of detention centers and all other services provided in support of CBP.

It is unclear whether DHS leadership is aware of the numerous mistakes it has made to date in the construction of the new border wall—or whether it cares. It is impossible to correct past errors if they are never recognized or acknowledged. This huge agency still seems to believe threatening property owners with legal proceedings is the best way to meet its objectives. Hiding behind legal proceedings does not encourage the landowners that DHS has their best interests at heart. What if DHS, driven during Secretary Chertoff's reign by completion schedules and hubris, finally completes the new border wall only to find that it has already begun to fall apart? And how can DHS expect border community residents to support its law enforcement officers and the policies they enforce when the department has so carefully and precisely fouled the field?

The laundry list of law enforcement agencies DHS depends on at the border wall is unwieldy and counterproductive. That list includes, in addition to the CBP, municipal police, county sheriffs, state police, the American military and its intelligence sections, and various units of the National Guard. Each has political constituencies. Add to them the Drug Enforcement Agency and the Federal Bureau of Investigation along with other DHS departments and divisions. The greater the number of players, the greater the opportunity for problems associated with communications, battles over turf, battles over intelligence, intelligence gathering, and other resources. Each agency or organization must also be concerned with its own public standing and credibility. The laundry list of military wannabes at the border increases the possibility of mistakes and errors, placing the general public, law enforcers, and illegal crossers at risk.

The use of nonmilitary law enforcers to patrol the line, gather intelligence, surveil, patrol public places, and, in general, participate in the enforcement of immigration policies warrants serious review. Local law enforcement institutions such as police departments are always motivated to spend federal funds for their own best interests in the impoverished borderlands. Are these funds being used to their greatest effect?

As demonstrated time and again in South Texas, local law enforcers are the most likely to employ the least trained and competent personnel. Such personnel are more susceptible to graft and corruption when for the *narcotrafficantes* money is no object. A voluntary melding of local, county, state, and federal law enforcement agencies, glued together by federal funds and dissimilar goals, may not be the best or only way to accomplish DHS objectives along the border. In fact, as suggested, this strategy may be counterproductive, reducing this amalgam of law enforcers to the lowest common denominator. Again, if everyone is in charge along the border wall, no one is in charge.

Mexico as a Failed State

Is Mexico's status as a failed state, whether true or not, a strategic justification for the necessity of a border wall, including militarized zones? In many ways such an argument follows the Cold War mentality of the necessity to act against, to deter, the threat of perceived enemies. In this case, the perceived enemy must be clearly defined as the Mexican criminal organizations and their subsidiary American-based gangs. The enemy is not the Mexican government or its people. Clearly, the American military should not be the only American institution, or even the first, to establish stronger binational ties with Mexico. What is notably absent in this regard is American leadership and political will.

In the absence of this leadership our military has attempted to do the best it can in establishing stronger ties with its Mexican counterparts. However, as suggested by the fiasco involving the hapless Mexican military convoy after Hurricane Katrina, diplomacy is frequently best conducted by diplomats. In their absence our military did the best it was able to do, but its best in this case was not good enough. The American military has vast resources it can call upon; it behooves the military to develop a pragmatic strategy to strengthen institutional and structural ties between itself and its Mexican military counterparts that are mutually beneficial. This strategy should extend well beyond a few rounds of golf, drinks, and the presentation of unwieldy mementoes to visiting Mexican dignitaries. Joint military exercises along the border are a beginning, not an end.

Our military leaders must, in short, forever jettison the legacy of distrust of Mexico in favor of establishing long-term binational strategies to combat the criminal organizations on both sides of the border. These strategies must go beyond the training of Mexican troops by American experts. These selfsame strategies, as suggested, should include an emphasis on the demand side of the criminal production, warehousing, and distribution of illegal drugs. What would happen to these Mexican criminal organizations if the products they sold were regulated and taxed? What would happen if drug dependence and addiction in the United States, as is increasingly the case in Mexico, were considered less a crime leading to incarceration than an issue of public health and safety? What would happen if we began treating the Mexican government and its military in the same way we treat the Canadians?

Congress and the President

Ultimately it is the U.S. Congress and our president who are responsible for providing oversight of DHS, CBP, and the construction of the new border wall. Since ISIS in 1998, Congress time and again has demonstrated that it is incapable of fiscal oversight. The taxpayers' bill for the border wall continues to grow each day of the year but still attracts little attention in Congress because, in part, it is dwarfed by other appropriations during these demanding times. As long as there are only a few congresspersons capable of reminding their respective committees and subcommittees of the excessive errors of ISIS, the repeated failures of subsequent DHS border fence programs, and the more recent failures of Boeing's Project 28 and its clones, the costs of the new border wall will continue to increase.

Boeing, Inc., will continue to grow fat off federal largesse as long as Congress and the president allow it. A largely uninformed and leaderless public cannot effectively serve as watchdog over intricate corporate ploys to increase profits winked at by the Department of Homeland Security. As suggested, completion of the border wall, both the low-tech one and any virtual components, does not guarantee operational control in the borderlands.

A Modest Proposal

Many of the concerns surrounding the Mexican border wall both suggest and reflect the complexity and challenges of American immigration. The more we understand the new border wall, the more we learn about these complexities and challenges, including the border wall's centrality in national immigration policy and its unintended consequences. This raises a preeminent question: Should the construction of the border wall be at least temporarily halted?

There are a number of reasons to consider this question. Chief among them is that by halting construction we will have time to discuss and debate the rationalizations and consequences of the border wall. Some of these rationalizations no longer have merit. Some of these consequences have never been considered. Such a national conversation benefits by an understanding of the previous history of attempts to build a Mexican border wall along with a detailed appraisal of its current status. This discussion would also examine the fortification of border communities and the attendant military zones as an integral part of a broader immigration policy.

A rush to defend the homeland against international terrorists is no longer a legitimate reason to construct and complete the border wall and militarized zones, of which the general public is unaware. Neither, too, is there a rush to gain operational control of the Mexican border—not when the wall itself may be creating consequences for which we are not prepared.

There is every indication to believe at this point that "operational control" is a blatant case of bureaucratic smoke and mirrors, a condition so poorly defined by DHS and Boeing as to be meaningless. There are no standards of measurement, no metrics, by which to judge operational control along our Mexican border. So when operational control is declared under existing standards, as it surely will be in spite of any factual basis suggesting otherwise, it will only serve the vested interests of the institutions involved. Everyone else, including the public, will be a loser. Providing time to consider judiciously what has been learned since construction began can only result in more inclusive and transparent policy decisions predicated on thoughtful discussion and debate by all those involved.

Those government agencies, programs, politicians, and ideologues with the most political capital invested and, therefore, with the most to lose by a public reconsideration of the border wall will, of course, be the loudest at the microphone to prohibit this process. We would expect DHS and CBP to develop brand new and innovative justifications to continue the wall construction. In such a case each and every federal dictate should be parsed, scrutinized, and checked against documented fact.

In a similar fashion, Boeing and other defense contractors can be expected to oppose strongly any suggestion of prudent action along the Mexican border that halts their financial gluttony. These same multinationals have been, and remain, in the forefront of the commodification of our national security and public safety. The more we neglect their fiscal oversight, the greater will be their corporate bottom lines. The feasting of these defense contractors on federal tax dollars should be brought into the light of public scrutiny.

Politicians representing these same constituencies certainly will also step forward to paint overdrawn scenarios based upon perceived threats to our national security and public safety. An authentic national debate, however, can give rise to voices never heard before and replace Congressman Sensenbrenner's theatrical mockery of the democratic process during his public field hearings.

Time masquerades behind many faces in the U.S.-Mexico borderlands, but in the years from ISIS in 1998 to the present, it is the master trickster. In the name of national security the border wall threatens the safety and lives of law enforcers even as it turns illegal crossings by undocumented workers into predictable death marches. In the name of national security the border wall may well undermine public safety even as it undermines the welfare and quality of life in borderland communities. And how exactly will militarized zones along the Mexican border impact the constitutional freedoms of citizens throughout our homeland? Finally, in the name of national security DHS and Boeing continue to demonstrate monstrous incompetency even as both remain mute about the price tag for their joint border folly. For all its appeal as a virtual American dream, this new border wall and the military zones have all the ingredients of an unheralded American nightmare.

It is in our own best national and binational interests to reconsider our rush to judgment before the congressional elections of 2006. Time in the case of the U.S.-Mexico border wall is not our enemy. We have only to look more closely and empathetically at our neighbors across the street, across our hometowns, and across our homeland to more clearly understand the role of immigration in our national history. In fact, the vast majority of all Americans have only to look more steadfastly at our own families—our parents, grandparents, and beyond—to be reminded of a simple truth: many immigrant Americans have grievously suffered from immigration policies in the past in order to gain a future foothold in our country. What we often know so well from our own family histories is the promise and potential of every honest immigrant seeking work in our country.

But however difficult these hardships in our history, no member of our families and extended families ever faced a monumental border wall with military zones and checkpoints, unregulated detention centers run by multinational corporations, or a federal strategy leading directly to death by dehydration in the desert.

The facts across Time are troubling from Brownsville, Texas, to San Diego, California. The new border wall impacts all Americans in one way or the other. Let us, therefore, take all the time necessary to reconsider what we are constructing, why we are constructing it, and what we hope to gain as measured against what we may lose. As a public we want to know how, if and when a border wall is completed, we will fairly and objectively judge its metrics for success. For whatever reasons, if the new border wall is in the end fairly judged a failure, we reserve the right to amend it, reconstruct it, or deconstruct it.

As we go about the modest political process of scrutinizing the ongoing construction of the Mexican border wall, as we consider the full meanings and impacts of the wall, militarized border communities, and nascent military zones upon our American democracy, we must ensure legitimate and inclusive public debate; there are many disparate voices yet to be heard. We must also develop ideas and strategies unfettered by the tacit assumptions of defense contractors and their engineers; there are many disparate voices yet to be heard. Finally, we must exhort Congress and our president to seize the reins of fiscal oversight and to provide leadership.

We have the Time to rethink all of these issues and their implications. If we fail in these efforts, we risk a foolishness of both monumental proportions and monumental consequences.

Epilogue

Updated Epilogue to the Paperback Edition

Hurricane Alex, the first hurricane of the 2010 season, slammed into the borderlands in the late hours of June 30th. The category-two storm spared those attempting to cap the British Petroleum oil rig in the Gulf of Mexico, site of the largest spill in U.S. history, but thousands in northern Mexican cities and towns, like Matamoros, were not so lucky.

Olga Rivera Garcia's aunt, by then in her eighties, was lucky. Decades earlier she had moved with her family to Matamoros because the Mexican border offered a higher standard of living than Guanajuato, where she was born and raised. Just before Hurricane Alex, Olga's aunt had finally returned to Guanajuato because it was her real home.

Olga and Carlos were also thinking of moving. Carlos was looking for a change, and Olga considered taking a leave of absence from her job at the university. In 2010 CBP was still growing. Carlos and Olga talked it over for three months. Carlos's new job offer in Customs promised a different set of responsibilities along with better job opportunities in the future. But Olga and Carlos would have had to move from their quiet street in Brownsville to Montreal.

At the last minute Carlos turned down the Canadian job. One big reason was their oldest daughter who, after earning her Ph.D. in clinical pharmacology, was finally moving back to the Valley from Dallas. Another was that Olga's doctor had a new diagnosis for her chronic illness and had begun a new course of treatment that might ease Olga's daily pain. "Carlos knows it would be hard for me in Montreal with the winters there," Olga explained. "I'm not used to the cold. As it is, the new medication seems to be working better."

Hurricane Alex spared Cameron and Hidalgo counties in 2010. At least at first. Hurricane Alex dumped two feet of rain in parts of northern Mexico, including three of the four river basins of the Rio Grande. Three weeks after Alex dodged South Texas, floodwaters from the hurricane were released into the Rio Grande from Falcon Dam near Zapata and upriver at Amistad Dam near Del Rio. The residents of some of the poorest river communities in the Valley, including Los Ebanos, Roma, La Grulla, and Sullivan City, were quickly inundated. Neighborhoods in low-lying areas in Zapata and Rio Grande City were also evacuated. The overall impact of the release of water upon Mexican communities is not yet known.

In late July FOS Omar Sanchez showed me the completed border wall at the new Donna International Bridge, then at Progreso and Pharr. The currents of the raging Rio Grande, fueled by Hurricane Alex, roiled against Judge Salinas's hydrowall—designed to be part levee, part barrier to border traffickers and costing in excess of one hundred million dollars. Hurricane Alex was the first real test of the hydrowall's ability to protect the homes of Valley residents from floodwaters. Not since Hurricane Beulah in the 1960s had floodwaters risen so high.

The Hidalgo hydrowall seemed to do its job in 2010. That is, except for Los Ebanos and Sullivan City, which lay squarely within Hidalgo County but were nevertheless inundated because no part of the levee's budget had been apportioned to them.

Even though work had stopped on the hydrowall, construction was far from complete in 2010. Ryan J. Scudder, Patrol Agent in Charge of the Weslaco CBP station, told me then that approximately sixty gates in the hydrowall were still not in place. In fact all along the new hydrowall there were twenty-foot gaps with no barriers to prohibit the crossing of undocumented workers or any kind of contraband. Scudder assured me that the absence of gates was not a real problem.

The other good news Scudder shared was that "the money has already been appropriated for the gates. We definitely have the money."

The bad news was that the Army Corp of Engineers had not finished the design or engineering of the hydrogates. Mr. Scudder explained that the engineering for the new gates was very complicated.

"How long until the gates are in place?" I asked Patrol Agent in Charge Scudder.

"One to three years."

When I returned in October 2011, I put the same question to another agent at the new Sector Headquarters in Edinburg, directly east of Highway 281. Shrugging his shoulders, that agent told me, "Maybe one or two years. We don't know."

By 2012 violence between the Mexican drug cartels has grown much, much worse. Two years earlier, when FOS Sanchez proudly showed me the Hidalgo hydrowall, he was already more concerned with the mounting gun violence en el otro lado and its impact on American communities than he was with any other issue. As we stood on the new Donna International Bridge, Omar Sanchez pointed out the elementary school a few hundred yards from the banks of the Rio Grande. Here a section of the Hidalgo border wall sat back a quarter of a mile from the Rio Grande, much closer to the elementary school than to the international border.

"This wall is protecting our kids," FOS Sanchez told me then as he pointed toward the imposing concrete and steel several hundred yards from where we stood. The pride in his tone was laced with growing concern. "I just hope and pray it [the hydrowall] will be enough."

His worry was more than justified. By 2012 drug-related violence has intensified on the other side of Hidalgo County's hydrowall with, for example, the mass beheadings of forty-nine victims discovered by the side of the major highway leading to Reynosa and the murders of fifty-two Mexican citizens in a fire set by armed thugs in a Monterrey casino.[1] Murders in Reynosa are commonplace, but both Mexican and American journalists have become too scared by the drug cartels to record the bloodshed. From week to week border residents may directly or indirectly experience extreme acts of violence that change the quality of their lives, changes that flawed crime statistics are incapable of measuring.[2]

In 2010, about the same time that Hurricane Alex pounded northern Mexico, President Obama, eighteen months into his presidency, gave his first major speech on immigration. In his speech at American University in July of that year, Obama outlined the need for comprehensive immigration legislation, emphasizing the history of immigrants and their role in our nation's accomplishments. Said President Obama, "We've always defined ourselves as a nation of immigrants—a nation that welcomes those willing to embrace America's precepts. Indeed, it is this constant flow of immigrants that helped to make America what it is."[3]

Even as he stressed the progress in immigration reform during his own administration, and during the Bush administration, President Obama admitted, "In sum, the system is broken. And everybody knows it. Unfortunately, reform has been held hostage to political posturing and special-interest wrangling—and to the pervasive sentiment in Washington that tackling such a thorny and emotional issue is inherently bad politics." "That is why," President Obama stated, "a broken and dangerous system that offends our most basic American values is still in place."[4]

Two years later, President Obama still hasn't jettisoned the majority of the Bush administration's immigration policies. One notable exception is President Obama's limited version of the Dream Act, announced by Secretary of Homeland Security Janet Napolitano on June 15, 2012, five months before the 2012 elections. This executive order by the president states that undocumented immigrant children who came to the United States before they were sixteen years of age would not be deported by ICE.[5] Besides this, President Obama continues to support Congressperson James Sensenbrenner and Congress's patchwork immigration bills quickly assembled after the national field hearings in 2006. The Obama administration, citing Republican obstinacy in the House, has put forward no detailed, comprehensive immigration legislation. As a result, myriad problematic immigration issues have flourished. Without legislative specifics, President Obama's rhetorical nods to immigration reform seem nothing more than random signals to his Latino supporters that he has not forgotten his campaign promises.

With no overall change in federal immigration law under Obama, no immigration-related issues have been more hotly contested than in the state of Arizona, where a Republican governor and Republican-dominated legislature easily passed SB 1070 in the spring of 2010. Arizona's bill may be essentially misguided; SB 1070, among other things, criminalizes anyone who is in the state without proper papers and, at the same time, potentially provides an ideal environment for racial profiling. But the intent behind the state bill, however wrongheaded or misrepresenting the fundamental problems facing the state, was to address a slew of immigration issues that have been ignored for decades at the federal level.[6]

The Obama administration's solution to states that would seek to create their own immigration laws was to sue Arizona. With the Arizona case now before the Supreme Court in 2012, it remains to be seen either what the nine justices will decide or, of equal importance, how the other sixteen states who support Arizona's legislation will respond to their decision.

Of course, the responsibility for federal legislation is not only the president's to address. Bipartisan leadership was, as President Obama emphasized, sorely lacking. Ted Kennedy is no longer in the Senate, and John McCain faced stiff opposition in 2010 and now stands strongly against earlier immigration legislation he initiated.

Shortly before President Obama's speech in 2010, Secretary Napolitano detailed the accomplishments of her agency. Her claims came down to a laundry list: an additional 1,200 National Guard troops assigned to the border, the majority going to the state of Arizona; additional DHS personnel ordered to the Tucson sector of the border; a beefing-up of law enforcement programs already in place; "unprecedented cooperation with Mexico" as embodied in the so-called Merida Initiative signed into law by Congress in 2008; and new drones to patrol the border skies.[7]

Secretary Napolitano measured the DHS's success by a 23-percent reduction in the apprehensions of illegal aliens from 2008 to 2009 and an increase in seizures of drugs, guns, and illegal cash. She also pointed to a 37-percent increase in the number of criminal illegal aliens deported, plus a tripling of audits of employers suspected of employing illegal workers.[8]

According to Secretary Napolitano, the last six miles of the Mexican border wall were completed in 2010.[9] This low-tech portion of the border wall, first mandated by Congress in 2006, now spans 625 miles of the borderlands. (However, as noted, this does not take into account the more than sixty gates in Hidalgo County that have yet to be installed.)

On the surface, the 2011 statistics from DHS continued to demonstrate marked successes after the border wall was constructed. Apprehensions of illegal aliens by the Border Patrol since 2008 decreased 53%. From 2009 to 2011 drugs, guns, and illegal cash seized by the Border Patrol and DHS substantially increased. As the number of agents in CBP exceeded 24,000, Secretary Napolitano also pinned her short-term hopes on the 2011 National Southwest Border Counternarcotics Strategy to further enhance security efforts with allocations for specific resources directed towards reducing the flows of illegal immigrants and illegal drugs into the country.[10]

What Secretary Napolitano fails to clarify in these newest numbers is that a significant portion of the decline in alien apprehensions is attributable not only to enforcement along the Mexican border but also to the direct impact of the Great Recession: fewer undocumented workers are motivated to enter the United States if fewer jobs are available or new laws, such as those passed in Arizona, make their lives more difficult. A certain number of undocumented migrants relocate from states like Arizona to other states with less stringent immigration laws. There are also an uncountable number who return to their countries of origin. Regardless of what factors caused the marked decline in illegal border crossings, the number of illegal aliens is estimated in 2012 to be at 11.2 million, down from an estimated peak of 12 million in 2007.[11]

Substantial increases in drug seizures and illegal cash, however, do not directly demonstrate that the amount of illegal drugs brought into this country is on the decline. In fact, given the price stability of marijuana and cocaine in most American cities and rural areas, these newest DHS statistics suggest that the international drug cartels are shipping more drugs across our borders. As always, drug interdictions become, in this decades' old scenario of our War on Drugs, simply an additional cost of doing business that the cartels find anything but prohibitive.

Under the Obama administration, ICE deportations designed to remove criminal aliens from our country have increased to an average of 400,000 a year. But to ICE's discredit, most of these arrests, detentions, adjudications, and deportations include undocumented aliens stopped by law enforcement for alleged misdemeanor offenses. Worse still, ICE's Secure Communities Program's statistics demonstrate that ICE stopped, detained, adjudicated, and deported 3,600 American citizens.[12]

For the second time in its short history DHS severed its contractual ties with the Boeing, Inc., virtual wall on January 15, 2010, including Project 28 and all its derivatives.[13] Secretary Napolitano assigned a study of Boeing's virtual border wall, and then subsequently announced on January 1, 2011, that DHS had permanently canceled the Boeing, Inc., contract. The Secretary failed to mention, however, that contract funds exceeding $1 billion had already been spent by Boeing.[14]

Twenty-five of Boeing's ninety-foot surveillance towers, along with other supporting communications facilities, stand outside of Nogales, Arizona, forming the sum total of Boeing, Inc.'s virtual wall and Boeing's designation as DHS's SBI-net Systems Integrator. This virtual wall—according to the agents with whom I talked in late 2011—remains as it is: of questionable utility and function in protecting the security of our Mexican border. Boeing's virtual wall never worked as promised, and now it is rotting in the wind.

According to Janet Napolitano's DHS, which very quietly released the announcement in late July 2011, Raytheon's Advanced Spectroscopic Portal (ASP) was also canceled. The contract called for a new gizmo that would identify dirty radioactive material (which could be used as weapons of mass destruction) at our ports of entry. Almost five years in development, Raytheon's turn at the corporate feeding trough was roughly $230 million. For $230 million DHS received 13 ASPs, which, according to a study by the National Academy of Sciences, constantly produced nothing but false positives. Luckily, DHS did save $300 million by canceling Raytheon's ASP contract.[15]

Customs and Border Protection promised that it would no longer offer border-security contracts to defense contractors with gizmos not fully developed or tested under real operational conditions.[16] Very soon after CBP's announcement, however, DHS announced a RFP almost identical to that awarded to Boeing, Inc., in 2006. (DHS's complex RFP appears to de facto allow a contractor to supply an undeveloped or unproven security system or component with no legal consequences.) To its credit, DHS claims at last, after more than eleven years since the events of 9/11, that it will no longer follow a "one size fits all" border surveillance strategy.[17]

CBP's strategic and tactical planning is tantamount to an optimum future, but remains problematic. For example, with a fleet of ten drones, including the One Predator at cost of nearly $20 million per unmanned aerial vehicle, CBP is well on its way to protecting geographically isolated parts of the Mexican border. But according to a GAO report, CBP drones are now frequently relegated to the tarmac because the CBP does not budget "resources to support its unmanned drones" for its new fleet of UAVs.[18]

Of even deeper concern is that CBP has now contracted the measurement—and by extension, the definition—of operational control of the Mexican border to a defense contractor. In testimony to Congress in May 2012, CBP promised as a part of its new national strategy that this subcontractor will develop scientific measurement of operational control against which future progress in protecting all our borders can be objectively compared and judged.[19] The catch? CBP stated that it will take two years to develop this new measurement.

When I visited Anzalduas County Park in the fall of 2010, the entire space was unrecognizable. Inundated by the floodwaters of the Rio Grande, the road from the highway was blocked off, so I left my rental along the muddy shoulder to walk a quarter mile to the new hydrowall. From the top of the border wall I could barely see the Butler building at the entrance to Anzalduas. The tops of palm and ebony trees swayed in the currents of a vast river at least a half-mile wide.

Below me the Rio Grande pounded against the concrete base of the Hidalgo County hydrowall. To my left, south toward the mouth of the river flowing into the Gulf of Mexico, the brand new Anzalduas bridge crossed over the flooded lands, still well above the reach of flood waters. Trucks loaded with NAFTA products motored noisily back and forth across the Rio Grande/Rio Bravo. Barriers and impressive fences bordered the new Anzalduas International Bridge that, along with the hydrowall, seemed to make any kind of smuggling all but impossible.

Weeds sprouted from the top of the new hydrowall and between cracks in the concrete. I think of how quickly the weeds in my yard in McAllen punched holes in my concrete drive. At that time no crews actually maintained the new hydrowall. And I was repeatedly told by CBP agents that the rust I saw and felt on the steel bollards atop the border wall was not rust, but a chemical process that actually protected the bollards from rusting.

Three fishermen trudged back to their truck with an ice chest loaded with fish they had caught from the Rio Grande. In Spanish a local television reporter asked them how long it took to catch their bounty of fish, which they displayed for a cameraman. "Only ten minutes," they told the reporter with pride. Had they heard that the Hidalgo County Health Department warned residents not to eat any fish from the river or even to wade in its toxic waters? No problem, said one of the fishermen, because they will grill the fish to kill any germs from the river.

Staring at the floodwaters covering Anzalduas Park, it was difficult to remember how for decades this popular recreational area was a major haven for smugglers of humans and drugs. During the daylight hours, Anzalduas was frequently a peaceful place, at least to the uninitiated who paid no attention to the jet skiers and the speedboats that often lined the Mexican park directly across from its American counterpart.

It was at night that Anzalduas came alive with the human traffic, the panicked dashes through the unyielding brush and cactus to waiting vans, the offloading from Mexican speedboats of burlap bags of cocaine and marijuana bricks. It was then that you heard the cries and shouts from the frantic chases, the headlights of CBP trucks and vans temporarily lighting up the park.

It was here in the summer of 2006 that President George W. Bush promised a crowd of supporters that new immigration legislation before Congress would put an end to national security problems along the border, drug smuggling, human trafficking, and other issues directly related to immigration. Very soon after President Bush and his entourage flew to his vacation ranch in Crawford, Texas, smuggling resumed at Anzalduas County Park.

Several days after visiting the flooded park in the fall of 2010, I asked an agent at the McAllen CBP Station who patrolled this particular piece of the border what Anzalduas was like, with the hydrowall in place and the Anzalduas bridge to Mexico finally completed.

"Before the flooding," the agent told me, "with the new wall Anzalduas was real quiet. Not like it used to be."

"Really?" I said.

"Yeah. It is no longer a hot spot." Then this CBP added, "The traffic just moved up river a little. A little west of Anzalduas."

"How hot is the traffic upriver from Anzalduas?" I asked the agent.

"Like before. Look, all that really happened is that the traffic moved a little west where there's no wall."

Notes

The author's original research records for this work, some of which are sealed until 2020, reside in The Southwest Collection / Special Collections Libraries, Texas Tech University (SWC/SCL-TTU).

Chapter 1

1. These border communities may not only be very different from those in the interior, but also very different from each other. The town of Eagle Pass, for example, has a unique history compared to the communities in Cameron County. See Paul Horgan's *Great River* for a historical perspective of the influence of the Rio Grande upon the people of the borderlands. Alan Weisman and Jay Dusard's *La Frontera: The United States Border with Mexico* presents a capable overview of the breadth of the border from Brownsville, Texas, to San Diego, California. Jorge G. Castañeda, in *Ex Mex: From Migrants to Immigrants*, suggests how the borderlands are envisioned from a Mexican historical perspective. Similar themes appear in *John Charles Beales's Rio Grande Colony*, translated and edited by Louis E. Brister, and Casey Walsh in *Building the Borderlands: A Transnational History of Irrigated Cotton along the Mexico-Texas Border*. Reverence by Mexican immigrants for the bandit Jesús Malverde over more than a century becomes more understandable in a broader historical and cultural perspective. See

Kate Murphy's article "Mexican Robin Hood Figure Gains a Kind of Notoriety in the U.S.," *New York Times*, January 8, 2008.

2. See Ted Conover, *Coyotes*, for one of the first insider views of human smuggling from Mexico to the United States. See also David Spener and Kathleen A. Staudt, eds., *The U.S.-Mexico Border: Transcending Divisions, Contesting Identities*. Whether one uses the term *undocumented worker* or *illegal alien* shapes the perspective of the discussion. In general, those who use the former term are more supportive of the rights of Mexican workers in the United States, while those using the latter are less so. More than twenty-five years ago I discussed the bias of both these terms. In these pages I use the terms interchangeably. See Robert Lee Maril, "Martian Fishermen," in *Cannibals and Condos: Texans and Texas along the Gulf Coast*.

3. Border Patrol agents in general find much less support for their efforts in border communities than in nonborder communities. See Robert Lee Maril, *Patrolling Chaos: The U.S. Border Patrol in Deep South Texas*.

4. This history of violence and bloodshed is discussed in detail in further chapters.

5. There are only a handful of examples of a first-world country directly bordering on a third-world country.

6. There are countless examples of resistance to unpopular laws in this region. One is reaction to the arbitrary enforcement of the Lacey Act by the U.S. Coast Guard against American shrimpers fishing in Mexican waters. See Robert Lee Maril, *Texas Shrimpers: Community, Capitalism, and the Sea*, 172–75.

7. There used to be two bridges, a "new" bridge linking Brownsville to Matamoros and an "old" bridge. Now there are three bridges. These include the International Bridge near the UTB-TSC campus, the Old Bridge, and the new Veterans Bridge. Mexican-Americans in the Lower Rio Grande Valley were systematically excluded from public higher education until the 1960s. See Robert Lee Maril, *Poorest of Americans: The Mexican Americans of the Lower Rio Grande Valley of Texas*, 114–37.

8. Along with the U.S.-Mexico borderlands, the Lower Rio Grande Valley of Texas is consistently one of the poorest regions in the United States. See Maril, *Poorest of Americans*, 4–14. Our research and methodology are in Robert Lee Maril and Anthony N. Zavaleta, "Drinking Patterns of Low Income Mexican-American Women," *Journal of Studies in Alcohol* 40 (1979): 480–85.

9. This topic is discussed in greater detail in later chapters.

10. For a history of the beginnings of border maquiladoras, see Ellwyn R. Stoddard, *Maquila*. A history of the maquiladoras in South Texas is detailed in Maril, *Poorest of Americans*, 65–72.

11. I personally observed the recycling of cardboard as building material for many years while I lived in Brownsville. For a detailed description of Mexican *colonias*, see Stanley R. Ross, ed., *Views Across the Border*. Quality of life indicators can be very low in *colonias* on the north side of the Rio Grande, where residents may lack basic services including potable water, sewers, and electricity, while *colonias* in Mexico widely vary, some much better than others.

12. The public denial of the existence of poverty in Oklahoma, the eighth poorest state, is very strong, as is the personal denial by many of the wealthy families that were once poor. This topic is discussed in Robert Lee Maril, *Waltzing with the Ghost of Tom Joad: Poverty, Myth, and Low Wage Labor in Oklahoma*, 107–29 and, more recently, Timothy Egan, *The Worst Hard Times: The Untold Story of Those Who Survived the Great American Dust Bowl*.

13. From 1975 to 1988 I lived in Harlingen and Brownsville. I returned to live in the Valley from 1999 to 2004, and I regularly visit that region since then. I have often been corrected in my usage of terms, particularly at academic conferences, by those who never lived in the Valley.

14. It was a common practice for many years to lunch in Matamoros between classes. My colleagues and I would walk across the International Bridge and then eat at one of any number of nearby Matamoros restaurants. While crossing and recrossing the International Bridge it was common to see men, women, and children wading from one side to the other. These individuals were regularly ignored by both American and Mexican authorities.

15. The role of immigration in Mexico and the United States is detailed in the comprehensive works of Douglas S. Massey, including *Beyond Smoke and Mirrors: Mexican Immigration in an Era of Economic Integration*. For an overview of Valley history, see Carlos E. Castañeda, *Our Catholic Heritage in Texas, 1519–1936*, along with Oakah L. Jones, Jr., *Los Paisanos: Spanish Settlers on the Northern Frontier of New Spain*. J. Lee Stambaugh and Lillian J. Stambaugh's *The Lower Rio Grande Valley of Texas* remains a classic study of South Texas but must be read today with reservation and diligence.

16. Deterrence theory is discussed in later pages. Statistics collected by the Border Patrol are highly politicized. For a more detailed account of the problems with the manipulations of these statistics, see Maril, *Patrolling Chaos*, 151–68.

17. On numbers of Border Patrol agents, see "Border Patrol Agents, 1975–2005," Transactional Records Access Clearinghouse, Syracuse University, http://trac.syr.edu/immigration/reports/143/include/rep143table3.html, and U.S. Customs and Border Protection, "CBP meets 18,000 Border Patrol Agent Hiring Commitment—Weeks Early," news release, December 17, 2008, www.cbp.gov/xp/cgov/newsroom/news_releases/archives/2008_news_releases/december_2008/12172008_9.xml. Numbers of illegal immigrants are based upon statistics from Aaron Terrazas et al., "Frequently Requested Statistics on Immigrants in the United States," *Migration Information Source*, October 2007. Estimates of the illegal alien population range much higher and lower; it is impossible to know the exact numbers of those living illegally in the United States. Statistics on drug traffic across the border are taken directly from U.S. Drug Enforcement Administration chart "DEA Drug Seizures," www.justice.gov/dea/statistics.html#seizures. According to recent statistics, 212,768 pounds of cocaine were seized in 2007 in the United States along with 806,238 pounds of marijuana. Significant amounts of heroin, methamphetamines, and "hallucinogenic dosage units" were also apprehended. Of these, the majority were seized along the Mexican border.

18. See Maril, *Poorest of Americans*, for a detailed description of the historical role of class in the Lower Rio Grande Valley of Texas. See also Evan Anders, *Boss Rule in South Texas*. The methodology used in this study consists of participant observation, including semistructured open interviews, historical analysis, and the analysis of secondary data, much of which comes from government documents and reports. Previous research experience facilitated access to government agencies and programs, elected officials, the private sector, and the military. Anonymous informants and whistleblowers were also used in this study. Elected and appointed officials are frequently named, but informants and whistleblowers remain anonymous. Privacy and confidentiality of respondents have been respected but in no way detract from the findings. I also drew heavily from a network of individuals and research first established in 1975. See the issues raised in conducting fieldwork in challenging settings as discussed at length by Ron Loewe and Jayne Howell, eds., *Practicing Anthropology* 31, no. 2 (Spring 2009).

19. This description is taken directly from the Honeywell, Inc., website at www .honeywell.com/sites/honeywell/.

20. Quote from the website of U.S. Customs and Border Protection: www.cbp.gov/xp/ cgov/border_security/border_patrol/border_patrol_sectors/. DHS's failed programs are extensively detailed in later chapters.

21. Maril, *Patrolling Chaos*.

22. In studying the Border Patrol, it is extremely important to remain outside their institutional sphere of influence and bias. This is only accomplished by maintaining scholarly independence and integrity. In part, I achieved this goal by adhering to the research methodology. Maril, *Patrolling Chaos*, 15–18.

23. Since 1981 I have worked with a variety of elected officials at the local, state, and federal level and also testified in civil trials, public hearings, and before the U.S. Congress. I have worked for the prosecution in criminal trials, and I have also contributed to state and federal legislation based upon my research findings, including Texas legislation to improve the quality of life in border *colonias* and, at the federal level, House Resolution 4044, House Resolution 715, and Senate Resolution 1348.

24. Maril, *Patrolling Chaos*. On the efforts of agents, see the daily actions of Noe Escondido, for example, at ibid., 73–88. Numerous problems with communications equipment, scope trucks, and ground sensors are discussed at ibid., 151–68. On the condition of the immigrants, see ibid., 59–72. This human suffering was not the exception; it was the rule (ibid., 122–34). Female immigrants were often told by their *coyotes* that, if caught by the Border Patrol, they would be sexually assaulted. Many undocumented workers were victimized before they ever reached the U.S.-Mexico border.

25. Border patrol apprehension rates and other statistics, as suggested earlier, are suspect.

26. This observation is discussed in subsequent chapters. The growth of the security industry since the events of 9/11 appears to have created experts out of many with modest military backgrounds having little to do with security or intelligence

work. This also appears to be the case among some academics in universities and think tanks.

27. Based on an interview in Greenville, North Carolina, with a Mexican official on March 21, 2007, concerning human rights abuses perpetrated by Mexican local, state, and federal authorities.

28. Ted Conover was one of the first to document the importance of Mexican remittances, now annually in the billions of dollars, upon certain regions of Mexico (Conover, *Coyotes*).

29. From unpublished research by the author conducted from 1999 to the present in South Texas.

30. In such cases the driver, the *coyote*, slows his car or van, jumps out while it is still moving, and hopes that his panicking passengers will divert the attention of the authorities, thus allowing his own escape. Many times this strategy works. Maril, *Patrolling Chaos*, 98–103.

31. Only as of spring 2009 has the smuggling of weapons to Mexican criminals, including the drug cartels, become a real concern among American law enforcement officials. As the violence between Mexican cartels intensifies, and more than five thousand people were killed in Mexico in 2008, attention is finally being directed to the decades-old smuggling of guns along the border. See Ginger Thompson, "A Shift to Make the Border Safe, from the Inside Out," *New York Times*, April 6, 2009, www.nytimes.com/2009/04/06/us/06napolitano.html.

32. The Border Patrol divides these "incidents" into three categories: "incursions," "encounters," and "sightings" (U.S. Office of the Border Patrol, *Mexican Government Incidents*, 2003–2005). These documents were obtained through the Freedom of Information Act initiated by Judicial Watch. See, more recently, Matthew Benson, "Guard Soldiers Back Off from Armed Men out of Mexico," *Arizona Republic*, January 6, 2007. I collected firsthand accounts of the role of the Mexican military in drug trafficking in South Texas in *Patrolling Chaos*.

33. The carjackers were eventually arrested, indicted, and convicted. See Maril, *Patrolling Chaos*, 183–90.

34. See the research conducted by the Center for Immigration Research, Department of Sociology, University of Houston.

35. Maril, *Patrolling Chaos*, 103–5.

36. Military units dressed in black periodically crossed the Rio Grande into the United States and avoided this system of sensors (Office of the Border Patrol, *Mexican Government Incidents*).

37. Agents who jumped into the Rio Grande to save drowning undocumented workers or rescued undocumented workers in other dangerous circumstances rarely received acknowledgment even in local media.

38. Discussions with Jacob Hockman have been beneficial in an understanding of how this process works at corporations other than Honeywell, Inc.

39. See John Newhouse, *Boeing versus Airbus: The Inside Story of the Greatest International Competition in Business*. See also Bill Yenne, *The Story of the Boeing*

Company. DHS's "business fair" and other details of the bidding process are discussed in detail in forthcoming chapters.

40. ISIS will be discussed in detail in a later chapter.

41. Susan Jacoby makes one of the most recent cases for the value of documenting history in *The Age of American Unreason.*

Chapter 2

1. The case of Border Patrol agents Jose A. Compean and Ignacio Ramos is discussed in a later chapter.

2. Recruitment to the Border Patrol, including academy training, is discussed in detail in further chapters.

3. My own congressman, Walter B. Jones, Jr., coined the concept "freedom fries" at Cubbie's Restaurant in downtown Greenville, North Carolina, just a mile from where I reside.

4. Frederic J. Frommer, "Air Marshals Put at Risk," *Greenville Daily Reflector,* May 21, 2006, A5. See also the series by Steve Losey documenting problems confronting the Air Marshals, including Stephen Losey, "Air Marshal's Firing Prompts Whistleblower Suit," *Federal Times,* November 7, 2006

5. For a report of the final accident investigation of this tragedy, see Sergio Chapa, "Border Agents Who Drowned Last Month in Rio Grande Were Not Wearing Life Preservers," *Brownsville Herald,* October 28, 2004, www.sergiochapa.com/files/bp.pdf.

6. The history of violence by the Border Patrol against those they apprehend is still remembered by many border residents in past and present *corridos,* popular Hispanic folk songs sung and handed down from one generation to another in Texas as well as California. A graphic example is "El Corrido del Ilegal" (or, in English, "The Ballad of the Illegal Immigrant"), which describes what happens to one illegal immigrant when apprehended by the Border Patrol. Inevitably encounters with the Border Patrol in *corridos* focus upon the agents' harsh treatment of undocumented workers. Tales of exploitation and brutality are a recurrent theme in these folk songs. A strong oral tradition, which includes the *corridos,* clearly represents a long standing perception of the Border Patrol as an agency of violence against undocumented workers. See Robert Lee Maril, *Patrolling Chaos,* 146, and, for a more detailed account, Maria Herrera-Sobeck, *Northward Bound: The Mexican Immigrant Experience in Ballad and Song,* 187–88.

7. See, for example, 10News, "Officials: Violence against Agents on Rise," *Homeland Defense News,* September 10, 2008, www.officer.com/web/online/Homeland-Defense-and-Terror-News/Officials—Violence-Against-Border-Agents-On-Rise/8$43145.

8. Mimi Hall, "Attacks against Border Agents on Record Pace," *USA Today,* February 27, 2008, www.usatoday.com/news/nation/2008-02-26-Borderviolence_N.htm.

9. Crucial statistics on occupational hazards, if documented, have not been made public by the Border Patrol. In my research of one Border Patrol station, all these problems were present, but because of the masculine culture in place, agents

rarely sought professional help. I documented the beginning of the trend in bribery attempts in 2000; see Maril, *Patrolling Chaos*, 188–90.

10. "OTMs" is an example of terminology that, over time, agents (like others in law
enforcement) have developed to aid them with problematic work situations. Such
terminology incorporates and reflects their biases.

11. Local police departments and county sheriffs are often part of the drug smuggling
problem. For example, since 2000 sheriffs in Cameron and Hidalgo Counties were
indicted, convicted, and served time in state and federal prisons for collaborating
with Mexican drug cartels. This topic is addressed in later chapters.

12. This problem, from the agents' point of view, is discussed in a later chapter.

13. This point is extensively detailed in further chapters.

14. The National Border Patrol Council is affiliated with the American Federation of
Government Employees.

15. For a readable description of the work of corrections officers, see Ted Conover,
Newjack: Guarding Sing Sing.

Chapter 3

1. I documented this same criminal activity, and the lengths to which certain agents
went to curtail it, in Robert Lee Maril, *Patrolling Chaos*, 169–82.

2. Ibid., 173–75; *Handbook of Texas Online*, s.v. "La Lomita Mission," www.tshaonline
.org/handbook/online/articles/LL/uql7.html. The Oblates raised grapes and pota-
toes, but neither their crops nor their proselytizing were very successful, and in
1907 they sold most of their land, excluding the park, to James W. Conway and
John J. Hoit. Soon after, these developers platted the nearby town of Mission.

3. During my field research from 1999 to 2001 I spent many days and nights in Anzalduas County Park with the Border Patrol. I returned to Anzalduas once in 2006,
twice in 2007, three times in 2008, twice in 2009, and twice in 2010. My observations in this chapter are based on some of those visits.

4. See Kyle Arnold, "Anzalduas Bridge Construction Slated to Begin in May," *McAllen Monitor*, April 7, 2007, 1.

5. A transcript of Bush's speech is at http://georgewbush-whitehouse.archives.gov/
news/releases/2006/08/20060803-8.html. The content and politics of his legislation, and the Congressional field hearing on immigration that was held in Dubuque,
Iowa, are discussed in later chapters. Hidalgo County politicians were particularly
identified as among the most enthusiastic supporters of President Bush. For example, Mission Mayor Beto Salinas was identified by President Bush in his speech
as "one of my dear friends." See Kaitlin Bell, "President's 2-Hour Visit to Valley
Includes Praise for Border Agents," *McAllen Monitor*, August 4, 2006, 1.

6. For example, in the spring of 2008 flooding along much of the river in this region
of South Texas made it impossible for the Border Patrol to patrol the line at Rio
Grande City and surrounding communities for several weeks. On the other side of
the river, the flooding was reported to be much more serious in nature.

7. Robert Lee Maril, *Poorest of Americans: The Mexican Americans of the Lower Rio
Grande Valley of Texas*, 19–34; Evan Anders, *Boss Rule in South Texas*. On the

violent history of the region, see, among others, Carlos E. Castañeda, *Our Catholic Heritage in Texas, 1519–1936*; Oakah L. Jones, Jr., *Los Paisanos: Spanish Settlers on the Northern Frontier of New Spain*; and J. Lee Stambaugh and Lillian J. Stambaugh, *The Lower Rio Grande Valley of Texas*.

8. See Maril, *Poorest of Americans*, 107–8, for a further description of the McAllen C Shift. See also the original, but limited, work of Arthur J. Rubel, *Across the Tracks*. This topic deserves further scholarly research and documentation. I remain grateful to Professor Dan Dearth at the Department of Criminal Justice at the University of Texas–Pan American for his detailed explanations of the McAllen C Shift. While the professional standards of the McAllen Police Department were elevated, graft and corruption among police officers directly related to illegal drugs remain a continuing problem.

9. This section relies heavily on the account in Gary Provost, *Across the Border: The True Story of the Satanic Cult Killings in Matamoros Mexico*. I also benefited from conversations on this topic with Antonio Zavaleta.

10. Ibid., 4. See also Himilce Novas, *Everything You Need to Know About Latino History*, rev. ed., 77–81.

11. The case of Juan Nepomuceno Cortina highlights these same points. Several studies of Cortina and his exploits show the various forces of violence in play in this region. See also Paul Horgan, *Great River*.

12. Several Civil War battles took place in the Valley. After the Civil War residents were again plagued by armed bands.

13. Evan Anders, *Boss Rule in South Texas*, 225.

14. See Maril, *Poorest of Americans*, 100–102.

15. See, for example, Mary Kidder Rak, *The Border Patrol*. More recent attempts by former agents focus frequently on the Special Operations Group of the CBP. See, for example, Erich Krauss and Alex Pacheco, *On the Line: Inside the U.S. Border Patrol*.

16. See the work of Maria Herrera-Sobeck, especially *Northward Bound: The Mexican Immigrant Experience in Ballad and Song*, discussed in a previous chapter.

17. I heard these same kinds of family stories from my students at the University of Texas–Pan American from 1999 to 2003 as I did at the University of Texas, Brownsville, from 1976 to 1988. Also, I documented these same kinds of stories from "old-timers" in the Border Patrol in South Texas.

18. This case was overturned, however, when the U.S. Attorneys Office was determined to have "engaged in prosecutorial misconduct." Former Agent Sipe admitted at trial that he struck the undocumented worker three times in rapid succession with his heavy flashlight. See Jeremy Roebuck, "Border Patrol Ordered to Reinstate Agent," *McAllen Monitor*, December 3, 2007, 1. Also see Maril, *Patrolling Chaos*, 96–97.

19. Agents pending trial in 2006 are listed in Pauline Arrillaga, "Sure Thing: Securing Homeland Difficult When Those Guarding Gates Corrupt," *Greenville Daily Reflector*, September 24, 2006, 1D. The case of Agent Oscar Antonio Ortiz is described in Associated Press, "Border Agent Gets Five Years for Smuggling," July 29,

2006, 18, and Steve Barnes, "Texas: Border Agent Pleads Guilty," *New York Times*, September 8, 2006, www.nytimes.com/2006/09/08/us/politics/08brfs-004.html. The documentary "Mexico: Crimes at the Border," *Frontline*, PBS, also documents these same trends. On arrests since 2006, see Rick Jervis, "Arrests of Border Agents on the Rise," *USA Today*, April 24, 2009, 3A, www.usatoday.com/news/nation/2009-04-23-borderagent_N.htm. Instead of arresting and charging managers, CBP frequently merely forces them to retire; see Maril, *Patrolling Chaos*, 183–85.

20. Maril, *Poorest of Americans*, 37–38.

21. Ibid.

22. County sheriff's departments were a crucial part of this system of peonage, as evidenced by a history of legal cases; ibid., 45–46.

23. The brutality of local police departments and county sheriff's departments is meticulously documented in the film *Strangers in Their Own Land*, narrated by Frank Reynolds, directed and produced by Hope Ryder. See also Maril, *Poorest of Americans*, 114–37.

24. Remnants of how this system worked were exposed in the Pharr Riot as documented in the film *Strangers in Their Own Land*. Through most of the history of this region the primary newspapers have been owned by Freedom Newspapers, one of the most conservative newspaper chains in the United States. I briefly worked for the *Valley Morning Star* in Harlingen in 1975.

25. See also Maril, *Poorest of Americans*, 46, 47–51.

26. Alejandro Portes and Ruben G. Rumbaut, *Immigrant America*, 15–16.

27. Maril, *Poorest of Americans*, 49.

28. Fortunately these events were documented in the film *Strangers in Their Own Land*.

29. From multiple interviews with law enforcement officials in the Valley.

30. This topic is discussed in a subsequent chapter.

31. Sergio Chapa, "Cantu Sentenced to 24 Years," December 14, 2006, *McAllen Monitor*, 1.

32. I served as a juror in this case and heard all testimony and saw all the evidence, including written documents, presented at trial. After the financial settlement was announced, a straw vote taken in the jury room showed that the jurors, if allowed to reach a verdict, would have voted unanimously against the defendants.

33. Jeremy Roebuck, "El Paso Contractor Linked to PSJA Bribery Case," April 2, 2008, *McAllen Monitor*, www.themonitor.com/articles/board-10528-sambrano-school.html. There is little research on white-collar crime in this region, particularly its impact on public schools, colleges, universities, municipal government, real estate, and not-for-profits. For a discussion of the impact of fraud by Valley real estate developers upon low-income homeowners, see Robert Lee Maril, "Contracts for Deeds," report for Texas RioGrande Legal Aid, Weslaco, Texas, 1995.

34. Chad C. Haddal et al., CRS Report 7–5700, Congressional Research Service, March 16, 2009, 1, 22–24. The validity of deterrence theory and its impact on immigrant flows is discussed in greater detail in subsequent chapters.

35. Ibid., 21, 22. Types of primary fencing other than these will be described in later chapters.
36. Ibid., 26.
37. Ibid., 14.
38. Ibid., 26.
39. Ibid.
40. A later chapter is devoted to ISIS.

Chapter 4

1. Some of this biographical information is taken directly from "President's Biography," http://pubs.utb.edu/president/Bio.htm.
2. See the proposed fenceline in "Border Fence Information," UTB-TSC, News Today, http://blue.utb.edu/newsandinfo/UpdateBorderFenceIssue.htm. Also, "Border Fence Information," International Technology, Education and Commerce Campus, UTB-TSC, at http://blue.utb.edu/newsandinfo/fence/itecc.htm.
3. Zachary Taylor was assigned to Fort Brown to harass Matamoros by firing cannon balls across the Rio Grande. One intention was to push Mexico into war. Hundreds of American soldiers died at Fort Brown from malaria and other tropical diseases before they ever invaded Mexico. See Robert Lee Maril, *Poorest of Americans: The Mexican Americans of the Lower Rio Grande Valley of Texas*, 19–34.
4. Before the 1980s the predominantly Mexican American student body was taught by an Anglo faculty, and the administration was almost entirely Anglo. Ibid., 114–37.
5. Ibid., 35–54.
6. From "President's Comments," May 6, 2008, http://blue.utb.edu/newsandinfo/2008_01_17ProposedFence_Map.htm.
7. "UTB/TSC and DHS Agree to Study Border Security Alternatives," March 19, 2008, https://blue.utb.edu/newsandinfo/2008%C2%AD%C2%AD_03_19BorderSecurity Alternatives.htm.
8. Randal C. Archibold, "Government Issues Waived for Fencing along Border," *New York Times*, April 2, 2008, www.nytimes.com/2008/04/02/us/02fence.html?_r=1&scp=1&sq=Government%20Issues%20Waive%20for%20Fencing%20along%20Border&st=cse.
9. This same view of "outsiders" has played out in Brownsville's federal court before. See Robert Lee Maril, "They Followed Us with Jets and My Own Country Arrested Us: The Arbitrary Enforcement of the Lacey Act," paper presented at the annual meeting of the Rural Sociological Society, 1984, College Station, Texas.
10. See Robert Lee Maril, "Contracts for Deeds," report for Texas RioGrande Legal Aid, Weslaco, Texas, 1995.
11. See Jackie Leatherman, "County Leaders Meet with Federal Officials to Discuss Fence, Levee," *McAllen Monitor*, October 23, 2007, www.themonitor.com/news/officials-6079-tuesday-county.html. Also see Jackie Leatherman, "County Moves Closer to Combined Levee–Border Fence," *McAllen Monitor*, April 14, 2008, www.themonitor.com/common/printer/view.php?db=monitortx&id=10955; Laura B.

Martinez, "The Fence is Coming, Levee or Not," *Brownsville Herald*, April 29, 2008, www.brownsvilleherald.com/news/fence-86264-county-border.html; and Kevin Sieff, "Border Fencing," *Brownsville Herald*, April 29, 2008.

12. See *United States of America v. 50.00 Acres of Land, More or Less, Situated in Hidalgo County, State of Texas, et al.*, Texas Southern District Court, McAllen, Texas, January 30, 2008. I would like to thank Texas RioGrande Legal Aid for providing me with this and other relevant documents.

13. Ibid., 60–62.

14. Ibid., 18–41.

15. Maril, *Poorest of Americans*, 5–7.

16. *United States of America v. 50.00 Acres of Land*, 79–84.

17. This tour of the proposed border fence site, which the CBP refers to as a "VIP ride along," took six weeks of correspondence to arrange. After repeated emails to the sector Public Affairs Office, during which time I was asked to submit detailed reasons for the tour, I was finally given agency permission. Before the events of 9/11, this request would immediately have been forthcoming from CBP. Subsequent requests to document the progress of the construction of the border fence were always met with agency resistance. These requests took from six weeks to two months to obtain. Professional researchers studying the CBP in California, Texas, New Mexico, and Arizona have dealt with this same difficulty in obtaining access to this federal agency.

18. Maril, *Poorest of Americans*, 55–90.

19. Maril, *Patrolling Chaos*, 286–305.

20. Ibid., 59–64.

21. Pumping stations siphon river water into the irrigation system that feeds the fertile Valley lands. The pumping stations, built in the 1920s, are frequently at bends in the river where the currents run slow. Such places are also frequently the best landing points for human and drug traffickers because the river is easier to cross and roads lead from the pumping station to Old Military Highway.

Chapter 5

1. See Stephen E. Brown, Finn-Aage Esbensen, and Gilbert Geis, *Criminology: Explaining Crime and Context*, 182–87.

2. Much of law enforcement work is, of course, based upon a tacit acceptance of the precepts of deterrence theory. I want to acknowledge the helpful discussions over a period of years with Capt. Ron Thrasher, Stillwater Police Department, Stillwater, Oklahoma.

3. Brown, Esbensen, and Geis, *Criminology*, 228.

4. Reliable research on terrorists that is available to the public is scant. The majority of research of Mexican drug cartels is based upon government reports.

5. Wayne A. Cornelius and Jesse M. Lewis, eds., *Impacts of Border Enforcement on Mexican Migration: The View from Sending Communities*; Wayne A. Cornelius et al., eds., *Migration from the Mexican Mixteca: A Transnational Community in Oaxaca and California*; Julia Preston, "Mexico Data Show Migration to U.S. in

Decline," *New York Times*, May 15, 2009, www.nytimes.com/2009/05/15/us/15immig.html?_r=1&hp.

6. See Cornelius et al., *Migration from the Mexican Mixteca*. Others strongly disagree with this interpretation, especially critics on the political right.

7. For reasons of public relations, Operation Blockade was soon renamed Operation Hold the Line.

8. Silvestre Reyes's biography is at his congressional website: http://reyes.house.gov/Biography/.

9. For additional information, see Timothy J. Dunn, *The Militarization of the U.S.-Mexico Border, 1978–1992*.

10. Statistics from 1997 through 2002 are from "Table 26, Deportable Aliens Located by Program and Border Patrol Sector and Investigations Special Agent in Charge (SAC) Jurisdiction: Fiscal Years 1997 to 2006," U.S. Border Patrol, 2007. Statistics from 2003 through 2007 are from personal communication with Ricardo Rosas, Public Information Officer, McAllen Sector Border Patrol, August 24, 2008.

11. Perhaps critics were willing to believe, at least in the first years of Reyes's new strategy, that the Border Patrol actually had discovered the magic formula for controlling the border. It is somewhat problematical why, as the numbers of apprehensions began to increase in spite of the new strategy, contrary to Border Patrol logic, Congress raised no serious concerns.

12. In 2007 the McAllen Sector reported 406,805 pounds of marijuana confiscated along with 7,342 pounds of cocaine. The McAllen Sector ranked the highest of all sectors in cocaine seizures. U.S. Border Patrol, "Table 26, Deportable Aliens Located by Program and Border Patrol Sector and Investigations Special Agent in Charge (SAC) Jurisdiction: Fiscal Years 1997 to 2006," 2007.

13. The majority of my informants estimated that from 30 to 40 percent of all agents left the Border Patrol, although the exact figures have not been made public. After a year or less as U.S. Air Marshals, some former Border Patrol agents transferred back, or attempted to transfer back, to the Border Patrol. Stephen Losey has written several articles about this topic and other problems faced by former Border Patrol agents working as U.S. Air Marshals. See, for example, Stephen Losey, "Air Marshal's Firing Prompts Whistleblower Suit," *Federal Times*, November 7, 2006; Frederic J. Frommer, "Air Marshals Put at Risk," *Greenville Daily Reflector*, May 21, 2006; and Eric Lipton, "Some U.S. Security Agents Chafe under Speech Limits," *New York Times*, April 26, 2005, http://query.nytimes.com/gst/fullpage.html?res=9E0DE1D81231F935A15757C0A9639C8B63&sec=&spon=&pagewanted=all.

14. From Migration Policy Institute, "The U.S.-Mexico Border," *Migration Information Source*, June 1, 2006, 2–3, www.migrationinformation.org/Feature/print.cfm?ID=407. Only recently have statistics on the number of dead illegal immigrants been collected from other local, county, and federal law enforcement agencies. For a variety of reasons these statistics most probably remain an undercount of the actual numbers of undocumented who die while attempting entry into the United States.

15. Ibid., 1.

16. See "Statement of Richard L. Skinner, Inspector General, U.S. Department of Homeland Security," Subcommittee on Management, Integration, and Oversight, Committee on Homeland Security, U.S. House of Representatives, Washington, D.C., 1. In addition to the reports authored by the DHS and the General Services Administration, the sworn testimony of various witnesses to congressional sub-committees, and the other literature cited, this chapter is based on a number of informants who wish to remain anonymous. See also John Mintz, "Probe Faults System for Monitoring U.S. Borders," *Washington Post*, April 11, 2005, www .mail-archive.com/medianews@twiar.org/msg00906.html; John Mintz, "Border Camera System is Assailed," *Washington Post*, June 17, 2005, www.nusd.k12.az .us/schools/nhs/gthomson.class/articles/border/news.HUM115/border.patrol/ Border%20Camera%20System%20Is%20Assailed.pdf; "Integrated Surveillance Intelligence System (ISIS)," *Global Security*, July 2, 2008, www.globalsecurity .org/security/systems/isis.htm; and Shruti Dat', "Immigration Service Patrols with Sensors and Video," *Government Computer News*, February 6, 2000, http:// gcn.com/articles/2000/02/06/immigration-servicepatrols-with-sensors-and -video.aspx?sc_lang=en.

17. Dat', "Immigration Service Patrols," 3.

18. One is left to assume that studies of the efficacy of the sensor system were not car-ried out prior to 2005 exactly because the Border Patrol did not want the public to know just how ineffective its sensor system was. It certainly possessed the re-search funds to analyze the data.

19. Border Patrol agents view the DEA agents as "hotshots" who rarely possess useful information. In turn, DEA agents have an equally low regard for agents of the Border Patrol. Cooperation between agencies has increased somewhat in recent years.

20. The political pressures that led to the decision to install ISIS require further research. It is unclear how ISIS was named; see Dat', "Immigration Service Pa-trols," 1.

21. Ibid.

22. Ibid.

23. "Statement of Richard L. Skinner," 1.

24. Dat', "Immigration Service Patrols," 1–2.

25. Ibid., 2. See also "Integrated Surveillance Intelligence System (ISIS)," *Global Se-curity*, July 2, 2008.

26. Dat', "Immigration Service Patrols," 3.

27. Website of Congressman Silvestre Reyes, http://reyes.house.gov/.

28. Testimony of Joseph Saponaro in "U.S. Representative Michael D. Rogers Hearing on Border Patrol Surveillance Technology," *Congressional Quarterly*, June 16, 2005.

29. Ibid. See also "Statement of James C. Handley, Regional Administrator, Great Lakes Region, U.S. General Services Administration, before the Committee on Homeland Security, Subcommittee on Management, Integration and Oversight," U.S. House of Representatives, Washington, D.C., February 16, 2006; and

"Statement of Richard Skinner, Inspector General, U.S. Department of Homeland Security, before the Subcommittee on Management, Integration and Oversight," U.S. House of Representatives, Washington, D.C., December 16, 2005. See also a number of articles in the mainstream media interpreting these reports, including John Mintz, "Probe Faults System for Monitoring U.S. Borders," *Washington Post*, April 11, 2005, www.washingtonpost.com/wp-dyn/articles/A42516-2005Apr10 .html.

30. "Statement of Richard Skinner," 2.
31. Ibid.
32. Ibid., 3. Emphasis added.
33. Ibid.
34. Ibid., 4.
35. Ibid., 5.
36. Ibid., 7.
37. Ibid. According to Inspector General Skinner, the Border Patrol, upon reviewing their report, including DHS's seven detailed recommendations, failed to respond adequately to five of the seven.
38. Saponaro testimony in "U.S. Representative Michael D. Rogers Hearing," 9.
39. Ibid., 10.
40. Ibid., 2. Emphasis added.
41. Interview with a Border Patrol supervisor, April 4, 2004.
42. The inspector general of GSA reported they had an "open investigation" of ISIS in 2005, but no charges were forthcoming (Saponaro testimony in "U.S. Representative Michael D. Rogers Hearing," 16).
43. Ibid., 14. In 2008 L-3 and Government Services, Inc., were reorganized yet again. "L-3 Communications has grown very quickly into the sixth largest defense company in the United States, and is a leader and prime defense contractor in Intelligence, Surveillance and Reconnaissance (ISR), secure communications, government services, training and simulation and aircraft modernization and maintenance. The company also is a leading merchant supplier of guidance and navigation products and systems, sensors, scanners, faxes, data links, propulsion systems, avionics, electro optics, satellite communications, electrical power equipment, encryption products, signal intelligence, antennas and microwave products" (quote from Michael T. Strianese, chairman, president, and chief executive officer, L-3 Communications, www.l-3com.com/about-l3/).
44. This information is from an interview with an anonymous source on February 2, 2008. I have not been able to verify these estimates from the DHS or CBP, although I believe the numbers to be accurate.

Chapter 6

1. See Rachel L. Swarns, "Critics Say Politics Driving Immigration Hearings," *New York Times*, August 7, 2006, www.nytimes.com/2006/08/07washington/07immig. html; Associated Press, "Lawmakers Bring Immigration Hearings to U.S.-Mexico Border," *USA Today*, July 7, 2006, www.usatoday.com/news/washington/

2006-07-07-immigration-hearings_x.htm; and Julia Preston, "House and Senate Hold Immigration Hearings," *New York Times*, July 6, 2006, www.nytimes.com/2006/07/06/washington/06immigration.html.

2. Terence P. Jeffrey, "Man of the Year: Jim Sensenbrenner," *Human Events*, December 22, 2006, www.humanevents.com/article.php?id=18622.

3. As early as July 8, Democrats noted the lack of bipartisanship in the field hearings. Congresswoman Sheila Jackson Lee, for example, began referring to the field hearings as "the big mockery." See Sylvia Moreno, "GOP Hearing Alleges Risks of Terrorism along Border," *Washington Post*, July 8, 2006:3. Some details of these hearings were collected from congressional staff members.

4. See the Democrats' position and opinion on both immigration bills as expounded in Congressman John Conyers, Jr., memorandum in "Is the Reid-Kennedy Bill a Repeat of the Failed Amnesty of 1986," Full Committee Oversight Field Hearing, 109th Cong., 2nd sess., September 1, 2006.

5. Ann E. Michalski, rough draft of testimony to be presented before House Judiciary Committee, Full Committee Oversight Field Hearing, 109th Cong., 2nd sess., Dubuque, Iowa, September 1, 2006, 2, copy in possession of the author.

6. Grassley's remarks are based upon my personal notes and a copy of testimony from Grassley entitled "Senator Chuck Grassley's Statement before the House Judiciary Committee Hearing on Immigration Reform," Dubuque, Iowa, September 1, 2006.

7. For a discussion of the overall effectiveness of IRCA, see Douglas S. Massey, Jorge Durand, and Nolan J. Malone, *Beyond Smoke and Mirrors: Mexican Immigration in an Era of Economic Integration*. While immediately after IRCA the number of illegal immigrants declined, soon the statistics met or exceeded previous figures. Campbell J. Gibson and Emily Lennon further demonstrate these points in *Historical Census Statistics on the Foreign-born Population of the United States: 1850–1990*, Population Division Working Paper No. 29. Grassley quote from "Senator Chuck Grassley's Statement," 1.

8. One example of such dissent is described in John Bicknell, "Month of Field Hearings Has Not Yielded Immigration Payoff House GOP Wanted," *CQ Today*, August 18, 2006. See also, T. R. Goldman, "The Man with the Iron Gavel," *Legal Times*, May 2, 2005.

9. "Financial Impact of Illegal Immigration along Southern Border," C-Span broadcast of House Committee on the Judiciary, El Paso, Texas, August 17, 2006.

10. Personal discussion with Josiah Heyman, Department of Anthropology and Sociology, University of Texas–El Paso, February 1, 2007.

11. For example, see House Committee on the Judiciary, "How Do Illegal Immigrants Impact the Costs of Healthcare, Local Education, and Other Social Services, and Would These Costs Increase under Reid-Kennedy," Full Committee Oversight Field Hearing, 109th Cong., 2nd sess., Concord, New Hampshire, August 24, 2006.

12. From my notes of Fonte's verbal testimony, September 1, 2006, and John Fonte, "Let us Not Repeat the Amnesty Mistake of 1986," Testimony before the House

Judiciary Committee, Full Committee Oversight Field Hearing, 109th Cong., 2nd sess., Dubuque, Iowa, September 1, 2006:3. The testimony of Robert Rector, "Amnesty and Continued Low Skill Immigration Will Substantially Raise Welfare Costs and Poverty," was very similar in substance and tone to Fonte's presentation. Rector is a senior research fellow, welfare and family issues, domestic policy studies, the Heritage Foundation.

13. Based upon my personal notes and a copy of testimony from Michael W. Cutler, "Testimony of Michael W. Cutler for the Hearing to Be Held on September 1, 2006, before the House Judiciary Committee," Dubuque, Iowa, September 1, 2006.

14. I had previously testified twice—the first time before the U.S. Senate Commerce and Banking Committee in 1998, and the second before the same committee in 1999. Senator John Ashcroft, Republican from Missouri, soon to become attorney general under President George W. Bush, chaired the latter session. In sharp contrast to Congressman Sensenbrenner, Senator Ashcroft allotted every member of the panel, regardless of party affiliation, the same period of time to give their presentation. Further, Senator Ashcroft did not immediately cut off presenters if they exceeded their time limits.

15. The economic impact of Latino immigrants has brought a new vitality to a number of rural and urban regions in the United States. In addition to the border states, I have personally observed this impact in North Carolina, Oklahoma, and Virginia. There is an extensive literature on this topic. See, for example, Frank D. Bean, Mark Leach, and B. Lindsay Lowell, "Immigrant Job Quality and Mobility in the United States," *Work and Organization* 31:499–518, and Frank D. Bean and Gillian Stevens, *America's Newcomers and the Dynamics of Diversity* (New York: Russell Sage Foundation, 2003). See also Richard Fry and B. Lindsay Lowell, "The Wage Structure of Latino Origin Groups Across Generations," *Industrial Relations* 45, no. 2:147–68.

16. Minutemen will be discussed in greater detail in a subsequent chapter. For an overview of their perspective, see Rudy Adler et al., *Border Film Project: Photos by Migrants and Minutemen on the U.S.-Mexico Border.*

17. This heavily scripted and staged production, which I witnessed on two different occasions, was intended by the Border Patrol to demonstrate to the naive observer the effective use of new technologies and equipment, including patrol boats. See Robert Lee Maril, *Patrolling Chaos,* 151–69.

18. Groups representing immigrants parsed certain segments of my research to find support for their specific positions. In a similar manner, Minutemen and others on the right of the political spectrum cited my research on the inefficiency of the Border Patrol in apprehending illegal workers. These tendencies, along with media bias covering immigration issues, are discussed in a later chapter.

19. A number of studies show similar findings. See, for example, Douglas S. Massey et al., "What's Driving Mexico-U.S. Migration? A Theoretical, Empirical and Policy Analysis," *American Journal of Sociology* 102, no. 4 (1997): 939–99, and Douglas S. Massey et al., *Return to Aztlan: The Social Process of International Migration from Western Mexico.*

20. This biographical information relies heavily on David Bacon, "Political Economy of Migration," *New Labor Forum*, June 2007, 1. It is also based upon information presented in Mark Leibovich, "Pit Bull of the House Latches On to Immigration," *New York Times*, July 10, 2006, A3. See Rep. Sensenbrenner's official website at www.house.gov/sensenbrenner. Also see an interview with the congressman in "House Republican Cites Guest-worker 'Amnesty'," *Washington Times*, January 25, 2006, along with Ruben Navarrette, Jr., "The Many Sides of James Sensenbrenner," *San Diego Union-Tribune*, August 10, 2006. Sparse biographical information, compared to other politicians on the national stage, is available on Sensenbrenner. For example, there is to date no official biography of him.

21. Terence P. Jeffrey, "Man of the Year: Jim Sensenbrenner." *Human Events*, December 22, 2006, www.humanevents.com/article.php?id=18622. *Rolling Stone* cited in *Wikipedia*, s.v. "Jim Sensenbrenner," March 12, 2008, http://en.wikipedia.org/wiki/Jim_Sensenbrenner.

22. At the time of this writing Jefferson had been found guilty and sentenced to more than a decade in prison.

23. Leibovich, "Pit Bull of the House Latches On to Immigration."

24. Bacon, "Political Economy of Migration."

25. I described one example typical of drug interdictions along the border in detail in Maril, *Patrolling Chaos*, 73–88. Although huge amounts of drugs are captured by the Border Patrol as well as other federal and state law enforcers, these interdictions represent a very small percentage of the illegal drugs reaching users throughout this country. This same point is summarized by Nicholas D. Kristof, "Drugs Won the War," *New York Times*, June 14, 2009, 10.

26. To his credit, Congressperson King was the only member of the committee of either party to ask a follw-up question of an invited panel member.

27. The Associated Press, "Texas: Did You See That Elephant Cross the Border?" *New York Times*, October 12, 2006, www.nytimes.com/2006/10/12/us/12brfs-002.html. See also "Now There's An Idea: Build the Wall on the Other Side," The 2007 Bum Steer Awards, *Texas Monthly*, January 2007, 102.

Chapter 7

1. I conducted all the field work described in this chapter. On this particular trip to the border my wife, Dindy Reich, accompanied me as a research assistant.

2. See the work of John McPhee, most notably *Basin and Range*.

3. See Jeremy Scahill, *Blackwater: The Rise of the World's Most Powerful Mercenary Army*. In 2009 a number of new criminal charges were alleged against this corporation and its CEO.

4. I first heard this strategy from a supporter of a senator in the spring of 2005. The politicians who made this argument are identified later in this chapter.

5. See *The 9/11 Commission Report: Final Report of the National Commission on Terrorist Attacks upon the United States*.

6. Stephen Dinan and Joseph Curl, "Bush Vows to Build Fence," *Washington Times*, October 12, 2006, www.washingtontimes.com/national/20061012-124422-1595r.htm.

7. See Blas Nuñez-Neto, "Border Security: Key Agencies and Their Missions," *CRS Report for Congress*, January 26, 2006. Julie L. Meyers was one of the many ideologues. Appointed by President Bush in 2005 as chief of Immigration and Customs Enforcement (ICE), Meyers was in charge of more than a large number of federal law enforcers. Before this appointment, the largest number of employees she had supervised was 170 while she was assistant secretary of commerce for export enforcement. Meyers had no previous law enforcement experience with the U.S. Border Patrol or U.S. Customs when she was appointed. One example of her questionable leadership occurred at an ICE Halloween party in 2007. Serving as judge of a costume contest, Meyers and two other managers awarded "most original" honors to an employee dressed in dark makeup, dreadlocks, and prison stripes. Other employees complained that the costume was racially insensitive. Secretary Chertoff reported that an inquiry was under way to determine if sanctions were necessary. See Suzanne Gamboa, "Employee on Leave over Costume," *New York Times*, November 7, 2007, http://query.nytimes.com/gst/fullpage.html ?res=9A02E5DA1E3DF934A35752C1A9619C8B63.

8. While I have been influenced by the ideas and concepts of Josiah McC. Heyman, Jason Ackleson, Rey Koslowski, Peter Andreas, Timothy Duncan, and David Spinner, among others, this present analysis is premised upon my own reading of existing federal documents, interviews with relevant politicians, and firsthand observation of the political process. See, for example, Josiah McC. Heyman and Jason Ackleson, "U.S. Border Security after September 11," in *Border Security in the Al-Qaeda Era*, ed. John A. Winterdyk and Kelly W. Sundberg, 37–74, and Josiah McC. Heyman, *Finding a Moral Heart for U.S. Immigration Policy*. See also Peter Andreas, *Border Games: Policing the U.S.-Mexico Divide*; Peter Andreas, *A Tale of Two Borders: The U.S.-Canada and U.S.-Mexico Lines after 9-11*, CCIC Working Paper 77; Jason Ackleson, "Fencing in Failure: Effective Border Control is Not Achieved by Building More Fences," *Immigration Policy in Focus* 4, no. 2 (April 2005); and Jason Ackleson, "Securing Through Technology? 'Smart Borders' after September 11th," *Knowledge, Technology, and Policy* 16, no. 1 (Spring 2003): 56–74. David Spener's *Clandestine Crossings*, on human trafficking, is also an excellent source.

9. I would like specifically to attribute the concept of a "perfect" border fence to Josiah McC. Heyman, chairman of the Department of Anthropology and Sociology, the University of Texas at El Paso.

10. Heyman and Ackleson's concepts of political "framing" and "focusing event," in their "U.S. Border Security after September 11," have been particularly helpful here.

11. Obviously, prima facie evidence is inconclusive, and this topic needs further research.

12. The specifications of Boeing's Project 28, when found, are ambiguous and open to different interpretations.

13. Local, state, and federal legislation was sometimes selectively enforced depending on the leanings of politicians and their constituents. The actions, for example,

of Sheriff Arpaio in Phoenix are noteworthy in this regard (Ryan Gabrielson and Paul Giblin, "Reasonable Doubt," five-part series, *East Valley Tribune* [Arizona], July 9–13, 2008). While this is a very important topic, it is not the central focus of my research.

14. A handful of articles rely on the facts of this case. For example, see Pauline Arrillaga, "What Really Happened in Border Shooting," *Washington Post*, February 16, 2007, www.washingtonpost.com/wp-dyn/content/article/2007/02/16/AR2007021601290.html.

15. See the CNN program host Lou Dobbs's discussion of Border Patrol agents who were convicted of shooting a "Mexican drug dealer" in the transcript from the broadcast dated January 9, 2007.

16. The National Border Patrol Council staunchly defended the two agents. See "National Border Patrol Council Rebuttal to the Misrepresentations of the U.S. Attorney's Office of the Western District of Texas Concerning the Prosecution of Border Patrol Agents Jose Alonso Compean and Ignacio Ramos," National Border Patrol Council of the American Federation of Government Employees, n.d., 1–9.

17. In contrast, former Border Patrol agent Michael Cutler, who has testified to Congress on numerous occasions, believes that Compean and Rosas made a "decision that was absolutely wrong, but that it does not constitute a crime, let alone a crime that will require them to spend more than a decade each behind bars" (Michael Cutler to the public, "My Commentary on the Imprisonment of the Border Patrol Agents," electronic communication, January 23, 2007).

18. Cutler, "My Commentary," 1.

19. Brad Heath, "Border Agent Killed," *USA Today*, July 27, 2009, 3A. The previous shooting deaths of agents Ricardo Salinas and Susan Rodriguez were in Cameron County, Texas, in 1998. T. J. Bonner, in the same article, says that about fifty agents were shot at in 2008. One, Luis Aguilar, died when he was run down by a suspected drug smuggler's vehicle.

20. Both Compean and Ramos had served approximately two and one-half years of their sentences. However, President Bush also believed, according to a White House source, that their sentences were "excessive, especially given the harsh conditions in which they have to serve their sentences." See Eric Lichtblau, "Bush Commutes 2 Border Agents' Sentences," *New York Times*, January 19, 2009, www.nytimes.com/2009/01/20/washington/20sentence.html.

21. The DHS was created under the Homeland Security Act of 2002.

22. U.S. Government Accountability Office, "Border Security: Key Unresolved Issues Justify Reevaluation of Border Surveillance Technology Program," Report GAO-06-295, Washington, D.C., February 2006.

23. To some degree this ignorance was a result of the events of 9/11. The major media and politicians who were familiar with ISIS demonstrated a general unwillingness to scrutinize seriously this new federal bureaucracy. Josiah McC. Heyman studied U.S. Customs until they made it very difficult for him to do so.

24. U.S. Customs and Border Protection, "CBP reaches 18,000 Border Patrol Agent Hiring Commitment—Weeks Early," news release, December 17, 2008.

25. This is not to say that U.S. Customs was without severe problems, only that it was the more functional of the two agencies. This conclusion is based upon interviews with several informants at different managerial levels. New CBP academy graduates in the BP and Customs were incompatible with the "old-timers" in both agencies.

26. One detailed case of this hostile work environment for female agents will be discussed in detail in the following chapter.

27. This was certainly not just true of the political appointees in the CBP, but in a wide range of federal bureaucracies.

28. Government Accountability Office, "Border Security," 22.

29. Ibid., 1.

30. Ibid. Emphasis added.

31. Ibid., 2.

32. Ibid.

33. Ibid.

34. Steven J. Pecinovsky, Director, Departmental GAO/OIG Liaison Office, Department of Homeland Security, to Mr. Randolph C. Hite, Director, Information Technology Architecture and Systems Issues, n.d., 1, cited in Government Accountability Office, "Border Security," 28.

35. Based upon interviews with informants at different levels within CBP.

36. Government Accountability Office, "Border Security," 1.

37. Ibid., 2.

38. Ibid., 2, 4. Emphasis added.

39. Heyman and Ackleson, "U.S. Border Security after September 11," 33.

40. U.S. Customs and Border Protection, "Public Affairs Guidance: SBInet Industry," news release, Office of Public Affairs, March 3, 2006, 1.

41. Ibid., 1–2.

42. Alice Lipowicz, "DHS bulks up Secure Border Initiative Procurement Oversight," *Washington Technology*, March 8, 2006, http://washingtontechnology.com/articles/2006/03/03/dhs-bulks-up-secure-border-initiative-procurement-oversight.aspx?sc_lang=en.

43. U.S. Government Accountability Office, "Secure Border Initiative Fence Construction Costs," Report to Congressional Committees, GAO-09-244R. Washington, D.C., January 29, 2008, 7, www.gao.gov/new.items/d09244r.pdf. A more detailed description of the different kinds of fences is found in chapter 3, "Anzalduas."

44. Pecinovksy to Hite, n.d. The private sector, however, knew about SBInet long before the national media and the general public. Emphasis added.

45. Ibid., 2. Emphasis added.

46. Ibid.

47. Rob Thormeyer and Alice Lipowicz, "DHS Awards Boeing SBI-Net Contract," *Government Computer News*, September 20, 2006, http://gcn.com/articles/2006/09/20/dhs-awards-boeing-sbinet-contract.aspx.

48. Griff Witte, "Boeing Wins Border Contract," *Raleigh News and Observer*, September 20, 2006, 12A.

49. U.S. Department of Homeland Security, Office of the Inspector General, *Department of Homeland Security's Procurement and Program Management Operations*, OIG-05-53, September 2005, 4, 6, 9, 8–10, www.dhs.gov/xoig/assets/mgmtrpts/OIG_05-53_Sep05.pdf. See in particular the chart on the report's page 21 entitled "Acquisition Staffing and Workload."

50. Chris Strohm, "Appropriators Skeptical of Promised Secure Border Initiative," *Government Executive*, April 7, 2006, www.govexec.com/dailyfed/0406/040706cdam1.htm.

51. Stephen Losey, "Hearing Reveals Significant Flows in SBInet Project," *Federal Times*, November 16, 2006.

52. U.S. Customs and Border Protection, "DHS Engages Private Sector on Border Technology: Industry Day, the First Step Toward a Strategic SBI Partnership," news release, January 26, 2006, www.cbp.gov/xp/cgov/newsroom/news_releases/archives/2006_news_releases/012006/01262006.xml. Photographs of this same event are at www.cbp.gov/xp/cgov/newsroom/multimedia/photo_gallery/archives/2006_newsphotos/industry_2.xml.

53. These names are from an Industry Day list provided by an informant. A list was made public.

54. Witte, "Boeing Wins Border Contract"; Alice Lipowicz, "3 Firms Will Compete to Build New Border Network," *Washington Post*, February 27, 2006, D3.

55. Industry lobbyists had informed their respective corporations of the upcoming RSP by DHS at least six months or more before the official announcement. Similarly, the winner was leaked weeks before the official announcement. Concerning the crash of the drone, see Spencer S. Hsu and Griff Witte, "Plenty of Holes Seen in a Virtual Fence," *Washington Post*, September 24, 2006, A3.

56. Based on the descriptions from Griff Witte, "Firms Vie to Provide the Future of Border Security," *Washington Post*, September 18, 2006, A1.

57. See chapter 1, "A Simple Solution."

58. In August 2009 President Calderon replaced fourteen hundred Mexican customs agents.

59. Wilson P. Dizard III, "DHS Puts Border Security on Fast Track," *Government Computer News*, February 3, 2006, http://gcn.com/Articles/2006/02/03/DHS-puts-border-security-on-fast-track.aspx.

60. Witte, "Firms Vie to Provide the Future of Border Security."

61. U.S. Department of Homeland Security, "DHS Announces SBInet Contract Award to Boeing," news release, September 21. 2006. Emphasis added.

62. Ibid., 1.

63. Stephen Losey, "New Border Protection System to Start Operation within Days," *Federal Times*, June 8, 2007.

64. The list of Boeing's problems is extensive, but will not be reviewed here. For an example, see Dave Carpenter, "Boeing, U.S. Reach Tentative Agreement," Associated Press, July 4, 2004.

65. Leslie Wayne, "Northrop, Airbus Ally Get Tanker Contract," *Memphis Commercial Appeal*, March 1, 2008, A6. Boeing, Inc., also had major problems with its 787 Dreamliner jet, which cost it billions. See, for example, Christopher Drew, "Boeing Cites Progress on Dreamliner, but No Test Flight Is Scheduled," *New York Times*, July 23, 2009, B3.

66. See a complete discussion of these problems in chapter 5, "ISIS."

67. L-3 Communications, "L-3 Announces Fourth Quarter 2008 Results," news release, January 29, 2009, www.l-3com.com/investor-relations/documents/earnings-presentations/Q4_08_EarningsFinal%201%2029%2009.pdf.

68. Losey, "New Border Protection System to Start Operation within Days."

69. Ibid., 1.

70. U.S. Customs and Border Patrol, "SBInet Completes Test of First Mobile Sensor Tower," news release, April 5, 2007, www.govtech.com/dc/104832.

71. Ibid.

72. Losey, "New Border Protection System to Start Operation within Days," 1.

73. Ibid.

74. Ibid.

75. These same concerns were raised by Spencer S. Hsu and Griff Witte in "Plenty of Holes Seen in a Virtual Fence," *Washington Post*, September 24, 2006.

76. See chapter 5, "ISIS."

77. Government Accountability Office, "Secure Border Initiative: DHS Needs to Address Significant Risks in Delivering Key Technology Investment," Testimony before the House Committee on Homeland Security, GAO-08-1148T, Washington, D.C., September 10, 2008, www.gao.gov/new.items/d081148t.pdf.

78. Ibid., 1. Emphasis added.

79. Ibid. Emphasis added.

80. See Deborah Bosick, "SBInet Project 28," news release, Boeing, Inc., March 28, 2008.

81. Government Accountability Office, "Secure Border Initiative: DHS," 1. Emphasis added.

82. Government Accountability Office, "Secure Border Initiative: Observations on Deployment Challenges," Testimony before the Committee on Homeland Security, House of Representatives, GAO 08-1141T, Washington, D.C., September 10, 2008.

83. Alice Lipowicz, "DHS, Boeing Move Closer to SBInet Rollout," *Washington Technology*, February 6, 2009, http://washingtontechnology.com/articles/2009/02/06/sbinet-update.aspx?sc_lang=en.

84. Government Accountability Office, "Secure Border Initiative Fence Construction Costs," Report to Congressional Committees, GAO-09-244R, Washington, D.C., January 29, 2008, 2, www.gao.gov/new.items/d09244r.pdf.

85. Ibid., 1. The GAO report cites one fence project as an exception to this claim.

86. See Elise Castelli, "For CBP, Challenge Is Secure Border Initiative," *Federal Times*, March 11, 2009, www.federaltimes.com/article/20090311/IT03/903110303/-1/RSS.

87. Ibid., 1.

88. Ibid.

89. Ibid.

90. Ibid.

91. From an interview with Texas CBP agents.

92. This section relies, except where cited, on the testimony of Timothy Peters, CBP's Interim Chief David Aguilar, DHS's Executive Director of SBInet Mark Borkowski, and Richard M. Stana before the U.S. House Committee on Homeland Security, Subcommittee on Border, Maritime, and Global Counterterrorism, September 17, 2009, Washington, D.C. A transcript is not at this time available to the public.

93. Peters also asserted that Boeing was losing money on this contract. In addition he asserted that since Boeing, Inc., now had a test site up and running in New Mexico, further additional problems could be tested and resolved. It is difficult to believe that Boeing, Inc., one of the largest corporations of its kind in the United States, did not figure into its contract costs of the site and operation of a test site. If it did not, then it is a further condemnation of Boeing's planning for Project 28.

94. Alice Lipowicz, "Building Work Starts on SBI-net."

Chapter 8

1. Characteristics about Agent Nora Muñoz have been changed to protect her privacy and anonymity. The labor force data on the Border Patrol in this chapter, unless otherwise noted, are derived directly from the U.S. Government Accountability Office, "Report to Subcommittee on Management, Investigations, and Oversight, House Homeland Security Committee," Washington, D.C., February 14, 2007.

2. The Border Patrol does not make public the exact percentage of its managers by gender. There are always exceptions, of course. In South Texas a long line of male sector chiefs was interrupted by the selection of a female sector chief shortly after 2001, but she served only a few years before retiring. She was replaced by another male. Gender discrimination is not unusual among law enforcement agencies, including federal agencies. My point here, however, is that the Border Patrol constitutes a special case because massive gender discrimination is, for the most part, totally denied and ignored.

3. U.S. Government Accountability Office, "Report to Subcommittee on Management, Investigations, and Oversight," 5.

4. The number of agents in 2007 is from an interview with Douglas T. Mosier, Public Affairs Officer, El Paso Sector Headquarters, Customs and Border Protection, February 1, 2007. At that time I did not foresee, of course, the recession that followed in 2008 and its impact on the labor force. As was the case with all the branches of the American military, the Border Patrol was able to meet its quotas as unemployment rose, making government service all the more attractive.

5. From Border Patrol statistics cited in Mimi Hall, "Border Agents Increasingly Targeted," *USA Today*, February 27, 2008. See also "Man Arrested in Agent's Death," *Greenville Daily Reflector*, January 24, 2008; Andres R. Martinez, "U.S. Authorities Fired On by Border Bandits," *McAllen Monitor*, July 13, 2006; and Zack Quantance, "Coyote Rams Truck into Border Patrol Agents' Cruiser," *McAllen Monitor*, October 16, 2007.

6. Most Arizona Hispanics do not refer to themselves as Mexican Americans.

7. No statistics are made public by the Border Patrol regarding divorce rates of their agents. My observations are based upon interviews with one station of three hundred agents and with agents at other sectors along the Mexican border.

8. One exception is religious institutions, which can provide significant support to individuals new to the community.

9. One of the perks of being a Border Patrol supervisor is that you avoid the heat, the other elements, the cuts, the falls, and the high-risk apprehension strategies. In their place supervisors are awarded a desk, hot station coffee, and relative power over their subordinates; they also get higher salaries. Most supes seldom venture outside the confines of the station, instead preferring to communicate over the radio to agents or, if privacy is required, on cell phones.

10. During my study of the Border Patrol, shift supervisors at muster announced on three different occasions they found code books in the hands of those arrested. Individual agents interviewed reported they frequently found maps on illegal crossers that pinpointed buried border sensors. It was commonly believed some retired agents or disgruntled active agents sold copies of the code books to criminals.

11. The National Border Patrol Council is part of the American Federation of Government Employees.

12. Sector chiefs in the past have had the latitude to make wide-ranging policy changes within their sector. One example is that of Silvestre Reyes. Under DHS they are more tightly controlled, but they still retain some latitude. When these same sector chiefs make a decision that might expose them to legal or public scrutiny, they frequently hide behind the agency by suggesting it is not their decision, but the decision of the "higher ups." This bureaucratic strategy of the Border Patrol is frequently used to buttress inappropriate organization policies and/or decisions at the sector and station level. It is, however, the sector chief who always remains directly responsible.

13. *Complainant [Border Patrol Agent] v. Defendant [Border Patrol Supervisor] et al. Bench Decision of Federal District Judge*, 15. Full identity of this EEOC decision in author's note at SWC/SCL-TTU.

14. Ibid.

15. Ibid.

16. The names of these particular employees of the Border Patrol have been changed.

17. Vehicular accidents while patrolling the line are common; some are serious, and some each year are fatal. Mechanical failures in isolated areas are common and

time consuming and temporarily can leave a particular area open to illegal border crossers.

18. At the time of this writing Agent Nora Muñoz's OIA case still remained open.
19. Exact percentages of the genders of agents at the Border Patrol station level are not public information.

Chapter 9

1. There are exceptions all along the border, including Nogales in Arizona. Nogales will be discussed in detail in a subsequent chapter.
2. See chapter 4, "Olga Rivera Garcia's Fence and Omar Sanchez's Fence."
3. From 1985 through 1997 I worked as a legal consultant to Valley legal firms and national firms based in Dallas and Houston.
4. This sense of political pressure is much less strong in Arizona and California than it is in Texas and New Mexico. But the point remains that local residents, regardless of their political views, have a major impact on the success or failure of the border fence. This point is emphasized in following chapters.
5. There were also citizens who welcomed the new border fence to Cameron County. While outspoken, they were a minority. Public opinion also varied by communities within Cameron County. For example, more residents of Harlingen, long dominated by Anglo politicians and interests, were in favor of the border fence than against it. Directly to the south of Harlingen the community of San Benito, long run by Hispanics and with a port of entry, was just as strongly against the fence.
6. Government Accountability Office, "Secure Border Initiative Fence Construction Costs," Report to Congressional Committees, GAO-09-244R, Washington, D.C., January 29, 2008, 1, www.gao.gov/new.items/d09244r.pdf.
7. Ibid., 2.
8. *Handbook of Texas Online*, s.v. "Mexican American Legal Defense and Educational Fund," www.tshaonline.org/handbook/online/articles/MM/jom1.html.
9. Research interviewing is a learned skill, which I learned while earning my master's degree in sociology from Indiana University and my doctorate in sociology from Washington University. Over the last thirty-five years, for the purposes of my research, I have personally interviewed and supervised interviews and surveys of thousands of individuals, including, among others, commercial fishermen, farm workers, collegiate wrestlers, sex offenders, ranchers and farmers, politicians, public school administrators and teachers, ship builders, juvenile offenders and their families, the American military, local and federal law enforcement officers, social workers, business leaders, religious leaders, public health workers, community activists, lawyers, residents of Mexico and France, and the citizens of the states of Arizona, Oklahoma, and Texas.
10. Antonio Zavaleta and Alberto Salinas, Jr., *Curandero Conversations: El Niño Fidencio, Shamanism, and Healing Traditions of the Borderlands*; Robert T. Trotter and Juan Antonio Chavira, *Curanderismo: Mexican-American Folk Healing*.

11. There is a clear need for more research into the exact nature of these programs, including fiscal oversight and program evaluation by researchers outside the influence of the institutions they study. One baseline question is whether these law enforcement agencies are directly using the federal money to supplement immigration laws. Another is whether these same monies are being used elsewhere in their policing budgets.

12. See Robert Lee Maril, *Texas Shrimpers: Community, Capitalism, and the Sea*; Robert Lee Maril, "The Impact of Raising the Truck Insurance of Migrant Farm Workers," public testimony before the Texas State Insurance Board, Austin, Texas, 1993; Robert Lee Maril, "An Analysis of Auto Insurance on Low Income Families," public testimony before the U.S. Senate Commerce and Banking Committee, Washington, D.C., September 9, 1999; Robert Lee Maril, "The Impact of Mandatory Auto Insurance upon the Residents of Maricopa County, Arizona," unpublished report for the National Association of Independent Insurers, Chicago, 1996; and Robert Lee Maril, "Contracts for Deeds," unpublished report, Texas Rio Grande Legal Aid, Weslaco, Texas, 1995.

13. See John M. Dement et al., "Surveillance of Construction Workers in North Carolina, Ohio, and Missouri." See also "Construction Deaths Rising in Wake County: Summary of Final Report to CPWR," Division of Occupational and Environmental Medicine, Duke University Medical Center, Durham, N.C., January 2001.

14. Sergio Chapa, "Deadly Blast Rips Nuevo Progreso," *Valley Morning Star*, Sunday, April 11, 2004.

15. See Robert Lee Maril, *Patrolling Chaos*.

16. See Jon Garrido, "Border Proves No Obstacle for Mexican Cartels," Latin America News, Jon Garrido News Network, February 23, 2009, www.lamnews.com/border _proves_no_obstacle_for_mexican_cartels.htm.

17. In certain places, pieces of brand new levee are also being constructed as a part of the wall.

18. Information on the detention of children is from interviews with a paralegal who daily meets his clients inside the detention centers. These interviews suggest unstudied and undocumented abuses of detainees. Much research needs to be done on this topic.

Chapter 10

1. Because of the catastrophic failure of the New Orleans levees after Hurricane Katrina, FEMA reevaluated all the nation's levees. Levees were deemed unacceptable if they were too low in height, improperly constructed, and did not meet other contemporary standards.

2. See Daniel Sutter, "Rio Grande Levee Failures and Flooding: The Economic Impact on Hidalgo," Center for Border Economic Studies, University of Texas–Pan American, March 2008.

3. See the website of the International Boundary and Water Commission at www .ibwc.gov.

4. Biographic details are based upon information provided at www.gsa.gov/Portal/gsa/ep/contentView.do?contentId=12904&contentType=GSA_BASIC.

5. Judge Salinas is not without his critics. See, for example, "Judge J. D. Salinas Buys into Border Wall," May 12, 2008, at http://notexasborderwall.blogspot.com/2008/05/judge-jd-salinas-buys-into-border-wall.html.

6. See, for example, Texas Border Coalition, "A Resolution Demanding Smart and Effective Security on the Texas-Mexico Border," October 1, 2007, www.texasbordercoalition.org/Texas_Border_Coalition/Resources_files/Resolution%20Demanding%20Smart%20and%20Effective%20Security%20on%20the%20Texas-Mexico%20Border.pdf. See also, McAllen, Texas, "Resolution Authorizing and Approving the Construction and Rehabilitation of Flood Control Levees with Respect to Alternative Approaches for Security the United States–Mexico Border," December 18, 2007, and Cari Lambrecht, "Levee Project Fact Sheet," Hidalgo County Commissioners' Court, Hidalgo County, Texas, n.d.

7. In fact, it is Judge Salinas who asks for and gets the legal interpretation of the Water Resources Development Act of 1996 allowing for the levee construction in Hidalgo County. See International Boundary and Water Commission, "Memorandum for Major Subordinate Commands and District Commands," December 7, 1997, for the legal basis justifying levee construction. Also, Beto Cardenas and Rene Gonzalez, in a personal communication, outlined the favorable legal interpretation. See "Innovative and Alternative: HCDD No. 1 DHS Levee-barrier Project," House Committee on Transportation and Infrastructure, January 26, 2009. See also, Dannenbaum Engineering Company, "Presentation of the Rio Grande River Lower Valley Levee Improvement Project within Western Hidalgo County," McAllen, Texas, n.d.

8. The second most important Valley dam is at Mercedes.

9. Residents of Eagle Pass were inundated by heavy rains prior to Hurricane Dolly. Flooding from the Rio Grande made it impossible for the Border Patrol to police the border area for several weeks.

10. The list of concerns was among the documents handed to me by Judge Salinas and his staff. It was marked only as "Concerns Submitted by Ann Carsons, 3/13/08." Concerning protests, see, for example, Sean Gaffney, "Protestors Take to Streets against Border Wall," *McAllen Monitor*, July 12, 2008, www.themonitor.com/news/wall-14507-county-border.html, and Christopher Sherman, "Town Survives Despite New Border Barrier," *McAllen Monitor*, February 26, 2009.

11. See "Concerns Submitted by Ann Carsons, 3/13/08."

12. Ibid.

13. Ibid.

14. The video, to the best of my knowledge, has not been completed.

15. Patient and an earnest listener, Judge J. D. Salinas has obvious political talents that may well be his ticket to much higher elected office.

16. See Robert Lee Maril, *Texas Shrimpers: Community, Capitalism, and the Sea*, and Robert Lee Maril, *The Bay Shrimpers of Texas: Rural Workers in a Global Economy*.

17. See John Woods, "Happenings in Precinct Two." Commissioner Wood is also a member of the Good Neighbor Environmental Board to the President and the Congress of the United States. See Good Neighbor Environmental Board to the President and Congress of the United States, "Natural Disasters and the Environment along the U.S.-Mexico Border."

18. When I lived in Brownsville in the 1970s and 1980s, it was a much smaller community. I have known Mayor Pat Ahumada for twenty years.

19. "Brownsville Mayor Declares Federal Government is Doing Irreparable Damage to Texas Border Region with Proposed Fence," Latina Lista, March 7, 2009, www .latinalista.net/palabrafinal/2008/01/brownsville_mayor_declares_federal_gover .html.

20. See Anonymous, "City Commissioner Accused of Abusing Time Sheets," KRGV, Harlingen, Texas, November 26, 2006, www.krgv.com/content/news/investigations/ story/City-Commissioner-Accused-of-Abusing-Time-Sheets/ZJjvU_zqI 0K25U95nhNGeA.cspx. While I lived in Brownsville, local accusations and reports of malfeasance among elected officials were rampant, always peaking just before elections.

21. I spent several night shifts alongside Border Patrol agents surveilling the Brewster property.

22. Maria Jimenez, "Humanitarian Crisis: Migrant Deaths at the U.S.-Mexico Border," report, ACLU of San Diego and Imperial Counties and Mexico's National Commission of Human Rights, San Diego, California, October 1, 2008, 15, www.aclu.org/ files/pdfs/immigrants/humanitariancrisisreport.pdf. These data are the most recent available. The statistics, as noted by Jimenez, are most likely undercounts of the actual number who die.

23. Ibid., 24.

24. Ibid.

25. Anonymous editorial, "Water in the Desert," *New York Times*, August 16, 2009, WK7. See also "No More Deaths Volunteers to Be Arraigned for Littering," *Catholic Sun* (Phoenix, Arizona), February 6, 2009, 1.

26. Brad Heath, "Border Agent Killed: U.S., Mexico Still Looking for Suspects," *USA Today*, July 27, 2009, 3A.

27. The details of this murder are to be found in Robert Lee Maril, *Patrolling Chaos*.

28. Heath, "Border Agent Killed."

Chapter 11

1. I come from a military family. I have shared my research on racism and gender discrimination with the military.

2. "About USNORTHCOM," www.northcom.mil/About/history_education/vision.html.

3. This conference is facilitated by Battelle, Inc., a corporation that carries on its letterhead the motto "The Business of Innovation."

4. See Abelardo Rodriguez Sumano, *En las entrañas de Goliat: La política estadounidense y su relación con México*.

5. The title of the conference was "U.S. Immigration Policy: A Public Forum." See news release, "League of Women Voters Greenville."

6. I contacted Mr. Gheen after this forum and requested an interview with him, but he did not respond. I again attempted to interview him in 2009, but again he did not reply to my request. See the website for his Americans for Legal Immigration PAC at www.alipac.us/.

7. See Steven M. Thomas, "The Minuteman Reconsidered," February 10, 2009, www.minutemanproject.com/immigration-topics/reconsidered.asp. See also Jim Gilchrist and Jerome R. Corsi, with foreword by Congressman Tom Tancredo, *Minutemen: The Battle to Secure America's Borders.*

8. I am indebted to Bob Edwards for his insights into American political movements; these insights inform this discussion.

9. Thomas, "Minutemen Reconsidered."

10. Pew Research Center for the People and the Press, "Press Accuracy Rating Hits Two Decade Low: Public Evaluations of the News Media, 1985–2009," September 13, 2009, http://people-press.org/report/543/.

11. Pew Research Center for the People and the Press, "America's Immigration Quandary: No Consensus on Immigration Problems or Proposed Fixes," March 30, 2006, http://people-press.org/report/274/americas-immigration-quandary.

12. Ibid., 3.

13. "G4S Wackenhut Custom Protection Officer," news release, Wackenhut Corporation.

14. To the west of Sasabe there are no border roads for at least a hundred miles.

15. See Timothy J. Dunn, *The Militarization of the U.S.–Mexico Border, 1978–1992.*

Chapter 12

1. I would hope other researchers would bring their expertise to the understudied and, in some cases, never studied topics discussed in these pages. This lack of interest, given the noted exceptions, is especially disheartening because several major research institutions are located within a modest car ride of the border. I hope this study will arouse the attention and interest of the scholarly community.

2. There are, in addition, any number of concerns raised by those interviewed and observed, many substantiated, others not, which I hope will serve as the basis for study by other researchers.

3. See, for example, David Johnston and Eric Schmitt, "Smaller-Scale Terrorism Plots Pose New and Worrisome Threats, Officials Say," *New York Times*, October 31, 2009, www.nytimes.com/2009/11/01/us/01terror.html.

Epilogue

1. See Karla Zabludovsky, "Police Find 49 Bodies by a Highway in Mexico," *New York Times,* May 13, 2012, www.nytimes.com/2012/05/14/world/americas/police-find-49-bodies-by-a-highway-in-mexico.html; and Randal C. Archibold, "Arson Fire

Kills 52 in a Casino in Mexico," *New York Times*, August 25, 2011, www.nytimes. com/2011/08/26/world/americas/26mexico.html.

2. Robert Lee Maril, "The Border Fear Index: How to Measure Border Security," *Homeland Security News Wire*, December 16, 2011, www.homelandsecuritynewswire. com/dr20111216-the-border-fear-index-how-to-measure-border-security.

3. "Transcript of Obama's Immigration Speech," *Wall Street Journal*, July 1, 2010, http:// blogs.wsj.com/washwire/2010/07/01/transcript-of-obamas-immigration-speech.

4. Ibid.

5. "Secretary Napolitano Announces Deferred Action Process for Young People Who Are Low Enforcement Priorities," Office of the Press Secretary, Department of Homeland Security, June 15, 2012, www.dhs.gov/ynews/releases/20120612 napolitano announces deferred action-process for young people.shtm.

6. Randal C. Archibald, "Pre-emption, Not Profiling, in Challenge to Arizona," *New York Times*, July 8, 2010, A15. Also, Monica Davey, "Nebraska City Torn as Immigration Vote Nears," *New York Times*, June 18, 2010, A1; and Marc Lacey, "Ilegales Siguen Arriesgándose," *El Sentinel*, May 21, 2010, 1–17.

7. "Fact Sheet Southwest Border Next Steps: Readout of Secretary Napolitano's Remarks on Border Security and Law Enforcement," Office of the Press Secretary, Washington, D.C., June 23, 2010, www.dhs.gov/ynews/releases/ pr_1277310093825.shtm.

8. Ibid.

9. Spencer S. Hsu, "Work to Cease on 'Virtual Fence' along U.S.-Mexico Border," *Washington Post*, March 16, 2010, www.washingtonpost.com/wp-dyn/content/article/2010/03/16/AR2010031603573.html.

10. "DHS' Progress in 2011: Southwest Border, Highlighting Our Progress in 2011," Department of Homeland Security, December 21, 2011, www.dhs.gov/ xabout/2011-dhs-accomplishments-southwest-border.shtm; and "Secretary Napolitano Highlights DHS' Progress in 2011," Department of Homeland Security Press Release, January 23, 2012, www.dhs.gov/ynews/releases/20111222-dhs-progress-2011.shtm.

11. Jeffrey Passel, D'Vera Cohn, and Ana Gonzalez-Barrera, "Net Migration from Mexico Falls to Zero--and Perhaps Less," Pew Hispanic Research Center, May 3, 2012, www.pewhispanic.org/author/jpassel.

12. Aarti Kohli, Peter L. Markowitz, and Lisa Chavez, "Secure Communities by the Numbers: An Analysis of Demographics and Due Process," Chief Justice Earl Warren Institute on Law and Society, October 2011, Research Report, Berkeley Law Center for Research and Administration, Berkeley, CA., www.law.berkeley.edu/ files/Secure_Communities_by_the_Numbers.pdf.

13. Spencer S. Hsu, "Work to Cease on 'Virtual Fence' along U.S.-Mexico Border," Washington Post, March 16, 2010, www.washingtonpost.com/wp-dyn/content/ article/2010/03/16/AR2010031603573.html.

14. Julia Preston, "Homeland Security Cancels 'Virtual Fence' after $1 billion is spent," New York Times, January 14, 2011, www.nytimes.com/2011/01/15/us/ politics/15fence.html?_r=1&ref=borderfenceusmexico.

15. Martin Matishake, "Homeland Security Cancels Troubled Radiation Detector Effort," *Global Security Newswire*, July 26, 2011, www.govexec.com/dailyfed/0711/072611-radiation-detector.htm; and David E. Sanger, "Nuclear-Detection Effort Is Halted as Ineffective," New York Times, July 29, 2011, www.nytimes.com/2011/07/30/us/30nuke.html.

16. Warren Stern, "The Last Line of Defense: Federal, State, and Local Efforts to Prevent Nuclear and Radiological Terrorism within the United States," Testimony Before the House Committee on Homeland Security, Subcommittee on Cyber security, Infrastructure Protection, and Security Technologies, July 26, 2011, www.dhs.gov/ynews/testimony/20110726-stern-last-line-of-defense.shtm.

17. Aliya Sternstein, "DHS vows to cancel border project if technologies seem high risk," *Nextgov*, February 21, 2012, www.nextgov.com/defense/2012/02/dhs-vows-to-cancel-border-project-if-technologies-seem-high-risk/50675.

18. Mickey Carter, "CBP Missing Equipment, Plans to Support Predator UAV Flights, IG Warms," *Homeland Security Today*, June 12, 2012, www.hstoday.us/focused-topics/border-security/single-article-page/cbp-lacks-equipment-plans-to-support-predator-uav-flights-ig-warns.html.

19. Robert Lee Maril, "Reliable Measurement, Program Evaluation, and Institutional Memory: The Border Patrol's New National Strategy," *Homeland Security News Wire*, May 24, 2012, www.homelandsecuritynewswire.com/dr20120524-reliable-measurement-program-evaluation-and-institutional-memory-the-border-patrol-s-new-national-strategy. See also Testimony of Michael J. Fisher before the House Committee on Homeland Security Subcommittee on border and Maritime Security, May 8, 2012, Washington, D.C., www.cbp.gov/xp/cgov/newsroom/congressional_test.

Bibliography

Ackleson, Jason. "Fencing in Failure: Effective Border Control Is Not Achieved by Building More Fences." *Immigration Policy in Focus* 4, no. 2 (April 2005). www.immigrationpolicy.org/sites/default/files/docs/Fencing%20in%20Failure.pdf.

———. "Securing Through Technology? 'Smart Borders' after September 11th." *Knowledge, Technology, and Policy* 16, no. 1 (Spring 2003): 56–74.

Adler, Rudy, et al. *Border Film Project: Photos by Migrants and Minutemen on the U.S.-Mexico Border.* New York: Harry N. Abrams, 2007.

Alba, Richard, and Victor Nee. *Remaking the American Mainstream.* Cambridge: Harvard University Press, 2005.

Alsup, Janet., ed. *Young Adult Literature and Adolescent Identity across Cultures and Classrooms: Contents for the Literary Lives of Teens.* New York: Routledge, 2010.

Anders, Evan. *Boss Rule in South Texas.* Austin: University of Texas Press, 1986.

Anderson, Jeffrey. "Napolitano Shifts Policy on Border Fence." *Washington Times*, March 17, 2010. www

.washingtontimes.com/news/2010/mar/17/napolitano-shifts-policy-on-mexico -border-fence.

Andreas, Peter. *Border Games: Policing the U.S.-Mexico Divide.* Ithaca, N.Y.: Cornell University Press, 2000.

———. *A Tale of Two Borders: The U.S.-Canada and U.S.-Mexico Lines after 9-11.* CCIC Working Paper 77. San Diego: The Center for Comparative Immigration Studies, University of California, San Diego, 2003.

Archibold, Randal C. "Government Issues Waiver for Fencing along Border." *New York Times*, April 2, 2008. www.nytimes.com/2008/04/02/us/02fence.html?_r=1 &scp=1&sq=Government%20Issues%20Waive%20for%20Fencing%20along%20 Border&st=cse.

———. "Pre-emption, Not Profiling, in Challenge to Arizona." *New York Times*, July 8, 2010, A15.

Arrillaga, Pauline. "What Really Happened in Border Shooting." *Washington Post*, February 16, 2007. www.washingtonpost.com/wp-dyn/content/article/2007/02/ 16/AR2007021601290.html.

Associated Press. "Lawmakers Bring Immigration Hearings to U.S.-Mexico Border." *USA Today*, July 7, 2006. www.usatoday.com/news/washington/2006-07-07 -immigration-hearings_x.htm.

———. "Texas: Did You See That Elephant Cross the Border?" *New York Times*, October 12, 2006. www.nytimes.com/2006/10/12/us/12brfs-002.html?_r=1.

Bacon, David. "Political Economy of Migration." *New Labor Forum*, June 2007, 1.

Benson, Matthew. "Guard Soldiers Back Off from Armed Men Out of Mexico." *Arizona Republic*, January 6, 2007, 2.

Bentham, Jeremy. *Political Thought.* New York: Barnes and Noble, 1973.

Bicknell, John. "Month of Field Hearings Has Not Yielded Immigration Payoff House GOP Wanted." *CQ Today*, August 18, 2006.

"Border Patrol Agents, 1975–2005." Transactional Records Access Clearinghouse, Syracuse University, 2006. http://trac.syr.edu/immigration/reports/143/include/ rep143table3.html.

Bosick, Deborah. "SBInet Project 28." News release, Boeing, Inc., March 28, 2008. Brister, Louis E. *John Charles Beales's Rio Grande Colony.* Austin: Texas State Historical Association, 2008.

Brown, Stephen E., Finn-Aage Esbensen, and Gilbert Geis. *Criminology: Explaining Crime and Context*, 4th ed. Cincinnati: Anderson, 2001.

"Brownsville Mayor Declares Federal Government is Doing Irreparable Damage to Texas Border Region with Proposed Fence," Latina Lista, March 7, 2009. www.latinalista .net/palabrafinal/2008/01/brownsville_mayor_declares_federal_gover.html.

Carpenter, Dave. "Boeing, U.S. Reach Tentative Agreement." Associated Press, July 4, 2004.

Castañeda, Carlos E. *Our Catholic Heritage in Texas, 1519-1936.* Austin, Texas: Von Boeckmann-Jones, 1936.

Castañeda, Jorge G. *Ex Mex: From Migrants to Immigrants.* New York: New Press, 2008.

Castelli, Elise. "For CBP, Challenge Is Secure Border Initiative." *Federal Times*, March 11, 2009. www.federaltimes.com/article/20090311/IT03/903110303/-1/RSS.

Chapa, Sergio. "Border Agents Who Drowned Last Month in Rio Grande Were Not Wearing Life Preservers." *Brownsville Herald*, October 28, 2004. www.sergiochapa .com/files/bp.pdf.

———. "Deadly Blast Rips Nuevo Progreso." *Valley Morning Star*, Sunday, April 11, 2004.

Conover, Ted. *Coyotes*. New York: Vintage, 1987.

———. *Newjack: Guarding Sing Sing*. New York: Vintage, 2001.

"Construction Deaths Rising in Wake County." WRAL, Raleigh, N.C., September 17, 1998. www.wral.com/news/local/story/129032/.

Conyers, John, Jr. Memorandum to House Committee on the Judiciary in "Is the Reid-Kennedy Bill a Repeat of the Failed Amnesty of 1986?" Full Committee Oversight Field Hearing, 109th Cong., 2nd sess., September 1, 2006.

Cornelius, Wayne A., and Jesse M. Lewis, eds. *Impacts of Border Enforcement on Mexican Migration: The View from Sending Communities*. Los Angeles: Center for Comparative Immigration Studies, 2007.

Cornelius, Wayne A., et al., eds. *Migration from the Mexican Mixteca: A Transnational Community in Oaxaca and California*. Los Angeles: Center for Comparative Immigration Studies, 2009.

Cutler, Michael W. "Testimony of Michael W. Cutler for the Hearing to Be Held on September 1, 2006, before the House Judiciary Committee," Dubuque, Iowa, September 1, 2006.

Dannenbaum Engineering. "Presentation of the Rio Grande River Lower Valley Levee Improvement Project within Western Hidalgo County." McAllen, Texas, n.d.

Dat', Shruti. "Immigration Service Patrols with Sensors and Video." *Government Computer News*, February 6, 2000. http://gcn.com/articles/2000/02/06/immigration-service-patrols-with-sensors-and-video.aspx?sc_lang=en.

Davey, Monica. "Nebraska City Torn as Immigration Vote Nears." *New York Times*, June 18, 2010, A1.

Dement, John M., et al. "Surveillance of Construction Workers in North Carolina, Ohio, and Missouri: Summary of Final Report to CPWR." Division of Occupational and Environmental Medicine, Duke University Medical Center, Durham, N.C., January 2001. www.elcosh.org/record/document/458/d000451.pdf.

Dinan, Stephen, and Joseph Curl. "Bush Vows to Build Fence." *Washington Times*, October 12, 2006. www.washingtontimes.com/national/20061012-124422-1595r.htm.

Dizard, Wilson P., III. "DHS Puts Border Security on Fast Track." *Government Computer News*, February 3, 2006. http://gcn.com/Articles/2006/02/03/DHS-puts-border-security-on-fast-track.aspx.

Drew, Christopher. "Boeing Cites Progress on Dreamliner, but No Test Flight Is Scheduled." *New York Times*, July 23, 2009.

Dunn, Timothy J. *The Militarization of the U.S.-Mexico Border, 1978–1992*. Austin, Texas: CMAS Books, 1996.

Egan, Timothy. *The Worst Hard Time: The Untold Story of Those Who Survived the Great American Dust Bowl*. New York: Mariner Books, 2006.

"Financial Impact of Illegal Immigration along Southern Border." C-Span broadcast of House Committee on the Judiciary, El Paso, Texas, August 17, 2006.

Fonte, John. "Let Us Not Repeat the Amnesty Mistake of 1986." Testimony before the House Judiciary Committee, Dubuque, Iowa, September 1, 2006. Hudson Institute. http://acc.hudson.org/index.cfm?fuseaction=publication_details&id=4182.

Frommer, Frederic J. "Air Marshals Put at Risk." *Greenville Daily Reflector*, May 21, 2006, A5.

Gaffney, Sean. "Protesters Take to Streets against Border Wall." *McAllen Monitor*, July 12, 2008. www.themonitor.com/news/wall-14507-county-border.html.

Gamboa, Suzanne. "Employee on Leave over Costume." *New York Times*, November 7, 2007. http://query.nytimes.com/gst/fullpage.html?res=9A02E5DA1E3DF934A35 752C1A9619C8B63.

Garrido, Jon. "Border Proves No Obstacle for Mexican Cartels." Latin America News, Jon Garrido News Network, February 23, 2009. www.lamnews.com/border_proves _no_obstacle_for_mexican_cartels.htm.

Gibson, Campbell J., and Emily Lennon. *Historical Census Statistics on the Foreign-born Population of the United States: 1850–1990*. Population Division Working Paper No. 29. Washington, D.C.: U.S. Bureau of the Census, 1999.

Gilchrist, Jim, and Jerome R. Corsi. *Minutemen: The Battle to Secure America's Borders*. Los Angeles: World Ahead Publishing, 2006.

Goldman, T. R. "The Man with the Iron Gavel." *Legal Times*, May 2, 2005.

Good Neighbor Environmental Board. *Natural Disasters and the Environment along the U.S.-Mexico Border*. Eleventh Report of the Good Neighbor Environmental Board to the President and Congress of the United States, March 2008. www.epa .gov/ocem/gneb/gneb11threport/English-GNEB-11th-Report.pdf.

Grassley, Chuck. "Senator Chuck Grassley's Statement before the House Judiciary Committee Hearing on Immigration Reform." Dubuque, Iowa, September 1, 2006.

Haddal, Chad C., et al. "Border Security: Barriers along the U.S. International Border." CRS Report 7-5700. Congressional Research Service, March 16, 2009.

Hall, Mimi. "Attacks against Border Agents on Record Pace." *USA Today*, February 27, 2008. www.usatoday.com/news/nation/2008-02-26-Borderviolence_N.htm.

———. "Border Agents Increasingly Targeted." *USA Today*, February 27, 2008.

Heath, Brad. "Border Agent Killed: U.S., Mexico Still Looking for Suspects." *USA Today*, July 27, 2009.

Hellyer, Clement David. *The U.S. Border Patrol*. New York: Random House, 1963.

Herrera-Sobeck, Maria. *Northward Bound: The Mexican Immigrant Experience in Ballad and Song*. Bloomington: Indiana University Press, 1993.

Heyman, Josiah McC. *Finding a Moral Heart for U.S. Immigration Policy*. American Ethnological Society Monograph Series, No. 7. Washington, D.C.: American Anthropological Association, 1998.

———, and Jason Ackleson. "U.S. Border Security after September 11." In *Border Security in the Al-Qaeda Era*, ed. John A. Winterdyk and Kelly W. Sundberg, 37–74. Boca Raton, Florida: CRC Press, 2010.

Hidalgo County, Texas, Commissioners Court. "Concerns Submitted by Ann Carsons, 3/13/08." McAllen, Texas, March 13, 2008.

Horgan, Paul. *Great River.* New York: Holt, Rinehart and Winston, 1954; reprint, Austin: Texas Monthly Press, 1984.

Hsu, Spencer S. "Work to Cease on 'Virtual Fence' along U.S.-Mexico Border." *Washington Post*, March 16, 2010. www.washingtonpost.com/wp-dyn/content/article/2010/03/16/AR2010031603573.html.

Hsu, Spencer S., and Griff Witte. "Plenty of Holes Seen in a Virtual Fence." *Washington Post*, September 24, 2006.

"Innovative and Alternative: HCDD No. 1 DHS Levee-barrier Project." House Committee on Transportation and Infrastructure, Chaired by Congressman James Oberstar, D-Minn., January 26, 2009.

"Integrated Surveillance Intelligence System (ISIS)." *Global Security*, July 2, 2008. www.globalsecurity.org/security/systems/isis.htm.

International Boundary and Water Commission. "Memorandum for Major Subordinate Commands and District Commands." December 7, 1997.

Jacoby, Susan. *The Age of American Unreason.* New York: Pantheon Books, 2009.

Jeffrey, Terence P. "Man of the Year: Jim Sensenbrenner." *Human Events*, December 22, 2006. www.humanevents.com/article.php?id=18622.

"Jim Sensenbrenner." Wikipedia, The Free Encyclopedia, March 12, 2008. http://en.wikipedia.org/w/index.php?title=Jim_Sensenbrenner.

Jimenez, Maria. "Humanitarian Crisis: Migrant Deaths at the U.S.-Mexico Border." Report, ACLU of San Diego and Imperial Counties and Mexico's National Commission of Human Rights, San Diego, California, October 1, 2008. www.aclu.org/files/pdfs/immigrants/humanitariancrisisreport.pdf.

Johnston, David, and Eric Schmitt. "Smaller-Scale Terrorism Plots Pose New and Worrisome Threats, Officials Say." *New York Times*, October 31, 2009. www.nytimes.com/2009/11/01/us/01terror.html.

Jones, Oakah L. *Los Paisanos: Spanish Settlers on the Northern Frontier of New Spain.* Norman: University of Oklahoma Press, 1979.

Kasinitz, Philip, et al. *Inheriting the City: The Children of Immigrants Come of Age.* Cambridge: Harvard University Press, 2008.

Krauss, Erich, and Alex Pacheco. *On the Line: Inside the U.S. Border Patrol.* New York: Citadel, 2004.

Kristof, Nicholas D. "Drugs Won the War." *New York Times*, June 14, 2009.

Lacey, Marc. "Ilegales Siguen Arriesgándose." *El Sentinel*, May 21, 2010, 1-17.

Lambrecht, Cari. "Levee Project Fact Sheet." Hidalgo County Commissioners Court, Hidalgo County, Texas, n.d.

Leatherman, Jackie. "County Leaders Meet with Federal Officials to Discuss Fence, Levee." *McAllen Monitor*, October 23, 2007. www.themonitor.com/news/officials-6079-tuesday-county.html.

———. "County Moves Closer to Combined Levee–Border Fence." *McAllen Monitor*, April 14, 2008. www.themonitor.com/common/printer/view.php?db=monitortx&id=10955.

Leibovich, Mark. "Pit Bull of the House Latches On to Immigration." *New York Times*, July 10, 2006, A3.

Lipowicz, Alice. "3 Firms Will Compete to Build New Border Network." *Washington Post*, February 27, 2006.

———. "Boeing Gets One-Year Extension on SBInet Contract." *Washington Technology*, September 18, 2009. http://washingtontechnology.com/articles/2009/09/18/cbp-extends-sbinet-contract-with-boeing-for-a-year.aspx?sc_lang=en.

———. "Building Work Starts on SBI-net," *Federal Computer Week*, May 8, 2009. http://fcw.com/articles/2009/05/08/sbinet-construction-started-this-week.aspx.

———. "DHS, Boeing Move Closer to SBInet Rollout." *Washington Technology*, February 6, 2009. http://washingtontechnology.com/articles/2009/02/06/sbinet-update.aspx?sc_lang=en.

———. "DHS Bulks Up Secure Border Initiative Procurement Oversight." *Washington Technology*, March 8, 2006. http://washingtontechnology.com/articles/2006/03/03/dhs-bulks-up-secure-border-initiative-procurement-oversight.aspx?sc_lang=en.

Lipton, Eric. "Some U.S. Security Agents Chafe Under Speech Limits." *New York Times*, April 26, 2005. http://query.nytimes.com/gst/fullpage.html?res=9E0DE1D81231F935A15757C0A9639C8B63&sec=&spon=&pagewanted=all.

Losey, Stephen. "Air Marshal's Firing Prompts Whistleblower Suit." *Federal Times*, November 7, 2006.

———. "Hearing Reveals Significant Flows in SBInet Project." *Federal Times*, November 16, 2006.

———. "New Border Protection System to Start Operation within Days." *Federal Times*, June 8, 2007.

"Man Arrested in Agent's Death." *Greenville Daily Reflector*, January 24, 2008.

Maril, Robert Lee. "An Analysis of Auto Insurance on Low Income Families." Public Testimony before the U.S. Senate Commerce and Banking Committee, Washington, D.C., September 9, 1999.

———. *The Bay Shrimpers of Texas: Rural Workers in a Global Economy*. Lawrence: University Press of Kansas, 1995.

———. *Cannibals and Condos: Texas and Texans along the Gulf Coast*. College Station: Texas A&M University Press, 1986.

———. "Contracts for Deeds." Unpublished report, Texas RioGrande Legal Aid, Weslaco, Texas, 1995.

———. "The Impact of Mandatory Auto Insurance upon the Residents of Maricopa County, Arizona." Unpublished report for the National Association of Independent Insurers, Chicago, 1996.

———. "The Impact of Raising the Truck Insurance of Migrant Farm Workers." Public testimony before the Texas State Insurance Board, Austin, Texas, 1993.

———. *Living on the Edge of America*. College Station: Texas A&M University Press, 1992.

———. *Patrolling Chaos: The U.S. Border Patrol in Deep South Texas*. Lubbock: Texas Tech University Press, 2004.

———. *Poorest of Americans: The Mexican Americans of the Lower Rio Grande Valley of Texas*. Notre Dame, Ind.: University of Notre Dame Press, 1989.

———. *Texas Shrimpers: Community, Capitalism, and the Sea*. College Station: Texas A&M University Press, 1983.

———. "They Followed Us with Jets and My Own Country Arrested Us: The Arbitrary Enforcement of the Lacey Act." Paper presented at the Annual Meeting of the Rural Sociological Society, 1984, College Station, Texas.

———. "Towards a Media Theory of the Lower Rio Grande Valley." *Borderlands Journal* 1, no. 1 (1977): 77–96.

———. *Waltzing with the Ghost of Tom Joad: Poverty, Myth, and Low Wage Labor in Oklahoma.* Norman: University of Oklahoma Press, 2000.

———, and Antonio N. Zavaleta. "Drinking Patterns of Low Income Mexican-American Women." *Journal of Studies in Alcohol* 40 (1979): 480–85.

Martinez, Andres R. "U.S. Authorities Fired On by Border Bandits." *McAllen Monitor*, July 13, 2006.

Martinez, Laura B. "The Fence is Coming, Levee or Not." *Brownsville Herald*, April 29, 2008. www.brownsvilleherald.com/news/fence-86264-county-border.html.

Massey, Douglas S. *Categorically Unequal: The American Stratification System.* New York: Russell Sage Foundation, 2007.

———, Jorge Durand, and Nolan J. Malone. *Beyond Smoke and Mirrors: Mexican Immigration in an Era of Economic Integration.* New York: Russell Sage Foundation, 2002.

———, and Kristin E. Espinosa. "What's Driving Mexico-U.S. Migration? A Theoretical, Empirical and Policy Analysis." *American Journal of Sociology* 102, no. 4 (1997): 939–99.

———, et al. *Return to Aztlan: The Social Process of International Migration from Western Mexico.* Berkeley: University of California Press, 1987.

McAllen, Texas. "Resolution Authorizing and Approving the Construction and Rehabilitation of Flood Control Levees with Respect to Alternative Approaches for Security of the United States–Mexico Border." December 18, 2007.

McPhee, John. *Basin and Range.* New York: Farrar, Straus and Giroux, 1982.

Michalski, Ann E. Rough draft of testimony to be presented before House Judiciary Committee, Full Committee Oversight Field Hearing, 109th Cong., 2nd sess., Dubuque, Iowa, September 1, 2006. Copy in possession of the author.

Migration Policy Institute. "The U.S.-Mexico Border." *Migration Information Source*, June 1, 2006, 2–3. www.migrationinformation.org/Feature/print.cfm?ID=407.

Miller, Michael V. *Economic Growth and Change Along the U.S.-Mexico Border.* Austin, Texas: Bureau of Business Research, 1982.

———, and Robert Lee Maril. "Poverty in the Lower Rio Grande Valley of Texas: Historical and Contemporary Dimensions." Technical Report No. 78-2. Texas Agricultural Experiment Station, College Station, 1979.

Mintz, John. "Probe Faults System for Monitoring U.S. Borders." *Washington Post*, April 11, 2005. www.washingtonpost.com/wp-dyn/articles/A42516-2005Apr10 .html.www.mail-archive.com/medianews@twiar.org/msg00906.html.

———. "Border Camera System Is Assailed." *Washington Post*, June 17, 2005. www .nusd.k12.az.us/schools/nhs/gthomson.class/articles/border/news.HUM115/ border.patrol/Border%20Camera%20System%20Is%20Assailed.pdf.

Moreno, Sylvia. "GOP Hearing Alleges Risks of Terrorism along Border." *Washington Post*, July 8, 2006.

Murphy, Kate. "Mexican Robin Hood Figure Gains a Kind of Notoriety in U.S." *New York Times*, January 8, 2008. www.nytimes.com/2008/02/08/us/08narcosaint .html?_r=2&scp=1&sq=jesus%20malverde&st=cse.

"National Border Patrol Council Rebuttal to the Misrepresentations of the U.S. Attorney's Office of the Western District of Texas Concerning the Prosecution of Border Patrol Agents Jose Alonso Compean and Ignacio Ramos." Press Release, National Border Patrol Council of the American Federation of Government Employees, 1–9.

Navarrette, Ruben, Jr. "The Many Sides of James Sensenbrenner." *San Diego Union-Tribune*, August 10, 2006.

Newhouse, John. *Boeing versus Airbus: The Inside Story of the Greatest International Competition in Business.* New York: Vintage, 2008.

The 9/11 Commission Report: Final Report of the National Commission on Terrorist Attacks upon the United States. New York: W. W. Norton, 2004.

"No More Deaths Volunteers To Be Arraigned for Littering." *Catholic Sun* (Phoenix, Arizona), February 6, 2009.

Novas, Himilce. *Everything You Need To Know about Latino History.* New York: Penguin-Putnam, 1994.

"Now There's an Idea: Build the Wall on the Other Side." 2007 Bum Steer Awards, *Texas Monthly*, January 2007, 102.

Nuñez-Neto, Blas. "Border Security: Key Agencies and Their Missions." *CRS Report for Congress*, January 26, 2006.

Pew Research Center for the People and the Press. "America's Immigration Quandary: No Consensus on Immigration Problems or Proposed Fixes." March 30, 2006. http://people-press.org/report/274/americas-immigration-quandary.

———. "Press Accuracy Rating Hits Two Decade Low: Public Evaluations of the News Media, 1985–2009." September 13, 2009. http://people-press.org/report/ 543/.

Portes, Alejandro, and Ruben G. Rumbaut. *Immigrant America.* Berkeley: University of California Press, 1996.

Preston, Julia. "House and Senate Hold Immigration Hearings." *New York Times*, July 6, 2006. www.nytimes.com/2006/07/06/washington/06immigration.html.

———. "Mexico Data Say Migration to U.S. Has Plummeted." *New York Times*, May 15, 2009. www.nytimes.com/2009/05/15/us/15immig.html?_r=1.

Provost, Gary. *Across the Border: The True Story of the Satanic Cult Killings in Matamoros, Mexico.* New York: Pocket Books, 1989.

Quantance, Zack. "Coyote Rams Truck into Border Patrol Agents' Cruiser." *McAllen Monitor*, October 16, 2007.

Rak, Mary Kidder. *The Border Patrol.* Boston: Houghton-Mifflin, 1938.

Rector, Robert. "Amnesty and Continued Low Skill Immigration Will Substantially Raise Welfare Costs and Poverty." Backgrounder on immigration, the Heritage Foundation, September 1, 2006. www.heritage.org/Research/Reports/2006/05/ Amnesty-and-Continued-Low-Skill-Immigration-Will-Substantially-Raise -Welfare-Costs-and-Poverty.

Rios, Larry. *The Fearful Humor of Border Patrol Agents*. Frederick, Md.: PublishAmerica, 2009.

Ross, Stanley R., ed. *Views Across the Border*. Albuquerque: University of New Mexico Press, 1978.

Rubel, Arthur J. *Across the Tracks*. Austin: University of Texas Press, 1966.

Scahill, Jeremy. *Blackwater: The Rise of the World's Most Powerful Mercenary Army*. New York: Nation Books, 2008.

Sensenbrenner, James Frank, Jr. Interview in "House Republican Cites Guest-worker 'Amnesty'," *Washington Times*, January 25, 2006. www.washingtontimes.com/news/2006/jan/24/20060124-111959-4121r/?page=1.

Sherman, Christopher. "Town Survives Despite New Border Barrier." *McAllen Monitor*, February 26, 2009.

Sieff, Kevin. "Border Fencing." *Brownsville Herald*, April 29, 2008.

Spener, David. *Clandestine Crossings: Migrants and Coyotes on the Texas-Mexico Border*. Ithaca, N.Y.: Cornell University Press, 2009.

———, and Kathleen A. Staudt, eds. *The U.S.-Mexico Border: Transcending Divisions, Contesting Identities*. New York: Lynne Rienner Publishers, 1998.

Stambaugh, J. Lee, and Lillian J. Stambaugh. *The Lower Rio Grande Valley of Texas*. Austin: University of Texas Press, 1954.

"Statement of James C. Handley, Regional Administrator, Great Lakes Region, U.S. General Services Administration, before the Committee on Homeland Security, Subcommittee on Management, Integration and Oversight." U.S. House of Representatives, Washington, D.C., February 16, 2006.

"Statement of Richard L. Skinner, Inspector General, U.S. Department of Homeland Security." Subcommittee on Management, Integration, and Oversight. Committee on Homeland Security, U.S. House of Representatives, Washington, D.C., December 16, 2005.

Stoddard, Ellwyn R. *Maquila*. El Paso: Texas Western Press, 1987.

Strohm, Chris. "Appropriators Skeptical of Promised Secure Border Initiative." *Government Executive*, April 7, 2006. www.govexec.com/dailyfed/0406/040706cdam1.htm.

Sumano, Abelardo Rodriguez. *En las entrañas de Goliat: La política estadounidense y su relación con México*. Mexico City: Aguilar, 2002.

Sutter, Daniel. "Rio Grande Levee Failures and Flooding: The Economic Impact on Hidalgo." Center for Border Economic Studies, University of Texas–Pan American, March 2008.

Swarns, Rachel L. "Critics Say Politics Driving Immigration Hearings." *New York Times*, August 7, 2006. www.nytimes.com/2006/08/07/washington/07immig.html.

10News (San Diego). "Officials: Violence against Border Agents on Rise." *Homeland Defense News*, September 10, 2008. www.officer.com/web/online/Homeland-Defense-and-Terror-News/Officials—Violence-Against-Border-Agents-On-Rise/8$43145.

Terrazas, Aaron, et al. "Frequently Requested Statistics on Immigrants and Immigration in the United States." *Migration Information Source*, October 2007.

Texas Border Coalition. "A Resolution Demanding Smart and Effective Security on the Texas-Mexico Border." October 1, 2007. www.texasbordercoalition.org/Texas _Border_Coalition/Resources_files/Resolution%20Demanding%20Smart%20and %20Effective%20Security%20on%20the%20Texas-Mexico%20Border.pdf.

Thormeyer, Rob, and Alice Lipowicz. "DHS Awards Boeing SBI-Net Contract." *Government Computer News*, September 20, 2006. http://gcn.com/articles/2006/09/20/ dhs-awards-boeing-sbinet-contract.aspx.

"Transcript of Obama's Immigration Speech." *Washington Wire Blog.* July 1, 2010. http://blogs.wsj.com/washwire/2010/07/01/transcript-of-obamas-immigration -speech.

Trotter, Robert T., and Juan Antonio Chavira. *Curanderismo: Mexican-American Folk Healing.* Athens: University of Georgia Press, 1983.

United Press International. "GAO: Each Extra Border Agent Costs $187,000." Washington, D.C., April 3, 2007. www.upi.com/Business_News/Security-Industry/2007/ 04/03/GAOEach-extra-border-agent-costs-187000/UPI-90761175605545/.

United States of America v. 50.00 Acres of Land, More or Less, Situated in Hidalgo County, State of Texas, et al. Texas Southern District Court, McAllen, Texas, January 30, 2008.

U.S. Customs and Border Protection. "CBP meets 18,000 Border Patrol Agent Hiring Commitment—Weeks Early." News release, December 17, 2008. www.cbp.gov/xp/ cgov/newsroom/news_releases/archives/2008_news_releases/december_2008/ 12172008_9.xml.

———. "DHS Engages Private Sector on Border Technology: Industry Day, the First Step Toward a Strategic SBI Partnership." News release, January 26, 2006. www .cbp.gov/xp/cgov/newsroom/news_releases/archives/2006_news_releases/ 012006/01262006.xml.

———. "Public Affairs Guidance: SBInet Industry." News release. Office of Public Affairs, March 3, 2006.

———. "SBInet Completes Test of First Mobile Sensor Tower." News release, April 5, 2007. www.govtech.com/dc/104832.

———, Border Patrol. *Mexican Government Incidents.* Vols. 2003–2005. Washington, D.C.: Department of Homeland Security, U.S. Customs and Border Protection.

U.S. Department of Homeland Security."Fact Sheet Southwest Border Next Steps: Readout of Secretary Napolitano's Remarks on Border Security and Law Enforcement." June 23, 2010. www.dhs.gov/ynews/releases/pr_1277310093825.shtm.

U.S. Department of Homeland Security, Office of the Inspector General. *Department of Homeland Security's Procurement and Program Management Operations.* OIG-05-53, September 2005. www.dhs.gov/xoig/assets/mgmtrpts/OIG_05-53_Sep05.pdf.

———. "DHS Announces SBInet Contract Award to Boeing." News release, Washington, D.C., September 21, 2006. www.dhs.gov/xnews/releases/pr_1158876536376 .shtm.

U.S. Drug Enforcement Administration. "DEA Drug Seizures," n.d. www.justice.gov/ dea/statistics.html#seizures.

U.S. Government Accountability Office. "Border Security: Key Unresolved Issues Justify Reevaluation of Border Surveillance Technology Program." Report to Congressional Committees, GAO-06-295. Washington, D.C., February 2006. www.gao.gov/new.items/d06295.pdf.

———. "Report to Subcommittee on Management, Investigations, and Oversight, House Homeland Security Committee." Draft report. Washington, D.C., February 14, 2007.

———. "Secure Border Initiative: DHS Needs to Address Significant Risks in Delivering Key Technology Investment." Testimony before the Committee on Homeland Security, House of Representatives, GAO-08-1148T, September 10, 2008, Washington, D.C. www.gao.gov/new.items/d081148t.pdf.

———. "Secure Border Initiative Fence Construction Costs." Report to Congressional Committees, GAO-09-244R. Washington, D.C., January 29, 2008. www.gao.gov/new.items/d09244r.pdf.

———. "Secure Border Initiative: Observations on Deployment Challenges." Testimony before the Committee on Homeland Security, House of Representatives, GAO-08-1141T. Washington, D.C., September 10, 2008.

U.S. House, Committee on the Judiciary. "How Do Illegal Immigrants Impact the Costs of Healthcare, Local Education, and Other Social Services, and Would These Costs Increase under the Reid-Kennedy Bill?" Draft report. Full Committee Oversight Field Hearing, 109th Cong., 2nd sess., Concord, New Hampshire, August 24, 2006.

"U.S. Representative Michael D. Rogers Hearing on Border Patrol Surveillance Technology." *Congressional Quarterly*, June 16, 2005.

Walsh, Casey. *Building the Borderlands: A Transnational History of Irrigated Cotton along the Mexico-Texas Border*. College Station: Texas A&M University Press, 2008.

"Water in the Desert." *New York Times*, August 16, 2009. www.nytimes.com/2009/08/16/opinion/16sun2.html.

Wayne, Leslie. "Northrop, Airbus Ally Get Tanker Contract." *Memphis Commercial Appeal*, March 1, 2008.

Weisman, Alan, and Jay Dusard. *La Frontera: The United States Border with Mexico*. New York: Harcourt Brace Jovanovich, 1986.

Wilson, William Julius. *More Than Just Race: Being Black and Poor in the Inner City*. New York: W. W. Norton, 2009.

Witte, Griff. "Boeing Wins Border Contract." *Raleigh News and Observer*, September 20, 2006, 12A.

———. "Firms Vie to Provide the Future of Border Security." *Washington Post*, September 18, 2006.

Wood, John. "Happenings in Precinct 2." News release, Cameron County Court, Texas, January 2007. www.co.cameron.tx.us/commissioner_pct2/docs/happeningsP2.pdf.

Yenne, Bill. *The Story of the Boeing Company*. Osceola, Wis.: Zenith Press, 2005.

Zavaleta, Antonio, and Alberto Salinas, Jr. *Curandero Conversations: El Niño Fidencio, Shamanism, and Healing Traditions of the Borderlands*. Bloomington, Ind.: AuthorHouse, 2009.

Acknowledgments

I would like to acknowledge the support of my colleagues Rebecca Powers, Joe Heyman, Ron Thrasher, Bob Edwards, Susan Pearce, Ben Sidel, David Griffith, Lorry King, and Arunas Juska. I also benefited from conversations with Genaro Gonzalez, Elena Bastida, Lauren Fisher, Royal Loresco, Tim Vanderpool, Stephen Losey, Rob Johnson, Erica Johnson, Jonah Sheridan, Dan Dearth, Carol Dearth, Charity Hall, Paul Marek, Jacob Hochman, Molly Sheridan, and Jordan Maril. Thanks to Travis Maril for transportation south of San Diego. Through his expertise in geovisualization, Tom Allen was particularly helpful in discussions of the impact of border geography upon immigration flows.

Margret Mulcahy, East Carolina University Center for Geographic Information Science, provided the maps. Cari Lambrecht provided several photos of the construction of the fence in South Texas. All other photographs are by the author. Jeanne Watkins and Becky Gardner were the administrative assistants who facilitated my work on this project. Research assistants Guillaume Bagal and Kacee Gore provided help with the end notes and bibliography. East Carolina University students in my 2010 graduate seminar in qualitative methods clarified a number of issues for me; I am grateful for their intellectual contribution. I especially want to thank the two anonymous reviewers. Jesse Peel was inspirational throughout the writing of this book through his life's work and his determination.

Finally, my gratitude goes to those interviewed who serve or have served in city, county, state, and federal agencies, programs, and institutions or in the private sector, without whom this book would not have been possible.

Page numbers in italics indicate images.

accountability, 292, 293, 295

Adams, Jeff, 161

Aguilar, David, 166

Ahumada, Pat, 242

Airbus, 165

aircraft, 286

Air Marshals, 97

Ajo-1, 173, 174, 176, 178

Alamo, Texas, 52

alcohol smuggling, 49

Aldrete Davila, Osvaldo, 144–47

Alemán, Miguel, 270

Alice, Texas, 10

Allee, Captain, 49

Americans for Legal Immigration, 272, 280

American Shield Initiative (ASI), 140, 147–53, 156, 158, 160, 162, 175, 176

American University, 303–4

Amigoland Mall, 64

Amistad Dam, 302

amnesty, 114

Anglos, 47, 48, 52, 53–54, 58, 66, 203

Anzalduas County Park, Texas, 38–39, 40–44, 58–59, 111, 114, 130, 209, 211–12, 218, 223; barriers in, *211*, 213, 215–16, 237–38; flooding in, 307–8; hydraulic walls in, *211*, 237–38

Arivaca, Arizona, 135, 136

Arizona, 4, 21, 94, 106, 135–38, 140, 162, 165, 167, 173, 180, 183–84, 221, 236, 251–56, *252*, *254*, 273, 275–78, *276*, 281, 284, 290–91, 305. *See also specific municipalities*; SB 1070, 304–5

Army Corps of Engineers, 71, 74–76, 121, 209, 214, 303

ARNORTH (U.S. Army North), 267

Artesia, New Mexico, 25, 181

ASI. *See* American Shield Initiative (ASI)

"assimilation," 118

Ballenger Construction, 239

Beccaria, Cesare, 91

Belfast, Northern Ireland, 215–16

Bentham, Jeremy, 91

Bentsen, Lloyd, Sr., 46, 51

Berlin Wall, Germany, 215, 229

Bhakta, Raj Peter, 130

binational health model, 268

binational issues, 281

biometrics, 33

Blackwater, Inc., 138

Boeing, Inc., 21, 135–36, 138, 161–76, 178, 203, 204, 250, 275, 277, 279, 285, 286, 291–93, 298, 299, 306–7,

bolios, 52

Bonner, T. J., 256

border communities, 289–90, 309–10n1. *See also specific communities*

bordercrossers, illegal, 9–10, 26, 49, 131, 224, 229, 249, 273, 284, 305. *See also* immigrants, illegal; workers, undocumented; apprehension rates, 96, 305; body counts of, 16–17; children, 222–23; commodification and, 292–93; deaths of, 98, 250–51, 255–56, 284, 286; dehydration of, 98, 250–51, 255–56, 284–85, 286; drowning of, 286; hydraulic walls and, 245–46; injuries of, 285; medical attention to, 285; motiva-tions of, 92; Reyes's strategy and, 94–95; risks to, 98; safety of, 284–85, 286; welfare of, 284–85, 286; women, 222–23

border gangs, 227–28. *See also* criminal organizations

Border Patrol academy, 25–27, 95, 181, 183, 220, 248, 295

Border Patrol agents, 4, 10, 12–17, 45, 50–51, 56, 58, 78, 83–90, 119, 122–23, 130–31, 273, 275, 277, 302, 306–7. *See also* Customs and Border Protection (CBP) agents; *specific agents*; at Anzalduas County Park, 40–41, 43; assaults against, 181–82; attrition of, 97, 320n13; Compean/Ramos case, 144–49; deterrence theory and, 91, 93; education of, 149; female, 34–35, 149, 248–49, 294–95, 331n2; former military, 149; gender discrimination against, 180–97; increased numbers of, 289; injuries of, 27, 28, 29, 286; ISIS and, 99–102, 107–10; legal authority of, 212–13; Mexican American, 248–49; Muñoz case, 179–97; occupational hazards for, 27, 28, 29; post-Reyes deterrence strategy, 98–99; recruit-ment of, 32, 34–35, 81, 181, 183–84, 195, 248, 294–95; Reyes's strategy and, 92–97; safety issues and, 249–52, 280, 283, 284–85, 286, 287; Stanton case and, 255–56; training of, 181, 220, 286, 293–94, 295; UTB-TSC and, 216–23; virtual fences and, 142, 166, 168, 177; welfare of, 284–85, 286; work life of, 24–37

Border Patrol managers, 102

Border Patrol Search, Trauma, and Rescue (BORSTAR), 285–86

Border Patrol Stations, 101. *See also specific stations*

border walls and fences, 12, 21, 38, 63, 69, 76, 80, 140, 213, 228, 231, 236, 239; alternative models, 291; at Anzalduas County Park, *211*, 215–16, 237–38; construction of, *210*, 282, 296, 298–99, 302–3; dearth of information about, 271; delays in construction of, 201, 209, 214, 302–3; effectiveness of, 284; environmental consequences of, 240; failure of, 178; funding of, 244, 275, 298; in Hidalgo County, *210–11*, 215–16, 230–31, 235, 237–41, 243–48, *247*, 291, 302–3, 307; high-tech, 110; impact of, 15–16, 217, 219–24, 280–81, 284, 287–89, 296, 303; kinds of, 156–57; "land acquisitions" and, 201; landing mat, 56–57; language and, 215–16; location of, 64; low-tech, 56, 174–77, 204, 221, 283–84, 290, 291; in Nogales, Arizona, 253; at Nuevo Progreso, 216–18; oversight of, 244, 297–98; pedestrian, 56, 58, 156–57, 174; politics of, 138–44; potential consequences of, 66–67; primary, 56; rationalization for, 282–83, 286–88, 298–99; reconsideration of, 298–300; Sandia, 56–57; in San Diego, California, 256; secondary, 56–57; secrecy surrounding, 142–43; strategy of, 285; in Texas, 250; at Tijuana, Mexico, *57*; types of, 290; at UTB-TSC, 198–200, 204–6, *205*, 241–42, 290–91; vehicle-barrier, 56, 57, 156–57, 174; virtual, 159, 165–66, 175–77, 221, 283–84, 290, 292, 306

Borkowski, Mark, 173, 175, 177, 279

bossism, 45, 46, 52, 53, 58

Bracero Program, 53, 270

Brand, Othal, 45, 46

Brewster Farm, 248

bridges, 310n7

British Petroleum oil rig, 301

Brownsville, Texas, 4, 5–10, 12, *15*, 27, *39*, 41, 47–48, 52–53, 130, 141, 239, 256, 268, 281, 290, 300, 302; Brownsville Police Department, 6, 64; UTB-TSC and, 62–64, 69, 71–72, 199–205, 207, 208, 234, 241–42

Brownsville Herald, 61

Brownsville International Bridge, 47

"bubbles," 98

Buenos Aires National Wildlife Refuge, 255–56

Bush, George H. W., administration of, 101

Bush, George W., 43, 44, 58–59, 111, 143, 266, 270, 304; administration of, 11–12, 33, 102–3, 115, 141, 155, 176–77, 181, 224, 237, 272, 281–83, 290, 291; immigration legislation by, 112, 114, 130, 138; pardoning of Compean and Ramos, 147; reelection of, 69; signing of Secure Border Fence Act, 234; signing of Secure Fence Act, 139–40; signing of USA Patriot Act, 125, 126; speech at Anzalduas County Park, 114, 308; State of the Union Address, 223

Calderón, Felipe, 226–27

California, 12, 94, 140–41, 146, 253, 275, 290, 300. *See also specific municipalities*

cameras, 140, 170, 177

Cameron County, Texas, *15*, 21, 71, 76, 110, 163, 205, 209, 241–45, 256, 291, 302. *See also specific municipalities*; Cameron County Mental Health Task Force, 241; Cameron County sheriff's office, 6; DHS and, 200–202, 212–14; Hispanics in, 52–55; human smuggling in, 41; potential flooding in, 44–45, 219–20, 238–39, 243–44

Canada, 141, 261–62, 266–67, 297

Canales, J. T., 49

Cantu, Conrado, 54–55

catch-and-release policy, 32–34, 143, 154, 184

Center for American Common Culture, 118, 119

Center for Immigration Studies, 119

Center for North American Strategic Studies, 268, 280

Charleston, South Carolina, 183

Chenevey, Jack, 174

Chertoff, Michael, 28, 33, 56, 58, 68–70, 76, 109, 140, 142, 147–57, 160–61, 163–64, 167, 172–78, 199–201, 209, 234, 236, 237, 275, 279, 281–84, 290, 292–93, 296

Chicanismo, 53

Chihuahuan desert, 14

citizenship status, 9, 47, 53, 66, 118–19

Ciudad Juárez, Mexico, 7–8, 93, 94, 118, 228, 229, 233, 253

civil rights movement, 53

Clark, Robert T., 267

class, 8–9

Clearwater, Florida, 18–19, 21, 279

Cleary, Tom, 167–72

Clinton, Chelsea, 61

Clinton, Hillary, 61

Clinton, William J., 125

Clinton, William J., administration of, 44, 100, 101, 102–3, 176, 281, 282, 291

CNN, 147

code books, 188, 190

Collins, Agent, 255–56

colonias, 70–71, 202, 214, 241

Colorado, 258, 259–64, 267

Colorado Springs, Colorado, 259–64, 267

Committee on Homeland Security, 172

commodification, 291–93

"common culture," 118

community policing, 290

Compean, Jose A., 144–47, 280

computers, 164

Congress, 129

Consolidated Appropriations Act of 2008, 56, 174

contractors and subcontractors, 104–5, 109–10, 143, 159, 161–67, 174–75, 214, 239, 244, 286. *See also* defense contractors

Cornyn, John, 28, 230–31, 233, 234, 237

Corpus Christi, Texas, 53

corridos, 49–50, 314n6

corruption, 54, 55, 109–10, 162–63, 226–27, 239, 240, 244, 296

Cortina Wars, 58

Costanzo, Adolfo, 46, 47

county government, 52

coyotes, 4, 12–13, 16, 29–31, 40, 42, 92–93, 98–99, 127–28, 224, 284

Crawford, Texas, 59

criminal organizations, 54, 284, 287–89, 297. *See also* drug trafficking

criminology, 91–92

Crocker, Sylvia, 262–63, 264, 267, 273

C Shift, 45, 46, 47, 58

C-Span, 117

Cuellar, Henry, 233, 234

Customs and Border Protection (CBP), 10, 12–17, 40–41, 44, 48, 53, 83–87, 122–23, 130–31, 228, 234, 237, 253, 256, 307. *See also* Customs and Border Protection (CBP) agents; access to, 319n17; apprehension policies, 283; apprehension rates, 220–21; BORSTAR, 285–86; brutality of, 49–50; budget of, 96–97; catch-and-release policy, 184; checkpoints of, 212; city duty, 185–88, 194; community policing and, 290; construction progress of, 57–58; contractors and subcontractors, 104–5, 109; creation of, 49, 148–49; criminal charges against, 50–51; desk jobs, 195–96; detention system, 143–44, 177, 222–23, 277, 283, 292, 295; deterrence theory and, 91–100; equipment, 177; executives of, 149–50; failures of, 293–95; financial motivations of, 291–93; funding of, 249; gender discrimination in, 180–97, 248–49, 294–95, 331n2; harassment of female agents, 149; hatred of, 49–50; in Hidalgo County, 239–40, 242–44; inability to plan, 288; institutional history of, 288; intelligence gathering by, 100, 185, 293; ISIS and, 101–10; leadership of, 166; lifesaving by, 285; managers, 102, 104–5, 293–95; manpower, 177; mortality reporting by, 284; organizational culture of, 149, 180–97, 293–94; oversight of, 297–98; policies of, 177, 183–85, 187, 220–21; political appointees to, 149; public affairs officers (PAOs), 191–92; racial discrimination in, 248–49; recruitment by, 181, 192, 195, 248; recruits, 220; safety and, 272, 282–87, 294, 299; San Diego sector, 56; SBI and, 151–52, 153, 154–56, 159, 161; scope truck assignments, 185–87, 188, 192–93, 194; subcontractors, 110; terminology to describe border crosser deaths, 250–51; at UTB-TSC, 64, 71–72, 76–79; UTB-TSC and, 198–205, 213, 216, 225, 228; vehicles of, 166, 177, 193–94; violence by, 314n6; violence directed toward, 286; virtual fences and, 144–47, 152, 154–57, 162, 169, 170, 172–78

Customs and Border Protection (CBP) agents. *See* Border Patrol agents
Cutler, Michael, 119, 123

Dallas, Texas, 267, 270
DEA. *See* Drug Enforcement Agency (DEA)

death by deterrence theory, 286
debt peonage, 51–52, 53
defense contractors, 11–12, 143, 158, 163, 165, 286, 291–93, 299. *See also* contractors and subcontractors
democracy, 280
Democratic Party, 113–14, 117, 123, 138, 141–42, 158, 283
Department of Homeland Security (DHS), 11–12, 21, 28, 33, 56, 58, 63–64, 70, 72, 77, 99, 169, 177–78, 231, 233–40, 242–45, 247, 249–50, 271, 275, 279–83; 287(g) program, 143; community policing and, 290; creation of, 54; dependency on law enforcement agencies, 296; ethnocentrism of, 286–87; failures of, 295–96; financial motivations of, 291–93; inability to plan, 288; incompetency of, 299; intelligence gathering and analysis at, 225–29; Investment Review Board, 150, 151; ISIS and, 103–10; joint programs with state and local governments, 213; justifications for the border wall, 282–83, 287; "land acquisitions" and, 200–201; lawsuit against private landowners, 200–201, 208; lawsuit against UTB-TSC, 67–69, 72, 200–204, 205, 209; lawsuits against property owners, 72–76, 214, 296; military model of, 291; operational control and, 298–99; oversight of, 297–98; Project 28 and, 172–76; property owners and, 296; SBI and, 152–67, 291–92, 293; statistics of, 305; strategy of, 285; UTB-TSC and, 199–204, 205, 209, 216, 219, 221–22, 224; virtual fencing and, 103–10, 140, 142, 144, 147–48, 150
Department of State, 233
deportations, 32–33, 53, 306
detainees, 292, 293

detention centers, 143–44, 177, 222–23, 277, 292–93, 295

deterrence, 31, 80, 90, 221, 282. *See also* deterrence theory

deterrence theory, 10, 91–100, 282, 286

Detroit, Michigan, 106

DHS. *See* Department of Homeland Security (DHS)

Dinh, Viet, 125

Dobbs, Lou, 24, 147, 272

"doing Xes," 94–95, 98

Donna, Texas, 4, 52, 79–80, 216, 218, 219, 223, 245, 302, 303

Donna International Bridge, 302, 303

Dotty, Dan, 76–83, 85

Douglas, Arizona, 94

Drabik, Walt, 101, 102–3, 104, 105, 107, 280

drones, 162, 164, 166

drug addiction, treatment of, 289–90

drug cartels, 50, 54, 162–63, 178, 212–13, 226, 287, 303

Drug Enforcement Agency (DEA), 54, 100, 296

drug interdictions, rates of, 96–97

drugs, illegal, 10–12, 17, 21–22, 34, 50, 283, 287–90, 305. *See also* drug trafficking

drug trafficking, 12–13, 34, 47, 76, 79–80, 107, 131, 171, 188, 248–50, 256, 270; at Anzalduas County Park, 40–42, 58–59, 213, 307; bribery and, 54–55; Compean/Ramos case, 144–47; deterrence theory and, 91, 92, 96–98; impact of barriers on, 15–16, 217, 219–21, 284, 287–89, 296, 303

drug users, incarceration of, 289–90

Dubuque, Iowa, 111–31, 138, 238

Dubuque, Julien, 121

Dubuque City Council, 115

Durham, North Carolina, 287

East Carolina University (ECU), 265, 266, 272, 273

Easterling, Lloyd, 256

economics, 92–93, 281, 305

Edinburg, Texas, 167–72

elections, 139, 140–41, 143, 300. *See also* presidential campaign of 2008

El Paso, Texas, 93–94, 113, 117–18, 130, 144–47, 155, 202, 228, 233, 253, 282, 289

El Paso Border Patrol, 144–47, 155

El Salvador, 10

El Salvadorans, 223

employment abuse, 214–15

endangered species, 240

environmentalists, 240

environmental laws, 154, 240

Environmental Protection Agency (EPA), 56, 154, 233, 234, 239

EOD Technology, Inc., 136–37

EODT Security, 136–37

Equal Employment Opportunity Commission (EEOC), 180–81, 189–90, 192, 193–94, 195

equipment, 17, 97, 106–7, 162–64, 166–67, 170, 177, 222, 278, 286. *See also specific kinds of equipment*

Ericsson, 161

ethnicity, 8–9

ethnocentrism, 286–87

Falcon Dam, 302

Falfurrias, Texas, 212

Farm Labor Organizing Committee, 272

FBI. *See* Federal Bureau of Investigation (FBI)

Federal Bureau of Investigation (FBI), 126, 296

Federal Emergency Management Agency (FEMA), 71, 232, 233, 239, 244, 267

Federal Legal Services, 54

FEMA. *See* Federal Emergency Management Agency (FEMA)

fences. *See* border walls and fences

Fernandez, Efraim, 53

feudalism, 51–52, 53

fiscal oversight. *See* oversight
Fish and Wildlife Service, 255–56
floaters, 16
flooding, 219–20, 232, 237–39, 302, 307–8
Flores, Alfonso, 53–54
Florida, 18–19, 21, 166, 279. *See also*
    specific municipalities
Fonte, John, 118, 119, 279
force multipliers, 228–29, 290
Fort Bliss, Texas, 259
fortification, 290
Fort Sam Houston, Texas, 267
Fort Walton Beach, Florida, 166
Fox, Vicente, 227, 270
Fox and Friends, 273
Fox network, 273
free will, 91
"friendlies," 238, 290

GAO. *See* Government Accountability
    Office (GAO)
Garcia, Carlos, 5–9, 61, 63, 65, 66, 301–2
Garcia, Juliet, 61, 62, 67–69, 198, 200,
    201, 202, 203–4, 241–42, 279,
    290–91
Garza, Godfrey, Jr., 230, 231, 232, 237,
    240
Garza, Joe E., 94–95
gates, 238, 242, 247, 285, 302–3
gender discrimination, 180–97, 248–49,
    294–95, 331n2
General Services Administration (GSA),
    103, 106, 108
George Bush International Airport,
    225–29
Germans, 122
Gheen, William, 272, 273, 280
Giddens, Gregory, 161, 167
G.I.s, Hispanic, 53
Gonzalez, Noel A., 74–76
Google Earth, 162
Government Accountability Office
    (GAO), 151–53, 156–57, 169,
    172–73, 177

Government Services, Inc., 103, 104,
    106, 109
graft, 54, 55, 109–10, 240, 244, 296
Grand River Center, 123
Granjeno, Texas, 4
Grassley, Charles "Chuck," 117
Great Depression, 52
Greenville, North Carolina, 271–72
ground sensors, 17, 81, 177, 188
Grupo México, 127
Grupo Río Juan, 43
GSA. *See* General Services Administra-
    tion (GSA)
Guajardo, Arturo, 55
Guanajuato, Mexico, 301
Guatemala, 10
Guerra, Manuel, 52
Gulf of Mexico, 301

Hall, David, 70–72, 76, 200, 209,
    213–15, 238, 280
Hanem, Andrew S., 68, 200–203, 214
Harlingen, Texas, 4, 10, 46, 52, 53
health care, 268
Herbswell, Charles, 191
Hidalgo, Texas, 10, 237
Hidalgo County, Texas, 21, 50, 79, 82,
    110, 163, 209, 280, 295. *See also* An-
    zalduas County Park, Texas;
    Hispanics in, 52–55; hydraulic walls
    in, 231, *236*, 237–41, 243–48, *247*,
    291, 302–3, 307–8; levees in, 71–72,
    231–32, 234–37, 243, *246*, 302;
    property owners in, 71–74;
    UTB-TSC and, 76–77, 201–2, 205–6
Hidalgo County Chamber of Commerce,
    212
Hidalgo County Commissioners' Court,
    205, 209, 211, 230, 234, 241, 243,
    250
Hidalgo County Drainage District
    Number One, 230, 233
Hidalgo County Health Department, 308
Highway 283, 239

Highway 286, 275

Hinojosa, Ricardo, 50

Hispanics, 9, 48–49, 51–53, 122, 130, 203, 241. *See also specific nationalities*

Homeland Security Appropriations Subcommittee, 160

Homeland Security Defense Education Consortium (HSDEC), 260, 264–65

Honduras, 10

Honeywell, Inc., 11–21, 110, 137, 143, 161–64, 279, 285; Honeywell Smart Lab, 12; Virtual Lab, 18–19

"hostiles," 238, 290

House Committee on the Judiciary, 112–15, 117, 125–26, 128, 130

House of Representatives, 129, 139. *See also* U.S. Congress

House Select Committee on Homeland Security, 106

House Select Committee on Intelligence, 102

Houston, Texas, 225–29

H.R. 4437, "Border Protection, Antiterrorism, and Illegal Immigration Control Act of 2005," 114, 115. *See also* Sensenbrenner Bill

HSDEC. *See* Homeland Security Defense Education Consortium (HSDEC)

Hudson Institute, 118, 279

Human Events, 126

human smuggling, 41, 59, 79, 127–28, 213, 220–21, 308

Hunt Valley Development, 43

Hurricane Alex, 301, 302, 303

Hurricane Beulah, 209, 232

Hurricane Dolly, 239

Hurricane Katrina, 267, 268–71, 297

hydraulic walls, *210*, *211*, 231, 236–48, *247*, 291, 302–3, 306–7

hydrogates, 303

hyperbole, 280

IBWC. *See* International Boundary and Water Commission (IBWC)

ICAD. *See* Intelligent Computer-Aided Detection (ICAD) system

ICAD II, 101, 102, 107

ICAD III, 102, 104, 107

ICBM (intercontinental ballistic missile) silos, 18–19

ICE. *See* Immigration and Customs Enforcement (ICE)

IDs, 64

Illegal Immigration Reform and Responsibility Act, 56

Illinois, 120, 122

IMC. *See* International Microwave Corporation (IMC)

immigrant rights groups, 286

immigrants, illegal, 9–17, 21–22, 26, 33, 123, 275, 283, 288–89, 310n2. *See also* bordercrossers, illegal; undocumented workers; workers, undocumented; amnesty for, 114, 139; decline in numbers of, 92–93; "voluntarily returned" (Vred) illegal immigrants, 56

immigration, 281. *See also* immigrants, illegal; immigration legislation; immigration policy

Immigration and Customs Enforcement (ICE), 143, 213, 221–22, 306, 326n7

Immigration and Naturalization Service (INS), 6, 33, 53, 99, 100, 102, 107, 130, 143–44, 150, 176, 223, 228–29; Electronic Systems Section, 101

immigration hearings, 111–18, 119, 123–24, 127–28, 138

immigration legislation, 36, 111–15, 117, 125, 127, 130, 138–42, 220, 275, 304–5. *See also specific legislation*

immigration policy, 139, 154–55, 158–59, 177, 178, 280, 282–83, 298, 305

Immigration Reform and Control Act (IRCA), 117

immigration reforms, 282. *See also* immigration legislation; immigration policy

Industry Day, 161–65

inflation, 164

information technology, 107–8. *See also* technology

INS. *See* Immigration and Naturalization Service (INS)

Integrated Surveillance Intelligence System (ISIS), 21, 58, 100–110, 139, 281–82, 298–99; failure of, 103–5, 109, 147–48, 150–53, 156, 158, 160–62, 165, 171, 175–76; force multipliers and, 228–29; funding of, 104

intelligence gathering, 100, 185, 296

Intelligent Computer-Aided Detection (ICAD) system, 101–2, 107. *See also* ICAD II; ICAD III

intercontinental ballistic missiles (ICBM), 137

International Boundary and Water Commission (IBWC), 233–36, 239

International Bridge, 27

International Microwave Corporation (IMC), 100, 102–6

International Technology, Education, and Commerce (ITEC) facility, 63–64

Iowa, 120, 122, 177, 238

IRCA. *See* Immigration Reform and Control Act (IRCA)

ISIS. *See* Integrated Surveillance Intelligence System (ISIS)

ITEC. *See* International Technology, Education, and Commerce (ITEC) facility

Jackson, Michael P., 161

Jackson Lee, Sheila, 115, 123, 128–30, 279–81

jargon, 280, 292

Jasso, Tony, 88–92, 99

Jefferson, William J., 126

Johnson, Robert, 53–54

Jordan, Barbara, 129

Kelly Air Force Base, 268, 269, 270–71

Kennedy, Edward M., 305

kickbacks, 239

Kiewit Construction, 245

Kilroy, Mark, 46–47

Kimberly Clark Company, 124

King, Steve, 128

Kingsville, Texas, 212

Korean War, 53

L-3 Communications Holdings, Inc., 103, 105–9, 161, 165–66

labeling, 8, 11

La Feria, Texas, 52

La Grulla, Texas, 302

La Joya, Texas, 233, 234

La Lomita Chapel, 42, 213

Lambrecht, Cari, 230, 238

language, 215–16, 220. *See also* jargon

La Paloma, Texas, 4, 243

Laredo, Texas, 25, 30, 118, 202, 234, 267, 268

Larry, 14

Latinos. *See* Hispanics; *specific nationalities*

law enforcement, 14, 16, 34, 280, 296. *See also specific jurisdictions*

law enforcement communications assistants (LECAs), 101, 104–5, 107, 171

League of United Latin American Citizens (LULAC), 53

League of Women Voters, 272

LECAs. *See* law enforcement communications assistants (LECAs)

levees, 217–20, 231–32, 234–38, 243–44, *246*, 302

lighting, 140

Limbaugh, Rush, 24

Lockheed Martin, 161, 162

Longhorn, 239

Lopez, Alonzo, 53
Lopez, Waldo, 268
Los Ebanos, Texas, 72, 302
Los Indios, Texas, 243
Los Rinches, 47–51, 58
Lowder, Michael, 267
Lugo, Adelcio, 272
LULAC. *See* League of United Latin American Citizens (LULAC)
Lulac et al. v. Richards et al., 202

magnetic sensors, 170
"mainstream America," 118
MALDEF. *See* Mexican American Legal Defense and Education Fund (MALDEF)
Mancow Show, 273–74
maquiladoras, 7, 118
Maril, Harry Aaron, 118–19
Maril, Robert Lee, 120, 255; in hometown, 271–72; on the *Mancow Show*, 273–74; at San Antonio conference, 265–71; testimony of, 123–24, 128–29; at USNORTHCOM, 259–60, 262–65; at UTB-TSC, 206, 207–8, 211–12, 216, 222–23
Marmolejo, Brig, 54
Matamoros, Tamaulipas, Mexico, 5–9, *39*, 47, 64–65, 67, 199, 203, 301
McAllen, Texas, 4, 8–9, 38, 43–50, 219, 223–25, 231, 234, 239, 268, 307; Hispanic population of, 45–46; McAllen Border Patrol Station, 58, 81–82, 85–86; McAllen Police Department, 45, 46, 47
McAllen Border Patrol Station, 81–82, 86
McAllen Construction, 239
McAllen C Shift, 58
McAllen Sector, 94–98, 99, 250–51
McAllen Station, 97–98, 308
McCain, John, 141–42, 215, 305
McKinney, Jeremy L., 272

McMann, Colonel, 260, 261–62, 264–65, 268
McVeigh, Timothy, 287
media, the, 144, 146, 147, 273, 274–75, 280
Medrano v. Allee, 49
Mercedes, Texas, 4
Merida Initiative, 305
Mexican American Legal Defense and Education Fund (MALDEF), 202
Mexican Americans, 9–10, 51–53, 66, 67
Mexican Ministry of Foreign Affairs, 233
Mexicans, 122, 178, 223, 264; deportation of, 53; discrimination against, 66; discrimination by, 66; exploitation of, 51–53; visas for, 123
Mexican War, 47, 58
Mexico, 10–11, 25, 93, 254–55, *254*, 260–62, 275, 303. *See also specific municipalities and provinces*; border gangs in, 227–28; corruption in, 226–27; criminal organizations in, 226–28; drug-related violence in, 178; as a failed state, 226, 297; government of, 289–90, 297; law enforcement in, 227; military of, 16, 227, 266–70, 297; relationship with the U.S., 269–71, 297, 305; response to wall in, 269, 271
Meyers, Juliet L., 326n7
Michalski, Ann E., 115–17, 123
Michigan, 106
microwave transmissions, 176
militarized zones, 281, 290, 291, 297, 299, 300
Miller International Airpoirt, 43, 59, 231, 234
minimum wage, 215
Minnesota, 130
Minutemen, 122–23, 130, 138, 140, 144, 146, 163, 272–73, 286
misinformation, 280
Mission, Texas, 10, 38, 43

Mississippi River, 120–22, 238

mobile towers, 166–67

money launderers, 54–55

Monitor, the, 86

Morningside, Herman, 81–82

multinational corporations, 162–63.
See also contractors and subcontractors

Muñiz, Baldomero, 72–73, 200, 279, 281

Muñoz, Cesar, 182, 183

Muñoz, Israel, 182, 189

Muñoz, Nora, 179–97

Naco, Arizona, 94

NAFTA. *See* North American Free Trade
Agreement (NAFTA)

Napolitano, Janet, 173, 178, 236–37,
243, 250, 256, 275, 279, 281, 284,
290, 293, 295, 305–6

narcotrafficantes. See drug trafficking

National Border Patrol Council, 35,
188–89, 256

National Guard, 266, 296, 305

National Guard armory, 63

National Hot Rod Association, 167–72

National Park Service, 117

National Public Radio, 273

national security, 299; profit motives
and, 291–93; public safety and,
282–91

nativity, 8–9

Navarro, Raul "Big Roy," 55

Newell, Annette, 272

New Mexico, 21, 25, 181, 220

newspapers, 52

Nogales, Arizona, 4, 94, 135, 228,
251–56, *252*, 253, *254*, 277, 281,
290–91

Nogales, Sonora, Mexico, 4, 252–55,
252, *254*

No More Deaths, 255–56, 280

nonborder cultures, 11

nonborder states, 32

NORAD. *See* North American Aerospace
Defense Command (NORAD)

North American Aerospace Defense
Command (NORAD), 261

North American Free Trade Agreement
(NAFTA), 43, 117, 270

North Carolina, 215, 287

Northrop Grumman, 161, 162, 163, 165

Nuevo Laredo, Tamaulipas, Mexico, 25,
28–29, 268, 270

Nuevo Progreso, Tamaulipas, Mexico,
216, 218, 219, 223

Obama, Barack, 147, 275, 303–4;
administration of, 33, 36, 142, 173,
177, 236, 236–37, 266, 281, 283,
290–93, 300, 304–6; Arizona SB
1070 and, 304–5; presidential
campaign of 2008, 141–42, 215;
speech on immigration at American
University, 303–4; stimulas package
of, 173, 236

Oblates, 42

OBP. *See* Office of the Border Patrol
(OBP)

Office of Internal Affairs (OIA), 195

Office of the Border Patrol (OBP), 104

OIA. *See* Office of Internal Affairs (OIA)

Oklahoma, 8, 11, 118–19, 311n12

Oklahoma City, Oklahoma, 8, 9, 118–19

Old Military Highway, 79, 88–89, 99,
209, 245

operational control, 283, 284, 298–99

Operation Blockade, 93–95, 97–98, 100,
155, 282

Operation Gatekeeper, 94

Operation Rio Grande, 94–95, 96, 98

Operation Safeguard, 94

Operation Streamline, 33

Operation Wetback, 53, 58

operator error, 171

opportunism, 143

OTMs (other-than-Mexicans), 31–32, 33,
221

oversight, 159–61, 239–40, 244, 290–293, 297–98

PAN. *See* Partido Acción Nacional (PAN)
Partido Acción Nacional (PAN), 227
Partido Revolucionario Institucional (PRI), 226–27
parts, 174–75
patronage system, 48, 55
Pearson, David, 198–200, 203–4, 206, 209, 239, 243
pedestrian fencing, 56, 58, 156–57, 174
Penitas, Texas, 237
peonage system, 52–53, 58
Peters, Timothy, 176, 279, 331n93
Peterson Air Force Base, 258–65
Pharr, Texas, 4, 53, 55, 58, 302
Pharr high school, 58
Pharr–San Juan–Alamo Public School District, 55
Philippines, the, 10
Pima County, Arizona, 275
politics, 223–24, 234, 235, 241, 244–45, 249, 280–81, 283. *See also* elections; presidential campaign of 2008
Polson, Houston, 259–60, 263–65, 279
Porter High School, 5
ports of entry, 287–88, 292
Posse Comitatus Act of 1878, 213
poverty, 7–8
Predator 2, 162
presidential campaign of 2008, 140–42, 215
Prevention through Deterrence strategy, 56
PRI. *See* Partido Revolucionario Institucional (PRI)
produce, transportation of, 79
profit motives, 291–93
Progreso, Texas, 4, 216, 245, 302
Prohibition, 49

Project 28 (P-28), 21, 135–36, 138, 140, 165–67, 168–74, 176, 178, 204, 250, 275–77, *276*, 279, 291–93, 298, 306
protests, 118
pseudosecrecy, 280
public safety, 282–91
punishment, 91
Putegnat, Michael, 202, 203

quality control, 239–40

race, 8–9
racism, 51–53, 281
radar, 140, 168–69, 175
Radio Shack, 174–75
Raleigh, North Carolina, 272
Ramirez, Alfonso, 53
Ramos, Basilio, 48
Ramos, Ignacio, 144–47, 280
rancheros, 47
Raytheon, 161, 162
Real ID Act of 2005, 56, 68, 125, 127, 154, 203
recession, 92–93, 141, 281, 284, 305
Reich, Dindy, 135, 138
Reid-Kennedy Bill, 114
Relampago, Texas, 4
remote video surveillance (RVS), 104, 105, 106, 107
Republican Party, 112–13, 115, 117, 119–20, 123, 126–29, 138, 142, 158, 283, 304
Reyes, Mary, 109
Reyes, Rebecca, 102
Reyes, Silvestre, 93–94, 95, 96, 97, 98, 100, 102, 114, 155, 280, 281, 282
Reyes, Silvestre, Jr., 102
Reynosa, Tamaulipas, Mexico, 43, 76, 94–95, 238
Ridge, Tom, 140, 147–48, 150, 152, 176, 281, 282
Río Bravo, 3, 7, 14–15, 38, 40, 43, 210, 213, 219–20, 233, 245, 270
Rio Grande City, Texas, 4, 10, 47, 302

Rio Grande Consolidated Independent School District, 74
Rio Grande floodplain, 232
Rio Grande, 3, 7, 9, 14–16, 26–27, 38–42, 45, 48, 63–64, 74–76, 89–90, 93–95, 144, 205, 209–10, 214, 217–18, 232, 234, 239–40, 281, 285, 302, 308
Rio Grande Valley, 6, 8–9, 38, 44, 47–48, 55, 58–59, 177, 202, 212, 214–15, 232–34, 279; flood control system in, 237–38; flooding of, 302; land transformation in, 51–53; levees in, 71–72, 77–78, 80, 82–83; property owners in, 200–201
Rio Grande Valley National Wildlife Refuge, 240
Rivas, Pamela, 73–74, 200
Rivera Garcia, Olga, 5–9, 60–67, 199, 203, 206–8, 279, 281, 301–2
Rocha, Henry, 88–92, 99
Rodriguez, Charles G., 266, 271, 279
Rodriguez, Manuel "Manny" A., 24–37
Rodriguez, Rogelio "Little Roy," 55
Rodriguez, Susan, 256
Rogers, Harold, 160
Rogers, Michael D., 106, 107, 109, 161
Rojo, Ricardo, 191, 192
Rolling Stone Magazine, 126
Roma, Texas, 47, 302
Rosas, Robert, 146, 256
RVS. See remote video surveillance (RVS)

S. 2611, "The Comprehensive Immigration adn Reform Act of 2006," 114. See also Reid-Kennedy Bill
Sabal Palm Grove Sanctuary, 208, 244
Sabo, Martin Olva, 160
safety, 250, 256, 294; occupational, 215; public, 282–91
Salinas, J. D., 71, 72, 77, 209, 230–41, 243, 250, 280, 291, 295, 302
Salinas, Ricardo, 256

San Antonio, Texas, 260, 265–71
San Benito, Texas, 4, 52
Sanchez, Omar, 76–83, 85, 216–23, 236, 245, 248–49, 280, 302–3
San Diego, California, 12, 48–49, 56–58, 111, 130, 141, 146, 253, 256, 273, 275, 290, 300
San Juan, Texas, 4, 52
Santa Ana National Wildlife Refuge, 218
Santa Maria, Texas, 4
Santa Rosa, Texas, 4
Saponaro, Joseph, 103, 106
Sasabe, Arizona, 135–38, 275, 276, 277–78, 279
satellite technology, 164, 170–71, 175, 176, 286
saturation flyovers, 286
SBI. See Secure Border Initiative (SBI)
SBI PMO (Program Management Office), 153, 156
SBI Program Executive Office, 156
SBI Program Management Program, 161
SBI Systems Integrator, 157–61, 163–66, 172–73, 175, 291–93, 306
SBI TI. See Secure Border Initiative Tactical Initiative SBI TI
scope trucks, 185–87, 188, 192–93, 194
Scudder, Ryan J., 302, 303
Secure Border Fence Act, 234
Secure Border Initiative (SBI), 12, 140, 150–55, 160, 167, 176, 240, 279
Secure Border Initiative Network (SBInet). See Secure Border Initiative Network (SBInet), 12–13, 21, 156, 158, 160, 163–64, 166–67, 172, 176–77, 306
Secure Border Initiative Tactical Initiative SBI TI, 156–57, 160, 174, 176
Secure Fence Act of 2006, 56, 139, 142, 144
Self-Help, 272

Sensenbrenner, Frank James "Jim," Jr., 111–13, 117, 119–20, 127–30, 138–39, 154, 203, 279, 281, 283, 299, 304; biography of, 124–26; immigration legislation by, 115, 127

Sensenbrenner Bill, 114–15

sensors, 17, 88–89, 90, 100, 104, 140, 174–75; ground, 17, 81, 177, 188; magnetic, 170; underground, 98–99

SER, 239

Sharyland Plantation, 43

Simpson-Mazzoli Bill, 117. See also Immigration Reform and Control Act (IRCA)

Sipe, David, 50

Skinner, Richard L., 103, 104, 160–61

smuggling, 16, 27, 29, 48, 49, 54, 57, 59, 213; of alcohol, 49; of drugs (see drug trafficking); of people, 41, 59, 79, 127–28, 213, 220–21, 308; of weapons, 313n31

social services, 52

soft Xes, 98

Sonora, Mexico, 4–5, 252, 254–55, 254

Sonoran desert, 14

South Carolina, 183

Sparrow, Agent, 83–87, 223–25

Spellman, Colonel, 265

Spero, Deborah, 161

Stana, Richard M., 177

Stanton, Walt, 280, 284

Starr County, 52, 74–76

Starr County School District, 74–76

Stanton, Walt, 255–56

stereotypes, 11. See also labeling

Stevens, Kevin, 161

subcontractors. See contractors and subcontractors

Sullivan City, Texas, 4, 302

Sumano, Abelardo Rodriguez, 268–70, 280

surface radar, 140, 168–69, 175. See also Project 28

surveillance equipment, 162, 278, 286, 290

Tamaulipas, Mexico, 5–9, 25, 28–29, 39, 40, 43, 46–47, 64–65, 67, 76, 94–95, 199, 203, 216, 218–19, 223, 238, 268, 270. See also specific municipalities

technology, 17, 107–8, 140, 154–55, 160, 163–64, 166–67, 283–84, 286, 290. See also specific kinds of technology

Terbush, James W., 265

terminology, 8–9, 215–16, 310n2. See also jargon

terrorism, 59, 80, 85, 91, 107, 119, 140–41, 225, 250, 270. See also terrorists; domestic, 287; sleeper cells, 224; terrorist attacks of September 11, 2001, 11, 54, 97, 98, 138–39, 142–43, 155, 212, 221, 282–83.

terrorists, 92, 138–39, 141, 225, 228, 287, 298

Texas, 4, 7, 12, 21, 25, 93–94, 106, 110, 117–18, 130, 141, 163, 167–72, 177, 198–229, 202, 214, 228, 250, 259–60, 281–82, 289–90, 296, 300, 303. See also specific counties and municipalities

Texas Border Coalition, 234

Texas Department of Public Safety, 49

Texas Fish and Wildlife Department, 239

Texas National Guard, 266, 279

Texas Rangers, 47, 49. See also Los Rinches

Texas RioGrande Legal Aid, 54, 70, 76, 200, 209, 214, 215, 238, 280

Texas Southmost College, 62

Thompson, Bennie, 159

Thrall Construction Rent-A-Fence, 204

Tijuana, Mexico, 7–8, 56, 57, 253, 275

time, 3–5, 7, 11, 21, 31–32, 280, 299–300

Torres, Superintendent, 31

tower poles, 106–7

towers, 166–67, 168–69, 170–71, 175, 176, *276*, 306

training, 286

transparency, 280

Treaty of Guadalupe Hidalgo, 47, 122, 267

tricky bags, 188

Truan, George, 208

Tubac, Arizona, 162

tube wranglers, 14–15

Tucson, Arizona, 21, 135, 165, 167, 180, 183, 251, 255–56, 277–78, 305

Tucson-1, 173, 174, 176, 177, 178

Tucson Sector, 251, 255–56

tunnels, 228

undocumented workers. *See* workers, undocumented

unemployment, 53

United States. *See also specific states*: relationship with Mexico, 269–71, 297, 305; U.S.-Mexico borderlands, *2*, 147

University of Texas, Brownsville–Texas Southmost College (UTB-TSC), 5, 9, 66–69, 76–77, 130, 198–204, *205*, 209, 239, 241–43, 290–91

University of Texas at Austin, 62, 65

University of Texas–Pan American, 202

University of Texas San Antonio (UTSA), 265

University of Texas system, 202

U.S. Air Force, 259–64

USA Patriot Act, 125, 126, 127

U.S. Army, 259, 267. *See also* AR-NORTH (U.S. Army North)

U.S. attorney general, 56

U.S. Border Patrol. *See* Customs and Border Protection (CBP); *specific locations*

U.S. citizens, deportation of, 53

U.S. Congress, 10, 43, 49, 53, 56, 59, 181, 201, 213, 231, 237, 275, 283, 300, 304, 305; deterrence theory

and, 96–98; ISIS and, 102, 104, 106, 109–10, 112–17, 120, 125–26, 129; lack of oversight by, 159–61, 290–93, 297–98; politics of fence building and, 138–40, 142; virtual fences and, 159–61, 165, 176, 178

U.S. Customs Service, 63, 148, 152. *See also* Customs and Border Protection (CBP)

U.S. Fish and Wildlife Service (USFWS), 240

USFWS. *See* U.S. Fish and Wildlife Service (USFWS)

U.S. Marshals, 49

U.S. military, 171, 267, 280, 296, 297. *See also* ARNORTH (U.S. Army North); USNORTHCOM (U.S. Northern Command); *specific branches*

USNORTHCOM (U.S. Northern Command), 258–62, 268, 270, 273, 278–79; Crocker, Sylvia, 260; Education Training Division, J-7, 259–60, 264; Interagency Coordination, 260, 262–63; Planning and Strategy Division, J-5, 260, 261

U.S. presidency, 297–98. *See also specific presidents*

U.S. Senate, 139. *See also* U.S. Congress

violence, 249, 256, 281, 303, 314n6; drug-related violence, 178; gun violence, 288–89; informal rules governing, 288–89

visas, 123

"voluntarily returned" (Vred) illegal immigrants, 32

vote-selling, 48

VRing, 184

Wackenhut Corporation, 277

walls. *See* border walls and fences

War on Drugs, 11, 128, 306

Warren, Cheryl, 125

Warren, Robert, 125
Washington State, 106, 117, 123
weapons smuggling, 313n31
Weber, Rebecca, 70–71, 76
Wells, James B., 52
Wells, Patricia, 225–29
Wendlandt, Charlie, 70
Weslaco, Texas, 52, 70, 77, 213–23, 245, 249, 302
Weslaco Border Patrol, 209
Weslaco Border Patrol Station, 76, 79, 220, 222, 223, 245, 249, 302
White House, 129
Williams Brothers, 239
Wisconsin, 120, 122, 125
Wood, John, 241–45
workers, legal, 214–15, 240
workers, undocumented, 4, 9–17, 26, 31–33, 55, 63, 76, 83, 98, 107, 177, 222, 240, 273, 303, 305–6. *See also* bordercrossers, illegal; immigrants, illegal; agricultural workers, 79; in

Anzalduas County Park, 41–42; deterrence theory and, 91–92, 94, 96; employers of, 306; employment abuse and, 70–71, 214–15; exploitation of, 70–71; politics of fence building and, 138–39, 142; safety of, 283–85
World War II, 53

Xe, 138

Younger, J. Arthur, 124

Zachry, 239
Zapata, Texas, 4, 302
Zavala, Leticia, 272
Zavaleta, Antonio "Tony," 6, 9–10, 41, 61, 63, 65, 199, 203, 204, 207–8, 209, 279
Zedillo, Ernesto, 227
Zenyon, Inc., 161
Zetas, 227

About the Author

Robert Lee Maril is professor of sociology and the founding director of the Center for Diversity and Inequality Research at East Carolina University. The author of many books, including *Patrolling Chaos: The U.S. Border Patrol in Deep South Texas* (TTUP, 2006) and *Waltzing with the Ghost of Tom Joad: Poverty, Myth, and Low-Wage Labor in Oklahoma*, he has testified three times on his research before the U.S. Congress, and his work has been widely cited both in scholarly publications and the national media. A resident of the Texas borderlands for seventeen years, he now lives in Greenville, North Carolina.